MILTON STUDIES

XXXVIII

M I L T O N
S T U D I E S

XXXVIII ❧ *Edited by*
Albert C. Labriola
and Michael Lieb

John Milton: The Writer in His Works

UNIVERSITY OF PITTSBURGH PRESS

MILTON STUDIES

is published annually by the University of Pittsburgh Press as a forum for Milton scholarship and criticism. Articles submitted for publication may be biographical; they may interpret some aspect of Milton's writings; or they may define literary, intellectual, or historical contexts—by studying the work of his contemporaries, the traditions which affected his thought and art, contemporary political and religious movements, his influence on other writers, or the history of critical response to his work.

Manuscripts should be upwards of 3,000 words in length and should conform to *The Chicago Manual of Style*. Manuscripts and editorial correspondence should be addressed to Albert C. Labriola, Department of English, Duquesne University, Pittsburgh, Pa., 15282–1703. Manuscripts should be accompanied by a self-addressed envelope and sufficient unattached postage.

Milton Studies does not review books.

Within the United States, *Milton Studies* may be ordered from the University of Pittsburgh Press, c/o CUP Services, Box 6525, Ithaca, N.Y., 14851, 607–277–2211.

Published by the University of Pittsburgh Press, Pittsburgh, Pa. 15261

CONTENTS

INTRODUCTION: POSTMODERN BIOGRAPHICAL STUDY OF MILTON

Albert C. Labriola

THE TITLE OF the present volume, *John Milton: The Writer in His Works,* highlights the revival of biographical criticism in Milton studies. Rather than biographical criticism as it was practiced in earlier eras or into and somewhat beyond the mid-twentieth-century, however, the present volume looks toward postmodern biographical criticism, the more multifarious commentary on the presences of authors in their works. Early biographical scholarship stressed the so-called life records of authors and produced what may be called documented and documentary lives. When in previous eras biographical scholarship elided into biographical criticism, what resulted was the positivist association between authors' lives and their writings. Dwelling on the manner by which experience was transformed into art, early biographical criticism added to our understanding of the lives of writers in at least two ways: juxtaposing events in their writings with episodes in their lives and enriching our interpretation of biographical topicalities in their works. Becoming at times more speculative, biographical criticism often created composite portraits of authors, whose traits of character and personality were inferred from their writings.

Postmodernist biographical criticism issues from a richer theoretical context, one informed by the various methodologies that have been propounded in the United States since the mid-sixties. These methodologies have achieved predominance in present-day critical and literary studies, and their tenets need not be recounted because they are well known and practiced almost universally in academe today. If one were pressed to assert the dominant trend of the postmodernist approach to texts, it would be a heightened awareness of subjectivity. By destabilizing the perceiving subject, postmodernism promotes a depth and diversity of interpretation previously unimagined. But the implications of postmodernism for biographical criticism and especially for biographies have not yet been fully realized; nor has a theory of postmodern biographical criticism been formalized or extensively forged because to do so is premature at this time.

In the recent past and at present, postmodern biographical critics have been at work to discern the presences of Milton in his writings in ways

1

previously unremarked. The major advance in this direction, to date, has been John T. Shawcross's *John Milton: The Self and the World* (1993), a biographical study whose emphasis is psychological and whose methodology and insights in many ways underlie the essays in the present volume. Appropriately, the ironic achievement of postmodern biographical study is that the subjectivity exercised on the part of the reader has been ascribed, in turn, to the writer. This process may be likened to the use of a kaleidoscope, a tube-like instrument held toward a source of light so that the loose bits of colored glass reflected by mirrors inside produce a symmetrical pattern. As the instrument is rotated, another pattern appears, accompanied by alterations in light and color. In other words, destabilizing the writer into various presences begets outcomes not unlike the changing patterns of organization, the various intensities and shadings of light, and the deployment and contrasts in colors in a kaleidoscope.

This analogy is apt, for it highlights a larger aim of postmodern biographical criticism. That aim runs counter to the positivist concept of objectifying the writer, of composing a canonical biography or even a canonical glimpse of a writer. To return to the analogy of the kaleidoscope, let us assume that it will produce five variations at successive rotations, each of which is numbered from one to five. Postmodern biographical criticism would assign a different perceiving subject or beholder to each of those variations. As a result, when the first pattern is being displayed, only one viewer would behold it; the second viewer would behold only the second pattern, and so forth. What all five beholders perceive is contained in the one tube, but no viewer ever perceives more than one (and only the same one) of the five displays. Though all the patterns in the kaleidoscope are different, there is no quantum difference between them. By that assertion I mean that the number of bits of colored glass is the same because postmodern biographical criticism does not aim to discover or include additional documentary evidence. Such incremental biography, if it may be so labelled, is peripheral to postmodern biographical criticism, which discerns in our present knowledge of an author what may be called a variety of patterns, gradations of lighting and shading, and contrasts in colors or in the hues of the same color. From my perspective, the foregoing assertion furnishes metaphors for the postmodern emphasis on an author's interior being and psychic life, in contrast to the more traditional emphasis on an externally documented life.

If, in pursuing the analogy of the kaleidoscope yet once more, we choose no longer to preserve the synchronism of a particular observer with a certain view in the tube, then the tube with all five patterns may become available to all five observers, as well as others. What the observers would learn is that no one view is more privileged than another, a situation manifested by the fact that there is no prescribed sequence for beholding the five patterns. Our previous numbering from one to five was purely arbitrary, for what is more important to postmodern biographical criticism is the permeability between and among the views that one acquires of an author. In effect, the reaction of observers to the views in the kaleidoscope anticipates the experience of readers of the present volume.

The postmodern engagement of a reader and an author might be described as one of intersubjectivity. What occurs is that the psychic experiences of a reader impinge on the perceptual understanding that he or she brings to bear on an author's life. Whereas some critics do advocate the so-called death of the author in the postmodern era, an amendment to that view might be that the author's resurrection is occurring through present-day biographical criticism. For the psychic traces discerned in an author's writings are visible because of a reader's own psychic experiences. The intersubjectivity that I am recounting may be perceived as a modified form of the psychological mechanisms of projection and displacement or even of Freudian transference. In effect, the reader uses his or her own psychic experiences as touchstones to access and assess the psychological verisimilitude of the biographical presences of Milton in his writings. At the same time, a postmodern reader has an acute awareness that his or her own subjectivity, not to mention Milton's, is culturally situated and mediated.

To transact an intersubjective relationship with an author, a reader must develop a model or paradigm—need I say theoretical framework?—that is tantamount to an epistemology. Central to this process are two issues: evidence and interpretation that bear on the interiority of an author. Informing this whole process or epistemology are various and interrelated tensions that come into play in any era and that become more problematic as a reader strives to engage an author of an earlier era.

In line with the foregoing, postmodern biographical critics shape their epistemologies by posing questions very different from those posed by more traditional biographers, questions such as the following: Who is the specular "I"? Is he or she knowable to himself or herself? If so, in what circumstances and when, prospectively or retrospectively? Does the specular "I" undergo self-formation; and if so, is it achieved by autonomous action or social conditioning, or by both means, and by others? How do social structures enable or inhibit the formation of the specular "I"? Do self and society have a relationship that is supportive or antagonistic, and how is self-formation affected by the relationship? Is it more important, not for an author to learn to write, but for an author to write to learn—to learn, that is, more about himself or herself? When and where do self-formation and self-disclosure occur in an author's writings? If the specular "I" of an author is a composite of several subjects that interact and unfold, not synchronously but asynchronously, how does a reader discern and chart such phenomena? In other words, when are the several subjects or presences of an author in states of fusion or fission? What is the formative impact of changing pressures brought to bear on an author—whether the pressures emerge from one's family and upbringing, one's marital life or lives, political or religious institutions, vocational aspirations, relationship with the godhead, and the like?

These questions in one form or another, and many more, are posed in the essays that follow. Engaging such inquiries becomes the means by which each essay develops an epistemology to discern the psychic life and interiority of Milton. From that threshold, each essay focuses, in turn, on the dual issues of evidence and interpretation; and in each essay, theoretical postulates eventuate in critical practices, from which the presences of Milton in his writings come into focus. Accordingly, the present volume aims to be both a prolegomenon and impetus to a systematic and widespread postmodern biographical study of Milton.

At the outset of the present collection, Joseph Wittreich's " 'Reading Milton': The Death (and Survival) of the Author" surveys most of Milton's best-known poems: the Nativity ode, the companion poems L'Allegro and Il Penseroso, Lycidas, Paradise Lost, Paradise Regained, and Samson Agonistes. Interrelated with his survey of the poems is a periodic consideration of selected prose works, notably Areopagitica, Tetrachordon, Defensio Secunda, Pro Se Defensio, A Treatise of Civil Power, and De Doctrina Christiana. Wittreich's coverage enables him to discern ongoing autobiographical impulses in the writings of Milton, which he initiated early in his career. By accenting these impulses first with the tone of apologia, then of self-defense, Milton ultimately enters into a realm tantamount to psychological autobiography. Wittreich likens Milton's ongoing psychic self-disclosure and its numerous inflections to a serial portrait, a panorama of self-images usually fragmentary, no one of which is definitive. In the visual arts, Wittreich cites Rembrandt's nearly seventy self-portraits as analogues for Milton's unfolding self-images. For Wittreich, moreover, the specular "I" of Milton evolves in the writings as kinetic and psychodynamic presences, unfolding rapidly and variously like a mind in motion. When identified, serially compiled, and analyzed in commentary like Wittreich's, these presences constitute a postmodern biographical study of the first order.

While Wittreich's study ranges far and wide, the essays that follow tend to dwell more specifically on fewer works by Milton, on a certain stage of his life, or on a recurrent manifestation of his particular presence(s) in his works. Thus, J. Martin Evans's "The Birth of the Author: Milton's Poetic Self-Construction" dwells on what Michel Foucault calls the "author function," specifically the "poet-as-imagined-presence-in-the-poem," which is distinct from, but interrelated with, the "poet-as-creator-of-the-poem." In particular, Evans discerns this poetic presence (and absence) across editions of Milton's poems, beginning with the 1645 collection and ending with the edition that includes *Paradise Regained*. In doing so, Evans identifies inside the texts of the poems, rather than in the editorial apparatus surrounding them, a poetic presence that alternates between being explicitly self-referential, on the one hand, and virtually self-negated, on the other. Most significant, however, is the evidence Evans unearths in the poems for his interpretation of the varied psychic life that this poetic presence enacts. He concludes that the self-assured poetic presence of *Paradise Regained* is the authorial self inside the poems toward which Milton was evolving across a lifetime. In sum, the poetic presence of Milton that Evans perceives inside the poems is also looking forward from them.

Related to Evans's study is that by Kathleen M. Swaim, " 'Myself a True Poem': Early Milton and the (Re)formation of the Subject," which dwells on Milton's lyric poems of the 1620s and 1630s. In these early poems, she discerns how Milton ventures into modern subjectivity and consequently forms an individuated voice at play. Swaim contends that Milton's experimentation in such heightened self-consciousness is the literary counterpart of the Continental philosophy of Descartes on subjectivity. In the early lyrics, as well, Swaim detects the influence of the English Reformation, which predates, of course, the writings of Descartes but anticipates his emphasis on subjectivity, self-formation, and veritable self-sufficiency. Her remarkable claim, boldly asserted but cogently argued, is that by the time he was twenty-one years old, Milton provides evidence in his poems of "fashioning a definitive, even a monumental self," a process that continues through the poems of his middle and later years, as well as in his prose. While Swaim only briefly hints at these later developments, which do not fall within the scope of her present coverage, she nevertheless establishes an epistemology for analyzing other works by Milton. In the early lyrics, her identification of multiple presences of Milton—a constructed self, a deferred self, and a dialogic self—is a major leap forward in establishing models of evidence and interpretation for postmodern biographical study.

Perhaps the most extraordinary approach to biographical study in the present volume emerges from John Leonard's essay, " 'Thus They Relate, Erring': Milton's Inaccurate Allusions." Leonard identifies so-called inaccuracies—historical and literary—in Milton's allusions, at times engaging the interpretations of editors on these very points. Unlike editors, whose interests, quite properly, are more narrow, Leonard frames an epistemology or "some methods and principles for determining when, whether, and how an authorial inaccuracy is intentional." As he executes his own epistemology, he focuses on cases where inaccuracies, if or when deliberate, provide glimpses into Milton's authorial presence in his writings. By engaging errant and revisionist treatments of allusions, Leonard strives to comprehend Milton's mind at work, so that the Foucauldian "author function" will include authorial intepretation embedded in the act of composition. For Leonard, such allusions are nodal points that provide evidence of the presences of an author in his works. Additionally, Leonard strives to pinpoint how and why in the contrived inaccuracies of Milton's allusions the author injects subversive irony and even instills in a character, who is central to an allusion, elements of his own personality or psychic life. Because Leonard attends to authorial traces and tracings in ways heretofore only partially realized, he breaks new ground for postmodernist biographical study of Milton.

Stella Revard's "Milton and the Progress of the Epic Proemium" puts new wine in old bottles by citing Milton's unfolding epic consciousness. Beginning with poems related to the Italian journey of 1638–1639 or works composed soon afterwards, Revard identifies therein the presence of Milton as a self-conscious prospective epic author. By extending her coverage to *Paradise Lost*, she notes the actual epic "author function" in the proemia or invocations at the outset of Books One, Three, Seven, and Nine. To access and assess the personality and psychic traces of Milton, she does a comparative study of his proemia and those of selected predecessors, two Greek and one Roman, respectively Hesiod and Pindar, on the one hand, and Vergil, on the other. Because of her selection of evidence and her model of interpretation, Revard is strikingly innovative, and will be deeply influential, in her insights. For she distinguishes Milton's personal voice in the midst of his adherence to tradition. She does so, in part, by examining the poetic genres that intermingle in the proemia and Milton's adaptation of them for self-referential expression. She notes, as well, the transitions in Milton's psychic life across the four proemia, a life that at some moments progresses along a particular axis of self-consciousness and at other times steers itself, or is steered, in other directions of self-analysis and self-realization.

In "*Paradise Lost* and Milton's Politics," Barbara Kiefer Lewalski comprehensively analyzes how and why the political views of Milton are central not only to his epic but to his presence in the poem as well. She has a much more profound understanding of the term "political," however, than traditional commentary on the poem manifests. Indeed, Milton's political self is a composite of various presences, one of which involves being a teacher inside *Paradise Lost*, a poem that, Lewalski contends, "undertakes a strenuous project of educating readers in the virtues, values, and attitudes that make a people worthy of liberty" and of republicanism. In line with the foregoing assertion, Lewalski cites evidence in the epic of Milton's advocacy of a republican commonwealth and his opposition to monarchy. Her emphasis is on the educative presence and function of the poet, on the readiness and aptitude of his readers to learn from him, and on the formative outcomes of their learning. Lewalski bores into the epic to interact with Milton's educative presence, which she finds all-pervasive: in the change from a ten-book to a twelve-book structure, the selection of blank verse as the prosodic (and political) medium of instruction, the integration of Arminianism into the educative presence and practice of the poet, representations of place in the epic (heaven, earth, hell), the account of episodes (e.g., the infernal consult in Book Two), speeches and rhetoric, gender representation, male and female psychology, and Michael's lesson to Adam couched in the form of history-as-prophecy.

Richard Strier in "Milton's Fetters, or, Why Eden Is Better than Heaven" perceives *Paradise Lost* "as a poem deeply divided against itself." This perception derives, in part, from the so-called Satanist outlook on the poem, attributable to Blake and Shelley. Adopting some, not all, of that viewpoint and its premises, Strier locates Milton's presences in the epic as twofold: fettered and unfettered. Milton is fettered when his biographical presence in the poem is that of a rational apologist pursuing the "Great Argument"—justifying God's ways to men, the avowed aim or intention of *Paradise Lost*. From this perspective, the rational apologetics of the epic and of the prose treatise *De Doctrina Christiana*, attributed to Milton, are similarly informed by Renaissance and Reformation theology. Bound by such fetters or, to put it another way, governed by the rationalistic and theological contexts in which he chooses to advance the "Great Argument" of *Paradise Lost*, Milton as an apologist encounters problems and limitations that he cannot surmount. Strier highlights evidence of where and why the "Great Argument" goes awry or is conspicuously flawed. On the other hand, the unfettered Milton is a counter-presence of Milton the rational apologist in *Paradise Lost*. Presenting Eden and unfallen human life, or nature and innocence, Milton is liberated from the contexts that govern his apologetics, and he becomes much more spontaneous and imaginative. Most illuminating is the evidence cited by Strier for contrasting treatments of the same topics by the fettered and unfettered Milton. While the topic of diffusion and the verbal imagery that the rationalist Milton uses to recount it focus on divine omnipresence, the spontaneous and imaginative Milton relates diffusion to, among other things, the pervasive power and virtue of the sun and the natural luxuriance of Eden.

If, as Strier contends, *Paradise Lost* is "deeply divided against itself," Michael Lieb in " 'A Thousand Foreskins': Circumcision, Violence, and Selfhood in Milton" perceives *Samson Agonistes* as a site where Milton's self-perception is entwined with the enactment of violence. Having already explored such a view as it pertains to bodily mutilation and dismemberment in Milton's writings and their bearing on the author's sense of self, Lieb now focuses on circumcision or the violence of the cut and its deployment in the dramatic poem. The patriarchal narratives of Scripture provide the framework for understanding the covenant of circumcision or *brit milah,* a central feature of a culture of violence. Adapting the *brit milah* to his theology, St. Paul both spiritualizes and internalizes this so-called savagery, reorienting it from its Hebraic focus on the flesh to a Christian concern with the heart. Though he advocates spiritual circumcision—in effect, faith incised in the human heart or sealed by sacramental celebration—St. Paul did not purge from his commentary on circumcision all elements of violence but in effect reoriented them by urging castration for the persecutors of his faithful brethren. Informed by such overtones of violence in the Hebraic and Christian Scriptures and among commentators in the early modern era, circumcision becomes a source of Freudian and other anxiety for Milton. In *De Doctrina Christiana* Milton expounds at length on his theology of circumcision, using biblical proof-texts, particularly from St. Paul's epistles, to undergird his views. Milton's other prose works likewise cite the Pauline epistles on circumcision; but genital mutilation and its displacements, including blindness, do haunt Milton and achieve their consummate expression and enactment in *Samson Agonistes* not only with reference to the protagonist but in relation to Milton's sense of self as a presence in the dramatic poem.

The apt conclusion to the volume is an essay on the prose, Stephen M. Fallon's "The Spur of Self-Concernment: Milton in His Divorce Tracts." Though the preceding essays deal at times with various prose writings by Milton, only Fallon's essay pursues postmodern biographical study wholly by reference to the tracts—in particular, the tracts on divorce. Composed after the antiprelatical tracts, in which Milton (re)presented himself as God's spokesperson, the divorce tracts provide psychic traces of what the author himself calls self-concernment. They do so, Fallon contends, in ways beyond the author's own ken, for they are not simply works by him but, in the postmodernist light, about him. Informed by a personal imperative and impressed by his own experience, the divorce tracts unfold a series of self-representations of Milton, a more psychodynamic process than that by which the less variegated and more consciously crafted unilateral self-image in the antiprelatical tracts was created and maintained. Two methods that Fallon employs to buttress his argument include a comparative study of the two editions of *The Doctrine and Discipline of Divorce* and a comparative study of the outlook on marriage in *The Doctrine and Discipline of Divorce* and *Tetrachordon.* By citing as evidence and then interpretively engaging similarities and differences—from the earlier to the later edition of the same work or from the one tract to the other—Fallon highlights how Milton's presences in his writings are dialectic, how the author disintegrates himself into multiple presences to conduct a dialogue with and within himself. Precisely here Fallon subsumes the essence of the preceding essays and points the project of postmodern biographical study of Milton in the direction it must inevitably take. When pursued, that direction may cause us to discover that (what I call) the "millennial Milton" is ironically a resurrected author, rather than a newly created one.

"READING" MILTON: THE DEATH (AND SURVIVAL) OF THE AUTHOR

Joseph Wittreich

I was confirm'd in this opinion, that he who would not be frustrate of his hope to write well hereafter in laudable things, ought him selfe to bee a true Poem, that is, a composition, and patterne of the best and honourablest things; not presuming to sing high praises of heroick men, or famous Cities, unless he have in himselfe the experience and the practice of all that which is praise-worthy.

—John Milton

John Milton himself is in every line of the Paradise Lost. . . . There is a subjectivity of the poet, as of Milton, who is himself before himself in every thing he writes.

In the Paradise Lost—indeed in every one of his poems—it is Milton himself whom you see; his Satan, his Adam, his Raphael, almost his Eve—are all John Milton; and it is a sense of this intense egotism that gives me the greatest pleasure in reading Milton's works. The egotism of such a man is a revelation of spirit.

—Samuel Taylor Coleridge

THAT MILTON ASSUMES a strong presence in his poetry is a presumption that, encouraged by the poet and especially his Romantic followers, survives as a core concept in much modern criticism, both in its theory and its practice. Yet where to locate Milton's presence, where it is most keenly felt, and the intricacies of that presence, remain mysteries, mysteries that are now, if not solvable, at least more readily explicable, through advances in literary theory coupled with ruminations in Milton criticism. Theory and criticism together afford complicating perspectives on a matter unwittingly posed by Milton in *Pro Se Defensio* (and still very much with us, and with us as a postmodern concern): "What now becomes of the author?" (YP 4: 746).[1] Milton seems to invite the undertaking of this essay: an overturning of centuries of conviction, undertaken with the aid of what many will recognize as postmodernist propositions whose sponsor, in this instance, is Milton himself. If Milton leaves his own imprint on the emerging genre of autobiography, it is by tilting this genre toward *apologia* and inflecting it with self-defense; then by converting the story from the details of everyday life to an autobiography of the human psyche. In this way, the author, even when supposed dead, preserves a presence in his writings.

I. Authorial Presence

Milton's early poems, containing many fragments of self-portraiture, and his prose works, rife with autobiographical reference and reflection, create the expectation of a persisting authorial presence in the late poems. Reading them, it has often seemed, is "reading" Milton: discovering him in those poems, then reading them as revelations of the poet's mental life and spiritual experience. However, a check is placed on such easy inferences, especially by the 1645 *Poems of Mr. John Milton*. Despite the various elements asserting authorial presence, including a frontispiece portrait and other front matter, plus epistles, headnotes, and endnotes to individual poems, the poems themselves seem to suggest that, often in hiding, the author must be sought out in unexpected places and sometimes will be found in curious postures, modifying earlier attitudes and correcting previously stated opinions, and even found in the interstices of a text in the guise of craftsman. At best, the poems offer flickering images in contrast with, and subversive of, both the stabilizing image of the frontispiece portrait and title-page message, each by insinuation aligning Milton with a royalist, cavalier line of poetry, while the accompanying poems effect a realignment of Milton with the traditions of prophecy and a poetics of both transgression and discovery.

If in *On the Morning of Christ's Nativity* the poet pleads that his muse rush to the manger, beating other gift-bearers there with the present of a "humble ode" (23), by the time he composes *Lycidas* (nearly eight years later), Milton forces a distinction, powerfully evident in *Paradise Lost* as well, between two poets (the one who sings the elegy, the other who speaks in its final words), this distinction emerging from the wrenching conclusion to the monody, a distancing operation, "Thus sang the uncouth swain" (186). That conclusion is a stunning reminder that "the 'I' of written discourse," as Louis A. Renza argues, "can never in itself signify the writer's self-presence."[2] Moreover, the forced distinction is eventually reinforced by the headnote elaborated from the *Lycidas* manuscript, one sentence of which appears in "The Table of the *English* Poems" as part of the poem's title and the whole of which is then added to *Lycidas* in its 1645 printing. One poet is inside the poem looking out, the other outside the poem looking in. Even as Milton the author or Milton the man seems to acknowledge a knit of identity with the uncouth swain, in effect saying "Been there! Done that!" he here creates a distinction that throughout *Paradise Lost* he maintains, developing a twin consciousness—or what Wordsworth in *The Prelude* describes as "two consciousnesses"—a consciousness of oneself and of some other being (2.32–33). To adapt words from *Tetrachordon*, he creates a consciousness of "*another self, a second self, a very self it self*" (YP 2:600).

In the Nativity ode, the poet is distinct from and subordinate to the muse, at least until the conclusion of the poem, when "thy . . . ode" (24) becomes "our . . . Song" (239). In *Lycidas,* two poets emerge: one is the piper and the other the bard; one is the poet's former and the other a new self; or as the poem implies, the one is the natural, the other the spiritual man, who emerges from this crisis lyric—a shipwreck of faith, over-tossed, without haven or shore—as the oracle of a better time. In *Paradise Lost,* one poet is the bardic narrator and the other the controlling consciousness of the poem, the one experiences an apocalypse of mind and the other effects an apocalypse of mind in his readers. Both poems, nonetheless, pit the gathering awareness of the poet within the poem against the enlarged consciousness of the poet who authors it, with the consequence that we see, as Blake saw in Wordsworth, the natural man continually rising up against the spiritual man.

This distinction asserts itself not only within the 1645 *Poems* but also on its more than ornamental frontispiece, where the mature poet of the main frame looks out upon the young poet in the window frame; where bard beholds piper, the poet at age thirty-seven (it is sometimes suggested) beholding the poet in his twenty-first year. More probably, the frontispiece is an example of illustration as much as portraiture in the tradition, let us say, of Chaucer depicted among his pilgrims or of John on Patmos attended by an eagle and taking in his vision, in which case the portrait / illustration is better read as emblematizing the double consciousness of *L'Allegro* and *Il Penseroso*, with the withered face of the portrait depicting the poet with a full acquist of experience, now in "weary age" (167), "attain[ing] / To something like Prophetic strain" (173–74). In this instance, it is not so much what John T. Shawcross calls the "performing self" and the "real self" but rather two different versions of the performing self that are pitted against one another.[3]

The mental progress inscribed within the frontispiece of the 1645 *Poems* is the progression mapped in the twin lyrics, encapsulated within *Lycidas,* and encompassed by the poetic volume itself. We can profitably think of this progress as an embedded narrative within the 1645 *Poems* and, doing so, will want to remember with Marshall Grossman that these narratives of the self relate not to the author as he "always essentially was," or even to the author as he now is, but rather to "the person he . . . will become by the story's end."[4] Moreover, these words encourage a refinement of what we have already said about *Lycidas:* the two poets within the poem, the singer of the elegy and the speaker of the epilogue, are different versions of the performing self, both distinct from the author who speaks through the title and headnote to his poem.

In *Paradise Lost* the situation is altogether more complicated. The prologues to individual books present different versions of the performing self, all of which bear similarity to and display difference from the poet's real self. The poem itself (in its own wily maneuverings) compounds these selves (again to use Shawcross's terms) with "hidden" and "inferential" selves.[5] Just as there are blurrings of characters, protagonists with antagonists, so in the four prologues, with autobiographical detail as the agent, there are repeated blurrings of the poem's narrator and its author, then of the author with various of his characters, even Galileo, who, John Guillory proposes, is "a cryptic self-portrait" of Milton himself.[6] Furthermore, as Robert Durling explains, from the author's perspective "the figure of the narrator is a role in which the author casts himself . . . [as] a dramatic projection," with the work itself revealing "the author . . . [as] it dramatizes and projects the structure of his consciousness." Harbored in this insight is the realization that when the author through a persona tells a story he is not "on the same level with the other characters. He exists above that level" because he is omnipresent in a narration, "the fabric" of which "is the *Author's* act of narration."[7]

The subtlety of Durling's observation, lost within the simplifications of Robert McMahon's more recent book, is caught nicely by Balachandra Rajan when he describes the epic voice of *Paradise Lost* as "the voice of the imperial imagination, of sumptuous orchestration, of metaphorical opulence, the encyclopaedic, outreaching, all-encompassing voice, the voice of the unifying imperative. No one articulates this voice more resplendently than Milton; and no one struggles against it more insistently."[8] Very simply, throughout *Paradise Lost* there is an entanglement of characters and voices, with Milton sometimes hinting at a knit of identity while always maintaining distinction—a point (as we shall see) that is equally pertinent to what is supposedly Milton's most autobiographical poem, *Samson Agonistes.* In the latter poem, the point is only graspable once we uncover a hidden self that forges unexpected alliances with others engaging the same materials and writing within the same traditions, with emphasis falling not on sameness but on difference, and not on continuities with but on departures from those traditions.

Within its fabric of narration, details of autobiography, like blindness, fearful circumstances, and treacherous enemies, link the narrator of *Paradise Lost* and its author; and as if to underscore the autobiographical impulse within this poem, autobiography (as Barbara Lewalski has shown) is invented by Eve, perfected by Adam, and parodied by Satan. Autobiography is inflected "as exemplum, a moralizing life" in the case of Eve and as "spiritual autobiography" in the instance of Adam,[9] but with the paradox that by the end of the poem Adam is the moralizing figure and Eve much more the spiritual presence. Jesus in *Paradise Regain'd* and Samson in Milton's tragedy will similarly use autobiography to relate their experiences, some details of which have led to the speculation that the autobiography of Samson especially is a projection of Milton's own autobiography. "Here Milton, in the person of Samson," writes Thomas Newton, "describes exactly his own case, what he felt, and what he thought," especially in those years after the Restoration.[10] A century later, David Masson follows suit: "The story of Samson must have seemed to Milton a metaphor or allegory of much of his own life in its later stages."[11]

The conclusion seems irresistible. What Andrew Marvell implied concerning *Defensio Secunda* applies to most of Milton's writings. As Marvell confides in a letter dated 2 June 1654, they are "imboss'd" with Milton's presence (YP 4:864)—so much so that in her fictional biography Ann Manning will have Deborah Milton report that her father's "Mind . . . too often ran upon Things around him, and made his Poem [she speaks specifically of *Samson Agonistes*] the Shadow and Mirrour of himself."[12] This conclusion would seem to be confirmed, even flagged, by the different frontispiece portraits to *The Poems of Mr. John Milton* (1645), *The History of Britain* (1671), and *Artis Logicae* (1672), and by the frontispiece portrait that is now a fixed feature of the second edition of Milton's epic prophecy (1674). Traditionally used to memorialize, the frontispiece portraits, as used in these books, function instead to define and aggrandize the artist, perhaps even as gestures toward laureateship.

It is as if these frontispiece portraits, facing title pages and casting Milton's image across them into the book, announce the interchangeability of the author and the work. They declare first that the author, now a felt presence, runs surveillance over his works, and second that the works themselves, more than representations of physical likeness, are portraits of the artist altogether more nuanced and shaded than the picture portraits of Milton accompanying them, which, if we are to believe John Aubrey, are "not *at all* like him."[13] As Jonathan Richardson Sr. had complained, because there are "so Few Good Pictures" of Milton, indeed so many "a Bad Picture," he is presenting this account of the poet's life: "This Picture of the Mind of *Milton,* Drawn by Himself Chiefly."[14]

The infamous legend accompanying the portrait to the 1645 *Poems* surely implies as much, and that, like a poem, the poet may be a pattern of honor and virtue, hence doctrinal to a nation and able, potentially, to turn an entire civilization into a nation of visionaries. Again like a poem, he may figure a process of change—a transformed self, an expanding consciousness—with the emphasis falling not on physical likeness but on the mental life of the poet, his spiritual form. No less so than a poem, the poet is an arena of forces, tensions, and contradictions; and it is in the gaps created by such that we are most likely to find him, rather than in the frontispiece portrait, which, as Milton indicates in later remarks on *Eikon Basilike,* are too often pieces of "conceited portraiture" that are there only "to befool the people" (YP 3:342–43). How an author acts upon a work, especially its narrative, is of more consequence and ultimately is more revelatory than how he acts within the work.

The works of Milton, taken together, create a serial portrait of their author analogous to the some sixty-two self-portraits by Rembrandt, which imply, as do Milton's word-pictures, that the artist, "never satisfied," says Georges Gusdorf, "acknowledges no single image as his definitive image." As Gusdorf goes on to suggest, such portraits, images of a changing self, possess an authenticity unmatched by portraits of the painter by other artists, the true image of which seems always to elude them. Both a means of self-definition and self-aggrandizement and a vehicle for self-defense, as well as a means of attaining self-knowledge, the serial portrait, never finished, always an ever expanding array of fragments, diagrams a life in motion, a mind evolving. In the words of Gusdorf, these portraits are "a revenge on history,"[15] and on one's enemies, quite literally so in the case of John Milton.

One thinks immediately of the Greek epigram below the William Marshall portrait—which has been called a "crude, Samson-like jest"[16]—rebuking the artist for the poor likeness of Milton, a more accurate and complex image of whom appears in the word-pictures of the accompanying poems, especially *Lycidas* and *Epitaphium Damonis,* and later of *Pro Se Defensio.* Through the legend to the portrait, Milton challenges its authenticity in the same way that T. Cross, in another epigram, will challenge a frontispiece portrait of Hugo Grotius:

> His outward figure heere you find—
> Of Grotius who hath drawne the mind—
> Whose Counterfeits how they agree
> With the Originalls, read and see.[17]

Through the last of the aforementioned titles, *Pro Se Defensio,* Milton identifies the driving force behind the inlays of autobiography in poetry and prose works alike: *apologia,* or in the words of Milton's preface to *Samson Agonistes,* "self defence, or explanation." One should at the same time remember that, calculatedly, the 1645 *Poems* segregate (as will not be the case in 1673) the efforts of Milton's right hand from those of his left, although, if only for an instant, Milton's two identities, as poet and polemicist, merge in the newly added headnote to *Lycidas*, which *"foretells* [prophesies] *the ruin of our corrupted Clergy then in their height."* Furthermore, the Virgilian epigraph on the title page, as Barbara Lewalski urges, "explicitly refus[es] the construction laid upon . . . [Milton] by Moseley's apparatus,"[18] even as it seems to refer to early receptions of Milton the polemicist by promising the predestined bard protection against the slanderous tongues likely to malign him.

If Milton taunted Marshall about the 1645 frontispiece portrait (and one can never be sure that Marshall himself was not "in" on the joke), he was himself taunted with it by Alexander More: "would I reproach with blindness . . . or with deformity," More asks in *Fides Publica*, "who even believed you handsome, especially after I saw that elegant picture prefixed to your Poems?" This comment provokes Milton's bitter complaint in *Pro Se Defensio*: "I did not wish to be a Cyclops, though you so depicted me, and because you have seen a picture totally unlike me 'prefixed to my poems' . . . at the suggestion and solicitation of a bookseller" (YP 4:750–51). Milton's presence in the form of a frontispiece portrait is the publisher's doing, but Milton's presence through the legend accompanying the portrait is his own doing. The legend, its authentic voice, rather than canceling authorial presence in the 1645 *Poems*, instructs the reader to look for that presence outside the portrait: in the accompanying legends and iconography, in other elements of the front matter (especially the Virgilian epigraph), in the poetry and annotation thereof that complete the volume, even in the elongated title accorded *Lycidas* on the contents page, both here and in the 1673 *Poems*.

Portrait and legend, Marshall and Milton, relate to one another here as contentious biography relates to self-serving autobiography. Milton's complaint about the Marshall portrait—"This image was drawn by an untaught hand, / you might perhaps say, looking at the form of the original. / But since here you do not recognize the modelled face, friends, / laugh at a bad imitation by a worthless artist"—finds its analogue in John Singer Sargent's quip: "A portrait is a likeness in which there is something wrong with the mouth."[19] From Milton's point of view the *form* is wrong, the whole *face* is wrong; and it is the form, after all, that registers the spiritual dimension of the figure represented and the face that is an index to the mind. In portraiture, as Richard Brilliant explains, the face is "the primary field of expressive action," with the portrait itself reflecting social expectations, if not realities, that seem at odds with Milton's conception of himself as both a poet and man of virtue.[20]

Portraits are idealizations. Yet Marshall and Milton are worlds apart when it comes to imagining the ideal, which for Milton has little to do with social trappings and standing and everything to do with greatness of mind, loftiness of spirit, and high intelligence. These features are not at all attended to in the facial iconography of the Marshall portrait, which, among other things, is missing the traditionally large cranium of, let us say, Albrecht Dürer's *Philip Melanchthon* (1526) or Martin Droeshout's *William Shakespeare* (1623). The seemingly contrary claims and competing signals of Marshall's portrait and Milton's legend to it anticipate the grounds of contestation involving the later prose works, particularly the three *Defenses*, where Milton as represented by others and then by himself is surrounded by a confusing range of contradictory images. For every action there is a reaction: whenever Milton is represented by another, he counters with a self-representation, as if to say that he knows himself and in self-portraiture is better revealed than in representations by the William Marshalls of the world. Over time, Milton's self-representations are so numerous that they constitute, as Brilliant might say, "a figured record of the subject over the years, providing, in the ensemble, a sense of the whole being as a changing constant."[21]

Indeed, by the time of Milton's three *Defenses*, the autobiographical impulse is so strong, his presence so powerful, that in *Fides Publica* More chides him for delivering "windy panegyric . . . by yourself upon yourself," in virtually the same breath suggesting as an alternative title for *Defensio Secunda*, "*Milton upon His Own Life*" (YP 4:1097)—a proposal Milton leaps at as he proceeds to fashion *Pro Se Defensio* (*His Defence of Himself*). These works, taken together, suggest the entanglement of defenses of himself and defenses of the English people, the interdependency and interchangeability of all these works. "*John Milton, Englishman*"—the poet's preferred signature, and part of the inscription in the oval surrounding the 1645 Marshall portrait, another indication of authorial collaboration in the design of this frontispiece—is reminiscent of scriptural convention whereby Abraham and Samson stand for both individual and nation, their reputations and national destiny irrevocably involved.

If there is any shock to be registered, it comes with the recognition that the conclusions Milton invites, the very contentions he elicits from his critics, then and now, concerning his seeming omnipresence in his poetry, are ones he himself challenges. The terms Milton employs are reminiscent of those used in our own time by Roland Barthes to question similar claims of authorial presence. As the theorist who proclaimed "the Death of the Author," who would subvert the very notion of authorship, has said, the "dead" writer still survives in characters who, though not the author, are "a secondary, derived fragment" of him. The author survives in the text not as host but as guest, "inscribe[d] . . . as one of his characters, drawn as a figure in the carpet; his inscription is no longer privileged . . . he becomes, one can say, a paper author . . . a paper *I*."[22]

That is just how the Milton of both *An Apology Against a Pamphlet* and *Pro Populo Anglicano Defensio* would have it. In the first instance, he declares that "the author is ever distinguisht from the person he introduces" (YP 1:880); and in the second: "we should consider not so much what the poet says, as who in the poem says it. Various figures appear, some good, some bad, some wise, some foolish, each speaking not the poet's opinions but what is appropriate for each person" (YP 4:439). Then quoting a passage from Seneca's *Hercules Furens* (922–24), Milton complicates, even confounds, this idea with the proposal that some voices in a poem or play may be privileged over others:

> if you take these as the words of Hercules, in whose mouth they are placed, they show the judgment of the greatest Greek of his time; if you take them as the words of the poet who lived in Nero's age—and it is the custom of poets to place their own opinions in the mouths of their great characters—he indicates what he himself and all good men in Nero's time thought should be done with tyrants; how righteous, how pleasing to the gods they held tyrannicide to be. (YP 4:446)

The proposition set forth in this last statement reminds us that Milton's poetry regularly exposes the limitations in critical systems that would contain and explain it.

In the first two of these instances, however, Milton formulates the proposition that a line of critics, which includes Anne Ferry, Robert Durling, Harry Berger, William Riggs, Boyd Berry, John Mulder, John Steadman, John Shawcross, and, most recently, Robert McMahon, has been driving home: "What the poem says at its various points and what its historical author thought or believed are not necessarily the same."[23] Yet Milton pushes further than his critics, as if to ask of them questions such as Barthes asks of Balzac:[24] Who speaks this way? Is it the hero of the tale (if we think we know who he or she is)? Is it Milton's poetic persona, Milton the author, or Milton the man? Does he speak universal wisdom? Or the politics and theology of his time? Or does he rather try to articulate a newly emerging (but still shared) understanding, or one unique to him as a sect of one? As an early modern writer, does Milton support or subvert the empire (some would say the *tyranny*) of the author? And if he is engaged in subversion, is it simply a gesture of iconoclasm effecting the removal of the author? Or does Milton make league with the reader—in the process, repressing the author in order to rescue the reader?

If it can be said that Milton's poetic career begins with the publication of the 1645 *Poems*, where his emergence as an author is, according to Humphrey Moseley, "*as true a birth, as the Muses have brought forth since . . . Spencer wrote*,"[25] then it should also be acknowledged that Milton's poetic career, culminating in the publication of *Samson Agonistes*, ends with the removal and death of the author effected by the lifting of a narrative frame and consequent annihilation of a narrative voice. Still, the author may say *no* to death, thereby announcing his survival, in the case of *Samson Agonistes,* within the recesses of the poem's epistle, as well as in the shadows of this poem's protagonist, although one must also ask if in Samson we behold Milton's current or his former self, a real or a fabled image of the author. A poetic career that begins with a conspicuous authorial presence ends with a rather more elusive one.

Milton discourages easy correlations between himself and his personae or between the author and various of his characters. Simultaneously, he lays down hints concerning where marks of his presence can be found; where that presence, unprecedentedly strong, yet highly amorphous, can be most felt and best observed. By steering us, in doing so, from pictures to the word, from portraits to poems and then to the writer writing, Milton displays his greatest affinity with postmodern theory. The New York artist Frank J. Boros is responsible for a whole series of portraits, some of them self-portraits, that, never depicting a human figure, instead map character by figuring the space the person or artist inhabits: by what is there and not there, by relative order and disorder—by accouterments. Revelations emerge from delineations of personal space, not persons, and by extension from poems by, not portraits of, the artist. Boros's conception, thus translated from painting back into literature, suggests that authors do not so much write themselves into their works as, through their very lives, afford a model for the new work, in Milton's case the poem.

Inlays of autobiography, rather than digressions, are integral to the prose and poetry alike. As Margaret Bottrall explains, they are aspects of "self-assertion, self-scrutiny, self-revelation" and, just as important, "pertinent replies to the abuse that had been flung at [Milton] . . . by political adversaries.[26] Yet these inlays, especially in the poetry, do not mean that Milton, even if blind and a prisoner like Samson, is writing autobiography. Rather, as Northrop Frye has said of the last published of these poems, "the link between Samson and Milton does not mean that *Samson Agonistes* is an autobiographical poem: it simply means that Milton was the only man who could have written it."[27]

II. The Author as Collaborator

We are in process of recovering an understanding that seems to have been widely held in the seventeenth century: "books were not the product of an isolated individual operating autonomously" but instead, as Stephen B. Dobranski observes, part of "a complex, dynamic, cooperative process"—a collaborative process between the writers of books and the makers of them.[28]

Moreover, it seems to have recently become self-evident to students of early modern texts that, in the 1645 *Poems,* Milton asserts a collaborative relationship with William Marshall, Henry Moseley, and typographers, the likes of which he would maintain in his later publications, quite remarkably so in both editions of *Paradise Lost.* On the 1645 frontispiece, through the devices of a legend in the oval frame of the portrait, an epigram beneath it, and iconographic embellishments in its margins, Milton, even as he hints that collaboration may be more extensive than we have supposed, and that Marshall himself may be privy to Milton's joke, contests the authorial identity projected through a portrait of a figure in academic regalia and aristocratic pose. At the same time, Milton uses such devices to begin the construction of an alternative identity hinted at in other elements of the front matter and confirmed by the poems themselves. Indeed, the poems contradict the claims of the frontispiece and title page, which would place Milton in the courtly tradition of Edmund Waller, and situate him instead within the Spenserian tradition claimed for him by Humphrey Moseley and, more broadly, within the Virgilian tradition insinuated through epigraphs on both the main title page and the 1637 title page for *A Mask.*

Since Milton never specifies, we will never know the extent of his collusion with printers or their typographers concerning the makeup of title pages or, for that matter, contents pages. Still, it becomes evident in *An Apology Against a Pamphlet,* then in *Areopagitica* and *Eikonoklastes,* and finally in *Pro Se Defensio,* that during the seventeenth century others, as well as Milton, scrutinized both titles and title pages (YP 1:876, 877; 3:343, 597; 4:733–34). As he worries over what is an apt title in *Areopagitica,* Milton notices how "Sometimes 5 *Imprimaturs* are seen together . . . in the Piatza of one Title page, complementing and ducking each to other" (YP 2:504), in the same work speaks of mischievous books with "dangerous Frontispices" (YP 2:524), and, if John Phillips is a reliable guide, also considers in what circumstances an author may publish anonymously, or nearly so, as Milton did with the 1637 edition of *A Mask,* the 1638 publication of *Lycidas,* the first edition of *The Doctrine and Discipline of Divorce,* and some issues of *Paradise Lost* that have a 1668 title page.[29]

It is folly to forget that "visually sophisticated" elements in texts like *Lycidas* and *Paradise Lost* are, in the words of Mark Bland, "more likely to have come from an author or a party acting on the author's behalf, rather than the printer" and folly, too, to overly credit Roy Flannagan's contention that the "blind Milton obviously exerted less control on the printing of what he wrote than the sighted Milton."[30] This first point is illustrated powerfully by the title page to *Areopagitica.* If the printer has suppressed his own name, Milton fearlessly showcases his identity, incorporating it into the subtitle of this work. The second point finds its best illustration in the expanding front matter for *Paradise Lost,* as that poem moves through different issues and eventually into a second edition.

Signatures of authorship become marks of honor for Milton. He complains, in *Defensio Secunda,* about engaging in polemic with those who publish "furtively and by stealth" and choose to remain "nameless" and who, doing so, are neither "devoted enough . . . nor loyal enough" to their cause. By contrast, Milton says of himself: "I was so far from being ashamed either of myself or my cause that I considered it disgraceful to attack so great a theme without openly acknowledging my identity" (YP 4:560–61). Any argument that the later Milton is hiding out when he publishes nearly anonymously, with initials only ("J. M."), the second edition of *The Readie and Easie Way,* as well as several early issues of *Paradise Lost,* needs to acknowledge that earlier titles of both works bear his full signature. Also to be acknowledged is that similarly anonymous works, like *A Treatise of Civil Power,* even if their title pages bear no more than an initialed signature, carry prefaces (in this instance, "To The Parlament") with a bold signature: JOHN MILTON. If, too often, not enough has been made of Milton's signatures, one should correspondingly not make too much of them either.

Given the centrality of *Lycidas* to Milton's canon, the privilege of place it was accorded in the 1695 edition of Milton's *Poems* (now printed first), plus its climactic place among the English poems in the 1645 edition, the title LYCIDAS, by virtue of its huge, boldfaced letters, leaps from the table of contents as if to assert its singular importance and as if to signal that, in matters such as these, Milton is very much in collaboration with printers and typographers (and will remain so throughout his publishing career). In this instance certainly, as well as in the typographic subordination of *A Mask* to "this Monody," which occurs in both editions published during Milton's lifetime, the best surmise, when it comes to the title pages for Milton's epic-prophecies, is that those title pages themselves constitute part of a collaboration between poet and printer. Hence, they should be regarded, on the one hand, as an act of mediation on the poet's part and, on the other hand, as an early reception deriving from publisher or printer (or both), indeed as an integral part of the poem's reception history. Milton's title pages, like seventeenth-century title pages generally, are themselves—with the texts they accompany, as they imply—sites for mediation (the title page for *Areopagitica* is a notable example). Or as Mark Bland remarks so discerningly: these title pages, together with the poem's front matter, are "point[s] of confluence where the constructions of meaning—the meetings of minds—" take place.[31]

It is clear from the printer's note to the reader in some later issues of the first edition of *Paradise Lost* that printer collaborates with poet to produce both the note on "why the poem rhymes not" and the arguments to its individual books, each reminding us that there is a poet behind this poem, overseeing, orchestrating the whole performance even to the point of revising it. The nature of the revisions (especially with regard to structure) is revelatory, no less so than inclusions as well as exclusions (dedicatory poems by "S. B." and Andrew Marvell in the first instance, and in the second the absence of a dedicatory page). When *Paradise Lost* goes into a second edition, this point is reinforced by the acknowledged revision of a ten-book into a twelve-book poem, then underscored by the expansion of the front matter to include the dedicatory—and mediatorial—poems by "S. B." and Marvell, as well as the addition of some fifteen new lines of poetry.

With the disappearance of the printer's note from the second edition, Milton himself, through his note on verse form, acts as mediator even as he now seems to enlist S. B. and Andrew Marvell, through their dedicatory poems, as additional negotiators with his readers. Taken together, the front matter constitutes a negotiation strategy crafted by Milton, who is, in this way, seen at the portal to his poem quite apart from the frontispiece portrait added to this second edition. He is also seen in his revisions to poems, with the "omissa" to *Samson Agonistes* further illustrating the point, as if flagging Milton's presence and thereby driving home Anne Middleton's proposition that "the author's labors as maker also situate the author himself within . . . [a poem's] reception history as reviser."[32] In the very act of mediating a poem to its audience, the author himself becomes a crucial player in the drama of its reception.

Particularly remarkable about Milton's title pages, together with the accumulating front matter, is that poet and poem, poem and reader, are bound inextricably in single compact so as to insist upon the poet's presence in a poem that completes itself in the mind of the reader; so as to establish outside the poem the dialectical relationship between poet and reader that is at its core. Moreover, as we proceed from the title pages to *Paradise Lost* where Milton's name (in initials only) is nearly anonymous to later ones (still belonging to the first edition) where the poet's name, even if muted by comparison with other elements of the title page, is nevertheless spelled out, and then onward to the second edition of *Paradise Lost*, where the poet's image is flashed across the title page from the frontispiece—when we take all this into account, the conclusion seems obvious. Initially, Milton mutes his presence through a practiced self-effacement explained by John Phillips in his "Response" to John Rowland as he perhaps borrows on Milton's wisdom. "It is by no means unusual for worthy men to withhold their names . . . [as does] St. Paul in the Epistle to the Hebrews," Phillips retorts to Rowland's remark. "He did, to be sure, write anonymously, but to a people bitterly hostile to his name about matters quite new and little credited" (YP 4:905). Nevertheless, *Paradise Lost* is a poem that, in its front matter, becomes increasingly self-referential, paving the way for our regular sightings of Milton in the multiple prologues to his epic-prophecy, in virtually all its characters, as well as within certain of the narrator's disruptive intrusions within the poem proper. The flashing images of Milton in the prologues and his flickering presence in each of the poem's characters both destabilize the portrait of Milton frozen into the frontispiece portrait. As we look for Milton's authentic image and voice in this poem, we are led repeatedly to the author's disruptive presence marked by a torn text; and if we continue to be haunted by Phillips's remark it is perhaps because it is so apt to the circumstances surrounding *De Doctrina Christiana*, indeed our best explanation as to why that work should remain without signature, apparently until after Milton's death.

III. Entering the Breach

One of the most provocative and, simultaneously, misguided claims of late-twentieth-century Milton criticism is that there is a "sequential principle" operating in and between Milton's epic-prophecies, and that it operates in such a way as to privilege the second over the first poem, and later books of *Paradise Lost* over earlier ones. What comes last, Robert McMahon argues, qualifies and corrects what precedes it; that is, "later utterances can modify earlier ones, but earlier ones cannot modify later ones."[33] By such calculation, coming late in Book Twelve, Adam's embrace of the felix culpa—"O goodness infinite, goodness immense! / That all this good of evil shall produce" (469–70)—would constitute this poem's final, definitive word on this topic. Interpreting according to this sequential principle, of course, evades Milton's own concept of privileged voices, his belief that a writer's own sentiments are given expression by the best of his characters. Adam's voice, according to McMahon's argument, takes precedence over God's, which earlier repudiates a doctrine that fallen Adam eventually embraces: "Happier, had it suffic'd him to have known / Good by it self, and Evil not at all" (11.88–89). The whole notion of a happy fall, even before these concluding books, is eroded by the narrator's declaration, "O yet happiest if ye seek / No happier state, and know to know no more" (4.774–75), and then by Raphael's insistence that no one needs to fall in order to rise. Rather, "body [will] up to spirit work, in bounds / Proportiond to each kind" (5.478–79), Raphael says, while explaining that the time will "come when men / With Angels may participate" (5.493–94). Then comes the acknowledgment of *unfallen* Adam that "In contemplation of created things / By steps we may ascend to God" (5.511–12) and his later admission to God that "[thou] Canst raise thy Creature to what highth thou wilt / Of Union or Communion, deifi'd" (8.430–31). Only the voice of the fallen Satan upholds the doctrine to which *fallen* Adam subscribes: "From this descent / Celestial vertues rising, will appear / More glorious and more dread then from no fall" (2.14–16) and, later, "happie though thou art, / Happier thou mayst be" (5.75–76). Milton's opinions, if they are to be found in his poetry, are, by his own admission, to be found in the mouths of his *great* characters, whose independence of mind steers clear of theological commonplaces.

Milton's opinions are also to be found, it would seem, in sites of contestation like the following. These are the words of Milton's Pauline narrator, who declares that, although Eve is "much deceav'd" (9.404), Adam is *"not deceav'd, / But fondly overcome with Femal charm"* (9.998–99, italics mine; cf. 1.35–36), his words contradicting those of God: "Man falls deceiv'd / By the other first: Man therefore shall find grace, / The other none" (3.130–32). God's words, moreover, are echoed here by Satan and there by Adam and Eve. "Man I deceav'd" (10.496; see also 41, 577), says Satan; and later, hurling recriminations at Eve while allowing for their mutual deception, Adam addresses Eve as "thou Serpent" who "Fool'd and beguil'd" him as the serpent also fooled and beguiled her (10.867, 879–80). In her response, which begins "Forsake me not thus, *Adam*" (10.914), Eve adapts Adam's rhetoric to her apology, where she owns up to having unwittingly offended, "Unhappilie deceav'd," him (10.917), prompting Adam, in his turn, to concede that "the Serpent hath contriv'd / Against us this deceit" (10.1034–35). Woman's deception of man registers as proverbial wisdom in *Samson Agonistes:* "wisest Men / Have err'd, and by bad Women been deceiv'd" (210–11). In this instance, Milton's tragedy observes the strategy and emphasis of *Christus Patiens,* the Christian tragedy cited in the preface to *Samson Agonistes,* with the Mother of God insisting that woman was deceived first— *never,* but for the serpent, "would the offspring of the rib, / . . . have been deceived / And dared to dare an over-daring deed" (4–6; cf. 943)—even as the verses of the poet-theologian, published as prologue to *Christus Patiens,* make all of mankind party to "the beast's deceit" (17). If Satan "contrived" by the error of woman "to defeat the human race, God contrived against him" (and with woman) to effect mankind's redemption (578–83).[34]

Milton mocks Satan's reading of the Genesis account of Creation according to the sequential principle, as Satan apostrophizes the Earth "as built / With second thoughts, reforming what was old" (9.100–101). By this logic Man as the center of the new creation surpasses the God who is at the center of the first creation (9.99–113). Similarly, a sequential principle for reading *Paradise Lost* forces us, presumptuously, to credit the narrator's conclusion over God's; indeed, to accept the narrator's conclusion as a corrective to and straightening out of God's crooked theology. Against such a position, it may be argued, first of all, that in *Tetrachordon* Milton privileged the Hebrew Bible over St. Paul's interpretation of it—indeed was chided for doing so by his early critics—and second, that by later commentators, both men and women, Hannah More as well as William Hayley, he was commended for just these swervings from Pauline orthodoxies.[35] The collective force of the statements by God and Satan, Adam and Eve, it would seem, overrules the words of the Pauline narrator: man is "not deceav'd" (9.998; cf. 404 and 1.35–36). In *Paradise Regained,* Satan reiterates his own stand on such issues, which is also God's stand: *"Adam* and his facil consort *Eve* / Lost Paradise *deceiv'd* by me" (1.51–52; italics in the second line mine).

If there is a Miltonic logic to be inferred from these examples, it is that when Satan agrees with God he speaks truth; and if there is a larger principle of interpretation, it is that the authentic Milton, an interrogator—and sometimes a transgressor—of orthodox opinion lurks in these sites of contestation from which he often reveals himself as a sect of one. He establishes precise inflections, makes crucial choices, all the while gently nudging us to do the same. Milton's poems may ultimately complete themselves in the experience of the reader; yet a vital part of their experience is of the writer writing. No less important than acknowledging a dialectic between the poet and his audience is determining the ethos of each and, hence, whether Milton's poetry encourages (as some would have it) a dialectic between a pietistic bard and a devout reader or, instead, sets against a text of platitudinous Christianity and submissive orthodoxy one of rebellion and subversion.

The aforementioned examples reflect correctively on much existing criticism in that, in our search for the author, they push us into often unvisited spaces, those breaches within poems created by inscribed contradictions. At the same time, the examples do not foreclose the possibility of finding Milton in the more usual places: in certain of his characters, including his narrator, especially in the multiple prologues, which, as John S. Diekhoff argued years ago, act as epistles in which Milton can fashion self-defenses and offer self-explanation.[36] On the one hand, the narrator acts as a second self, "whose similarity to the author," says Foucault, "is never fixed and undergoes considerable alteration within the course of a single book. It would be as false to seek the author in relation to the actual writer as to the fictional narrator; the 'author-function' arises out of their scission—in the division and distance of the two."[37] On the other hand, the prologues to individual books of *Paradise Lost,* where the narrator is so conspicuous a presence, have not only a narrative but a rhetorical function: they are centers of ethical proof through which the narrator, and Milton through the narrator, establishes himself as "a composition, and patterne of the best and honourablest things"—in words from

An Apology Against a Pamphlet, as having "in himselfe the experience and the practice of all that which is praise-worthy" (YP 1:890).

Such an understanding is traceable to Jonathan Richardson Sr., who finds in the accumulation of passages like this one not merely delineations of Milton's mind, or vindications of his character, but the hope of exciting others "to be Enamour'd, as Hee, with the *Beauty of Holiness*."[38] This multifaceted agenda, not restricted to the prologues of *Paradise Lost*, spills over into the narrative proper, which itself functions at times as *apologia*, particularly in its representations of Satan wherein comparisons involving shimmering likenesses are usually overruled by forced distinctions. If there is a rhetoric to Milton's prologues, there is likewise a rhetorical component to his narratives, Satan's here and Samson's later.

IV. "ALWAYS A KNIT OF IDENTITY . . . ALWAYS DISTINCTION"

If at the time of the Restoration Milton was occasionally elided with Samson, because of his supposed revenge fantasy of toppling the restored monarchy, he was also—and even more persistently—mythologized as Satan, because of his participation in rebellion and sedition. With John Goodwin, he was numbered among the "Rebellious Devils" and "Blinde Guides" of a now-stumbling nation. Speaking with the devil's mouth and sorted with the devil's party, this "Infamous," "Sacrilegious *Milton*" was called a *"Diabolical Rebel"*—"altogether a Devil" posing as a saint, a compendium of the most hated villains and their various villainies—and presumed already to have "gone to hell."[39] Long before William Blake, Milton was thought to be of the devil's party.

Within this context we can best assess Milton's audacity in beginning *Paradise Lost* in hell and in then presenting so alluring a portrait of Satan. Milton responds effectively to a horizon of expectation, established by a swarm of adversaries, but with some surprises as he pulls their whiskers before tearing them out. In what must be a carefully calculated gesture, Milton, as if he were blurring his own persona into the character of Satan, begins *Paradise Lost* with a descent into the underworld, but he also, with equal calculation, completes the depiction of his journey with an allusion to the Orpheus story. Returning from hell, "now with bolder wing," the poet-narrator, as if on Milton's behalf, claims to be singing "With other notes then to th' *Orphean* Lyre," having been "Taught by the heav'nly Muse to venture down / The dark descent, and up to reascend" (3.77, 19–20), and emphasizing, as if in response to Milton's critics, that he is no less differentiated from Satan than are Prometheus, Achilles, Aeneas, and Odysseus. Milton's narrator, moreover, has journeyed into hell without making of himself a hell or, more important, without (as Orpheus had done) entering into a contract with Pluto—or the devil.

In the very act of shifting the network of classical allusion from parallels with Satan's role to parallels with his own, the narrator would seem to invite the further conjecture hazarded earlier in this century by Denis Saurat and implied earlier still by William Blake: that the author of *Paradise Lost* is his own hero.[40] If heroism in this poem is to be ascertained and measured by a character's resemblance to classical paradigms, then this strategic shift of reference from Satan to the narrator and, through the narrator, to Milton makes the poet himself the surest choice and standard for heroism. In his 1671 poetic volume, Milton shifts the standard of comparison from classical to biblical exemplars of heroism, finding in Samson's life multiplying parallels with his own, yet finally suppressing their likenesses by emphasizing their still more striking differences. With Samson's story as with Satan's, Milton is telling not an exemplary tale but a cautionary one, which requires him to distance himself from those with whom he had been aligned (often by his adversaries). And that is the crucial point here.

Likening Milton to Satan and Samson through creative analogy is the doing of Milton's adversaries. These analogies Milton sets about undoing in *Paradise Lost* and *Samson Agonistes* as part of his *apologia*. In the process, Milton parodies a venerable tradition of portraiture exemplified quite notably by a portrait of the third-century Roman emperor Commodus as *Commodus-Hercules*—a mode of portraiture in which historical persons are shown possessing the attributes of figures in legend and mythology by way of aggrandizing them through the comparisons. Milton's enemies employed the counter-strategy of invoking analogies and, through them, ascribing to Milton attributes that would diminish and demean him. In turn, Milton's strategy is to define himself by differentiation and, through differentiation, to fashion and mediate an alternative image of himself.

Milton is joined in this work of mediation through an *apologia* by Andrew Marvell, whose dedicatory poem for the second edition of *Paradise Lost* addresses six charges, most of them deriving from Milton's adversaries: the first that his blindness, coming upon him suddenly, is a mark of divine disfavor; the second that, driven by revenge, Milton, Samson-like in his sedition, is poised to hurl down the pillars of church and state; third, that Milton's projects always seem to involve a twisting and turning of Scripture and a consequent mutilation of God's word; fourth, that Milton is a pretender to prophecy; fifth, that in an act of enormous hubris Milton claims to "soar aloft" (37); and sixth that his rhymeless verse is both artless and politically charged.

The prologue to Book Three, with "the Bard's confession of blindness," is slighted by Robert McMahon as an irrelevancy ("no literary necessity"), despite the fact that, as we have seen, it undermines, quite intentionally, earlier attempts to identify Milton with Satan.[41] It also provides Marvell with the arguments he thinks will undermine identification of Milton with Samson. This is the prologue that, through persistent echo and allusion, is foregrounded by Marvell's poem, which, in defense of the poet, argues, on the one hand, that Milton is no spiteful Samson and, on the other, that apparently unlike Samson but certainly "like *Tiresias*," "Heav'n . . . / Rewards with *Prophesie* . . . [Milton's] loss of Sight" (43–44). As early as *Tetrachordon*, Milton took it for "a generall precept" of all the "Sages, not to instruct the unworthy and the conceited who love tradition more then truth, but to *perplex* and stumble them purposely with contriv'd obscurities" (YP 2:643; italics mine). In *Defensio Secunda*, Milton confronted his accusers head-on: theirs is a blindness that, "deeply implanted in the inmost faculties, obscures the mind" so that they "see nothing whole or real"; his, a blindness that only deprives him of "superficial appearance" but leaves him with "intellectual vision," as well as "the light of the divine countenance" (YP 4:589–90).

At the same time that he is blind, then, Milton is "most keen in vision" and prays, again in *Defensio Secunda*, in language anticipating the prologues to Books One and Three of *Paradise Lost*, that by his infirmity he "may . . . be perfected, by this completed," "in this darkness, . . . clothed in light," in "an inner and enduring light" of "divine favor" (YP 4:589–90). In *Paradise Lost*, therefore, far from perplexing God's word, Milton performs as, in Marvell's judgment, an inspired interpreter of it: one whose darkness has been illumined by the irradiating power of celestial light, and who thus sees and tells of things invisible to mortal sight; one whose rhymeless (unpremeditated) verse is both a token of and testimony to his prophetic office. Even when Samson was admitted to the company of prophets, it was to exemplify the lowest order of prophecy, not the order of prophecy with which Milton aligns both his narrator and himself in comparisons with Moses and John of Patmos.

Milton's own life has been a steady progress toward the truth and, unlike Samson's, stands free of, instead of being shot through with, sometimes suspect conversion experiences. Again unlike Samson, Milton, not driven by revenge fantasies and motives, is providentially spared the life that Samson loses. Nor was Marvell alone in defending Milton against charges of vindictiveness. Witness, for example, Edward Phillips, whose "Life" of the poet speaks of Milton's own very "generous nature, more inclinable to Reconciliation than to perseverance in Anger and Revenge."[42] More important, witness Milton himself, who, while chastising others for the "divine vengeance" they "rashly and absurdly invoke on others," in *Defensio Secunda* says of himself: "Far be it from me to have so little spirit . . . , or so little charity that I cannot . . . easily pardon [my enemies]" and thereupon allows that he "bear[s] no grudge whatever . . . against any man" and "endure[s] . . . with the greater equanimity all the curses that are uttered" against him (YP 4:599, 591, 596).

Compare to Milton's posture here that of Samson, who sharply rebukes Dalila when she pleads for forgiveness and, indeed, mocks those who forgive (759–65)—an episode that stands in sharp contrast to the poem's epistolary reference to *Christus Patiens* (or *Christ Suffering*). There the mother of God, addressing Peter, assures him that, though he "has done great evil," as well as "terrible things," he "can still obtain forgiveness," Peter here "sin[ning] for fear of the mob" (814–19) as Dalila herself sins out of fear that her threatening countrymen will treat her as cruelly as they had Samson's Timnian bride.

A pardoner of others, Milton himself, probably owing to Marvell's intervention, won a pardon in 1660, without which we would probably not have any of his last poems to engage in such points of contestation. What Milton says of himself and what his biographers say of him set the poet apart from the unforgiving, unpardoning Samson, thus questioning the proposition argued most forcefully by Michael Lieb that, because Samson is Milton's chosen hero, the poet projects himself into him, becoming what he beholds, in the process adopting Samson's violence as his own signature as he turns his enemies' "theater of assault" into his own (and Samson's) "theater of destruction." For Lieb, then, "Milton's defense of the regicides is a defense of himself, his support of their cause, a support of his own. In that defense, he himself becomes the strong man."[43] Behind Lieb's argument is a whole tradition of Milton criticism that sees Samson's duplicity and wiliness as of a piece with Rahab's noble lying, Ehud's justifiable deceptions (justifiable because Ehud clearly "acted upon divine prompting"), and Jael's "pious fraud"; that is, as a part of Milton's ongoing "self-justification," which is as evident in *De Doctrina Christiana* as in *Samson Agonistes* (see YP 6:764 and n.10).

Milton and Samson shared certain circumstances, to be sure. Both men were seemingly chosen for high exploits, in Milton's words from *Pro Se Defensio*, "now to venture into the sun, and dust, and field of battle, now to exert real brawn, brandish real arms, seek a real enemy" (YP 4:795). In Milton's case, not before but in the aftermath of blindness, these words themselves are heightened to metaphorical meaning. Engaged in mental fight, both here and in *Defensio Secunda,* Milton exalts battle by the pen over battle by the sword, extolling "that truth . . . defended by reason—the only defence truly appropriate to man" (see YP 4:553, cf. 624). Likewise, both Samson and Milton, only one of them forgiving, were unfortunate in their marriage choices, each having been stung by women; and both in later life, having been briefly incarcerated, felt dejected and defeated. For many of Milton's critics, however, it was not just common circumstances that linked Samson and Milton but the shared feelings and opinions that were their outgrowth.

If initially it seemed that "Milton made the best" of "very indifferent

subject matter" by choosing the Samson story and unleashing its satiric po-
tentiality against bad women and bad wives, before the end of the nineteenth
century, the screen of autobiography had been greatly enlarged. *Samson
Agonistes* was now being read by David Masson, for example, as "a represen-
tation of Milton in his secret antagonism to all the powers and all the fashions
of the Restoration" and, still more broadly, as a poem in which Samson's
tragedy affords "a metaphor for the tragedy of Milton's life."[44] Yet in an
enormous swing of this pendulum, insisting that "Milton had no thought of
creating a personal or political allegory," William Riley Parker (as the first
reception of the poem, by Marvell, had done) stresses the differences be-
tween Samson and Milton, as if to say that poetry sometimes approaches but
seldom replicates autobiography.[45]

Rarely does a critic mention (Lieb is the most notable exception) that
Samson's volatile rhetoric finds its parallels not in Milton's attacks upon his
opponents but rather in their attacks upon him.[46] When, in his dedication to
du Moulin's *Clamor,* More promises its readers that they are about to witness
Salmasius "tearing to pieces this disgrace [Milton] to the human race" (YP
4:1045),[47] he uses the same language of intimidation Samson deploys against
Dalila when she pleads, "Let me approach at least, and touch thy hand": "Not
for thy life, lest fierce remembrance wake / My sudden rage to tear thee joint
by joint" (951–53). When, in turn, du Moulin in his *Clamor* imagines Milton
being "whirled . . . into the air" and, once felled, "bestrew[ing] the rocks far
and wide with his shattered brain" (YP 4:1078), he attacks Milton with the
same language Samson hurls at Harapha: "Go baffl'd coward, lest I run upon
thee . . . / And with one buffet lay thy structure low, / Or swing thee in the Air,
then dash thee down / To th' hazard of thy brains and shatter'd sides" (1237,
1239–41).

More telling still are passages from 1 Corinthians 15:32 and 15:33 cited
no fewer than five times by Milton, very importantly in *Pro Se Defensio* (see
also YP 2:507–8; 6:403, 620, 751) and again in the preface to *Samson Ago-
nistes*—a passage that reinforces the point made in the first of the earlier
examples:

If after the manner of men I have fought with beasts at Ephesus, what advantageth it
me, if the dead rise not? let us eat and drink; for tomorrow we die.
    Be not deceived: evil communications corrupt good manners.

In *Pro Se Defensio,* Milton says of Alexander More:

you wickedly attribute to yourself that glorious martyrdom of the Apostle when you
say that you fought with beasts, . . . not as a man with a beast, but, yourself a beast, with
a human being—that is, with a woman. (YP 4:751)

That Samson, who had earlier torn the lion as the lion tears the kid, should address Dalila as a beast, then threaten to destroy her as earlier he had destroyed the lion, speaks volumes. "Out, out *Hyaena*" (748), Samson rails, as he later acknowledges learning from this woman the "Adders wisdom" (936) and as he now fears that, in a fit of "sudden rage," he will "tear . . . [Dalila] joint by joint" (953). When the Chorus (at Samson's prompting) describes Dalila as "a manifest Serpent" (997) and Samson, in his turn, calls her a "viper" (1001), Samson invites from us the very kind of rebuke that Milton delivers to More: you, Samson, are now fighting with beasts *"not as a man with a beast, but, yourself a beast, with a human being—that is, with a woman."*

In turn, Milton's rebuke of More recalls an earlier one from *The Doctrine and Discipline of Divorce* aimed at any man who, in his perverse imaginings, turns "this bounty" of God's creation, women, into a stinging "Scorpion, either by weak and shallow constructions, or by proud arrogance and cruelty to them" (YP 2:595–96). Here, of course, Milton is talking about bad husbands and good wives, as opposed to what some think is the reverse situation in *Samson Agonistes*, although the complexity of this poem and the force of its interrogations, together with the stinging rhetoric of both Samson and the Chorus, allow for the questions of just how good a husband is Samson and how bad a wife is Dalila? Is she "the most bird-brained woman ever to have gotten herself involved in major tragedy" or, instead, "a deeply wronged wife"?[48] Milton, the so-called woman-hater, often said to return to the fold by giving women their due in *Samson Agonistes*, by sleight of hand, seems instead to be giving Samson his due as he reminds us, yet again, that the author of a work is always distinguished from the character he introduces.

Milton's practice here finds an analogy in Caravaggio's depiction of his own features on the head of Goliath held by David and thrust at the viewer by way of "inviting the spectator to read him."[49] One may read Caravaggio's features in the face of Goliath, Samson's in Harapha, and Milton's in Samson. In each projection, we observe versions of the selves of David, Samson, and Milton, respectively—versions of the self sacrificed in each disfiguration, in each self-mutilation. In Caravaggio's painting, we witness, in effect, the decapitation of the artist; and in *Samson Agonistes*, we witness his death or, rather, the death of Milton's violent self, Milton's "repristination" not within a culture of violence, as Lieb argues, but with the extirpation of a culture of violence that is as much the signature of Harapha as of Samson but no longer that of Milton. While Lieb presents *Samson Agonistes* as "the expression of Milton's attempt to deal in poetic form with the crisis that faced him during the time the Defenses were produced,"[50] in a process that turns both Samson and Milton from victim into victimizer and celebrates each in this transformation, my point is otherwise: *Samson Agonistes* mounts a critique of, it does not celebrate, a culture of violence; it shows Milton embracing an ethical system to which Samson is a stranger, one trumpeting in poetry the lamentation and declaration of *De Doctrina Christiana:* "Violence alone prevails; . . . it is disgraceful and disgusting that the Christian religion should be supported by violence" (YP 6:123).

The distinctions between Samson and Milton forced by the poem itself are maintained by the pairing of poems in the 1671 poetic volume, reminiscent of the wisdom (perhaps Milton's own?) articulated by John Phillips in his "Response": "He is not Christ's, but the devil's deputy who does not imitate Christ's example" (YP 4:943). And it is that example, thrust upon *Samson Agonistes* by virtue of the reference to *Christus Patiens (Christ Suffering)* in the poem's epistle, that drives the final wedge between Samson and Milton; that uses differences implied by, or stated within, this epistle to underscore the differences emerging from the poem, with the epistle itself announcing itself as an *apologia,* this term explaining one function of the poem itself.

V. "MUCH BEFORE-HAND MAY BE EPISTL'D"

One of the wisest of Milton's critics, Joan S. Bennett, would have us understand this of Milton's prefatory epistle: "[It] tells us that in the tragedy we will find ourselves in the same Christian humanist world to which the epics belong . . . and that, in submitting ourselves to this tragedy, we will enter an experience graver, more moral, and to our greater spiritual good than even that of *Paradise Lost* and *Paradise Regained.*"[51] Milton's preface states immensely—and otherwise. It is impossible to read the 1671 poetic volume and not remember, when coming upon the title page and preface to *Samson Agonistes,* that this critic represents Milton's tragedy to us just as Satan, in *Paradise Regain'd,* represents the genre to Jesus: as teacher "best / Of moral prudence, . . . High actions, and high passions best describing" (4.262–63, 266). Representing tragedy as one of nature's fallen forms, Jesus, in turn, exalts those forms by "God inspir'd" as "better" teachers (4.350, 357).

Here, it is important to notice that the citations of *Christ Suffering* and of 1 Corinthians 15:33 in the preface to *Samson Agonistes* are of a piece, each citation, however differently, bringing Euripides to the fore. By most accounts, St. Paul's struggle with the wild beasts is metaphorical, referring to taming the beast within or to conflicts with other men who in their condition and manners are like wild beasts. Moreover, the exhortation, "Be not deceived: evil communications corrupt good manners," now attributed to Menander but in Milton's day printed in editions of Euripides as well as Menander, allows that by evil communications and conversations—by false doctrines and bad examples—the morals of the people (or in some translations, the manners, dispositions, or minds of the people) are corrupted since, in words from *Christus Patiens*, "evil goes in competition with evil" (43).[52] Here in 1 Corinthians 15:32–33, the views of one heathen poet rival those of another.

The words just quoted from *Christus Patiens* epitomize an interpretation of 1 Corinthians 15:32–33 that Calvin himself would inch beyond and that Milton would push far away from. A mid-seventeenth-century Bible, twice printed, creates a hinge between Calvin's and Milton's different understandings of 1 Corinthians 15. In this heavily annotated Bible, it is said that St. Paul refutes one poet (Epicurus) with the words of another (Menander) in a strategy that would repeal the foolish thinking of one heathen "by the testimonies of the better sort of heathen." Or, as Theodore Haak explains: "This is a verse taken out of a Heathen Poet *Menander*, wherewith *Paul* confutes the former speech of the Epicureans," which is right only if there is no resurrection. But Paul, confident of one, thus advises, "suffer not your selves to be seduced by such speeches of Epicureans."[53]

It is just this sort of interpretation on which Calvin and his followers would put a check; and that check, in turn, explains why Milton, seemingly alone among early modern commentators, displaces Menander with Euripides. As Calvin explains, the oddity of God's countering (through St. Paul) a saying of the Epicureans by words taken from Menander is that the latter, a comic poet of Athens, foolishly drowned himself because a rival poet, receiving more attention, bruised his ego. If Calvin is suspicious of any interpretation that would use verse 33 to illustrate how God put truth into the mouth of the wicked, he embraces the notion, contrary to the Jesus of *Paradise Regain'd*, that Greek philosophy and literature afford important sources of proverbial wisdom for Christianity; that because everything emanates from God we can draw wisdom indiscriminately and promiscuously from every quarter. Even less Miltonic is Calvin's insistence that, through Paul, God here warns against "glid[ing] into profane speculation, under the pretext of inquiry," meaning that, first, it is not God's but Satan's way to engage in "disputation with a view to the investigation of truth" and that, second, following from this proposition, "nothing is more pestilential than corrupt doctrine and profane disputations, which draw us off . . . from a right and single faith."[54]

Writing across the grain of Calvin's commentary, Milton slides by the suicidal Menander, invoking Euripides instead as the classical poet whose words speak prophetically of Christianity, of the consolation of the resurrection. Moreover, Milton does so within a context that, like this one developed by John Trapp, invokes an analogy with Samson by way of saying: "Go forth and shake yourselves (as *Samson* did) out of that dead lethargy whereinto sin hath cast you: your enemies are upon you, and you fast asleep the while."[55] But it is also a context in which, like Haak, Milton is forcing typological differences, thus making the point with Haak that all men die in Adam, and even the faithful may fall asleep in Christ: "For although Christ shall raise up all men in general, even to the ungodly and unrighteous, as their just Judge, so [may he] punish them eternally in body and soul."[56] That is, Samson is here to illustrate not a person's awakening into a new life but his or her awakening from spiritual death and sinful lethargy for judgment, good or bad. Milton's typological play, enforcing difference, would seem to pit Adam / Samson or the natural man against Jesus the spiritual man, with those like Christ who remain steadfast in their faith prevailing over those like Adam and Samson who waver.

To worry over Milton's supposed misattribution of the rebuke, "Be not deceived: evil communications corrupt good manners," is quite to miss the mark. The authority for Milton's attribution is early modern editions of Euripides apparently unknown to, because uncited by, most biblical commentators of the same period. In one of his paraphrases, Erasmus urges his readers to beware of "philosophers and false Apostles . . . beware lest theyr tales deceyue you, and bryng you into a perylouse erroure, always remembring, what was truly sayd of a certaine poete of yours: evyll wordes corrupte good maners," the "certaine poete" being Epicurus.[57] In the seventeenth century, the silence of David Dickson, Samuel Cradock, and Samuel Clark is filled by one of Matthew Poole's annotators, who speaks generally of the verse as belonging to "one of the Pagan Poets; but containing in it much truth."[58] Other commentators such as William Fulke, Hugo Grotius, and Theodore Haak, following the Geneva Bible, attribute that verse to "Menander in Thaidi" or, as Grotius will insist: "Est versus ex Thaide Menandri."[59]

Thus shifting the attribution from Menander to Euripides, Milton eliminates the possible linkage of Menander and Samson through their alleged suicides. More important, he exalts a pagan prophet of Christianity and of the resurrection even as he underscores the spirit of interrogation he shares with Euripides and here brings to the Samson story. Milton is like St. Paul in threading the example of Euripides into his poem and like Euripides in submitting received legends and myths to careful scrutiny—and then to reinterpretation. Enforcing typological differentiation through a scriptural text that stresses the differences between Adam and Christ, then stresses differences between Samson and Christ, and Samson and Milton, Milton springs free of the Samson analogy, of any association with the natural man, aligning himself instead with Jesus and the spiritual man.

The passage from Corinthians also crystallizes the question lurking between the covers of the 1671 poetic volume—whose life is to be imitated, that of Jesus or that of Samson?—a question reinforced by the separate title-page references, in Greek, then in Latin, to Aristotle's insistence that *tragedy is imitation;* that through action, especially climactic action, character (or ethos) reveals itself. Grotius remembers that "Some of these *Jews* would admit of one only case, wherein it was lawful for a man to kill himself, namely, rather than live to be a perpetual reproach and scorn of the Enemies of God":

For seeing the Power over our lives is not in our selves but in God . . . , They presume that it is the will of God that they should put an end to that reproach by a voluntary death. And hither they refer the Examples of *Sampson.* . . . And that also of *Saul.*

Infinite examples can be adduced, says Grotius, with St. Ambrose extolling these people, St. Jerome allowing only the example of Jonas, and with "St. Augustine . . . be[ing] of another mind"; for, if he concedes that these examples may be "guided by some Divine Instinct, . . . he [would] not have any Christian draw this into a Precedent."[60]

Grotius then draws the following conclusion from all this disputation: no man should destroy another or himself in any circumstance: Abraham his son, or Samson himself. Yet our humanity, together with the example of Christ, requires that we forgive them, while never invoking them as models. Grotius cites not only Christ as the ultimate model but also Euripides as an authority within his argument that, always, anger and revenge derive from a feebleness of intellect and weakness of understanding; that, even in circumstances where revenge is not evil or forbidden, patience is always the better recourse; and, when eventually turning to the Book of Judges, that the standard for judging judges and approving tribal activity is best evident when the judges themselves move against rather than act as perpetrators of "barbarous inhumanity."[61] Here, again, Euripides is a constant point of reference, a regularly cited authority.

The passage from Corinthians and the citation of *Christus Patiens* shift the emphasis toward Euripidean tragedy as affording the principal paradigm for *Samson Agonistes.* In *De Doctrina,* let us remember, Euripides is exalted, as he had been in *The Tenure of Kings and Magistrates,* as a "far better" interpreter of Scripture than some of Milton's contemporaries, even if "without knowing it"; and this judgment comes in the same paragraph where Milton, perhaps recollecting the precedent afforded by John Trapp, makes a usually unnoticed reference to the Samson story—"Judges xv. 19: *his spirit returned and he lived"*—by way of urging, *not* that the Spirit once again rushes upon Samson, but that the Judges redactor here employs "an idiom applied to recovery from any kind of unconsciousness" (YP 6:407–8); to an awakening, as Milton explains earlier, *"some to eternal life, some to shame and eternal contempt"* (YP 6:406). This paragraph, surely not coincidentally, is framed by citations of 1 Corinthians 15 and the distinction drawn there between those who now have the promise of the resurrection and those (like Samson presumably) who without hope for, or belief in, the resurrection "despaired of the soul as well as of the body" (YP 6:406). The citation from Judges is one of many, as Milton explains, whose subject is "the death of the spirit" (YP 6:408).

Warning that those who do not have the promise may promote wrong life styles, that those "who were denying the resurrection may have gotten their alternative eschatology . . . by dining in temples" with those of another persuasion, St. Paul's exhortation rebukes those going to false temples, as if to say: "They should know God better. There will be eschatological consequences to their actions, a judgment of deeds."[62] Come to your senses, awake from your death sleep, sin no more, Paul seems to be saying, as he prosecutes his argument within a context of Christian suffering and Christian ethics in the face of dangerous tendencies at work in both the church and the state. In the bolder language of Samuel Clark: "Don't think that you can entertain . . . rotten principles, and yet keep your selves free from corrupt Practices."[63]

Milton comments more temperately, in *De Doctrina* deducing from the example of Naaman the Syrian that it may be better not to go to false temples: even "when the performance of some civil duty makes it necessary," it may be "safer, and more consistent with reverence for God, to decline any official duties of this kind . . . , or even relinquish them altogether" (YP 6:694). The God of *Samson Agonistes,* apparently both contrarious and contradictory, is ready to dispense with his laws and to compel people to conform to his ways. Milton's God, in contrast, governs by "the generall rule of charity"; again in words from *Tetrachordon,* He "cannot contradict himself"; and in contrast with Samson, God's Son "exercis'd force but once," as Milton explains in *A Treatise of Civil Power,* "and that was to drive profane ones out of his temple; not to force them in," not "by . . . force" to impose his ways and, even if expelling, not destroying people, although their presence was "an offence" and their praying "an abomination" (YP 2:596; 7:269). Samson at the temple stands in striking contrast with the Son when he is at the same site, a contrast reinforced by the climactic episodes in both poems of the 1671 poetic volume: the Son atop the pinnacle, Samson at the pillars of a temple the Messenger dubs "a spacious Theatre" (1605).

The quotation from Corinthians quietly slides a story from the Hebrew Bible into the context of New Testament ethics and Christian suffering. *Christus Patiens,* on the other hand, punctuates the New Testament contextualization of this Old Testament story. Additionally, the allusion to fighting with beasts recalls the praise of Samson in the Epistle to the Hebrews where he is celebrated for having "stopped the mouths of lions" and for having "waxed valiant in fight" (11:33–34), but where it is also acknowledged that these men, including Samson, "received not the promise [of the Resurrection]: God having provided some better thing for us, that they without us should not be made perfect" (11:39–40). In conjunction, the passages from Corinthians and Hebrews put the brakes on unconditional claims for Samson's heroism and certainly on any reading that would translate *Samson Agonistes* into *Samson Patiens,* even as these passages distance those like Milton who live with the promise of the Resurrection from those like Samson who lived—and acted—without it.

When within Milton's poem Samson and the Chorus bestialize Dalila with the images of serpent and viper/adder, they displace the images attached to Samson himself in Jacob's prophecy in Genesis: "Dan [read Samson] shall judge his people. . . . Dan shall be a serpent by the way, an adder in the path" (49:16–18). The Semichorus, of course, returns those images to their rightful bearer when Samson, "rouz'd / From under ashes into sudden flame," appears "as an ev'ning Dragon [a flying serpent or adder] . . . , / Assailant on the perched roosts, / And nests in order rang'd / Of tame villatic Fowl" (1689–90, 1691–95). Samson himself, in this flickering moment, is seen as some of Milton's adversaries saw him: as the serpent, the image of which Milton had already divested himself in *Paradise Lost* and the image that here, with no little irony, now holds Milton separate from Samson even as it suggests that, rather than unbound, Samson may still be bound.

The same irony pertains, then curdles, when we remember that, in *Areopagitica,* the eagle flying into the sun is Samson's emblem, just as the spread eagle was the emblem of Milton (an image, as William Riley Parker explains, on the coat of arms with which Milton sealed his letters).[64] On the other hand, in *Pro Se Defensio,* Milton's image for his adversary is the phoenix—"you who were till now a phoenix" (YP 4:784)—an image that once plucked away from Alexander More exposes this nemesis for what he really is. In *Paradise Lost,* the images of phoenix and eagle blur in the description of Raphael entering Eden and then attaining to the altitude "Of Towring Eagles, to all the Fowls . . . seem[ing] / A *Phoenix*" (5.271–72). In each instance, the figure who seems to be a phoenix proves otherwise. Moreover, not since *Epitaphium Damonis* has Milton used the image of the phoenix to signify the divine bird, hence an awakening and a resurrection; and in popular usage, judging from John Donne, to call every man a phoenix is to say no more than that every man is a phoenix (a resurrected spirit) potentially with the still unanswered question of *Samson Agonistes* remaining: is the potentiality to which Samson aspires, are the expectations the Chorus has for him, not to mention those of many of his poem's readers, actually achieved?

The dispute over whether the image of the phoenix was appropriate in sacred poetry problematizes Milton's use of that image here. In a translator's note to Grotius' *Sophompaneas*, it is said that the tragedians' borrowings come more appropriately from "the sacred oracles of Truth" than from Greek "Fable." It is thereupon urged that, when drawing upon Scripture, tragedians should eschew its errors and fablings such as one finds when David mistakenly invokes the phoenix in Psalm 92: "The just shall flourish as a *Phaenix;* where he should have said, as a Palme tree." That is, except where there is textual corruption, the fable of the phoenix "is no where, [when] he seeks to illustrate those things which belong to heavenly truth."[65] When—and if—the phoenix appears within a biblical poem, then, its traditions and connotations are secular, not sacred—civil rather than religious. Hence Milton's conclusion in *Samson Agonistes:* the phoenix, "though her body die, her fame survives, / A *secular* bird ages of lives" (1706–07; italics mine). No sign of the resurrection of the spirit here, the phoenix emblematizes earthly fame within a tragedy whose poet is unswerving in his conviction from *Lycidas* to *Paradise Regain'd,* that "Fame is no plant that grows on mortal soil" (78) in anticipation of what Jesus will say in the latter poem: "For what is glory but the blaze of fame" (3.47).

In *Samson Agonistes* no less than in *Paradise Lost,* parallels exist, as William Riggs insists, both imagistically and typologically, "not as ends in themselves but . . . as means to the forcing of distinctions."[66] For our purposes, it might be said that Riggs does no more than assert one of Georges Gusdorf's guiding principles of autobiography: "The man who takes the trouble to tell of himself . . . has become more aware of differences than of similarities; . . . and he believes it a useful and valuable thing to fix his own image so that he can be certain it will not disappear."[67] The first two books of *Paradise Lost* and *Samson Agonistes* are not only Milton's response to, but his revenge upon, his critics. Furthermore each is driven by the same strategy that gets foregrounded in the prefatory epistle to Milton's tragedy: character definition by differentiation, including character definition of the poem's author, who finally distinguishes himself from the figures, most notably Satan and Samson, with whom his adversaries compare him.

The preface to *Samson Agonistes* is doubly important, first of all, because as Milton observes, it allows for "self defence" and "explanation." Or as Martial, whom Milton cites, explains: the "prefatory epistle" is essential to tragedy where poets "cannot speak for themselves" in the poem proper. The epistle is thus a "crier" for poems where the poet is prevented from speaking in his own behalf;[68] it is the place for an *apologia,* as well as a site for laying down interpretive clues. Milton defines himself by differentiation and, simultaneously, implies that he will define Samson similarly. Second, and even more importantly, in the prefatory epistle to *Samson Agonistes,* with its strong authorial presence, Milton emerges as an interpretive guide, quietly pointing back its companion poem and its tradition of heroic drama as a continuous literary context for the last poems. But more important still, in this epistle, Milton invites us to ponder unexpected yokings like that of Euripides and Seneca, even more than of Aeschylus and Sophocles, thus fixing our attention upon the former pair, both of whom have been, for most of the twentieth century, something of a forbidden context for *Samson Agonistes*. Through the examples of Euripides and Seneca, Milton, like the biblical redactors before him, foregrounds and focuses contradictions instead of eliminating them, and promotes interrogation of scriptural stories instead of easy submission to inherited readings of them. He does not dogmatize one reading but, instead, dramatizes competing interpretations, in the end advancing *Samson Agonistes* as a tragedy of both religious and political thinking: of Christian doctrine, of Calvinist theology, and of Royalist as well as Puritan ideology.

So what are we to conclude, what can we infer from these observations? *Conclusions first.* Milton emerges from his writings as a "plurality of egos"—in the words of Foucault, as a self that "fragments . . . into a plurality of possible positions and functions."[69] His self-portraits are, in one sense, like those of Pierre Bonnard: they blur. In another sense, they are much more like those paintings, not of himself, in which Bonnard asserts a presence: a knee juts from the frame into the space of the painting. *Only a knee.* Milton's presence in the prose writings, where he appears as orator / preacher, is more palpable than his appearance, often as an actor, in his poems. In the first instance, Jacques Derrida, following Jean Jacques Rousseau, argues that when the orator / preacher "represents himself, . . . the representer and the represented are one." On the other hand, "the actor is born out of the rift between the representer and the represented: . . . He signifies nothing. He hardly lives, he lends his voice. It is a mouthpiece. Of course the difference between the orator or preacher and the actor presupposes that the former does his duty, says what he has to say."[70]

In *Pro Se Defensio,* Milton complicates such a distinction—complicates it enormously—by allowing himself, once invoking "the public theatre," to say that "we have completed the fourth act of this drama," the "theatre" being a place where orators parry in debate and don different masks (YP 4:781, 783). Paul Stevens states the case exactly: "in his prose, when he most seems to be speaking in his own voice, and when he is most insistent on his identity and integrity, he says different things in different styles at different times to different people."[71] Even in his prose writings, Milton can be a masked presence, although even there he realizes that the risk is in wrapping oneself in a forest of fables, hence deceptions, the phoenix image being a case in point. In the poetry, more often he is a hidden presence—someone who must be sought out in unexpected places, usually in shadows, fragments, or glimpses, seldom in full-blown portraits. Moreover, as early as in *The Reason of Church-Government,* Milton indicates that, even if his more real self is evident in the prose writings, it may be an inferior self. In "this manner of writing," an effort of his "left hand," Milton admits to "knowing my self inferior to my self" (YP 1:808); to revealing a real self that falls far short of the idealized self-portraits in the poetry.

The self that he is *is* inferior to the self that he aspires to be, except perhaps in *De Doctrina,* his "dearest and best possession" (YP 6:121). What the preface to *Samson Agonistes* establishes conclusively is that, at strategic junctures, the same mind-set producing the poem is also evident in *De Doctrina,* where within a couple of pages, as we have seen, Milton invokes 1 Corinthians 15, then (as St. Paul had done) slides a passage from Euripides into his text in order to interpret the biblical passage and thereupon explains a biblical idiom with specific reference to the Samson story in the Book of Judges. No single citation but this collocation of the same three citations, both in *De Doctrina* and in the preface to *Samson Agonistes,* is sufficiently distinctive of Milton so as to argue that the same hand which wrote the preface to Milton's poem is evident, powerfully so, in *De Doctrina,* Book One, chapter 13.

Now for the inferences. We must do more than just ask: where is Milton the author to be found? For this question typically yields to another: what specifically is *Milton's* function as an author? That is, we need to know what is at stake in authorship, especially when some folks in Milton studies are now in a phase of denying Milton's authorship of *De Doctrina Christiana,* thus refashioning not only the canon of English literature but also Milton's place therein, in the process turning a poet of liberty into one tyrannized by a craving for certainties and by comforting orthodoxies similar to our own. If we are going to deny Milton authorship of *De Doctrina* on the grounds that his radicalism here does not easily conform to the supposed orthodoxies of his last poems, that Milton's so-called "*genuine* ideas are at odds with those in *De Doctrina Christiana*"—a work that we are then told makes Milton "the most incoherent thinker in history"[72]—we will necessarily reduce Milton's status from one who, besides authoring books, fashioned a whole tradition of understanding as he altered received readings of the stories of Creation and the Fall, as well as those of Jesus tempted and Samson triumphant. We will, that is, starch Milton into conformity with the very traditions he resists and, in the act of denying *De Doctrina* as a context for his last poems, hinder and crop the discovery of the nineteenth century that sheds so much light on the poems of the seventeenth century. Milton's status as transformational author, creating his own traditions, then using them as provocations for individual expression and as incitements for the formation of whole schools of criticism—this Milton is put at risk when, as an author of many books, he becomes, because some of us cannot recognize him in *De Doctrina,* the author of one less book.

After all, it is not as if, once this theological treatise was discovered and published, there were no readers ready to say they found Milton in it; who would not echo the words of Milton's daughter: "I see him! 'tis Him! . . . 'tis the very Man!"[73] Discontinuities, inconsistencies, eccentric theories; discrepancies and contradictions; modifications of earlier thinking, regular revision of it, refinements, as well as striking out in new directions—these features are not menacing to authorship, much less denials of it, but evidence a life in motion and a mind on the stretch. These features are the badge of an inquiring spirit, the trademarks not of every author but of Milton as an author. Milton at odds with Milton, this text vying with that one, fissures within texts—surely these are not arguments against but signs of Milton's authorship; of his lifelong project of engendering controversy through which, as he explains in *Of True Religion,* "Senses [are] awakt, . . . Judgement [is] sharpn'd, and the truth . . . more firmly establish't" (YP 8:437–38).

Milton's aesthetic, in prose works and poetry alike, is derivative from Scripture, and, as understood and practiced in the seventeenth century, was founded upon disputation and enquiry. Then, as now, there was a "crisis of meaning" emanating from a fear not shared by Milton, but very much in the air today: that a "maelstrom" of knowledge—its vying factors and data, its arrayed theories, each gesturing toward a different and differently nuanced meaning—serve only "to aggravate . . . radical doubt," which, in its turn, leads to "skepticism, indifference or to various forms of nihilism." *On the contrary,* Milton seems to be saying: when contradiction contradicts itself out of existence, or is displaced by "the principle of noncontradiction"; when "dialectical structures" of truth—what the Milton of *Areopagitica* calls "the wars of Truth" (YP 2:562)—wither into what Pope John Paul II now describes as the "unity of truth," then the *truths* of poetry get overrun and overruled by the truth of religion.[74] In such moments, Milton's (as well as our) steady, unstoppable search for truth, if not completely halted, is severely impeded, as opposing ways of viewing and interpreting the world and human life get lost.

Milton's own rebellious writings, one of which and the dearest of which is *De Doctrina Christiana,* invite us to read rebelliously: to scrutinize theological no less than political systems; to sift and winnow and puzzle out beliefs for ourselves; in free discussion, to move against certain conventional opinions, to study sites of conflict and controversy, and, in the process, to wipe away superstition and tyranny both from those systems and from the minds they manacle. If we remember these words as constituting Milton's agenda in *De Doctrina,* a work that resists both spiritual arrogance and religious dogmatism, we may then experience a dawning awareness of what is at stake in denying Milton authorship of the work and, as a consequence thereof, denying Milton's readers this crucial context for his later poems.

Names of authors signify; they are both "description and designation." Hence, as Foucault explains, someone's "disclosure that Shakespeare . . . had not written the sonnets . . . we attribute to him . . . would constitute a significant change and affect the manner in which the author's name functions."[75] Let there be no mistake about it: the same is true, the consequences would be the same, were we now to dislodge *De Doctrina* from Milton's canon. This looting of Milton's canon may result in the loss of Milton the author. Milton as speculative theologian, creating a new system that would deliver us from existing systems—this Milton, a sect of one—would be removed from the landscape of cultural history, his removal modifying that landscape significantly. If the orator's voice gives us a more authentic voice than that of the poet, if an image of Milton emerges from the prose writings in greater clarity and with more certainty, then to deny Milton authorship of *De Doctrina* is to rid the world of Milton's heterodoxy, as we exchange the relatively authentic voice of the orator for the fictions and occasional subterfuges of the poet.

If we are going to deny Milton's authorship of *De Doctrina* now because the treatise shuns the millenarianism of the early prose works, because its apocalypticism is so much tamer than that of *Of Reformation, Areopagitica,* and *Eikonoklastes,* and now because *De Doctrina* is not easily brought into conformity with the last poems, because its radicalism does not match with their supposed orthodoxy, we should confess immediately that we are privileging what in fact may not exist, an *unchanging* mind, and simultaneously banishing from Milton's canon the work that best evidences the writer's mind in transition. In the same breath, we should acknowledge that a logical extension of the practice of embedding contradictions within a work is to put them at play between works even as we, first, wonder whether Milton's deferral of an apocalypse in history is really a denial of it, whether revisions of apocalyptic thinking should be construed so easily as rejections of millenarianism, and then ask just how conforming to orthodoxies Milton's last poems really are, how much time elapsed before they were so perceived and why *eventually* they were thus understood. What was, what continues to be at stake?

As the eye alters it may find congruence where some see only contradiction; and where there is contradiction, real not feigned, it may be more aptly explained as a staple of the scriptural books, as an aspect of their poetics, hence as a predictable element in any secular scripture (like Milton's) in-formed by a poetics that says, in effect, *if you ask no questions you receive no answers.* As Euripides was wont to say: where there are answers, they "manifest themselves in unpredictable ways. / What we most expect / does not happen. And for the least expected / God finds a way."[76] Or as the poet of *Christus Patiens* will say, echoing Euripides: "God dispenses unexpected things / And often accomplishes what could not be hoped / And things which seemed inevitable do not happen" (1130–32). The answers themselves may be tentative, inconclusive, which is but to say that the questions, and our reiteration of them, are what really matters. In these assertions, Euripides and the poet of *Christus Patiens* help to formulate what will likely emerge as the distinctive features of a revitalized Milton criticism, which comes to appreciate *Samson Agonistes* not as a spiritual triumph but as a mental agon; not as a tragedy with a fortunate outcome but as one readying mankind for reversals of fortune even as it gestures toward a world of new possibilities—a world, as Alfred Kazin might say, that finally does away with tragedy; that, running deeper than tragedy, would extirpate it from history.[77]

NOTES

This essay was written with assistance and support, here gratefully acknowledged, from the PSC-CUNY Research Foundation, and probably never would have been written at all without the invitation from Albert C. Labriola to present a paper to "The Milton Seminar" and the encouragement both from him and Michael Lieb to revise that lecture for this special issue of *Milton Studies.*

1. I have here adapted Milton's words from another context to articulate what will become the chief concern of this essay. Whenever possible, all quotations of Milton's prose writings and poetry are given parenthetically within the text of this essay. Those quotations come, respectively, from *The Complete Prose Works of John Milton,* 8 vols., ed. Don M. Wolfe et al. (New Haven, 1953–83), hereafter designated YP; and *The Complete Poetry of John Milton,* 2d rev. ed., ed. John T. Shawcross (Garden City, N.Y., 1971). For the epigraphs to this essay, see Milton, *An Apology Against a Pamphlet,* in YP 1:890, and Coleridge, *Table Talk,* in *The Romantics on Milton: Formal Essays and Critical Asides,* ed. Joseph Wittreich (Cleveland, 1970), 270, 277.

2. Louis A. Renza, "The Veto of the Imagination: A Theory of Autobiography," in *Autobiography: Essays Theoretical and Critical,* ed. James Olney (Princeton, N.J., 1980), 292.

3. John T. Shawcross, *Intentionality and the New Traditionalism: Some Liminal Means to Literary Revisionism* (University Park, Pa., 1991), 170. Similarly useful distinctions are formulated by Mikhail M. Bakhtin, *Art and Answerability: Early Philosophical Essays,* ed. Michael Holquist and Vadim Liapunov, tr. Vadim Liapunov (Austin, 1990), 12–14.

4. Marshall Grossman, *The Story of All Things: Writing the Self in English Renaissance Narrative Poetry* (Durham, N.C., 1998), xiv.

5. Shawcross, *Intentionality and the New Traditionalism,* 170, 179.

6. John Guillory, *Poetic Authority: Spenser, Milton, and Literary History* (New York, 1983), 161.

7. Robert Durling, *The Figure of the Poet in Renaissance Epic* (Cambridge, Mass., 1965), 2, 4.

8. See Robert McMahon, *The Two Poets of "Paradise Lost"* (Baton Rouge, La.,1998) and Rajan, "The Imperial Temptation," in *Milton and the Imperial Vision,* ed. Balachandra Rajan and Elizabeth Sauer (Pittsburgh, 1999).

9. Barbara Lewalski, *"Paradise Lost" and the Rhetoric of Literary Forms* (Princeton, N.J., 1985), 186, 214, 218.

10. See Newton's comments as reprinted in *The Poetical Works of John Milton,* 7 vols., ed. Henry John Todd (London, 1801), vol. 4, 403–4; and see the comments of others on 402, 413–14, 469.

11. *The Poetical Works of John Milton,* 3 vols., ed. David Masson (London, 1874), vol. 2, 91.

12. See Ann Manning, *The Maiden and Married Life of Mary Powell . . . and the Sequel Thereto Deborah's Diary* (London, 1898), 351.

13. John Aubrey, "Minutes of the Life of Mr. John Milton," in *The Early Lives of Milton,* ed. Helen Darbishire (1932; rpt. London, 1965), 3.

14. Jonathan Richardson, "The Life of the Author," in *The Early Lives of Milton,* 231, 254.

15. Georges Gusdorf, "Conditions and Limits of Autobiography," in *Autobiography,* ed. James Olney, 35, 36.

16. See William Riley Parker, *Milton: A Biography,* 2 vols. (Oxford, 1968), vol. 1.289. Parker here refers to this portrait as "Milton Agonistes."

17. See Grotius, *His Sophompaneas, or Joseph. A Tragedy. With Annotations by Francis Goldsmith* (London, 1652).

18. Barbara Lewalski, "How Radical Was the Young Milton?" in *Milton and Heresy,* ed. Stephen B. Dobranski and John P. Rumrich (New York, 1998), 66.

19. See both *The Complete Poetry of John Milton,* ed. Shawcross, 200, and Sargent's comment as quoted by Richard Brilliant, *Portraiture* (Cambridge, Mass., 1991), 13.

20. Brilliant, *Portraiture,* 10.

21. Ibid., 132.

22. Roland Barthes, "The Death of the Author" and "From Work to Text," in *The Rustle of Language,* tr. Richard Howard (New York, 1986), 51, 61–62.

23. McMahon, *The Two Poets,* 3.

24. Barthes, "The Death of the Author," 49.

25. Humphrey Moseley, "The Stationer to the Reader," *Poems of Mr. John Milton* (London, 1645), sig. [a4v].

26. Margaret Bottrall, *Every Man a Phoenix: Studies in Seventeenth-Century Autobiography* (London, 1958), 3.

27. Northrop Frye, *Fearful Symmetry: A Study of William Blake* (Princeton, N.J., 1947), 325–26.

28. Stephen B. Dobranski, "Licensing Milton's Heresy," in *Milton and Heresy,* ed. Dobranski and Rumrich, 140, 150; cf. 146, 154.

29. See the essay by Robert J. Griffin, "Anonymity and Authorship," forthcoming in *New Literary History.*

30. Mark Bland, "The Appearance of the Text in Early Modern England," *Text* 11 (1998): 100; and Roy Flannagan, ed., *The Riverside Milton* (Boston, 1998), 1135.

31. Bland, "The Appearance of the Text," 127. See also Gary Spear, "Reading before the Lines: Typography, Iconography, and the Author in Milton's 1645 Frontispiece," in *New Ways of Looking at Old Texts: Papers of the Renaissance English Text Society, 1985–1991,* ed. W. Speed Hill (Binghamton, N.Y., 1993), 187–94.

32. Anne Middleton, "Life in the Margins, or What's an Annotation to Do?" in *New Directions to Textual Studies*, ed. Dave Oliphant and Robin Bradford (Austin, Texas, 1990), 108.

33. McMahon, *The Two Poets*, 24; see also 155.

34. *Christus Patiens*, referred to in the preface to *Samson Agonistes* as *Christ Suffering*, is here translated by Alan Fishbone, of the Greek and Latin Institute of the Graduate School and University Center of the City University of New York, from *Christus Patiens, Tragoedia Christiana*, ed. J. G. Brambs (Leipzig, 1885). In his Trinity Manuscript plans for biblical tragedies, Milton contemplates writing a play of the same title and provides a thumbnail sketch for it (see YP 8:562).

35. See Joseph Wittreich, *Feminist Milton* (Ithaca, N.Y., 1987), 20, 164; see also 67, 76.

36. See John S. Diekhoff, "The Function of the Prologues in *Paradise Lost*," *PMLA* 57 (1942): 697–704, and *Milton's "Paradise Lost": A Commentary on the Argument* (1946; rpt. New York, 1958), 13–27.

37. Michel Foucault, "What Is an Author?" in *Language, Counter Memory, Practice: Selected Essays and Interviews*, tr. Donald F. Bouchard and Sherry Simon (Ithaca, N.Y., 1977), 129.

38. Jonathan Richardson, "The Life of the Author," in *The Early Lives of Milton*, ed. Darbishire, 247.

39. See Roger L'Estrange, *No Blinde Guides* (London, 1660), sig. A2; Thomas Long, *Dr. Walker's True, Modest and Faithful Account Of The Author of Eikon basilike* (London, 1693), 2–3; Joseph Jane (1660), in William Riley Parker, *Milton's Contemporary Reputation* (Columbus, 1940), 105; G. S., *Britains Triumph, for her Imparallel'd Deliverance* (London, 1660), 15; and anon., *A Third Conference Between O. Cromwell And Hugh Peters in Saint James's Park* (London, 1660), 8.

40. See Denis Saurat, *Milton: Man and Thinker* (1944; rpt. New York, 1948), 184, and Blake's epic-prophecy titled *Milton*.

41. For McMahon's contrary arguments, see *The Two Poets*, 39, 41.

42. See Edward Phillips, "Life of Mr. John Milton," in *The Early Lives of Milton*, ed. Darbishire, 67.

43. See Michael Lieb, *Milton and the Culture of Violence* (Ithaca, N.Y., 1994), 236, 260, 263; see also 235, 240. And see Francis Barker, *The Culture of Violence: Essays on Tragedy and History* (Chicago, 1993), which, although it never mentions *Samson Agonistes*, affords an important qualifying context and perspective for Lieb's book.

44. See *The Complete Poetical Works of John Milton*, 5th ed., ed. Henry John Todd, 4 vols. (London, 1852), vol. 3, 323. Masson, *The Life of John Milton: Narrated in Connexion with the Political, Ecclesiastical, and Literary History of His Time*, 7 vols. (1881; rpt. Gloucester, Mass., 1965), vol. 6, 664, 674, 676, 677.

45. Parker, *Milton*, vol. 1, 314. Again, Bakhtin is immensely helpful in his comments on "the author's position of being situated outside the hero" and in his insistence that "the author experiences the hero's life in value-categories that are completely different from those in which he experiences his own life"; see Bakhtin, "The Problem of the Author's Relationship to the Hero," *Art and Answerability*, ed. Holquist and Liapunov, tr. Liapunov, 15; also 17–22.

46. Lieb, *Milton and the Culture of Violence*, 159–263.

47. As Lieb explains, the implicit allusion here is to Achaemenides' description of the Cyclops smashing bodies and bloodying them against the rocks (ibid., 167).

48. See Irene Samuel, "*Samson Agonistes* as Tragedy," in *Calm of Mind: Tercentenary Essays on "Paradise Regained" and "Samson Agonistes*," ed. Joseph Wittreich (Cleveland, 1971), 248; and William Empson, *Milton's God* (London, 1961), 211.

49. See Leo Bersani and Uysse Dutoit, *Caravaggio's Secret* (Cambridge, Mass., 1998), 2.

50. Lieb, *Milton and the Culture of Violence*, 227; see also 181–200.

51. Joan S. Bennett, "A Reading of Samson Agonistes," in *The Cambridge Companion to Milton*, ed. Dennis Danielson (1989; rpt. New York, 1994), 225.

52. On different translations of 1 Corinthians 15:33, see, e. g., John Locke, *A Paraphrase and Notes on the Epistles of St. Paul*, ed. Arthur W. Wainwright, 2 vols. (1707; Oxford, 1987), vol. 1, 251, 454.

53. See anon., *Annotations Upon all the Books Of The Old and New Testament*, 2 vols. (1645; rpt. London, 1651), sig. ff; and Theodore Haak, *The Dutch Annotations Upon the New Testament* (London, 1657), sig. Ll3v.

54. Calvin, *Commentary on the Epistles of Paul the Apostle to the Corinthians*, 2 vols. (1577; rpt. Edinburgh, 1848–49), vol. 2, 42–43.

55. John Trapp, *A Commentary Or Exposition Upon All the Epistles* (London, 1647), 121. Cf. *De Doctrina Christiana* (YP 6:408).

56. See Haak, *The Dutch Annotations*, sigs. Ll3–[Ll4v].

57. See *The Paraphrase of Erasmus upon the new testamente*, 2 vols. (London, 1548–49), vol. 2, annotation to 1 Corinthians 15:33.

58. See Matthew Poole (and his followers), *Annotations Upon The Holy Bible*, 2 vols. (London, 1683, 1685), vol. 2, annotation to 1 Corinthians 15:33.

59. See both *The Bible and Holy Scriptures* (Geneva, 1560), pt. II, fol. 82, and Grotius, *Annotationes in Vetus & Novum Testamentum*, 2 vols. (London, 1627), vol. 2, 308.

60. Grotius, *His Three Books Treating of the Rights of War and Peace*, tr. William Evats (London, 1682), 219.

61. Ibid., 23, 365, 370.

62. Ben Witherington, *Conflict and Community in Corinth: A Socio-Rhetorical Commentary on 1 and 2 Corinthians* (Grand Rapids, Mich., 1995), 306. See also William F. Orr and James Arthur Walther, *1 Corinthians* (Garden City, N.Y., 1976), 338–40.

63. Clark, *The New Testament Of Our Lord and Saviour Jesus Christ* (London, 1603), sig. [Rr4].

64. See Parker, *Milton*, vol. 2, 1097.

65. See Grotius, *His Sophompaneas . . . With Annotations by Francis Goldsmith*, sig. B3 and p. 96.

66. Riggs, *The Christian Poet in "Paradise Lost"* (Berkeley, 1972), 28.

67. Georges Gusdorf, "Conditions and Limits of Autobiography," in *Autobiography*, ed. Olney, 30.

68. Martial, *Epigrams*, ed. Walter C. A. Ker, 2 vols. (Cambridge, Mass., 1919), vol. 1, 109.

69. Foucault, "What Is an Author?" 130.

70. Derrida, *Of Grammatology*, tr. Gayatri Chakravorty Spivak (Baltimore, 1976), 305.

71. Paul Stevens, " 'John Milton, Englishman': Soliloquy, Subject, and the Modern Nation State," *Elizabethan Theatre* 16 (1999).

72. William B. Hunter, *Visitation Unimplor'd: Milton and the Authorship of "De Doctrina Christiana"* (Pittsburgh, 1998), 153 (italics mine).

73. See Richardson, "Life of the Author," in *The Early Lives of Milton*, ed. Darbishire, 229.

74. I have used Milton and the current pope to contrast the poet's with the theologian's truth, drawing phrases from the reprinted encyclical of 15 October 1998: "John Paul Words: '2 Modes of Knowledge Lead to Truth in All Its Fullness,' " *The New York Times*, 16 October 1998, A10.

75. Foucault, "What Is an Author?", 121.

76. Euripides, *The Bacchae*, tr. Michael Cacoyannis (New York, 1987), 85.

77. Alfred Kazin, "Introduction," in *The Portable Blake* (New York, 1946), 55.

THE BIRTH OF THE AUTHOR: MILTON'S POETIC SELF-CONSTRUCTION

J. Martin Evans

Writing is that neutral, composite, oblique space where our subject slips away, the negative where all identity is lost, starting with the very identity of the body writing.

Roland Barthes, "The Death of the Author"

FOR A WRITER with such a notoriously strong personality, Milton was surprisingly reticent about taking public credit for his poems. His first published work, *On Shakespeare,* was printed anonymously in the second Folio (1632), his second, *A Mask Presented at Ludlow Castle* (1637) was "not openly acknowledged by the Author," as Henry Lawes put it in the dedication, and his third, *Lycidas* (1638), had affixed to it only his initials, "J. M." Not until the collected edition of 1645 was "Mr. John Milton" openly acknowledged as the author of any of his published poems, and even there his identity was immediately problematized by the Greek epigram that was printed under what purports to be his portrait:

> That an unskilful hand had carved this print
> You'd say at once, seeing the living face;
> But, finding here no jot of me, my friends,
> Laugh at the botching artist's misattempt.[1]

No sooner does Milton appear in person, as it were, than we are told that it really isn't him at all. Now you see him, now you don't. Even as late as 1667 there is some typographical hesitancy about affirming Milton's authorship. On the first two title pages of the first edition of *Paradise Lost,* we are told that the poem was "Written in TEN BOOKS By JOHN MILTON," but Milton's name shrinks visibly between the first and second issues, and on the title page of the third it has been reduced once again to his initials: "The Author J. M." "The Author JOHN MILTON" is announced for the first time on the title page of the fourth issue of the epic in 1668, and his name appears thus in all his subsequent poetic works. It is almost as if the poet had gradually materialized before our eyes during the course of his career. A similar progression from initial anonymity to ultimate self-assertion, I will argue, takes place within

47

Milton's poems themselves. What we seem to be witnessing as we read his non-dramatic verse is exactly the opposite of the process Roland Barthes describes in the epigraph: the birth of the author.[2]

In an area as hotly contested as that of literary authorship a few preliminary distinctions and caveats are in order. The first and most important is the distinction between what Patricia M. Spacks calls the "poet-as-creator-of-the-poem" and the "poet-as-imagined-presence-in-the-poem."[3] I will be concerned almost exclusively with the latter, with Milton's "author function," as Michel Foucault would have it.[4] As a result, I will have little to say about the vexed question of the relationship between the two figures. In a sense, of course, they can never be the same person, for as C. S. Lewis pointed out a long time ago, it is impossible "for anyone to describe himself, even in prose, without making of himself, to some extent, a dramatic creation," and it is consequently "quite impossible that the character represented in the poem should be identically the same with that of the poet."[5] To take a concrete instance, the Milton who grieves for the death of Edward King in *Lycidas* is not the same person as the Milton who put that grief into words. Between the "poet-as-creator-of-the-poem" and the "poet-as-imagined-presence-in-the-poem" yawns the unfathomable mystery of composition.

On the other hand, it seems to me that Robert McMahon pushes this argument rather too far when he insists that the speaker in *Paradise Lost* is a purely fictional character whose intellectual and moral growth is one of the poem's major themes.[6] Granted that it may be misleading to conflate Milton with his authorial persona, the fact remains that the correspondences between the two figures are remarkably close, far closer than those between, say, the narrator of *Troilus and Criseyde* and the still shadowy figure of his creator.[7] The characteristics that Milton the historical author attributed to Milton the narrator of *Paradise Lost*—blindness, old age, social and political isolation, religious faith—positively invite us to identify the one with the other. As Janet Adelman notes, "it is clear that the narrator is a consciously controlled character in the poem; but it is equally clear that Milton is anxious to ensure that we recognize him in the narrator."[8] It is probably no accident that, despite what Leah Marcus has called the "vast interplay of poststructuralist energies" that has been brought to bear on the issue of "the writing subject,"[9] Milton for the most part remains Milton "without the deauthorizing bracket of quotation marks."[10]

Finally, the "poet-as-imagined-presence-in-the-poem" may present himself to us in two quite different ways. On the one hand, he may simply be the unidentified source of the voice that utters the poetic text. We know someone is there because we can hear the words he is speaking, but because he never talks about himself we have no idea who he is or what he looks like.

To borrow the cinematic vocabulary Herbert Phelan uses to analyse *L'Allegro* and *Il Penseroso*, he is an invisible "off-screen" presence, projecting a scene which he either witnessed or imagined but in which he does not himself appear. On the other hand, the poet may be an identifiable character in his own poem, an "on-screen" figure whom we can both hear and see.[11] Using the first person singular, he presents himself to us as a self-referential reality, an actor whose thoughts and deeds, feelings and appearance, are themselves part of the poem's subject matter. He no longer simply produces the text; he actively participates in it. If the first kind of poetic presence remains steadfastly outside the poem, this second kind of authorial persona operates inside it as well.

I. THE 1645 *POEMS*

Bearing these distinctions and qualifications in mind, I propose to trace the gradual emergence of an individualized poetic presence in the editions which appeared in public under Milton's name, beginning with the 1645 collection of his shorter works.[12] According to Marcus, this extraordinary volume presents us already with a full fledged portrait of the artist as a young man, a portrait which is constructed partly by the order in which the texts are printed, partly by the poet's running commentary on his own poems. No other English poet, she points out, "had so overtly inserted his own voice in the text as a commentary on what he had achieved (and even the age at which he had achieved it)." His authorial interventions "are quite unprecedented in an English volume of poems" and would have "looked much newer . . . to his contemporaries" than they do to us today. Their effect, she concludes, is to inaugurate "a new view of literary subjecthood," namely "the invention of an individual literary life."[13] The Milton of the 1645 edition is a highly self-conscious imaginative construct, the precursor of all those "authors" whose "lives and works" furnished the material for the kind of literary biography that became so popular in succeeding centuries.

So far as the volume as a whole is concerned, Marcus's argument seems to me to be entirely persuasive. As John K. Hale put it in an almost contemporaneous article on "Milton's Self-Presentation in *Poems . . . 1645*," "the editorial acts of selection and grouping and sequential arrangement . . . add up to a major personal statement. They declare, so to speak, 'This is my self; these are its powers.'"[14] But both critics base their arguments almost exclusively on evidence that resides *outside* the poems themselves, the order in which they appear and the external prefaces ("In this monody the author laments") and postscripts ("This subject the author finding to be above his years") that enclose but rarely, if ever, penetrate them. The "new historical subject" that Marcus describes presides over the poems like a guardian angel, but he does not appear inside them. His relationship to the texts themselves is not unlike that between the portrait of Milton gazing out from the foreground of Marshall's engraving and the youthful figures cavorting in the pastoral background, inhabitants of a contiguous but separate world.

The texts of the poems themselves, free of the editorial apparatus that surrounds them, tell a rather different story, and it is on this story that I would like to focus. (All quotations are from Merritt Y. Hughes, editor, *John Milton: Complete Poems and Major Prose* [New York: 1957].) To begin at the beginning, the first poem in the 1645 volume, *On the Morning of Christ's Nativity*, has often been described as a kind of literary epiphany, either heralding Milton's coming of age as a poet, or, still more egocentrically, using "the occasion of Christ's birth to announce his own poetic nativity."[15] Attractive as they may be from a purely historical point of view—Milton did indeed reach the age of twenty one in December of 1629, when he composed the poem, and he did place it at the front of his volume, ahead of several earlier works— these autobiographical readings begin to seem rather less plausible once we start reading the opening stanzas. For Milton emphatically disclaims any responsibility for the poem at all. The "voice" (27) that welcomes the Christ-child, and the "humble ode" (24) with which it celebrates his birth, both belong to the "Heav'nly Muse" (15). No sooner do we hear "Mr. John Milton" begin to speak than he abruptly silences himself and consigns the rest of the poem to a third party, who begins a new poem in a new verse form. Like the "holy song" that promises to "run back and fetch the age of gold" in stanza fourteen, the author's speech is interrupted and displaced by a stronger force which takes over the rest of the poem—"this must *not yet* be so" (150). It is almost as if Milton had made his entrance too soon.

The hymn that follows consistently enacts the premise that it is being sung by the Heavenly Muse, in concert with "the angel choir" (27), rather than by the individual who spoke the proem. For the notion that the "joyous news of heav'nly Infant's birth / My muse with Angels did divide to sing," as Milton put it later,[16] is powerfully reinforced by the fact that their song is simultaneously an "ode" (24) and a "hymn" (17), both of which are essentially choric in nature. As the insistently plural pronouns keep reminding us— "our" ears, "our" senses, "our" fancy, "our" song (126, 127, 134, 239)—we are listening to "a choir-poem that harmoniously effaces the individual."[17] Indeed, the *Nativity Ode* is the most rigorously depersonalized of all the poet's nondramatic works, with not a single "I," "me," or "my" in its entire thirty-one stanzas. If Milton ever wrote a poem in which "the very identity of the body writing" is lost, as Barthes put it, this surely is it. In one of the most recent studies of the poem to appear in print, Richard Halpern argues that "by putting off epic expansiveness to dwell in the 'humble ode'" Milton enacts a *kenosis* or "emptying out" analogous to "Christ's decision to forego heaven and lie 'meanly wrapt in the rude manger.'" Milton's *kenosis* is even more radical than Halpern recognizes: he has effectively erased himself from his own poem.[18]

Having withdrawn at the end of the introduction, he never makes his presence felt again. One of the most striking features of the *Nativity Ode* is the absence of any closing epilogue in which the poet might reassume the authorial control he gave away in the prologue. The next time we encounter him is not at the end of the *Nativity Ode,* as we might have expected, but at the beginning of *The Passion,* where he emphatically asserts both his own presence and his responsibility for the ensuing poem:

> For now to sorrow must *I* tune *my* song,
> And set *my* Harp to notes of saddest woe.
>
> (8–9; italics mine)

The disembodied voice we heard in the opening four stanzas of the *Nativity Ode,* still speaks to us in the same verse form, but it has now assumed a concrete physical identity. In both grammatical and existential terms, the speaker has become a "person" that we can see as well as hear. Yet despite the bardic pose he attempts to strike, he looks and sounds like nothing so much as a nervous young child performing for the first time in front of an audience of grown-ups, striving self-consciously to assume the right posture and to compose his features into the appropriate expression:

> Befriend me Night, best Patroness of grief,
> Over the Pole thy thickest mantle throw,
> And work my flatter'd fancy to belief,
> That Heav'n and Earth are color'd with my woe;
> My sorrows are too dark for day to know:
> The leaves should all be black whereon I write,
> And letters where my tears have washt, a wannish white.
>
> (29–35)

In this stanza alone there are six first person singular pronouns, and the poem as a whole is so relentlessly self-referential that we can scarcely glimpse its ostensible subject through the veil of the poet's "woe" (32). In W. R. Parker's words, "Milton was writing a poem about himself writing a poem."[19] The passion that he describes is his own rather than Christ's.

After this unsuccessful debut, in the following eight poems the poet disappears from view almost entirely. With the exception of a fleeting appearance in the *Epitaph on the Marchioness of Winchester,* where Milton writes "So have I seen some tender slip / Sav'd with care from Winter's nip" (35–36), we don't see him again until *L'Allegro* and *Il Penseroso*. What is more, in the first three of the poems following *The Passion*, the odes *On Time*, *Upon the Circumcision*, and *At a Solemn Music*, we hear not the voice of the poet himself but a communal voice that sounds very much like those of the Heavenly Muse and the angel choir in the *Nativity Ode*. For here, too, in strict accordance with generic decorum, the first person pronouns are consistently plural:

> For *we* by rightful doom remediless
> Were lost in death, till he that dwelt above
> . . . .
> Emptied his glory, ev'n to nakedness;
> And that great Cov'nant which *we* still transgress
> Entirely satisfi'd,
> And the full wrath beside
> Of vengeful Justice bore for *our* excess.
>
> (*Upon the Circumcision*, 17–24; italics mine)

This is the voice of fallen humanity rather than that of John Milton; once again the individual poet has been submerged in a multiple consciousness that transcends any specific personal identity.

In a radical change from the *Nativity Ode* and *The Passion*, the three odes are addressed, not to the reader, but to a series of superhuman entities: to Time, to the angels who celebrated Christ's nativity, and to Voice and Verse. As a result, our relationship to the text is transformed from that of a direct participant to that of an eavesdropper: we are no longer the recipients of the speaker's utterance but its overhearers, no longer the silent partners in a potential dialogue but its auditors. And this shift from what we might call the declarative to the dramatic lyric affects the speaker, too, for it opens up the possibility that the voice we are listening to belongs not to the poet but to a dramatis persona, a purely imaginary construct whose thoughts and feelings do not necessarily correspond to those of the author any more than the sentiments uttered by a character in a play correspond to those of the dramatist.[20] In the odes this possibility remains largely unexploited—in all three cases, the feelings the voice expresses and the values it celebrates are clearly Milton's own—but as we shall see shortly it has a crucial bearing on the way we interpret *L'Allegro* and *Il Penseroso*.

The five poems that follow the odes revert to the anonymous voice we last heard in the proem to the *Nativity Ode*, but in the first three of them it is now directed to two quite different audiences, first to the reader, and then to the poet's subject. In line 47 of *Epitaph on the Marchioness of Winchester*, for instance, the poet suddenly stops referring to the dead woman in the third person and turns to address her directly in the second:

> And those Pearls of dew *she* wears,
> Prove to be presaging tears
> Which the sad morn had let fall
> On *her* hast'ning funerall.
> Gentle Lady, may *thy* grave
> Peace and quiet ever have;
> After this *thy* travail sore
> Sweet rest seize thee evermore.   (43–50; italics mine)

The same thing happens, albeit less dramatically, in line 5 of *Song on May Morning:*

> Now the bright morning Star, Day's harbinger,
> Comes dancing from the East, and leads with her
> The Flow'ry May, who from *her* green lap throws
> The yellow Cowslip, and the pale Primrose.
>   Hail bounteous May that dost inspire
>   Mirth and youth and warm desire!   (1–6, italics mine)

And again in the short tribute to Shakespeare:

> What needs my Shakespeare for *his* honor'd Bones
> The labor of an age in piled Stones,
> Or that *his* hallow'd relics should be hid
> Under a Star-ypointing Pyramid?
> Dear son of memory, great heir of Fame,
> What need'st *thou* such weak witness of thy name?
>   (*On Shakespeare*, 1–6; italics mine)

In each case, the sudden change of direction calls attention to the role of the unidentified speaker by creating a second discursive coordinate by which we can plot his position in the text. He acquires, as it were, an extra dimension; we see him both head-on and in profile.

In none of these poems, however, whether they are declarative (like the two Hobson elegies), dramatic (like the three odes), or both (like the three works I have just discussed), does the poet appear in person, as he did, so disastrously, in *The Passion*. Not until *L'Allegro* and *Il Penseroso*, which immediately follow the twin tributes to the university carrier, does he finally reenter the text, albeit somewhat cautiously. When we first encounter the poet in line 37 of *L'Allegro*, for instance, his presence is hedged about by a condition that has not yet been completely fulfilled:

> And if I give thee honor due,
> Mirth, admit me of thy crew.   (37–38)

For most of the remainder of the poem he is a mere shadow, a "generalized receiver of shifting impressions," in Louis L. Martz's memorable phrase,[21] whose participation is implied but never clearly affirmed by the repeated infinitives—"to live" (39), "to hear" (41), "to come" (45)—and present participles—"list'ning"(53), "walking" (57)—that describe his various activities. Indeed, the very process of seeing is described in terms so depersonalized— "Straight mine eye hath caught new pleasures" (69)—that it can be narrated in the third rather than the first person: "it measures" (70), "it sees" (77). And when the speaker, for only the second time, refers to himself directly in the final lines, his presence is once again deprived of any significant impact by the surrounding conditional:

> These delights, if thou canst give,
> Mirth, with thee, I mean to live.   (151–52)

As Dana Brand has noted, the self of *L'Allegro* lacks psychological as well as physical substance.[22]

Initially, at least, the speaker in *Il Penseroso* is far more fully realized. The "walking" and "listening" are now performed by a visible "I" who "not only receives impressions from without, but also actively addresses and 'woos' their action."[23]

> Thee Chantress oft the Woods among
> I woo to hear thy Even-Song;
> And missing thee, I walk unseen
> On the dry smooth-shaven Green,
>
> . . . .
>
> I hear the far-off Curfew sound,
> Over some wide-water'd shore.   (63–75)

But as the poem continues, this energetic presence becomes increasingly passive as the mood shifts from indicative to hortative—"Or let my lamp at midnight hour / Be seen" (85–88), "And let some strange mysterious dream / Wave at his Wings" (147–48), "But let my due feet never fail / To walk" (156–57), "There let the pealing organ blow" (162)—and the speaker becomes in turn the object rather than the subject of the desired actions—"see me" (121), "me goddess bring" (132), "Hide me" (141), "Dissolve me" (165). After the last two requests, for concealment and dissolution, respectively, it comes as no surprise when the speaker concludes with a variation of the same self-effacing formula that his mirthful predecessor had used to bring his address to a close:

> These pleasures Melancholy give,
> And I with thee will choose to live.   (175–76)

The consciousness presented in *Il Penseroso* may be more continuous than that in *L'Allegro* as Brand has persuasively argued,[24] but it is ultimately just as tentative in its self-assertion.

Which brings us to a question that critics have been debating since the eighteenth century. Are *l'allegro* and *il penseroso,* "the same man as he is differently disposed," in Theobald's words, or are they two different people, as Dr. Johnson appears to have believed?[25] To put the question in a slightly different way, was Milton speaking in his own voice in both poems, or was he impersonating two quite different fictional characters, neither of whom represented his personal values and beliefs?[26] The external evidence is thoroughly ambiguous. Whereas the obvious similarities of phraseology and verse form suggest the first alternative, the titles themselves argue for the second. For our purposes, however, it does not really matter how we answer the question. For whether or not James Holly Hanford is right that "there is, of course, no question of two individuals. *L'Allegro* and *Il Penseroso* are equally Milton,"[27] we are confronted by an authorial presence that has split into two competing selves. The poetic "I" we last encountered in *The Passion* has become not the kind of unified "we" who sang the three odes but a radically divided dual consciousness.

The process of reintegration begins in the first of the ten sonnets that follow the two companion poems—"Whether the Muse or Love call thee his mate, / Both them I serve, and of their train am I" (13–14)—but it achieves its most complete realization in sonnet seven on the poet's twenty-third birthday. This is by far the most deeply personal poem up to this point in the volume. The nervous schoolboy of *The Passion,* who attempted unsuccessfully to treat a topic "above the years he had when he wrote it," has given way to a steadfast young man, fully aware now of the lack of "inward ripeness" (7) that made the earlier poem a failure and determined to wait patiently upon the will of heaven. The passiveness that undermined the last part of *Il Penseroso* has become "wise," as the poet declares that his growth:

> shall be still in strictest measure even,
> To that same lot, however mean or high,
> Toward which Time leads me, and the will of Heav'n. (10–12)

And the conditionality which qualified the self-assertions at the end of both *L'Allegro* and *Il Penseroso* has been transformed into a pious recognition of human dependence upon divine providence:

> All is, if I have grace to use it so,
> As ever in my great task Master's eye. (13–14)

Yet powerful as it may be in comparison with the poems that preceded it in the collection, sonnet seven is finally about a self that is still unformed and unproductive. The poet is "near" his "manhood" (6), but he has not yet arrived. His spring is "late" and the tree has not yet blossomed. "The Author John Milton" is still a work in progress. Indeed, in the very next poem, sonnet eight, he splits once again into two distinct entities, the confident speaker issuing a series of orders to the military officer who has captured the poet's home—"Guard them, and him within protect from harms" (4)—and the silent (though potentially eloquent) occupant on whose behalf the speaker has intervened as if he were quite literally another human being—"He can requite thee" (5), "he knows" (5), "he can spread" (7). With the exception of the editorial comment at the end of *The Passion,* this is the first time Milton has referred to himself in the third person. It is almost as if he had become simultaneously the magisterial reader who announced that the poem's topic "was above the years [the author] had when he wrote it" and the youthful writer who actually "left it unfinished."

After two sonnets addressed to virtuous women and a masque presented to the countess of Derby, the "poet-as-imagined-presence-in-the-poem" makes his final appearance in the famous elegy that concludes this section of the volume. Referring to himself once again in the third person, Milton informs us in the headnote that *Lycidas* is a "monody" sung by a single "author," and indeed the poem begins as if it were a species of personal monologue delivered by an "on-screen" speaker in the dramatic present:

> Yet once more, O ye Laurels, and once more
> Ye Myrtles brown, with Ivy never sere,
> I come to pluck your Berries harsh and crude.   (1–3)

But as the authorial voice continues to speak, it gradually begins to shed its initial identity. The first hint that we are not in the presence of a stable and unified self comes in line 56, when the speaker suddenly corrects the question he has just posed:

> Where were ye Nymphs when the remorseless deep
> Clos'd o'er the head of your lov'd Lycidas?
>
> . . . .
>
> Ay me, I fondly dream!
> Had ye been there—for what could that have done?   (50–57)

As I have noted elsewhere, the second thoughts open up a tiny fissure in the poet's consciousness between the self that interrogated the nymphs and the self that subsequently realizes the pointlessness of doing so.[28] The fissure widens in line 76, when Phoebus Apollo intervenes to remind the rebellious poet that true fame is to be found in heaven:

> But the fair Guerdon when we hope to find,
> And think to burst out into sudden blaze,
> Comes the blind Fury with th'abhorred shears,
> And slits the thin-spun life. "But not the praise,"
> Phoebus repli'd, and touch'd my trembling ears.   (73–77)

The unexpected preterite verbs create a temporal and epistemological gap between the speaker who revolted against the Muse's discipline (64–76) and the speaker who learns to submit himself to the authority of "all-judging Jove" (76–84).[29] The two figures are still the same person—Phoebus touches "my trembling ears" not "his"—but from this point on, his perspective has been transformed by the revelations of the god of poetry.

What is more, Phoebus's interruption—advice from a source outside the speaker's consciousness—momentarily deprives the poet of his authorial function. He heard these words, and recorded them, but he did not compose them; for a few lines, the "author" has disappeared, just as he did at the end of the proem to the *Nativity Ode*. The same thing happens on an even larger scale when the "Pilot of the Galilean lake" (109) arrives on the scene to condemn the hireling shepherds and predict the day of judgement. As Stanley Fish has pointed out in a brilliant analysis of the first person voice in *Lycidas,* this rival speaker completely ignores the grieving swain and addresses his diatribe not to the poet, as Phoebus Apollo had done, but to the dead Lycidas.[30] Milton has virtually ceased to be a presence in his own poem, or, to put it slightly differently, he has so completely submerged himself in the figure of St. Peter that he has left a temporary vacuum in the rhetorical space he once occupied.

By the time he returns to invoke the assistance of Alpheus (132), his identity has been compromised to such an extent that it has apparently disintegrated, for, as the plural possessive pronouns imply, the "frail thoughts" that "dally with false surmise" (153) and the "moist vows" that are eventually "denied" (159) belong not to a single but to a multiple personality. For a few lines, at least, the choric voice we last heard in the ode *At a solemn Music* has taken over a poem that began as a monologue. At line 165, however, the poet suddenly reasserts himself by abruptly silencing the speakers who had just displaced him:

> Weep no more, woeful shepherds, weep no more,
> For Lycidas your sorrow is not dead.   (165–66)

So violent is this reentry that more than one critic has attributed these words to a completely new character.[31] But as the rhythmic and verbal echoes of the opening line seem to insist, this is the same voice we heard addressing the laurels and myrtles at the beginning of the elegy. The poem is starting all over again.

No sooner has the speaker regained control of his authorial role, however, than he undergoes a still more drastic transformation. Once again the tense changes from the dramatic present to the narrative past, but this time the author and the genre of *Lycidas* change with it:

> Thus sang the uncouth swain to th'Oaks and rills,
> While the still morn went out with Sandals gray;
> He touch't the tender stops of various Quills,
> With eager thought warbling his Doric lay.   (186–189)

The historical "author" bewailing "a learned friend" has become a fictional "swain," and his "Doric lay" has become part of a larger meta-narrative, the existence of which Phoebus Apollo's earlier interruption had only hinted at. Fish describes this phenomenon solely in terms of the speaker's disappearance from the scene of his own poem,[32] but there is more involved here than a disappearance. As the old speaker disappears, the poem acquires a new author, who begins what is essentially a new poem in a new verse form. As I have shown elsewhere, the unidentified voice that speaks the final ottava rima belongs to a speaker we have never heard before, either in *Lycidas* or in the poems preceding it, a speaker who hails from the violent and erotic world of sixteenth-century romantic epic.[33] The elegy and the poet who sang it fade away into the distance, together with the rest of Milton's youthful creations, and we are left with the sense that for the second time in this volume we have witnessed a "nativity." A mysterious new self has been born out of the speaker's anguish, but we will have to wait until "Tomorrow" (193) before we find out who he is.

As even this brief analysis may suggest, *Lycidas* repeats in miniature most of the evasive maneuvers I have traced in the poems that preceded it. The shifts back and forth between a single and a multiple consciousness, the recurring disappearances and reappearances of an authorial persona, the unexpected changes of direction in the speaker's discourse, and the pervasive impression that these are the words of someone who is not yet "too much of a poet," as Milton put it in the verse letter to John Rouse,[34] all combine to create a poetic presence that is radically unstable, a tentative and hesitant self whose position is finally usurped by the anonymous figure who invades line 186 of *Lycidas*. Far from painting a coherent "portrait of the artist" as Marcus suggests, or telling the story of a "rising poet" steadily advancing towards maturity, as Martz has argued, the constantly shifting forms of poetic selfhood we encounter in the poems of the 1645 volume call into question the very possibility of a unified and fully realized poetic consciousness.[35] Like Montaigne's *Essays*, the poems read like a series of experiments in self-presentation, sometimes visible, sometimes invisible, sometimes singular, sometimes plural, sometimes direct, sometimes oblique, but always inherently provisional in their efforts to construct the "poet-as-imagined-presence-in-the-poem." As the Virgilian motto on the title page seems to imply, Milton is still only a "future bard."

II. *Paradise Lost*

A seventeenth-century reader familiar with *The Poems of Mr John Milton* might well have expected to encounter a rather more fully developed and mature authorial persona when he began to read *Paradise Lost. A Poem Written in Ten Books By John Milton* (or *J. M.*) some twenty-two years later. This expectation would be sadly disappointed, at least in the opening lines. For the self-confident epic narrator who expelled the swain in the final ottava rima of *Lycidas* has disappeared, along with the verse form in which he spoke. In his place we are confronted with a speaker who has adopted the verse form associated with the one genre in which the figure of the author normally plays no role whatsoever: drama. What is more, this speaker almost immediately excludes himself from the poem he has just begun:

> Of Man's First Disobedience and the Fruit
> Of that Forbidden Tree, whose mortal taste
> Brought Death into the World, and all our woe,
> With loss of Eden, till one greater Man
> Restore us, and regain the blissful Seat, . . .   (1.1–5)

At this point of the epic's opening sentence, as Janet Adelman has observed, anyone with the slightest knowledge of either classical or Renaissance epic would have expected the next line to begin "I sing."[36] Instead, the unidentified voice invites an external force to assume the narrative burden: "Sing heavenly Muse" (1.6). As in the proem to the *Nativity Ode,* a self-effacing speaker has consigned the rest of the poem to a third party.

In this case, however, the poet's abdication is less clear-cut, for shortly afterwards he relegates the Muse to the role of assistant in an enterprise in which he is still the prime mover:

> I thence
> Invoke thy aid to my advent'rous Song,
> That with no middle flight intends to soar

Above th'Aonian Mount

. . . .

Instruct me

. . . .

What in me is dark
Illumine, what is low raise and support;
That to the highth of this great Argument
I may assert Eternal Providence,
And justify the ways of God to men.   (1.12–26)

In the *Nativity Ode* the Heavenly Muse was asked to present *"thy* humble
ode" (24) to the infant Christ-child. Here she is only invoked as an aid to *"my*
adventurous song."* The burden of authorial responsibility has shifted signifi-
cantly. Not for very long, though. Just two lines later the speaker once again
surrenders control of the poem to the Muse as he urges her not only to assist
him but also to take over the role of narrator herself:

Say first, for Heav'n hides nothing from thy view,
Nor the deep Tract of Hell, say first what cause
Mov'd our Grand Parents in that happy State,
Favor'd of Heav'n so highly, to fall off
From thir Creator

. . . .

Who first seduc'd them to that foul revolt?   (1.27–33)

Strictly speaking, everything that follows is an answer to that question, pro-
vided by the poet's divine informant.[37] Hence the repeated references to
"Men," in lines 685 and 740 of Book One and in lines 496–97 of Book Two;
the voice that describes human folly and corruption in these passages clearly
belongs to a higher order of being than the human.

The authorial persona here behaves in much the same way as the figure
of the poet in the 1645 edition, continually vacillating between self-erasure
and self-assertion as he struggles to find a place for himself in his own text.
But as *Paradise Lost* continues, the speaker gradually begins to assume a
rather more stable poetic identity. In the proem to Book Three, for instance,
we learn that he himself has voyaged with Satan to the shores of hell and back
again:

Thee I revisit now with bolder wing,
Escap't the Stygian Pool, though long detain'd
In that obscure sojourn, while in my flight
Through utter and through middle darkness borne
With other notes than to th' Orphean Lyre
I sung of Chaos and Eternal Night,

> Taught by the heav'nly Muse to venture down
> The dark descent, and up to reascend,
> Though hard and rare, thee I revisit safe.   (3.13–21)

The Muse has served as his Sibyl, guiding him through the underworld, but both the infernal experiences and the words that have described them have been his, not hers. And from this point on the narrator writes consistently as if he has been physically present in the various locales he portrays. In the prologue to Book Seven we learn that the Muse has conducted him up to the heaven of heavens where he has drawn "Empyreal Air" (7.14) and then back to earth, his "Native Element" (7.16), where:

> More safe I Sing with mortal voice, unchang'd
> To hoarse or mute, though fall'n on evil days,
> On evil days though fall'n, and evil tongues;
> In darkness, and with dangers compast round
> And solitude.   (7.24–28)

A second-hand third-person narrative has turned into a first-hand first-person account of a story in which the poet is himself involved,[38] and in which he turns from the reader to address his characters directly just as he had done in the elegies for Shakespeare and the Marchioness of Winchester:

> These lull'd by Nightingales imbracing slept,
> And on *thir* naked limbs the flow'ry roof
> Show'r'd Roses, which the Morn repair'd. Sleep on,
> Blest pair; and O yet happiest if *ye* seek
> No happier state, and know to know no more.
>   (4.771–75; italics mine)[39]

"The Author John Milton" has finally taken charge of his own poem, with the result that in the prologue to Book Nine he no longer prays directly to the Muse, as he had in the prologues to Books One, Three, and Seven, but delivers a literary manifesto to his readers:

> No more of talk where God or Angel Guest
> With Man, as with his Friend, familiar us'd
> To sit indulgent, and with him partake
> Rural repast, permitting him the while
> Venial discourse unblam'd: I now must change
> Those Notes to Tragic.   (9.1–6)

He acknowledges his "Celestial Patroness" (9.21), but in the third person, and no longer does he ask her for further information. Now the story resumes on its own, without the customary act of interrogation: "The Sun was sunk, and after him the Star" (9.48).[40] By Book Ten, the mortal voice that began the poem so diffidently has acquired almost superhuman authority, scolding the fallen pair for their forgetfulness and bullying the reader with strident rhetorical questions:

> For still they knew, and ought to have still remember'd
> The high Injunction not to taste that Fruit,
> Whoever tempted; which they not obeying,
> Incurr'd, what could they less, the penalty,
> And manifold in sin, deserv'd to fall.   (10.12–16)

The poet has begun to sound like his Muse.

III. *Paradise Regained*

Four years later the evolution of Milton's literary persona reaches its climax in the opening lines of *Paradise Regained:*

> I who erewhile the happy Garden sung
> By one man's disobedience lost, now sing
> Recover'd Paradise to all mankind,
> By one man's firm obedience fully tried.   (1.1–4)

Here for the first (and last) time in Milton's poetic career is a full-blooded authorial presence, a self-assertive "I" who takes immediate responsibility not only for the poem we are about to read but for the great poem that preceded it as well. Shortly afterwards, to be sure, he pays tribute to the Muse's inspiring power. But even though his song may be "prompted," it is unequivocally "my" song (12). Unlike his previous incarnations, this speaker is in total control of the poem from the very beginning, freely editorializing in his own person—"Alas how simple, to these cates compar'd, / Was that crude apple that diverted Eve" (2.348–49)[41]—and on at least one occasion turning his back on the reader in order to relate part of the story to the character who actually lived it:

> ill wast thou shrouded then,
> O patient Son of God, yet only stood'st
> Unshaken; nor yet stay'd the terror there.
> Infernal Ghosts, and Hellish Furies, round
> Environ'd thee, some howl'd, some yell'd, some shriek'd,
> Some bent at thee thir fiery darts, while thou
> Satt'st unappall'd in calm and sinless peace.   (4.419–25)

It is an extraordinary moment. For a few lines, at least, we are completely excluded from the narrative scene while the poet engages in a private act of reminiscence with his hero. The rhetorical device that gave an extra dimension to the speaker in the elegies on Shakespeare and the Marchioness of Winchester has been enlisted in the service of a narrator so powerful that he can turn his protagonist into his audience. The birth of the author is finally complete.

In Milton's literary career, Stanley Fish wrote, "the poet's fierce egoism is but one half of the story."[42] The other half, I have suggested, is a long, drawn-out process of somewhat tentative experimentation which produced an authentic and fully integrated poetic self only after a lifetime of false starts, unexpected retreats, and detours into passivity and plurality. The slowly evolving figure whose various twists and turns, entries and exits, divisions and unifications I have traced was anything but the self-confident patriarch we have recently been taught to discern in his poetry. "The Author John Milton" took a long time to be born.

Stanford University

NOTES

1. David Masson, *The Life of John Milton* (Gloucester, Mass., 1965), vol. 3, 459. The relationship between the portrait and the Greek text underneath it has been the subject of a good deal of critical attention in recent years. See, in particular, John Hale, "Milton's Self-Presentation in *Poems . . . 1645*," *MQ* 25 (1991): 37–48; Leah Marcus, "Milton as Historical Subject," *MQ* 25 (1991): 120–27; Gary Spear, "Reading before the Lines: Typography, Iconography, and the Author in Milton's 1645 Frontispiece," in *New Ways of Looking at Old Texts: Papers of the Renaissance English Text Society, 1985–1991,* ed. W. Speed Hill (Binghamton, N.Y., 1993), 187–94; and Randall Ingram, "The Writing Poet: The Descent from Song in *The Poems of Mr. John Milton, Both English and Latin (1645),*" in *Milton Studies* 34, ed. Albert C. Labriola (Pittsburgh, 1996), 179–97.

2. I do not treat either Milton's translations or his dramatic works, because, of course, for these texts, questions of authorial presence would be irrelevant. For reasons of length I omit any consideration of his poems in languages other than English.

3. Introduction to Louis L. Martz and Aubrey Williams, *The Author in His Work: Essays on a Problem in Criticism* (New Haven, 1978), x.

4. Michel Foucault, "What Is an Author," in *Textual Strategies: Perspectives in Post-Structuralist Criticism,* ed. Josue V. Harari (Ithaca, 1979), 148.

5. C. S. Lewis and E. M. W. Tillyard, *The Personal Heresy* (Oxford, 1965), 9–10.

6. Robert McMahon, *The Two Poets of Paradise Lost* (Baton Rouge, 1998), especially the introduction and chapter 5.

7. See Robert M. Durling, *The Figure of the Poet in Renaissance Epic* (Cambridge, 1965), ch. 2.

8. Janet Adelman, "Creation and the Place of the Poet in *Paradise Lost*," in *The Author in His Work: Essays on a Problem in Criticism,* ed. Louis L. Martz and Aubrey Williams (New Haven, 1978), 65, n. 4. Cf. Annabel Patterson's comment in the introduction to *John Milton*

(London, 1992): "Yet the fact remains that anyone reading *Paradise Lost* . . . runs up against the irreducible and insistent presence of Milton the author, 'presence,' 'Milton' and 'author' all, of course, being subject to our inference that Milton was (carefully or anxiously) constructing them for us and for himself" (7).

9. Foucault, "What Is an Author?" 143.

10. Marcus, "Milton as Historical Subject," 120.

11. Herbert J. Phelan, "What Is the Persona Doing in *L'Allegro* and *Il Penseroso?*" in *Milton Studies* 22, ed. James D. Simmonds (Pittsburgh, 1986), 3–19.

12. A rather different pattern might emerge if the poems were treated in the order in which Milton actually wrote them, and if my interests were psychological and biographical that would no doubt be the appropriate way to proceed. My concern here, however, is with the way in which Milton presented his authorial persona to his readers, and for that reason I have focused on the poems as they appeared in print in the seventeenth century. As Cleanth Brooks and John Edward Hardy put it many years ago, "from the viewpoint of literary history there are clear reasons for preserving and emphasizing [the 1645 edition] as a volume in its own right, keeping the arrangement which Milton himself made" (*Poems of Mr John Milton: The 1645 Edition with Essays in Analysis* [New York, 1951]), vi.

13. Marcus, "Milton as Historical Subject," 121, 124.

14. Hale, "Milton's Self-Presentation," 41.

15. Richard Halpern, "The Great Instauration: Imaginary Narratives in Milton's 'Nativity Ode,'" in *Re-membering Milton: Essays on the Texts and Traditions,* ed. Mary Nyquist and Margaret W. Ferguson (New York, 1987), 6. See also C. W. R. D. Moseley, *The Poetic Birth: Milton's Poems of 1645* (Aldershot, U.K. 1991), 97–114.

16. *The Passion,* lines 3–4.

17. Paul H. Fry, *The Poet's Calling in the English Ode* (New Haven, 1980), 44.

18. "The Great Instauration," 4.

19. W. R. Parker, *Milton: A Biography,* 2 vols. (Oxford, 1968), vol. 1, 72.

20. It is theoretically possible, of course, that the voice in a declarative poem belongs to a persona rather than to the author, as I have argued it does in the hymn in the *Nativity Ode*. The sentiments of the "Heav'nly Muse" correspond so closely to Milton's, however, that it is difficult, if not impossible, to distinguish them from each other.

21. Louis L. Martz, "The Rising Poet," in *Poet of Exile: A Study of Milton's Poetry* (New Haven, 1980), 47. Cf. Dana Brand's observation that "Everything appears as a pure, spontaneous experience, not as an experience 'had' by a self-conscious observer" ("Self-Construction and Self-Dissolution in 'L'Allegro' and 'Il Penseroso,'" *MQ* 15 [1981]: 117).

22. Brand, "Self-Construction and Self-Dissolution," 116–19.

23. Martz, "The Rising Poet," 48.

24. Brand, "Self-Construction and Self-Dissolution," 116–19.

25. *Lives of the English Poets,* ed. by George B. Hill, 3 vols. (Oxford, 1905), vol. 1, 165–67.

26. The recurrent use of the term "persona" in recent discussions of the two poems suggests that the latter alternative has come to dominate critical thinking about them.

27. James Holly Hanford, "The Youth of Milton: An Interpretation of His Early Development," in *Studies in Shakespeare, Milton, and Donne* (New York, 1925), 131–33.

28. J. Martin Evans, *The Road from Horton: Looking Backwards in Lycidas* (Victoria, 1983), 68.

29. John Crowe Ransom originally called attention to this anomaly in his essay "A Poem Nearly Anonymous," in *The American Review* 1 (1933), 179–203, 444–467.

30. Stanley Fish, "*Lycidas:* A Poem Finally Anonymous," *Glyph* 8 (1981): 12.

31. In "The Dread Voice in *Lycidas,*" in *Milton Studies* 9, ed. James D. Simmonds (Pitts-

burgh, 1976), 238, W. B. Madsen argues that they are spoken by the archangel Michael whose protective powers the shepherds had invoked in lines 162–64. Fish, too, believes that "these are entirely new accents spoken by an entirely new voice" ("*Lycidas*," 14), but he does not attribute them to Saint Michael.

32. Fish concludes that *Lycidas* is "a poem that relentlessly denies the privilege of the speaking subject . . . and is finally, and triumphantly, anonymous" ("*Lycidas*," 16).

33. See Evans, *The Road from Horton*, 71–72.

34. *Ad Ioannem Rousium*, line 6.

35. In a trenchant critique of Martz's argument, Randall Ingram points out that, in order to read the 1645 volume as a narrative of poetic development, Martz is forced to discuss the poems themselves in reverse order, concluding rather than beginning with the *Nativity Ode*. See "The Writing Poet," 192.

36. Adelman, "Creation and the Place of the Poet in *Paradise Lost*," 58.

37. The poet makes a brief reappearance in Book One, 376, to renew his questions; "Say Muse, thir Names then known, who first, who last, / Rous'd from the slumber?" The Muse replies in line 381ff.

38. Stanley Fish notes that the announcement "I sing" is "in marked contrast to the more deferential yielding of agency in the invocation to Book I" ("With Mortal Voice: Milton Defends against the Muse" *ELH* 62 [1995]: 518).

39. In Book Nine, 404–407, the narrator intervenes again: "O much deceiv'd, much failing, hapless Eve, / Of thy presum'd return! event perverse!" On neither occasion, however, can Adam and Eve actually hear him.

40. Adelman contends that the prologue to Book Nine contains both "the strongest statement of the muse's aid" and "the strongest statement of Milton's doubt of the muse's aid" and that this "radical combination of self-assertion and self-denial" is "characteristic of Milton's stance throughout the poem" ("Creation and the Place of the Poet in *Paradise Lost*," 57). It seems to me, rather, that as the poem continues, the self-assertions become progressively stronger and the self-denials progressively weaker, and that the prologue to Book Nine marks a key moment in this process.

41. See also Book Two, 264, 295; Book Three, 443; and Book Four, 6–7, 563–64.

42. Fish, "*Lycidas*," 17.

MYSELF A TRUE POEM: EARLY MILTON AND THE (RE)FORMATION OF THE SUBJECT

Kathleen M. Swaim

WHETHER UNDERSTOOD AS AN event in religious history or as the triumph of logocentricism, the English Reformation constituted its citizenry as readers and, by extension, defined the best of readers as the best of men. Under the influence of grace, its model individual elevated himself or herself ever higher through interaction with the Word. This enduring system constituted a Protestant—for example, the late exemplar of the Puritan extreme of Protestantism, John Milton (1608–74)—as a unique individual believer who had the capacity and responsibility to process biblical texts independently and creatively and to develop a unique relationship with the divine therefrom. In this vein, Milton's "Of True Religion" commends those who "use all diligence and sincerity of heart, by reading, by learning, by study, by prayer for Illumination of the holy Spirit, to understand the Rule and obey it, they have done what man can do."[1] Milton's *Christian Doctrine* carries such textual processing to a systematic extreme. Indeed, from his earliest days, readerly heroism took on the status of family myth, when John Milton's father was disinherited for owning a Bible.

In the fine phrasing of *Areopagitica*, the mid-seventeenth century undertook the "reforming of Reformation itself" (YP 2.553), and for Milton—as for many contemporaries—this extension constituted the hero not just as Reformation reader but as Revolutionary writer. The late 1620s and the 1630s were the years of Milton's coming of age, and more broadly a time when a revolutionary Protestant spirit was abroad in the land, dictating new possibilities and new responsibilities for every citizen. In what he understood to be an ultimately logocentric universe, Milton devoted himself to embodying and heroicizing readerly and writerly skills.[2] This essay will consider a series of Milton's lyrics written during the late 1620s and the 1630s that evidence his wrestling with the process of defining himself as a poet, for him a role compounding reading with writing. Within the broad recognition of education as initiation into the status of autonomous wielder of intellect,[3] Milton's early poems go out of their way to display the learning he was in the process of amassing even as they wrestle with educational issues and limitations. At school and beyond, Milton sought to incorporate in himself a universal knowledge, and he labored with passionate intensity to sharpen a voice. He understood that if his ambitions were answered, that voice would be the voice of his nation and his faith as well. At the height of his fame, he knew himself to be addressing the audience of all learned Europe, as his *Second Defense* makes clear (YP 4.1.557–58).

Milton's early—and in some ways apprentice—lyrics of the late 1620s and the 1630s manifest the development of several elements of an individuated voice. These elements will remain in play throughout his poetry and prose productions. Early and late they do so within the energy field of René Descartes (1596–1650) and his publication of *Rules for the Direction of the Mind* (1628), *Discourse on the Method* (1637), *Meditations on First Philosophy* (1641), and *Principles of Philosophy* (1644), milestone documents theorizing the emergence of modern subjectivity and crystallizing some ways in which—across the Channel—the English Reformation had been moving to constitute its citizens for nearly a century. That subjectivity is available to us as the texts Milton produced—texts that manifest his unique and original consciousness. We compose "John Milton" through the reading of his texts just as he was composing himself and crafting his presentation of that self as heroicized poet with their composition.

A range of varied recent commentary has clarified the modern self as "the power to impose a shape upon oneself,"[4] as performing itself, as essentially split or conscious of itself as an autonomous, aware, discontinuous (and therefore growing) being, and as a self in play, that is suspended, provisional, and continuously renegotiating its own nature and boundaries. Its limits are always undergoing formation and re-formation as it projects fictions, retrospectively producing a coherence that the process is simultaneously abandoning. Albert W. Fields theorizes: "The *created* Self, by urgency of its paradigm, becomes at once the *creator* of an emerging plastic Self, a Self undergoing endless shaping; and although external forces, including the hand of God, were eventful and forceful in this fashioning, the most significant emergent force was the Self's 'Will.'"[5] Francis Barker historicizes the process in *The Tremulous Private Body:* "Not only is it now possible and necessary to narrate the outer world from an inner place, by means of a clarified and transparent instrumental language, and similarly to reflect on others as Others, but—more insidiously—the subject can, and now must, reflect on itself in the same fashion." After Milton's lifetime, subjectivity was to take fuller shape in Lockean empiricism, in which the subject understands itself as producing knowledge from internal resources, by processing experience rather than receiving it from the deity and His creation: "The subject consequently takes the place of God and becomes the author and guarantee of its own (subjective) truth."[6]

With John Milton, emerging modern subjectivity takes on a certain momentum—reaches a point from which there is no turning back. John Milton was twenty-one years old in 1629 and already showed evidence of fashioning a definitive, even a monumental, self.[7] He had early come to see his educational advantages and the inherent talents they nourished as securing for himself an essential individuation in a world he understood as a meritocracy, where qualities of mind and spirit defined worth and hierarchical positioning. Such status is repeatedly shadowed in his works by the parable of the talents (Matthew 25:14–30). In *On the Morning of Christ's Nativity* and *Lycidas*, as in *The Reason of Church Government* (1642), the worthy poet speaks as the enchanted son of the muses and also as the human instrument through which the Christian deity sounds its trumpet blasts of prophecy, its jeremiads and its "unexpressive" joys. To complicate the process, the Miltonic voice, like other issues of self, operates always within the radical Christian principle of losing oneself in order to find oneself.[8]

Late in his career Milton would dramatize the first moment of a suddenly mature thinking person's first consciousness in the essentialized Cartesian formulation his epic hero Adam voices:

> Myself I then perus'd, and Limb by Limb
> Survey'd, and sometimes went, and sometimes ran
> With supple joints, as lively vigor led:
> But who I was, or where, or from what cause,
> Knew not; to speak I tri'd, and forthwith spake,
> My Tongue obey'd and readily could name
> Whate'er I saw
>
> .   .   .   .
>
>   fair Creatures tell,
> Tell, if ye saw, how came I thus, how here?
> Not of myself; by some great Maker then,
> In goodness and in power preëminent;
> Tell me, how may I know him, how adore,
> From whom I have that thus I move and live,
> And feel that I am happier than I know.   (8.267–73, 276–82)[9]

For Milton, the individual is made in the image of God, and thus the creature bears a rational resemblance to his creator even as he is himself not just an image or imitator but a maker in his own right, a producer or potential producer of good out of evil.

The lines just cited record Milton's most Cartesian formulation with Adam as essentially "self-knowing" (7.10) and definitively not "self-begot" (5.860). They dramatize the moment enacted biographically in *On the Morning of Christ's Nativity*—and amplified in the 1630s lyrics to follow, when consciousness becomes, not a stable, but a multiple and fluid function, and the thinking being simultaneously apprehends itself from both outside and inside. Additionally, the consciousness becomes divided, split between a projection of an unlimited deity in which it participates and a self-conscious realization of its own limitation, and therefore a realization that it should aspire to abandon a lesser self in favor of one that more fully partakes of the deity it expansively apprehends.[10] Nowadays we may not automatically recognize the extent to which Descartes' articulation of modern consciousness insists upon aligning self-awareness with the divine awareness that constitutes it, but a much cited sentence from *Apology for Smectymnuus* (1642) records the fluid complexity of this essentially Reformationist subjectivity: "I conceav'd my selfe to be now not as mine own person, but as a member incorporate into that truth whereof I was perswaded, and whereof I had declar'd openly to be a partaker" (YP 1:871).[11] The transaction negotiates the question of which comes first: the truth or the "I," "mine own person" or incorporate membership, persuasion or conception, the owning or disowning of the self, with *own* here signaling both the verb of possession and a pronoun intensifier.

My argument begins with *On the Morning of Christ's Nativity* of 1629. Of course, Milton had produced a number of poems and translations in earlier years, but with *Christ's Nativity* what had before been merely youthful promise becomes transcendent achievement. Here for the first time for him theological grace and the psychological imagination it tropes produce a "true poem"—both in the sense of a fully articulated lofty rime and in the sense that an autobiographical passage from *Apology for Smectymnuus* (1642) was to spell out: "he who would not be frustrate of his hope to write well hereafter in laudable things, ought him selfe to bee a true Poem, that is, a composition and patterne of the best and honourablest things; not presuming to sing high praises of heroick men, or famous Cities, unlesse he have in himselfe the experience and the practice of all that which is praise-worthy" (YP 1:890). For himself, the pamphlet goes on to explain, the practice combines "a certain niceness of nature, an honest haughtiness and self-esteem . . . [and] modesty." In *Paradise Lost* the archangel Raphael voices an auxiliary principle: "Oft-times nothing profits more / Than self-esteem, grounded on just and right / Well manag'd" (8.571–73).

Coming as it does at the threshold of modern subjectivity, Milton's great epic of the 1660s was to celebrate the transformation of the Western psyche by conflating theological and psychological / philosophical fields and enfolding that compound into the role of epic poet, the most readerly and writerly of Reformation heroes. *Paradise Lost* offers "Omnific Word" and "Divine Similitude"—the dominant vehicles of all poetry, the goal of true poetry—as epithets for the second person of the Trinity. In early ode as in late epic, interactions between a poem's image and theme, or vehicle and tenor, adumbrate the relationship between Christ as man and Christ as God, between accessibility and transcendence, between accommodational security and provocative insight. In the late Milton's idiosyncratic version of the Trinity, the second person modulates into the third. If the second equates with poetic elements—Word, Similitude—the third impels the reader and reading process. In *Paradise Lost* it is "a Comforter . . . / The Promise of the Father" who *writes* upon the hearts of believers and thereby "guide[s] [readers] in all truth" (12.486–90, italics mine). In *Christian Doctrine,* this third person is sometimes God the Father himself and sometimes the Son, "a divine impulse, light, voice or word sent from above" (*Christian Doctrine* 1.6; YP 6:282–83, 284). The Christian writer / reader exists as and within a continuous process of transformation. In its interactions with the Word and the world, such a vital self progressively dissolves and reforms; intellectually and spiritually, it multiplies and accumulates talents and divine approbation.

I. *On the Morning of Christ's Nativity* and the Constructed Self

From his early youth, Milton understood himself as destined to be a poet, likely to "leave something so written to aftertimes, as they should not willingly let it die" (*Reason of Church Government,* YP 1.810). *On the Morning of Christ's Nativity,* written in the Christmas season of 1629, a few weeks after his twenty-first birthday, confirmed this literary promise. The treatise describes an apt poetic purpose that "celebrate[s] . . . the throne and equipage of Gods almightinesse" (YP 1.817). Behind Milton lay adolescent years of skilled versification and translation as his father's prodigy, years too of rigorous discipline in his studies and in virtue, years of aspiration and hope and passionate labor, years in which Milton pursued what *The Reason of Church Government* describes as "industrious and select reading, steddy observation, insight into all seemly and generous arts and affaires" (YP 1.821). With *Christ's Nativity,* the twenty-one-year-old author found himself not just ready but suddenly able to generate a text worthily harvesting that arduous construction of an educated self.

With *On the Morning of Christ's Nativity,* Christianity and poetry—unified in a literary, spiritual, and Cartesian self—simultaneously come alive for the fledgling author. As a product and a process, this ode defined Milton's heightened understanding of what it meant, and what it felt like, to be a poet of the highest order, and articulated his sudden and singular perception of harmony and order, his coinciding spiritual and poetic creation and recreation. Here writing becomes for him a discovery of and a production of the self at the same time that it opens that temporary achievement to meanings in excess of the author's input and control. Milton's is an art, as Catherine Belsey keenly observes, in which "meanings are produced not given," and Linda Gregerson speaks of its *transitive* literary gestures that open and signal beyond themselves.[12] Milton had long since learned that the poet should be impelled by inspiration from classical muses representing the Christian Word—but here he learns that signification exceeds representation because the poet is a prophet and the prophet is the voice of God.

Christ's Nativity is appropriately also about beginnings. It is about a moment in time and a moment outside of time and a moment reenacted through time—that is, at each Christmastide—and reenacted within the hearts of all Christians. *On the Morning of Christ's Nativity* is literally about the birth of the theological Word, the moment of Incarnation and Christ's transforming of human history and human consciousness. Milton is himself biographically in the process of replicating these categories—both within and outside of contemporary expectations of the individual as *imitatio Christi*. The opening verses of the Gospel of John authorize the linguistics of such an enterprise: "In the beginning was the Word, and the Word was with God, and the Word was God. . . . And the Word was made flesh, and dwelt among us, (and we beheld his glory, the glory as of the only begotten of the Father,) full of grace and truth" (1:1, 14). The gospel verses speak too of a man named John—whether the Baptist or Milton—who is a chosen precursor rightly receiving, empowered by, and bearing witness to true light. Externally at the Incarnation, grace overwhelms nature to define a new logocentric universe; internally, the poet synthesizes his own past and powers, all his educational cumulation and theological belief, and gives a Pythagorean harmony to his classical learning, the Old and New Testaments, and his own place in history (1629) and eternity.

Perhaps the most profound lesson Milton learned from writing *On the Morning of Christ's Nativity* was that a true poem is a verbal construct whose "answerable style" (*PL* 9.20) reconstitutes its thematics. The poet must precisely calibrate the disparate elements of a poem's art with the themes he wishes to convey. For Incarnation themes, an answerable style must represent language and reality in the process of at once expressing and transcending their limitations. Artistically, *On the Morning of Christ's Nativity* must therefore inaugurate a new literary form, a new system of naming, and a new mode of apprehension for the poet and his audience. This poem fundamentally keeps decorum when the dynamics of its form and content align the poet's voice, the angelic choiring, the music of the spheres, and the reader's psyche. The poetic agent waits to receive the apprehension, to be literally *in-*

spired, whether through the pagan myths of Apollo and the Muses (daughters of Memory) or the Christian myth of prevenient grace. Theology dictates the governing promises, but authors and readers put them into practice through acts of remembering (re-membering). In the language of *Paradise Lost* it becomes a matter of body turning all to spirit, of the "Umpire Conscience," of Christ as mediator and similitude, and of the paradise within. Of course, all such theological and linguistic categories offer analogies of modern selfhood.

To begin with, an answerable style should reconstitute old modes within a new literary dispensation. The classic muse collapses into the "heav'nly Muse" and classical ode into Christian hymn.[13] Milton's innovative form defies logical as well as chronological sequence. Destabilized tenses fluctuate between the mundane and the transcendent; images likewise fluctuate between earthly and heavenly elements to convey the mystery of the arriving transformative order, with its inevitable erasure of preceding norms. Data often have to register their points through negations of the old order. Whatever is confinable within experiential matter or within recorded names gravitates downward and is insistently closured; what is not confinable opens upward and outward toward expansive possibilities. The poem dismisses the unworthy mundane, now truly seen and valued, and affirms the new standard of measurement that enables and then transcends such distinction and moral sorting.

Christ's Nativity's wondrous new song captures the world, the mind, the whole human enterprise just at the instant when a new imaginative dispensation begins in history as well as in its creator. *Peace* illustrates the basic linguistic and chronological difficulty as well as the breakthrough layering. At the poem's transitional moment, the deity sends down "the meek-ey'd Peace" (46). In a traditional register, this feminized figure may be dressed in "Olive green" (47), divide the clouds with "Turtle wing" (50), and wave a "myrtle wand" (51). Historically, as during the reign of Caesar Augustus, contemporary with Christ's birth, the earth may experience "a universal Peace through Sea and Land" (52). Mythically, it is a time of Ovid's "Birds of Calm" (68; Met. 9.745–46). The all too lamentable human norms, however, define peace chiefly as "*No* War, or Battle's sound" when "The [military] Trumpet spake *not*" (53, 58, italics mine), or as a natural world that has "forgot to rave" (67). None of these vocabularies can express the arriving Prince of Peace (Isaiah 9:6), but they are the only vocabularies available to serve as vehicle of any expressive effort.[14] When the Word of John 1:1 locks fully into place, appropriate expressive possibilities will become available, and they will do so not just because Christ has come but also because his coming redeems human imaginations—that is, opens humanity to poetic, layered linguistic resonances and to typological simultaneity of understanding. It will open readers to the mode of redemptive imagination into which the newly post-incarnational poet is inducting himself.

The homologue *sun/son* carries this transformative and resonating art and linguistics to new reaches. It exploits the coincidence of the sun's birthday (the December solstice) and, a few days later, the Son's birthday (December 24–25),[15] as both institute a new light and a new era and an inevitable format for growth of that light, temporally definable as a new year and theologically definable as a New Dispensation. Chronologically, *Christ's Nativity* reifies the literal meaning of *solstitium,* "to stand still" (*OED*). "Greater Sun" (83) expresses the new agency of spirit and grace by simultaneously retaining and transcending the outmoded language system. On the one hand and before the critical pause, the sun was Nature's "lusty Paramour," wantoning seasonally with the beloved earth (35–36); it was also Ovid's chariot of Phoebus (Met. 2.59–69), with its "bright Throne" (84), "burning Axle-tree" (84), and team of horses brightly treading the pathway of the sky (19). The arriving vocabulary overwrites this sun with the "greater Sun" of Christ, "the son of Heav'n's eternal King" (2), and "the Prince of Light" (62), in other words with wholly new Christian meanings of love, light, life, and perception. Accommodationally, the word *Son* elevates *sun* as "that glorious Form, that Light unsufferable, / And that far-beaming blaze of Majesty" (8–9), but also as emissary to darksome earth and man from "Heav'n's high Council-Table . . . of Trinal Unity" (10–11) and from "the Courts of everlasting Day" (13). Both *Son* and *sun* are what *Paradise Lost* calls "Divine Similitudes." In their "conspicuous count'nance, without cloud / Made visible, th' Almighty Father shines, / Whom else no Creature can behold" (3.385–87). It is the true poet's role to facilitate that beholding.

In an analogue of the rhetorical figure of antimetabole (of which more in a moment), Milton's careful layering of language and meaning and myth systems in *Christ's Nativity* simultaneously deconstructs the old order. In its most continuous sequence of ideas, the poem's final third dismisses the pagan gods who are not susceptible to Christian transformation—unlike "Peace" and "greater Sun" and, of course, "Mighty *Pan*" (89). A sometimes formulaic catalogue mimics misguided worship. The new Christian light of Bethlehem highlights what is wrong with previous modes of deity and worship, including their weightedness toward things of the earth, their insistence upon binding rather than freedom, their bestial demeaning of both gods and worshippers, and their vanity (see "In vain" in lines 204, 208, and 219). In the light of the newly incarnate Christian truth, "The Oracles are dumb" (173) and Apollo and other passé pagan deities "can no more *divine*" (177, italics mine). Because the new order transforms human perceptions and human aspiration, such agencies can no longer impose upon human credulity. This new light damns their darkness; this new music negates their deceptive voice, whether hum or shriek; this new consciousness erases the fraud and hysteria they inspired.[16]

The boldest example of this practice, Apollo's pagan "divining" in stanza 19, both collects Milton's educational resources and anticipates his brief epic of some forty years later. The Delphic Oracle depended upon accidents of nature and deliberate human irrationality. Specifically, it communicated through rocky echoing chambers ("arched roof," "steep of *Delphos*") as interpreted by attendants under the spell of hallucinogenic laurel leaves. The new "divining" mode aims to redeem, not consecrate, earthly matters; it demands active aspiration, not passive submission to the laws of matter and gravity. *Paradise Regained* revisits the ceasing of oracles with a fuller theorization of Christ's transformative linguistics:

> God hath now sent his living Oracle
> Into the World to teach his final will,
> And sends his Spirit of Truth henceforth to dwell
> In pious Hearts, an inward Oracle
> To all truth requisite for men to know.   (1.460–64)

Oracle proves to be another of those terms—like Peace or sun/Son—that *On the Morning of Christ's Nativity* both deconstructs and reconstitutes within the spiritualized vocabulary of Incarnation. In both early ode and late brief epic, and for the reader as well as the poet, Christ's spirit quickeneth (John 6:63); it is able to pierce "dead things with inbreath'd sense" (*At a Solemn Music*, 4 [1633]).[17]

The formal order of *Christ's Nativity* follows the model of the rhetorical figure antimetabole (e.g. 1-2-3-4-3-2-1), a serial sequence progressing to a hinge after which the regressive sequence unwinds toward its starting point. In its largest thematics, such antimetabole formats the Christian loss of self in order to find the new (reborn) self. In stylistic terms—to cite one additional category of evidence—it formats the investment of data with new meaning, this time through evidence from the whole range of the poem. By the end of *On the Morning of Christ's Nativity*, "Heav'n's youngest-teemed Star" (240) has become a metonym for the Christ-child as well as the cosmological event recorded in Matthew, the guide of the wise men, the cosmic hieroglyph of New Dispensation. *Youngest teemed Star* replaces the deeply amazed stars of the old order of nature (stanza 7, where *bespake* means gave order). Antimetabolically, the poem's ending returns us to the dawn that will jail the "flocking shadows" of false deity. This dawn, like all dawns, is a point of transition between darkness and light. This dawn—and all dawns if one chooses to read them so—marks a moral and spiritual transition. The poem stops rather than concludes to reflect the promise that, prior to ultimate perfection, there is no end to the process of Incarnation here beginning, ultimately in the words of *Paradise Lost,* that time when "God shall be All in All" (3.341). The subjective equivalent would be the time when the self has achieved the stability, completeness, coherence, finality, and closure it is always pursuing.

The Bethlehem star collapses into "greater Sun" in the poem's closing image of the sun pillowing his chin upon an orient wave just as the Christ-child is resting in the manger. The poem constitutes the event as both climactic and anticlimactic, multiplying and collapsing layers of data. In its extreme silence and potentiality, it marks the birth of the Word, that transcendental signified that absorbs all mundane layers and that ultimately guarantees all meaning. The stanza types the infant Hercules (though not by name) to heroicize the transformation of consciousness. An analogous newborn, Hercules, like Pan a type of Christ, overcomes the poem's final and typological beast, the Typhon serpent. Since Typhon figures in Egyptian and Greek mythology, this heroic action puts into play the preceding pagan pantheon even as it again—and conclusively—commands the newly instructed Christian reader's imaginative, typological, interpretive reading. Where pagan snakes are merely reptilian, Judeo-Christian snakes evoke interpretations ranging from A to Z, so to speak, from Genesis to Revelation.

What in the old order of nature and psyche is capable of Christian transformation is so transformed in the poem; what is not capable of transformation is confined through time. The sun and stars, natural conveyors of light and thus potential forms into which deity may be infused, can partake of new light as *être* and *raison d'être* because they earlier embodied that aspect of deity. The order of grace redefines the traits Pan shares with Christ—love, shepherding, and all-ness—so that the redemptive ideas within Pan's nature may be newly apprehended. Along with Pan, the sun and stars may be poetically perceived and positively redirected, as the fays, for example, may not, for sun and stars too have always embodied aspects of the true God. The positive redirection of vocabulary rewards a Christian reading of images; it layers historical perspective, mythographic knowledge, and typological interpretation. The poem thus rewards the imaginations it has structured into its readers. Poetic perception, as characteristically throughout Milton's poetry, entails the ability to see through the object to the full idea behind it, and the joyful transcendent awareness of the relationship of the object and idea to encompassing Christian truth. Milton will differently distribute the two dimensions of such a poetic—as we shall see in a moment—in *L'Allegro* and *Il Penseroso,* and indeed the "sublime" for which Milton was to become famous depends upon his lively responsiveness to experiential data and his capacity to reconstitute data and instruct audiences to the transcendent resonances implicit in them. It is a process that Milton both received and bequeathed via *On the Morning of Christ's Nativity.*

Poetry-making is a cooperative, inspired activity and as such both confirms and expands the self and its options. As grammatical evidence of this, the authorial first person singular of *On the Morning of Christ's Nativity* melds into first person plurals and thence into the angelic choir. The poet's voice here is choric, and *Christ's Nativity's* central stanza (13), its antimetabolic climax, re-presents the Gloria of the Gospels. *The Reason of Church Government* similarly proposes that poetry is obtained "by devout prayer to that eternall Spirit who can enrich with all utterance and knowledge, and sends out his Seraphim with the hallow'd fire of his Altar to touch and purify the lips of whom he pleases" (YP 1.820–21). Poetry-making is thus a combination of meditating and mediating. The divine descends to mortals and mortal forms in order to raise them toward its own transcendent nature. In a linguistic environment, the result will be both *expressive* and *unexpressive.*[18] The meaning of the latter is *not able* to be contained in discursive forms, but also *not needing* to be thus confined. The term *unexpressive*—both here and in *Lycidas* (176)—embodies the excess of meaning that escapes the control of the author, who enables a mimetic experience for his readers. In both ode and pastoral elegy, *unexpressive* instances full presence and obliterates the différance of representation (Belsey, *John Milton: Language, Gender, Power,* 31). *Christ's Nativity* is thus a project that both defines and defies the nature of language. The Word in *On the Morning of Christ's Nativity* establishes the standard of measurement by which all merely earthly singing, including this Christmas rapture, becomes tedious, forcing the singer to move on to pastures new as happens similarly in the finale of *Lycidas.*

On the Morning of Christ's Nativity celebrates not just the author's achievement of creative consciousness but also his freedom from isolated self-consciousness, precisely the purposes of the Incarnation. Early lines describe *Christ's Nativity* itself as "a present to the Infant God" (16) and in Milton's description of this poem's production to his friend Charles Diodati (during the Christmas season of 1629) as "my gifts for the birthday of Christ— gifts which the first light of dawn brought to me" (*Elegia Sexta,* Hughes, 53). Multiple references produce excessive meanings within both *present* and *gift,* with *present* fluctuating between immediacy and donation. The *gifts* are at once given to Milton from the muses and given from Milton to the divine babe—and given again from Milton to Diodati and to us in the form of this breakthrough production. His gifts, his productions, are at once given and received and given again. The parable of the talents necessarily haunts the word *gift* as well.

Christ's Nativity treats formation and reformation, at once construction of the artifact and transformation of the self. Descartes' *"cogito ergo sum"*— alternatively *scribo ergo sum*—hovers always in the background of the action of *Christ's Nativity*, for here the authorial subject—the Smectymnuan true poem that is his self along with his linguistic product—comes fully into being. Here John Milton has been able to produce relations of representation and signification and thus produce access to truth for himself and—he projects— for the audience of his self-consuming construct. Artistically and theologically he is able to find and to lose and then to re-find himself. He has seized control of his own "industrious and select reading" and in the process been able to lay proprietary claim to all of reality. He has projected a representational absorptive fiction from his mind that becomes a newer, higher reality. In a breakthrough moment, he has become a controlling, thinking, reflective being—reflective upon God and reflective of God, both a thinking and a spiritual agent. With this poetic production he both recognizes and transcends his own limitations.

II. *L'Allegro* and *Il Penseroso* and the Deferred Self

A few years after completing *On the Morning of Christ's Nativity*, while still a student at Trinity College, Cambridge, Milton constructed a pair of remarkable poems—or a remarkably paired poem—in *L'Allegro* and *Il Penseroso* (1631?). If *On the Morning of Christ's Nativity* grew out of a reciprocation between Milton's poetic and theological comings-of-age, *L'Allegro* and *Il Penseroso*—in the words of *The Reason of Church Government*—analyze and thereby "allay the perturbations of the mind, and set the affections in right tune" (YP 1.816–17). The paired poems stage the experience of interiority, distinguishing complementary ways of collecting and processing experiential data and acting out the right relation between the self and the external world. Ultimately, if they are less about achieving a self, they are more about negotiating a thinking person's relationship with external and internal realities within a Cartesian subjectivity. All poems are to some extent about their own making (*poesis*), and *L'Allegro* and *Il Penseroso*, like *Christ's Nativity*, again enfold the process of the poet's subjective self-definition into their own essentiality. The present tense and future thrust of both poems mark the texts as process rather than product.

The paired poems embrace an answerable style to "realize" two contrasting and complementary psychic states. Put simply and traditionally, the 152-line *L'Allegro* celebrates how it feels to experience "heart-easing Mirth" or care-less ease and thus represents the psychic principle of happiness. It does so by reviewing a series of discrete data formatted as what an alert young man—*L'Allegro* and *Il Penseroso* present a distinctly masculine subjectivity—might experience in the course of a day's journey from morn to night amidst country and city scenes. Again put simply, the 176-line companion poem, *Il Penseroso*, reviews the serial experience of a no less alert but now definitively thoughtful young man whose predominantly nocturnal experience normatively "commerc[es] with the skies" (39). His psyche comprehends what the age called Melancholy.

Spenser taught Milton—as he continues to teach—that the feminine tropes a male agent's motives, desires, and aspirations. After their dismissive prologues, each of Milton's paired poems begins with an emblematic or static representation of a presiding Lady embodying "what is universally pleasurable and universally desired by men." "[Each] portrays not pursuer or pursuit but that bodiless thing itself which the freely delighting mind or the meditative mind tirelessly seeks to ally itself with. . . . [S]he is not a person; she is a personification . . . a way of talking about the absolutely not the contingently real."[19] Each then exfoliates into detailed scenes that trigger dynamic, essentializing responses in the speaker and readers. Through inherited troping devices, both *L'Allegro* and *Il Penseroso* stage the immediacy of thought's self-representation; they discover and reveal the action and process of thought. They affirm the existence of the perceiving self as coinciding and simultaneous with the occurrence of thinking, and they stage thought as a forward-flowing arrangement of signs, images, and ideas that both do and do not necessarily relate to their ostensible triggers. *Il Penseroso* in particular performs the discovery of the thinking self and of the self's capacity to think of itself as thinking, the thinking subject producing order and unity out of a flow of data and thereby also producing the Cartesian self who manages that construction and risks its disruption.

Both *L'Allegro* and *Il Penseroso* thematize their own operating principles and force readers to reenact them. In one vocabulary, *L'Allegro* enacts what the logic and rhetoric of the age called *invention,* that is, discovery of data, while *Il Penseroso* enacts the complementary process of *disposition,* that is, determining how data may be related to each other and to the whole scheme of things. *L'Allegro* is dominated by the optical; the more aural *Il Penseroso* is dominated by (in)sight or access to invisible realms. *L'Allegro* opens up vistas; *Il Penseroso* turns inward to enclosed spaces, and its diminished visual field intensifies data through learned intertextualities as well as through contrastive exercises (Christopher, "Subject and Macrosubject," 27, 28). *L'Allegro* targets the present and diurnal, *Il Penseroso* the future and eternal; *L'Allegro* the "care-free," *Il Penseroso* the committed. *L'Allegro* aims to recreate the experience of "the happy one," un-selfconsciously receiving the pleasurable data of the world his senses register; *Il Penseroso* similarly targets "the pensive one" who filters the world's data through capacious intellectual and spiritual resources and aspires to the "Prophetic strain" (174), and to what Prolusion #7 calls "the cycle of universal knowledge" (Hughes, 625). *Il Penseroso* filters its data and processes through learning and letters; *L'Allegro* goes out of its way to resist such resonances. Although *L'Allegro* may appear the easier project to put together, such erasures must have been a severe challenge to the richly provisioned Miltonic mind.[20]

Each poem interplays immediate acts of perception with its own and its companion poem's systems, relative to the serial data they share. The relationship of the two to each other is both complementary and oppositional, both dialectical and dynamically interactive. Psychologically, each poem does the dream-work of its companion, compressing and displacing elements that are at once both familiar and alien. After the first reading of *L'Allegro,* all levels of data in both poems call attention to, first, the likenesses and, then, the telling differences between the two efforts. For differing purposes, each, for example, features theatrical experience: *L'Allegro* views modern comedy (Shakespeare, Jonson) in a public theater in the afternoon; the solitary *Il Penseroso* reads ancient classical tragedy in his quiet study at night. *L'Allegro* hears the morning Lark and the strutting Cock; *Il Penseroso* meditates upon a book-filtered Nightingale (Philomela). In parallel syntax, *L'Allegro*'s parents "met once" (20) while *Il Penseroso*'s "met oft" (27–28). The female agency impelling *L'Allegro* is "buxom, blithe, and debonair" (24) while *Il Penseroso*'s syntactically parallel one is "Sober, steadfast, and demure" (32). *L'Allegro* characteristically "walk[s] not unseen" (57), while *Il Penseroso* "walk[s] unseen" (65). The poems are thus devised so as to encourage and reward the reader's pursuit of parallels of form or syntax as well as content, and as Merritt Hughes wisely commented long ago, "structural analysis will never exhaust the correspondences" between the two (67).

Il Penseroso's mode of aspiration is always shadowed by a denial of the material in *L'Allegro* upon which it builds, and, in the terms of Georgia Christopher's psychoanalytic projection, the latter poem practices sublimation, and the former, gratification ("Subject and Macrosubject," 25, 30). The reading of one thus always imports the remembrance and anticipation of the other. In a Derridean vocabulary, they impel a continually deferred resolution in which presence emphasizes absence and difference emphasizes likeness. *L'Allegro* builds up to "un-twisting" the chains of harmony (143), and *Il Penseroso* strives to "unsphere" or "unfold" Plato and the soul (88–89). Ultimately, what is untwisted or unsphered is the other poem, as the poems necessarily locate meaning in the site of the reader rather than in the text(s) themselves.[21] The end of *Il Penseroso,* and thus of the compound, invites a return to the beginning of *L'Allegro* as each of these basic psychic states creates the need for its opposite. The resulting oscillation between their polarities, as well as their continuous, mutually refreshing cycle, is aptly imaged by a Möbius strip.

The unique genre of these poems thus enacts the différance of destabilized modern subjectivity. *Il Penseroso's* narrative retrospection reads *L'Allegro* as dramatizing a single, always previous psychic unity and enacts its displacement by heightened consciousness, by provisionality and infinite regression. When one poem valorizes a temporarily stable self, it is also valorizing the Other (what the self lacks and must grow toward). *Il Penseroso* foregrounds the advantage of thoughtful being but also its exhaustion—hence the refreshment of immersion in the simpler sensoriness and temporary, illusory stabilities of *L'Allegro,* to fortify the psyche for a subsequent cycle of destabilization or growth.

Not inappropriately, Milton manufactured the genre for the paired pieces by compounding academic systems and discourses from his primary— that is, his academic—life experience at the time of their composition (c. 1631). In one such system, the paired poems proceed, as even modern debating competitions do, as matching responses to a contested question. As it happens, several of Milton's surviving school exercises treat materials similar to those of *L'Allegro* and *Il Penseroso:* Prolusion #1, *Whether Day or Night Is the More Excellent;* Prolusion #6, *That Sportive Exercises Are Occasionally Not Adverse to Philosophic Studies;* and Prolusion #7, *Learning Makes Men Happier Than Does Ignorance.* Contemporary education taught all schoolboys various devices for mastering both sides of a question at a deep level. When their dialectics pressured students to "realize" an item or issue and its opposite from as many angles as possible and to express either or both as eloquently and learnedly as they could, however, it was also instructing them in stepping outside their own positioning and looking at themselves from an alternative site. Thus the debating exercise genre necessarily taught deferrals of data and response in the poems' presentations of self.

Milton conscripts educational practice to format the poems' data in a complementary way as well. The schooling of the times set templates for particular argumentative exercises, in this case specifically the genre of the encomium. Schoolbooks of the day spell out the procedure very clearly:

Begin with an exordium. Then subjoin what stock the person is, divided as follows: of what people, of what country, of what ancestors, of what parents. Then explain his education under the heads of instruction, art, laws. Then introduce the chief of all topics of praise, his deeds, which you will show to be the results of 1. his excellences of mind as fortitude or prudence, 2. his excellences of body as beauty, speed, vigor, 3. his excellences of fortune as his high position, his power, wealth, friends. Then bring in a comparison in which your praise may be heightened to the uttermost. Finally conclude with an epilog urging your hearers to emulate.[22]

To construct encomia, these paired poems begin with the contrastive parentage of Mirth (Venus and Bacchus, or Zephyr and Aurora) and of Melancholy (Saturn and Vesta). Milton then moves to the auxiliary populations, that is, "of what people, of what country." For *L'Allegro* these consist of "Jest and youthful Jollity, / Quips and Cranks, and wanton Wiles, / Nods, and Becks, and Wreathed Smiles . . . And Laughter holding both his sides" (26–28, 32); and for *Il Penseroso* of "Peace and Quiet, Spare Fast," and "retired Leisure" (45–46, 49). Contemporary Ramistic textbooks of Logic—one of which Milton himself authored—specified that a subject would encompass all such adjuncts, but that a subject would also reciprocate precisely with its proper adjunct.[23] Both *L'Allegro* and *Il Penseroso* thus move from general populations to individuals that embody their subject: "The Mountain Nymph, sweet Liberty" essentializes *L'Allegro* as the "Cherub Contemplation" does *Il Penseroso*. A similar distribution between pagan and Christian marks *L'Allegro's* opening invocation of "come thou Goddess fair and free" (11) and *Il Penseroso's* of "Come, pensive Nun" (31). In keeping with encomium theory, the data of both poems then flow into expansive equivalences of something like their ideas' deeds and excellences of mind, body, and fortune.

At their climax, both poems move beyond such stabilities to heighten musical comparisons "to the uttermost" and, thus, not only to stretch beyond strict rationality, but also to signify the receding openness that beckons the subject's growth into the space it produces. *L'Allegro's* delectable couplets enact the musical theory they describe:

> And ever against eating Cares,
> Lap me in soft *Lydian* Airs,
> Married to immortal verse,
> Such as the meeting soul may pierce
> In notes, with many a winding bout
> Of linked sweetness long drawn out,
> With wanton heed, and giddy cunning,
> The melting voice through mazes running:
> Untwisting all the chains that tie
> The hidden soul of harmony.   (135–44)

The "winding bout" escapes syntactical norms in the excess and fluidity of a "giddy, melting, untwisting" forward flow of energy. *Il Penseroso's* musical invocation takes parallel form:

> But let my due feet never fail
> To walk the studious Cloister's pale
>
> . . . .
>
> There let the pealing Organ blow
> To the full voic'd Choir below,
> In Service high and Anthems clear,
> As may with sweetness, through mine ear,
> Dissolve me into ecstasies,
> And bring all Heav'n before mine eyes. (155–56, 161–66)

Here a more controlled syntax frames a complex aural interplay that likewise enacts the dissolution and ecstasy of Melancholy's aspiration, at the same time that it is staging a more formed and dedicated subject position for the speaker.

A similarly destabilized subjectivity impels the paired poems' heightened comparisons with the great poet Orpheus' career, with *L'Allegro*'s in an optative modality (*may, would have, quite,* and *half-regained*), while *Il Penseroso*'s verbs register their forcefulness upon the action and readers (*bid, sing, Drew, made, grant,* and *seek*). They conclude with matching invitational epilogues:

> These delights if thou canst give
> Mirth, with thee I mean to live.
>
> (*L'Allegro* 151–52, and see 37)

> These pleasures *Melancholy* give,
> And I with thee will choose to live.
>
> (*Il Penseroso,* 175–76)

"If" keys the *L'Allegro* project at various points, as does "choose" for *Il Penseroso*. *Il Penseroso* moves forcefully beyond the simple conditional to a future imperative that encapsulates the preceding enterprise.[24] The repeated rime of give and live, along with the shared combination of command, exhortation, and future conditional subjunctives, completes the cycle they reinforce. The conditionality of these endings fluctuates between what the speaker can do and what the category can do to the speaker, between giving and receiving (see also "talents" and "gift" in *Christ's Nativity*).

The prolusions document Milton's educational praxis, just as his short treatise *Of Education* spells out his pedagogical theory. Both reiterate the deeply felt Miltonic assumption that, in the words of Prolusion #3 (*Against Scholastic Philosophy*): "your mind should not consent to be limited and circumscribed by the earth's boundaries, but should range beyond the confines of the world. Let it reach the summit of knowledge and learn to know itself and at the same time to know those blessed minds and intelligences with whom hereafter it will enter into eternal fellowship" (Hughes, 607). Prolusion #7 speaks similarly of a spiritual restlessness after "the cycle of universal knowledge" has been completed (Hughes, 625); *Of Education* aspires to "an universall insight into things" (YP 2.406); and *The Reason of Church Government* retrospectively personalizes the achievement as "the full circle of my private studies" (YP 1.807). Milton believed deeply in education, and in particular that the poet should be "instructed and perfected in an all-around foundation in all the arts and in every science" (Hughes, 622). The ideal education his pedagogical treatise espouses builds hierarchically and chronologically from the rudiments of grammar and nature, through studies in philosophy, mathematics, and politics, to culminate in "that sublime art" of poetry (YP 2.404). The theory echoes the construction of an autonomous knowing self voiced earlier in *Christ's Nativity*—compounding the vantages of apprentice poet, serious student of literature, and pilgrim en route to eternity.

L'Allegro and *Il Penseroso* may map disjunctive systems along the way, but both projects inhabit the same epistemology here theorized. They assume, in phrasing from *Of Education,* that "because our understanding cannot in this body found it selfe but on sensible things, nor arrive so clearly to the knowledge of God and things invisible, as by orderly conning over the visible and inferior creature, the same method is necessarily to be follow'd in all discreet teaching" (YP 2.367–69). This modelled growth of the mind functions always with an eye to the classical ideal: "I call therefore a compleate and generous Education that which fits a man to perform justly, skilfully and magnanimously all the offices both private and publicke, of peace and war" (YP 2.377–79). It assumes a beginning "with Arts most easie, and those be such as are most obvious to the sence" (YP 2.374)—and it culminates in a "confirm'd and solidly united . . . body of . . . perfected knowledge" (YP 2.407). Progress is from simple and sensory to complex, intellectual, and divine.

The hero of *Il Penseroso* performs a similar method and goal:

> And may at last my weary age
> Find out the peaceful hermitage
>
> . . . .
>
> Where I may sit and rightly spell
> Of every Star that Heav'n doth shew,
> And every Herb that sips the dew;
> Till old experience do attain
> To something like Prophetic Strain. (167–68, 170–74)

If *L'Allegro*'s hero is collecting data, *Il Penseroso*'s is devoutly processing it, always with the intention of constructing the Smectymnuan true poem of himself. Both poems enact the process of an author simultaneously harvesting and interrogating his recent readings, simultaneously trying to discover his poetic and cultural inheritance and to remake it—to create a new and "answerable" poetics and to fashion a valid productive self or "authority." Both force the reader to enact, or to reenact, the speaker's fluctuation and growth, his endless curiosity and delight in new data and new possibilities.

On the surface, L'Allegro erases the speaker's subjective presence. By omitting pronouns and syntactical markers and, when it lists the data of the external world, insistently using detailed substantives, dangling participles, and unattached dependent clauses. Its syntax is predominantly paratactic, heavily dependent upon the linguistics of "and" (Christopher, "Subject and Macrosubject," 24–25). But its disjunctions (paradoxically) establish a continuous flow. Paradoxically too, the elision of first person pronouns conveys not merely the surface absence but also a subversive presence that haunts the selective "turn-ons" of a single continuous consciousness. Il Penseroso's more secured pronouns and syntax, and hence the evidence of (some) narrativity and teleology, provide the companion poem with a more articulate, continuous subjectivity. Indeed, this project insists upon that subject's essential isolation, and thus its fluid and centripetal self-development and self-knowledge. It goes out of its way to manifest the Cartesian principle that the essence of self is the mind and its processes and constructs.

In summary, subjectivity in these paired poems takes the recognition of a multiple self as foundational, but that multiplicity is always defining itself vis à vis a (fictional) unity. Together L'Allegro and Il Penseroso dramatize at once a subject reviewing external data and a fluid, multiplying subjectivity interplaying less with reality than with its own re-productions of data or mental fictions. The pair allow us to watch their compound speaker in the process of studying, externalizing, and creating its self. So understood, L'Allegro and Il Penseroso represent stages in the seventeenth-century construction of a modern self—by contrast with the medieval self as a stage on which divine forces play (Christopher, "Subject and Macrosubject," 24, 29, 23). The modern self, or modern subjectivity, is always in process, split into dynamic interplays of paradox and of consciousness and self-consciousness. The selected and doubly re-presented data of L'Allegro and Il Penseroso allow the speaker to trope his data—make figures out of them, give them a spin—and in so doing manifest himself as a maker (poet) who is both inside and outside of his materials as they are both outside and inside of him.

III. LYCIDAS AND THE DIALOGIC SELF

Lycidas, the pastoral elegy Milton wrote in 1637 to honor the untimely death of his fellow Cambridge student Edward King, marks the completion of the first phase of Milton's literary production and of his poetic definition and presentation of self. *Lycidas* is arguably the most exhaustively annotated and the most variously commented upon lyric in the English literary canon, by critics of all stripes. For New Critics it is "a poem more intricately articulated than even the most elaborate dissections of it suggest"; for Humanists, "the very criterion and touchstone of poetical taste," implying an entire liberal education; and for more recent critics, an indeterminate, highly intertextualized puzzle.[25] Like *Paradise Lost, Lycidas* articulates the problems of knowledge and subjectivity. Here, as with *Christ's Nativity* and *L'Allegro* and *Il Penseroso,* author and reader together retrospect their educational equipment and inheritance—but this time in search of answers to the ultimate questions of life, order, and value. Finally, like *Paradise Lost, Lycidas* is designed for a fit audience, though few, and requires a comparably athletic curiosity and memory. The reading of either poem is necessarily exclusive, or more precisely the text compels the reader's choices, dedication, action, and capacity for growth.

Between the debilitating self-consciousness with which *Lycidas* opens and the third-person projection of self with which it ends, *Lycidas* is a poem of *reflection,* as that term suggests contemplation, or more largely as it signifies a process of casting light or thought and receiving back the effect and the reversal of what was cast. The narrator projects a train of dramatized characters and fragments from his learned memory upon a kind of screen, from which they speak back to him what he knows but may have temporarily forgotten of their meaning and contexts. His thought proceeds by leaps between one fictional presentation or encoded memory and another, leaps that he seems at once to drive and be driven by. *Lycidas* thus dramatizes the fragmentation of consciousness, its waves and waverings, its conflictedness, its temporary stabilities and persistent openness to growth. Through a series of developmental dialogues with separate aspects of himself, the speaker gradually progresses toward a more stable relationship to reality and history. In sum, the poem both performs and fictionalizes the dialogics of the narrator's conflicted subjectivity.

The answerable style of *Lycidas* gives yet another form to the self as Smectymnuan true poem, a form that builds on the educational construction of a modern self and the division and reciprocal deferral that we have seen in the two productions previously examined. Like Milton's other poetry, *Lycidas* takes its genre very seriously, and indeed its 193 lines reconstitute almost the whole tradition of the pastoral elegy and echo each previous practitioner. The narrator's present grief re-presents and re-processes the secure accumulation of his earlier learning and builds out of that trauma a higher synthesis that makes a future possible. *Lycidas* traces the speaker's loss of innocence, his horrified sense of betrayal, his gradually reconstructed hopes, and his eventual leap of faith, in a combined Christian and artistic triumph. It arrays a plethora of inherited, academic, and personal data and aperçus, fragments that oscillate between the familiar or even generically trite, on the one hand, and the opposite extreme of personalized terror, fierce inquiry, and triumphant insight on the other.

Clashes between the fictions that the self temporarily inhabits are dramatized successively in the poem's three sections. Structurally the three sections (lines 15–84, 85–131, and 132–185) stage an interlocked series of psychic acts. The first foundational section, as suggested above, interrogates a mythological cast of characters (those projected mental fictions) on the great human questions: Why death? Why this death rather than another? Why no natural or supernatural preventive agencies? Why dedication or sacrifice in the face of elemental, inescapable purposelessness? As earlier, the promises within the parable of the talents inevitably haunt the inquiry. The interrogated fictions of section II progress from the classical to the Christian, and from ancient Ortygia and Lombardy via Galilee to modern England (Camus), to culminate in the deliberately baffling images of the grim wolf and two-handed engine, mystified images that "by occasion foretell the ruin of our corrupted Clergy then in their height." Thus at a basic level, *Lycidas*, like other great tragic works of literature—*Oedipus the King*, *Hamlet*, or *King Lear*—asks large numbers of large questions, and a question by definition positions heroic inquirers at the edge of an abyss that may consume them.

In its pursuit of answers, *Lycidas* acts out the dependency of *cognition* upon *re-cognition* (Gregerson, *Reformation of the Subject*, 150). This poem foregrounds the self as absorptive reader, interacting with its commonplace book of instructed memory. In a commonplace book, a student collects redeployable pieces of his reading, to be retrieved through his kaleidoscopic apparatus of re-cognition for use as apt occasions arise in the future. Because of the distinct stages of this process—not to mention Milton's industrious reading and disciplined and capacious mind—*Lycidas* is almost always heavily annotated. Indeed, in important ways *Lycidas* is about footnotes and footnoting and not merely decorated or explicated by them. Individualized, cumulative, allusive data re-present the speaker's mind and quest while they are teaching the reader the rules of this reading game. As a general principle, in *Lycidas'* invitational artistry, directions proceed by indirections or, moving from the language of *Hamlet* to that of *Henry V*, we are to piece out the poet's imperfections with our thoughts. Globally as locally, the narrative continuity of *Lycidas* depends upon what is not said, upon the ways speaker and reader fill in the gaps between foregrounded units of ostensible content.

So familiar is the speaker with the myths that he invokes them indirectly, using epithets or descriptors rather than names. Some references substitute a traditional classical epithet for a familiar name—"Sisters of the sacred well" (15) for Muses, or "Herald of the Sea" (89) for Triton, or *"Hippotades"* (96) for Aeolus. Others draw upon modern intertextualities, as when *"Mona"* (54) derives Anglesey, and *"Deva"* (55) derives from Dee, by way of Michael Drayton and William Camden. With a boost from similar sources, the phrases "sanquine flower inscrib'd with woe" (106) and "the great vision of the guarded Mount" (161) both substitute poetic descriptors for the Hyacinth and St. Michael to which we eventually work our way back. At a late stage, the reference to "him that walk'd the waves" (173) filters the strategy through the complex intertextualities of Matthew (14:25–26) to promote the simultaneous candidacies of Christ and a doubting Peter. Peter carries a (negative) Roman Catholic valence for seventeenth-century English Puritan readers, but Peter also invites identification as a normatively human recipient of divine advice and support. The process stages the subtle equipment and unique processes of the speaker's mind at the same time that it defers the reader's recognition by one or more stages. Ultimately, the reader's mimesis of the speaker's deferred consciousness operates in relation to the poetic construct itself. His or her dialogics are with the poem, its sources, and its interpretive tradition.

Some similar verbal counters are held in a deliberately ambiguous or conflated solution—for example, "blind *Fury*" (75), "Blind mouths" (119), and sucking eyes (139–40). Several puzzles, such as the "grim Wolf" (128) and the notoriously fertile "two-handed engine" (130), overwhelm rational solution altogether. The narrator—perhaps normally, perhaps just at this psychic crisis—thinks through such elusive counters, while the reader must reconstruct—that is, footnote—the process. But both are demonstrating the deferred and fluid consciousness appropriate to this poetic enterprise. The narrator is reprocessing his whole educational history and mind; the reader is reprocessing the poet's process, the poem itself. Both are destabilized as they pursue elusive understanding of the incomprehensible and cling temporarily to any sort of security against mortality's insistent terror. In what grows to be a repeated rhythm of *Lycidas,* the opening of section II retreats from the edge of an interrogative void to restabilize by way of another conventional poetic site and agent, with Arethuse and Mincius matching the invocation of the Sisters of the Sacred Well at the beginning of section I. Structurally, the invocations of Arethuse and Alpheus for poetic inspiration at the openings of sections II and III force the reader to collect or re-collect the broken pieces of this deliberately fragmented myth to reproduce the poem's healing force.

Lycidas stages sequentially its foregrounded stabilities alternating with instabilities. Section I concludes with a fictional projection of the classical deity of poetry and order, Phoebus Apollo, offering what appears to be an ultimate evaluation from

> those pure eyes
> And perfect witness of all-judging *Jove;*
> As he pronounces lastly on each deed,
> Of so much fame in Heav'n expect thy meed.   (81–84)

It is no wonder, after the speaker's shattering interrogation of human and divine purpose, that Apollo's answer should now fail where once it satisfied, exposing the fictions of the speaker's educational treasury as what they are, mere fictions. To make matters worse, here, as Catherine Belsey has observed, God has come to function not as authorizing principle but as judge of true poetry (Belsey, *John Milton: Language, Gender, Power*, 30).

   Lycidas' first two sections relate to each other as past to present, as reward to punishment, as positive to negative, and as thesis to antithesis. The interrogations of section II end with "hungry Sheep" looking upward without satisfaction, finding "Blind mouthes" agape and threatening where they looked for security and nourishment. Verbally, the shift is from Jove's easy pronouncements to the awful "nothing said," from an exposed fiction to empty silence. The first the poet-narrator had evaluated as "That strain . . . of a higher mood" (87), but the second performs as "the dread voice" (132)— simultaneously the dread silence—that annihilates expression and fiction alike. Section II, like section I, ends with another teetering on the brink of the void. After another retreat to the safety of pastoral convention (this time in the form of Alpheus), section III accepts the frail but freshly envisioned comfort of a floral bouquet—now acknowledged as fictive—and also accepts the grim reality of any corpse hurled for weeks about the Irish Channel. Like earlier sections, section III resolves with an evaluative process and a distribution of justice, ultimately in the blest kingdoms, penultimately not in reward (I) or punishment (II) but in *recompense* (meaning "compensation [received or desired] for some loss or injury sustained" or "compensation or return for trouble, exertion, services or merit" [*OED*]). *Recompense* embraces both author's and reader's investments of sympathy, study, and self-study. In a complementary resolution, the speaker moves from the newly achieved layered understanding of past and present realities to a moment of special creativity and to the prospect of an artistically as well as spiritually redeemed future. The poem that has touched on a wide range of inherited learning now performs its own mythopoetic action when it adds Lycidas as the Genius of the shore (183) to its layers of classical and Christian myth.

   To turn from section I to section III is to turn from past to future, from memory to imagination, from uncertainty to triumphant success, from an old to a New Dispensation, and from despair to grace. As we saw with the layered "true poetics" of *Christ's Nativity*, the day-star of *Lycidas* layers cosmos, classical Phoebus, and Christian savior, and focuses hopes of resurrection upon the figure of Edward King. The phrases "watry floor" (167), "drooping head" (169), and "where'er thy bones are hurl'd" (155) recall Orpheus's "gory visage" (62), while, cosmically, "the opening eyelids of the morn" (26) and "the Star that rose, at Ev'ning, bright" (30) are reshaped within a day-star that is also both Phoebus Apollo and the Sun of Righteousness. The analogy, "So sinks the day-star . . . So *Lycidas* sunk" (168, 172), gives way to a revelation that is also Revelation (e.g. 19:9, 7:17, 21:4), and the blest kingdom vision catches up previous motifs of language and image within the new vocabulary of the Logos. "Him that walk'd the waves" relieves us of anxiety about the pilot of the Galilean lake—whether the epithet points to Jesus or Peter.

Together the three sections of *Lycidas* capture the process whereby the speaker shapes the insistent flux of fragmented consciousness into a controlled but fluid or open-ended design. As we saw with *L'Allegro* and *Il Penseroso*, the achievement of one mode of psychic security generates fresh and rewarding instabilities. Together the three parts of *Lycidas*, however, move toward stability, and do so by actively abandoning the lesser insights of earlier psychic sites. Throughout, *Lycidas* has sought security by intertextualized reaches to stability elsewhere. As the elegy draws toward its end, of course it privileges biblical texts over others because in them the fluidity of expression and receptivity are of divine origin and promise. Where earlier diction was often harsh and uncertain and earlier imagery was fractured, the poet now conveys his heightened spiritual vision in a language of remarkable verbal and syntactical freshness and sweetness, clarity and assurance. His own, now *unexpressive* song answers that of the

> sweet Societies
> That sing, and singing in their glory move,
> And wipe the tears for ever from his eyes   (179–81),

and that song has now achieved full expression and explicit narrative flow and control. It is no accident that the speaker is now both at his most eloquent and at his most allusive. But his stylistic ingenuity now chiefly refreshes the Christian alphabet familiar from the Bible, especially from its final book Revelation. The academic complexities, earlier multiplied, and the earlier centrifugal fragments now can be seen to have fed a single and certain wholeness that layers Protean Word and Divine Similitude. Here again any stable reader-self takes on the lineaments of provisionality when the classical (literally) collapses into the ever-receding layers of the Christian. But instability is itself redeemed in the heightened achievements that the author, text, and reader have now earned. The Christian loses a self to find a self in what is both a more creative and more absolutely sure provisionality.

The coda makes explicit the subjectivity of such a moment as the speaker both does and does not achieve closure for the text and the self that produced it. The poem has moved chronologically away from the backward-looking "Yet once more" (1), through "the heavy change" (37) of immediate loss, through several stages of "Now," to emerge from the poem with a "Henceforth" (183), as the speaker anticipates his own enlightened future in tomorrow's "fresh Woods, and Pastures new" (193). When the poem earlier promised that "*Fame* is no plant that grows on mortal soil" (78), it was deferring recognition (the self as others' icon and the isolation and self-consciousness such status imports) to an indeterminate future time and place. The coda voice of *Lycidas* frames the author as himself an achieved fiction, and its third-person projection acknowledges such iconics while translating isolation and self-consciousness into future potentiality. By performing the speech act, the "tear" of *Lycidas* (14), he has—at least temporarily—stabilized his text and his psyche. In the fruitful dynamics of subjectivity, to stabilize is to be able to move beyond.

Lycidas—and later *Paradise Lost*—is a poem that, once truly participated in and absorbed, cannot thereafter be separated from the reader's consciousness. This is perhaps why both texts have stimulated such a wide and Protean range of fully articulated responses. *Lycidas*, then, thoroughly demonstrates the first as well as the second of Fredric Jameson's foundational propositions that "we never really confront a text immediately, in all its freshness as a thing-in-itself. Rather, texts come before us as the always-already-read; we apprehend them through sedimented layers of previous interpretations, or—if the text is brand-new—through the sedimented reading habits and categories developed by those inherited interpretive traditions."[26] *Lycidas* by its very nature layers the pastoral and literary traditions it enfolds, but also answering to its very nature, to read *Lycidas* is to read the history of others' readings of the poem, starting perhaps with Samuel Johnson's critique of its too easy collection of exhausted, improbable, and unsatisfying pastoral counters that mingle "trifling fictions [with] the most awful and sacred [Christian] truths" to produce unskilful, indecent, and blasphemous equivocations. Overall, for Johnson "the true meaning is so uncertain and remote that it is never sought because it cannot be known when it is found."[27]

The epistemics, indeed the politics, of the latter is the key issue. Johnson did not—indeed with his whole being could not—endorse the principle that impels so much of Milton's thinking, that "A man may be a heretick in the truth" if truth for him is fixed rather than in process (*Areopagitica*, YP 2.543).

Johnson needs a text to be a secured product, while for Milton the fluid text is "the pretious life-blood of a master spirit, imbalm'd and treasur'd up on purpose to a life beyond life, . . . the breath of reason it selfe, . . . an immortality rather then a life" (YP 2.493). Milton requires that the text be alive so that the reader can be alive through interacting with it. For an heir of the Reformation like Milton, the Bible offers the textual model. *Paradise Lost* describes an essentialized reading transaction that begins with "those written Records pure," but—it is the archangel Michael here speaking—those written records are "not but by the Spirit understood," and it is "the Spirit within" that does the interpreting (12.513, 514, 523). As the preface to *Christian Doctrine* makes clear, the spiritual understanding thus enjoined upon every Reformationist individual requires the most athletic endeavor, whether in the active contextualizing and concordancing of individual passages and words, or in an apparently passive, but really equally athletic patience. The logocentric truth which Milton and his Protestant/Puritan culture celebrated as absolute was in fact essentially unstable, its fluidity always encouraging and rewarding the individual's growth, always looking toward an ultimate fulfillment—that moment in (or at the end of) time in *Paradise Lost* when "God shall be All in All" (3.341). *Areopagitica* images the same occasion as the moment when all the scattered fragments of the body of Truth shall have been re-collected (YP 2.549, see *recollection* as memory), a moment of personal and universal completion that paradoxically beckons the modern subject's growth.

CONCLUSION

Milton commentary has occasionally, and wittily, observed that, early and late, Milton was always reworking the same poem, the script of its author's and its reader's active, performed spiritual enlightenment. Even when the materials of his poem are coded as secular—as with *L'Allegro* and *Il Penseroso*—Milton clearly understands poetry to be "the inspired guift of God rarely bestow'd" (*Reason of Church Government*, YP 1.816). Certainly Milton set himself always to reinscribe his wide classical and Renaissance learning, and he defined his place in the literary tradition as overwriting and underwriting these materials with the data and processes of Christian truth. For him, the latter meant enlivening the textual transaction by deferring cooperative creativity onto the poem's readers. True poetry leads its readers, as its author, to redemptive vision and rededicated spiritual (and therefore also personal and public) service.

Lycidas actively seeks to "imbreed and cherish in a great people the seeds of vertu, and publick civility" (*Reason of Church Government*, YP 1.816). In a final extension of the inquiry into the modern subject, we must note that the term's political dimension foretells the shape that the ensuing three decades of Milton's life were to take, decades in which the "complete and generous education" described in *Of Education* can be seen to have fitted the mature author "to perform justly, skilfully and magnanimously all the offices both private and publicke of peace and war" (YP 2.378–79). When Milton attached the explanatory headnote to *Lycidas* in his Trinity manuscript (and for the political purposes of the edition of his *Poems* in 1645)— "And by occasion foretells the ruin of our corrupted Clergy then in their height" (Hughes, 120)—he was marking *Lycidas* as a work that "deplore[s] the general relapses of Kingdoms and States from justice and Gods true worship" (*Reason of Church Government*, YP 1.817). Claims for individual agency sound John Milton's characteristic note—the authorial self as controlling originator of meaning—but this added headnote reinterprets the learned aesthetic within the political. Such broadened public purposes signal a move from issues of the personal subject to the political subject, the civil and prophetic citizen and agent.

If the constructions of the subject we examined earlier savor of self-fashioning, this *Lycidas* headnote signals a self-focusing in response to sociopolitical forces. The broader movements of his era were thus writing themselves upon and through this extremely individuated spokesman. As Puritanism hardened in the decades immediately following the 1630s, it proved itself not merely a private phenomenon. While the whole process of Puritan conversion was affirming the existence of a new kind of interiority, of a private, unique, inner space—the space of self-consciousness, of subjectivity—it was at the same time demanding participation in the world. In the polis as in the Puritan psyche, it was leaving behind an old, secure, traditional world in favor of new systems of discipline and labor; it was valorizing duty and a sense of civic mission, an uncompromising and sustained commitment to public ideals, and the systematic and enthusiastic labor to realize those ideals in this world. In theory and practice, Milton sought variously to register poetry as apt labor for such an agenda. For others more than and after him, conscience translated into energetic commitments to progress and the re-formation not only of religion but of society and social structures of all kinds. But, soon enough, the Restoration world view was recognizing order not as divine and natural but as humanly and artificially constructed and manifestly more political and social, increasingly empirical and threatening, and in need of the sort of restraint mechanisms Hobbes had codified in 1651. Even as the late Milton was giving epic form to the spiritualized subject, around him the modern self and modern state were taking shape by displacing earlier transcendental signifieds as the basis of psychological identity and by privileging new social values and ethics, and new political realities based on those two great Foucauldian principles of power and repression.[28]

University of Massachusetts—Amherst

NOTES

1. "Of True Religion," in *Complete Prose Works of John Milton*, 8 vols., ed. Don M. Wolfe et al. (New Haven, 1953–82), vol. 8, 423–424, hereafter cited parenthetically in the text as YP, followed by volume and page number. References to Milton's poetry and Prolusions draw from *John Milton: Complete Poems and Major Prose*, ed. Merritt Y. Hughes (New York, 1957).

2. In *The Reformation of the Subject: Spenser, Milton, and the English Protestant Epic* (Cambridge, Eng., 1995), Linda Gregerson comments on how "the readerly evolution of subjectivity . . . in *Paradise Lost* . . . derives its considerable force and its world-altering potential from a cornerstone of the Reformation: salvation by means of direct and individual access to the Word" (148). Gregerson captures much of the complexity of the Protestant Reformation's determinations of individuality and community in the series: "Manifestations material and immaterial, theological and political, accidental and purposive, suasive and coercive, liberationist and oppressive, opportunistic and principled, inconsistent, contradictory, impure" (229).

3. Hassan Melehy, *Writing Cogito: Montaigne, Descartes, and the Institution of the Modern Subject* (Albany, 1997), 15.

4. Stephen Greenblatt, *Renaissance Self-Fashioning: From More to Shakespeare* (Chicago, 1980), 1.

5. Albert W. Fields, "The Creative Self and the Self Created in *Paradise Lost*," in *Spokesperson Milton: Voices in Contemporary Criticism*, ed. Charles W. Durham and Kristin P. McColgan (Selinsgrove, Pa., 1994), 156. See Fields (156) on the trial by contraries as the shaping force of identity so eloquently theorized in *Areopagitica* and so variously dramatized in *Paradise Lost*.

6. Francis Barker, *The Tremulous Private Body: Essays in Subjection* (London, 1984), 53; Catherine Belsey, *The Subject of Tragedy: Identity and Difference in Renaissance Drama* (London, 1985), 65. Katherine Eisaman Maus takes these and associated critics to task as she pursues her own distinction between inward disposition and outward disposition in the English Renaissance theater. For her, " 'Subjectivity' is often treated casually as a unified or coherent concept when, in fact, it is a loose and varied collection of assumptions, intuitions, and practices that do not all logically entail one another and need not appear together at the same cultural moment" (*Inwardness and Theater in the English Renaissance* [Chicago, 1995], 29).

7. By contrast with what Keats called Shakespeare's negative capability, John Milton demonstrates what Harold Bloom captures as "positive capability," an insistence on insinuating a sense of the stable essential self into every statement. Virtually each of his published words calls attention to Milton as its author[ity]. Harold Bloom, *The Anxiety of Influence: A Theory of Poetry* (New York, 1973), 34.

8. See Matthew 10:39, "He that findeth his life shall lose it; and he that loseth his life for my sake shall find it" (similarly, see Matthew 16:25, Mark 8:35, Luke 9:24, and John 12:25). See also

Christian Doctrine 2.8: "A man's charity towards himself is what makes him love himself next to God, and seek his own temporal and eternal good" (YP 6:719). The *OED* cites Milton's works for the earliest usage of *individuality* (1645) and of one sense of *individual* (1641). See Man as an individual soul in *Christian Doctrine* 1.7.

9. Gregerson analyzes Eve's articulated emergence of selfhood, her invention of herself from memory, in *Paradise Lost*, Book Four, in comparable terms.

10. Clearly, the scope of the present project does not allow for a full alignment of Cartesian propositions and Milton's poetic practice, but as a sample, Descartes treats the subject's self-definition vis à vis an empowered apprehension of the deity in *Discourse on the Method* 1.128; *Principles of Philosophy* 1.197–203; and *Third, Fourth,* and *Fifth Meditations* 2.24–49. *Of Education* shares an incremental epistemology with Descartes' *Rules for the Direction of the Mind,* e.g. Rules 5, 6, and 7 (1.20–28); and *Discourse* (1.120). René Descartes, *The Philosophical Writings of Descartes,* 3 vols., trans. John Cottingham, Robert Stoothoff, and Dugald Murdoch (Cambridge, 1985).

11. See Jonathan Goldberg, *Voice Terminal Echo: Postmodernism and English Renaissance Texts* (New York, 1986), 124.

12. Belsey, *John Milton: Language, Gender, Power* (Oxford, 1988), 104; Gregerson, *Reformation of the Subject,* 162.

13. An ode is a carefully wrought formal, public, or social poem (literally "a singing") of dignified celebration and reflection. See Carol Maddison, *Apollo and the Nine: A History of the Ode* (Baltimore, 1968). As a hymn, *On the Morning of Christ's Nativity* is quite literally "a praise" whose celebration of the deity absorbs a liturgical intention.

14. As I have argued elsewhere (*Studies in Philology* 68 [1971]: 484–95), the linguistics of "mighty *Pan*" (line 89) undergo a similar transformation. If the Shepherds possessed the imminent awareness, they would be able to call the deity of the new order, Christ, by his right name. Since they do not, they must cast their tribute in the language of their governing experience. "The mighty *Pan*" is *kindly* come, and according to their human *kind,* the shepherds *can* receive him appropriately. Being men, that is, they can receive grace as well as change.

15. It is apt too that on December 9, 1629, Milton had celebrated his own twenty-first birthday, then as now the traditional coming of age.

16. Rosemond Tuve, *Images and Themes in Five Poems by Milton* (Cambridge, Mass., 1962), 63; David Daiches, *A Study of Literature for Readers and Critics* (New York, 1964), 44.

17. Belsey notes that "the Incarnation-as-signifier and the textuality of meaning" are the same concern, "the question of différance," and permeate Milton's poetry from *Christ's Nativity* through *Paradise Regained* (*John Milton: Language, Gender, Power,* 105).

18. *Christ's Nativity* appropriates the wonderful word *unexpressive* from *As You Like It* (3.2.10) to describe the song of the heavenly choir in line 116 (and again, Milton uses it in *Lycidas,* 176).

19. Georgia B. Christopher, "Subject and Macrosubject in *L'Allegro* and *Il Penseroso,*" in *Milton Studies* 28, *Riven Unities: Authority and Experience, Self and Other in Milton's Poetry,* ed. Wendy Furman, Christopher Grose, and William Shullenberger (Pittsburgh, 1992), 31; Tuve, *Images and Themes,* 15, 17.

20. Stanley E. Fish, "What It's Like to Read *L'Allegro* and *Il Penseroso,*" in *Milton Studies* 7: *"Eyes Fast Fixt": Current Perspectives in Milton Methodology,* ed. Albert C. Labriola and Michael Lieb (Pittsburgh, 1975), 85.

21. Casey Finch and Peter Bowen, "The Solitary Companionship of *L 'Allegro* and *Il Penseroso,*" in *Milton Studies* 26, ed. James D. Simmonds (Pittsburgh, 1991), 11, 17.

22. Donald L. Clark, *John Milton at St. Paul's School: A Study of Ancient Rhetoric in English Renaissance Education* (New York, 1964), 240, quoting Apthonius.

23. See *A Fuller Course in the Art of Logic Conformed to the Method of Peter Ramus* (YP 8:247).

24. Marc Berley, "Milton's Earthy Grossness: Music and the Condition of the Poet in *L'Allegro* and *Il Penseroso*," in *Milton Studies* 30, ed. Albert C. Labriola (Pittsburgh, 1993), 154.

25. Balachandra Rajan, *The Lofty Rime: A Study of Milton's Major Poetry* (Coral Gables, Fla. 1970), 55; Paul Elmer More, "How to Read *Lycidas*," in *Lycidas: The Tradition and the Poem*, ed. C. A. Patrides (New York, 1961), 87.

26. Jameson, *The Political Unconscious: Narrative as a Socially Symbolic Act* (Ithaca, N.Y., 1981), 9.

27. Samuel Johnson, "The Life of Milton," in *Lycidas: The Tradition and the Poem*, ed. C. A. Patrides (New and Revised Edition, Columbia, Mo., 1983), 60–61.

28. The propositions within this last paragraph draw heavily upon Michael Walzer, *The Revolution of the Saints: A Study in the Origins of Radical Politics* (Cambridge, 1965), passim, and upon Stephen L. Collins, *From Divine Cosmos to Sovereign State: An Intellectual History of Consciousness and the Idea of Order in Renaissance England* (New York, 1989), 28, 29, 36.

"THUS THEY RELATE, ERRING": MILTON'S INACCURATE ALLUSIONS

John Leonard

M ILTON IS A LEARNED POET who usually gets his facts right. But he can get them wrong. His history is sometimes faulty and his literary allusions often misrepresent well-known poems and myths.[1] This essay will examine several real and alleged errors in Milton's poetry. All the passages I cite have moved readers to protest: "But it wasn't like that!" My question is this: "Are Milton's mistakes simple howlers, or do they reveal something more interesting about the author in his works?" Many have found it hard to believe that Milton's mistakes are just mistakes. Some critics see them as deliberate ironies planted in the poems for a subversive purpose. This view is especially popular at the present time, when it is fashionable to be suspicious of everything. Other critics see Milton's inaccuracies as Freudian slips. For Harold Bloom, Milton's misreadings of earlier poets (especially Spenser) spring from "no mere lapse in memory" but are "a strong defense" against the "poetic father."[2] Bloom's theory might be convincing in some instances, but it is finally unpersuasive because it concentrates exclusively on literary inaccuracies and ignores historical ones. We need an account that attends to both.

It is always difficult, and sometimes impossible, to answer the question: "Is this error just an error?" No theory can resolve every case in advance. Each case must be judged on its merits. But we can see some common patterns. My purpose is to find some principles that will help us to tell when an inaccuracy says something interesting about the mind that produced it. Not all errors are deliberate or psychologically significant. We cheapen an author's art if we do not admit this. We need to recognize the possibility of dross if we are truly to appreciate gold. The critic who writes about inaccuracy in literature faces two equal and opposite dangers. The first is that of dismissing authorial errors as a trivial matter which high art easily transcends.[3] The second is that of overestimating an author's subtlety. Milton's inaccuracies are especially difficult because they have a strange way of courting both dangers at once. The problem is that they usually involve some kind of clash between high-minded idealism and wry irony. Many of Milton's inaccuracies follow the same pattern. They make historical or literary persons

96

more heroic or virtuous than they really were. This presents the critic with a peculiar challenge. We must decide whether wishful nostalgia or subversive pessimism has prompted Milton to change his sources. Has he got his facts wrong because he yearns for a golden world that never existed or has he deliberately bent the facts for an ironic or iconoclastic purpose? Critics have generally approached this question (specific instances of it) as if it were easy, but much of what follows will suggest that it is difficult.

The essay is divided into three sections. In section one I give a representative sample of historical errors and try to clarify some issues. In section two I focus on *Sonnet X* and Milton's allusion to "that old man eloquent," Isocrates. Annabel Patterson has recently drawn attention to what she believes is a deliberate error in this allusion—one that renders Milton's tribute to the Earl of Marlborough "decidedly suspect."[4] Although I am unpersuaded by Patterson's argument, I share her view that *Sonnet X* should be central to any discussion of historical inaccuracy in Milton. The poem forces us to formulate first principles. In my third and final section I take the principles formulated in section two and apply them to the clash between idealism and irony in Milton's inaccurate literary allusions.

I. "Slightly Viewed, and Slightly Overpassed"

The critic who presumes to write about historical inaccuracy must take special care with his or her own accuracy. If Milton can make mistakes, we can too, so we should check our own facts thoroughly before we either blame or praise him for getting his facts wrong. We should not assume that editors are always right when they tell us that Milton is wrong. Sometimes it is the editor's correction that stands in need of correction. *Sonnet VIII* is one poem where Milton indubitably knows best:[5]

> and the repeated air
> Of sad Electra's poet had the power
> To save th' Athenian walls from ruin bare.   (12–14)[6]

The allusion is to the end of the Peloponnesian War as described in Plutarch's *Lysander.* The Spartans and their allies met to decide the conquered Athenians' fate. The Thebans wanted to raze Athens and enslave its people. This proposal was about to prevail, when a man from Phocis sang one of Euripides' odes. The conquerors were so moved that they spared the city. So far, so good, but Thomas Warton in 1785 introduced a jarring note. Milton says that poetry saved the "walls"; Plutarch goes on to say that the Spartans tore the walls down to the cheerful sound of flutes. Warton briefly corrected Milton.[7] Dennis Burden in his 1970 edition adds a note of censure and calls Milton's version "inept," since Lysander "did destroy the fortifications of Athens."[8] Peter Goldstein, writing in 1990, tries to get Milton off the hook by arguing that the slip is deliberate.[9] Goldstein believes that Milton put it there to undermine his own claims for the power of poetry. Milton, it turns out, was not the high-minded idealist of myth but a respectably jaded pessimist and sly obscurantist. Or was he? For two hundred years critics have told us that Milton is wrong and that Lysander destroyed "th' Athenian walls." Thus they relate. Erring, for it was not the city wall that Lysander destroyed in 404 B.C., but the umbilical Long Walls that linked Athens to its harbors in the Piraeus. Lysander *did* spare the city wall. Plutarch is quite clear on this point, as are Xenophon, Isocrates, Lysias, Diodorus Siculus, and Arrian.[10] Milton's accuracy is on this occasion unbreached, and it is the would-be underminers who are hoist with their own petard.

That said, there are times when the inaccuracy is Milton's. One of Alastair Fowler's great strengths as an editor is that he candidly acknowledges this without being condescending about it. His note on Fontarabbia typifies his many triumphs. Where previous editors follow Newton and cite Mariana as the source of Milton's statement that "Charlemagne with all his peerage fell / By Fontarabbia" (*PL* 1.586–87), Fowler states the facts: "The Spanish historian Juan de Mariana put the defeat at Fuenterrabia, but there was no version in which Charlemagne fell." So did Milton nod? Fowler thinks not. Noting that Fuenterrabia was where Charles II "went to plot with the French and Spanish" in 1659, Fowler conjectures that Milton is deliberately contrasting "this dubious diplomacy with the greater Charles's honest chivalry."[11] In this instance Fowler persuades me that the error is deliberate and that it serves an ironic purpose. But there are times when it is better (not just simpler) to suppose that Milton made a mistake.

One such moment occurs in *Paradise Regained* when Satan urges Jesus to ally himself with Parthia rather than Rome:

> one of these
> Thou must make sure thy own, the Parthian first
> By my advice, as nearer and of late
> Found able by invasion to annoy
> Thy country, and captive lead away her kings
> Antigonus, and old Hyrcanus bound,
> Maugre the Roman.   (3.362–68)

The problem with this is that it lumps Hyrcanus and Antigonus together as defeated Roman allies. Hyrcanus did side with Rome, and was led captive, but Antigonus was on the Parthian side. He deposed Hyrcanus with Parthian help and reigned over Judaea for three years until Herod and Mark Anthony defeated and crucified him.[12] John Carey notes that "Satan is inaccurate" but declines to say whether Milton is also inaccurate.[13] Walter MacKellar, taking Carey's hint, confidently declares that the error is deliberate. MacKellar believes that Satan rewrites history so as to exaggerate Parthian power.[14] Attractive at first sight, this reading entails a price. If Satan's error were indeed deliberate, we should expect Jesus to correct it. Jesus elsewhere shows himself to be an expert on Jewish history, and he never hesitates to correct Satan. It is odd that Satan should think he can get away with this lie, and still more odd that he does get away with it. But the most telling point against Carey and MacKellar is this: the true history would serve Satan's purpose better than the false one. Satan is trying to convince Jesus that the Parthians can crown him king in Rome's despite. That is exactly what they did with Antigonus. Rather than invent a spurious abduction, Satan would do better to emphasize Antigonus' real historical triumph. Antigonus' subsequent crucifixion would, I readily admit, be an embarrassment to Satan, but it would also be a golden opportunity for either Jesus or Milton to turn the tables with a proleptic remark foreshadowing Jesus' own, very different, crucifixion. Jesus had done something like this at the end of Book Two when he dismissed earthly kingship as a "wreath of thorns" (459). Jesus when he speaks these words does not know that he will die wearing a crown of thorns, but we do, and our knowledge makes his words poignant. Satan's error about Antigonus creates a golden opportunity for just such an effect, but Milton misses it. It is this, more than anything else, that convinces me that the error is Milton's rather than Satan's. Milton is not the kind of poet to let pass an opportunity as good as this. It is understandable that Carey and MacKellar should want to give Milton credit, but in this instance their ingeniousness only makes things worse.

I am not saying that we should never give Milton the benefit of the doubt. Other things being equal, we should give him the benefit of the doubt, but we should also ask ourselves whether there is a real benefit to give. It is often hard to tell—harder than critics have generally been willing to admit. One particularly difficult case occurs in *Paradise Regained* when Belial proposes to set women in Jesus' path. Satan promptly puts him down ("Belial, in much uneven scale thou weigh'st / All others by thyself," 2.173–74) and reminds him of a great worthy who could not be "taken with such toys" (2.177):

> Remember that Pellean conqueror,
> A youth, how all the beauties of the East
> He slightly viewed, and slightly overpassed.   (2.196–98)

The allusion is to Alexander's self-control after the battle of Issus. Darius had fled the field, leaving his beautiful wife and daughters in the Persian camp.

Alexander, who could have taken the women as booty, treated them with honor. Plutarch says that they lived as though in "inviolable virgins' chambers instead of in an enemy's camp."[15] He goes on to tell how Alexander sent Parmenio to Damascus to seize the rest of the Persian wives. They too were beautiful, but Alexander displayed "the beauty of his own sobriety and self-control" with the jesting remark that Persian women "were torments to the eyes." He then "passed them by as though they were lifeless images."[16] Milton's editors duly note the source and Carey quotes generous portions of it. Orgel and Goldberg report that "Plutarch reports [Alexander's] sexual abstinence."[17] But there is a problem. Despite reports to the contrary, Plutarch does *not* say that Alexander abstained. One captive was so captivating that even the great Pellean could not resist her beauty. "The beauty of his own sobriety and self-control" notwithstanding, he decided to play the conqueror after all. Casually, even indifferently, Plutarch lets this awkward detail slip into his glowing encomium:

But Alexander, as it would seem, considering the mastery of himself a more kingly thing than the conquest of his enemies, neither laid hands upon these women, nor did he know any other before marriage, except Barsiné. This woman, Memnon's widow, was taken prisoner in Damascus. And since she had received a Greek education, and was of an agreeable disposition, and since her father, Artabazus, was son of a king's daughter, Alexander determined (at Parmenio's instigation, as Aristobulus says) to attach himself to a woman of such high birth and beauty. But as for the other captive women . . .[18]

"Slightly viewed, and slightly overpassed"? By Miltonists maybe. Not by Alexander. Barsiné caught *his* eye. But did Milton notice her?

The answer we give this question will largely determine our judgment of the inaccuracy. If Milton simply missed Barsiné, I think we have to admit that his oversight damages the poem. The allusion makes the serious claim that Alexander was a paragon of continence. Paragons of continence do not have sex-slaves. Perhaps Milton was led astray by Plutarch's ebullience. Plutarch's tribute certainly is sincere. Alexander *was* abstemious by Macedonian standards. But those are not the right standards for judging the Son of God. Even one lapse would be disastrous in his case. Since Alexander did lapse, it is hard to see why Belial should be cowed by Satan's allusion to him. Alexander's behavior tells for Belial's hopes, not against them. Even if we close our eyes to Barsiné, the goings-on after Issus were not so chaste that "the fleshliest incubus" need despair of a fleshly temptation. Plutarch at once goes on to tell how Philoxenus offered to buy Alexander "two boys of great beauty," and Hagnon offered to buy him "a Corinthian youth named Crobylus." True, Alexander was outraged—but by the word "buy," not "boy." He had no scruples when Nabarzanes made him a free gift of "Bagoas, a eunuch of remarkable beauty and in the very flower of boyhood."[19] This detail comes from Quintus Curtius, not Plutarch, but even Plutarch describes a drinking party at which Alexander kissed Bagoas to the delight of his cheering soldiers. He also describes Alexander's intemperate behavior after his beloved Hephaestion had died of fever. "Transported beyond all reason," Alexander crucified Hephaestion's doctor.[20] Alexander's grief was understandable, maybe even forgivable, but it is not what we should expect from one who "with a smile made small account / Of beauty and her [and his?] lures" (*PR* 2.193).

But what if Milton *did* notice Barsiné? It is Satan, after all, who praises Alexander. Might not the error be his? I raise this possibility with some trepidation because I think we Miltonists are often too quick to load our problems on Satan's back. Whenever anything awkward crops up (such as Milton's sexual politics or the horrors of Chaos) critics conveniently trot out "Satan's perspective" to take the fall. My point is not that we should never suspect Satan, but that we should exercise suspicion cautiously, and with a healthy suspicion of our own need for scapegoats. It would be absurdly ingenious, in the case before us, to suppose that Satan intentionally distorts the truth about Alexander. Satan is a liar, but he always lies for a purpose. Lying to Belial would serve no useful purpose at this time. But it is just possible that Milton foists the error onto Satan because he wants to expose Satan's limited imagination. Satan, like Plutarch, exalts Alexander as a paragon, but he fails to see that even this high estimate of the Son of God (so rashly has he "weighed / The strength he was to cope with," 4.8–9) is woefully inadequate. Satan sneers at Belial's lusts but fails to see that Alexander had the same lusts, albeit in milder measure. Ingenious as this argument might seem, two things support it. Firstly, there is the well-attested fact of Alexander's bisexuality. Milton is most unlikely to have forgotten that even if he did forget Barsiné. Secondly, there is the strange detail, puzzling to critics, that Satan *does* employ beautiful women and boys in the banquet temptation even though he had scoffed at Belial's suggestion that he do just that. Lovely women saunter under the trees while "Tall stripling youths . . . of fairer hue / Than Ganymede or Hylas" wait at table (2.352–53). Critics have sometimes seen a contradiction between Satan's expressed contempt for sex and his subsequent offering of a spicy banquet, but if my hunch is correct there need be no contradiction. Satan consistently pitches his temptation at Alexander's level, either not seeing or not caring that Alexander was less than perfect. He knows better than to make Barsiné or Bagoas the center of his temptation. Fame is the best lure for a new Alexander; but Barsiné and Bagoas still have their place. I do not pretend that this reading solves all the difficulties. Some might still feel that Milton's inaccuracy is a simple error. They might be right.

My immediate concern is not to urge any one interpretation. My point is simply this: we should not ignore Satan's error. We should allow it to collide with, and ignite against, the facts. Editors have not done this. Carey's note quotes Plutarch but omits the detail about Barsiné. Most editors take Satan's history on blind trust.

II. "That Dishonest Victory"

If there is one critic who does not take things on trust it is Annabel Patterson. In her groundbreaking essay "That Old Man Eloquent" she goes out of her way to find awkward facts, and she refuses "to sweep them under the rug of a high-minded idealism."[21] In particular, she urges critics to face the implications of an historical inaccuracy in *Sonnet X*. The alleged inaccuracy occurs in Milton's simile comparing James Ley, "that good Earl," to Isocrates, "that old man eloquent." The earl, having led a virtuous life, lived

> more in himself content,
> Till the sad breaking of that Parliament
> Broke him, as that dishonest victory
> At Chaeronea, fatal to liberty,
> Killed with report that old man eloquent.   (4–8)

Milton claims that King Charles's decision to rule without Parliament in 1629 ended the life of the seventy-nine-year-old Earl of Marlborough in the same way that Philip of Macedon's subjugation of Athens in 338 B.C. ended the life of the ninety-eight-year-old Athenian orator Isocrates. Both men died of grief. The problem here is that Isocrates might not have felt any grief. He had spent the last half of his long life urging the Greeks to unite in a Panhellenic crusade against Persia, and he had recently called on Philip to lead it. Philip's victory at Chaeronea made Isocrates' impractical dream practicable. Milton once again gives us a story from Greek history that appears not to fit the facts. What are we to make of this?

Although I am unpersuaded by Patterson's reading, and will take issue with it here, I should say at once that I have nothing but admiration for her inspired recognition that *Sonnet X* must be the central text and test case for any study of Milton's inaccuracies. The Isocrates simile brings several critical issues into clearer focus. Three questions immediately present themselves: 1) Is Milton *really* inaccurate? 2) If so, is he being deliberately ironic? 3) If there is a deliberate irony, does it enhance or spoil the poem? These questions go to the heart of the matter, and I think we can ask them profitably whenever we encounter a seeming authorial error. I shall have occasion to ask them again. Patterson asks none of the questions explicitly, but it is clear what her answers would be. She never doubts that Milton is in error and she repeatedly uses the words "ironic" and "disingenuous" to describe his intentions.[22] In Patterson's view, Milton deliberately planted the error in his simile so as to subvert his own tribute to the earl. Milton ostensibly praises Isocrates as a champion of liberty, but his real message (for those in the know) is that Isocrates was a collaborationist scoundrel, and his implication is that the earl was one too. This is a bold and original argument, and it goes to the heart of my present topic. Can it stand up to scrutiny?

Let us start with the first question. Is Milton's history *really* inaccurate? With *Sonnet VIII* I was able to answer this question confidently. Matters are not so straightforward with *Sonnet X*. This time I cannot refute the charge of inaccuracy with a confident "not guilty." The best that can be hoped for is a cautious "not proven." The nub of the matter (though Patterson never mentions it) is a letter to Philip, supposedly written by Isocrates shortly after Chaeronea. This letter, "Letter III," congratulates Philip on his victory and urges him to unite the now-humbled Greeks in a Persian war. Some classicists (including Friedrich Blass, Sir Richard Jebb, and Leslie Smith) have accepted the letter as genuine, but others (including Arnold Schaefer, Ulrich von Wilamowitz-Moellendorf, and Karl Münscher) have rejected it as an ancient forgery.[23] Several scholars have hedged their bets. In 1989 Michael Grant cautiously remarked that the letter "may or may not be genuine."[24] The issue has not been resolved to everyone's satisfaction, but most classicists do now accept "Letter III." If they are right, Milton's version of events would obviously be wrong, and in some sense "ironic"—but in what sense? The word "irony" has its dangers for it can refer to very different things. Specifically, we need to distinguish the irony of intent from the irony of circumstance.

Which brings us to our second question: "Is Milton being deliberately ironic?" If Milton knew that Isocrates welcomed Philip's victory, Patterson would have a good prima facie case for suspecting him of being disingenuous. But not all ironies are disingenuous. Milton might have complimented the earl in good faith, not knowing that future classicists would dig up some dirt on Isocrates. The irony of intent would make Milton sly and slippery; the irony of circumstance would make him a high-minded idealist circumvented by history. My own view is that *Sonnet X* is untouched by deliberate irony. Patterson skews the issue because she never admits that Milton's version of Isocrates' death was standard in the Renaissance. From her account, an uninformed reader might infer that Milton had just made the story up, in brazen defiance of universally known and acknowledged facts. Milton did not make the story up. His version accords with all the ancient lives of Isocrates. Dionysius of Halicarnassus, Lucian, Pausanias, and Philostratus all say that Isocrates died because he would not outlive the liberty of Athens. The *Lives of the Ten Orators,* once attributed to Plutarch, tells the same story, and so does the anonymous biography of Isocrates now attributed to Zosimus of Ascalon.[25] Dionysius says that Isocrates chose to die with his city's heroes. Pausanias, pseudo-Plutarch, and Zosimus add the detail that he starved himself. Lucian and Philostratus say that the mere news of Athens's defeat was enough to finish him. Lucian says he groaned, quoted a line from Euripides, sighed the words "Greece will lose her liberty," and "quitted life." This is very close to Milton. "Broke him" suggests a sudden stroke rather than a hunger strike, while "fatal to liberty" looks like a paraphrase of "Greece will lose her liberty." I suspect that Lucian was Milton's primary source, but Milton had easy access to all the ancient lives, which were regularly printed in Renaissance editions of Isocrates. Hieronymus Wolf's 1553 Basel edition (reprinted in 1570, 1587, and 1651) and Henri Stephanus' 1593 Paris edition both contain the lives by Dionysius, Philostratus, and pseudo-Plutarch. Wolf's edition also contains a life by Wolf himself that follows pseudo-Plutarch's account of Isocrates' death. Wolf appends a brief collection of famous men's comments. The last of these, by Juan Vives, reports that Isocrates was "so great a lover of his country" ("tantus patriae amator") that he died of grief when the news of Chaeronea was announced at Athens.[26] The entry for "Isocrates" in Carolus Stephanus' famous dictionary repeats Philostratus' account of Isocrates' death.[27]

Ignoring these sources, Patterson rests her case on *The Oxford Companion to Classical Literature*—a useful text but a dangerous guide to the ironic intentions of Renaissance poets. It is dangerous because it tells us too much. It draws on a body of scholarship unknown to Milton. Milton was learned, but he was not acquainted with nineteenth- and twentieth-century debates about "Letter III." So far as I have been able to ascertain, the first person to invoke "Letter III" against the ancient lives was Friedrich Blass in 1865.[28] Milton's version of Isocrates' end did not look odd in the eighteenth century. Newton and Warton both repeat the traditional story in their editions of Milton, and John Lemprière repeats it in his *Classical Dictionary* (1792). If Patterson is to make a convincing case for deliberate irony in *Sonnet X,* she will need to produce at least one Renaissance author who cast doubt on the ancient lives.

If the *Oxford Companion* tells us too much, it also tells us too little. Constraints of space force it to compress and distort the scholarship it cites. It does this in its account of Isocrates' death. Following the *Oxford Companion,* Patterson concedes that Isocrates might have committed suicide, but "the reason for that suicide, if truly historical" would not have been what Milton says it was. The real reason, she claims (quoting the *Oxford Companion*), was not that Philip had won but that "Athens was still determined to resist him."[29] This theory, first proposed by Ernst Curtius in 1867, was given wide currency by Sir Richard Jebb, who took it up in *The Attic Orators* (1893). Rejecting the traditional, patriotic motive for Isocrates' suicide, Jebb writes: "It is more conceivable that Isocrates should have destroyed himself because he saw Athens still resolved to resist, and because he dreaded the conflict, when Philip should be at the walls, between his duty to Athens and his duty to Greece. If the tradition of the suicide is considered too strong to be set aside, this seems the most reasonable account of it."[30] Jebb wants a version of Isocrates' suicide that consists with "Letter III." Unfortunately, "Letter III" works no better with Jebb's argument than with the ancient versions of Isocrates' death. The problem lies in Jebb's claim that the Athenians were "still resolved to resist." There had been some talk of resistance in the panic immediately following the battle. Hypereides proposed to arm all disenfranchised citizens, metics, and slaves. But all such talk evaporated when Philip offered to withdraw his army and free his two thousand Athenian prisoners without ransom. The Athenians were so grateful for these unexpectedly generous terms that they made Philip an Athenian citizen and raised his statue in the marketplace.[31] When Philip's envoy Antipater arrived at Athens to negotiate the peace and return the ashes of the Athenian dead, he was received with honor. It is this that sinks Jebb. Jebb's argument could hold only if Isocrates killed himself before Philip's terms were known. Yet the very first sentence of "Letter III" refers to Antipater's presence in the city and goes on to speak warmly of the peace negotiations then in progress. It follows that Isocrates could not have killed himself in protest at Athenian bellicosity. The Athenians had ceased to be bellicose by the time "Letter III" was written. Jebb finally admits the truth in a footnote, 226 pages after he had seemed to accept Curtius' theory. Acknowledging that his earlier argument would work only if "Letter III" were written before the peace treaty, Jebb concludes: "Now I confess I think the Third Letter was written *after* the conclusion of the peace."[32] This retraction changes everything, but a surprising number of scholars, including the editors of *The Oxford Companion,* have missed it. Jebb concludes by offering yet another explanation for Isocrates' suicide. "The real motive," he writes, "may have been an access of [Isocrates'] disease." Jebb conjectures that "some friend," perhaps Isocrates' adopted son Aphareus, "may have invented the heroic motive," perhaps "availing himself of the coincidence" that Isocrates died on the burial day of the Athenians who fell at Chaeronea.[33] I will not presume to pick holes in this conjecture. It is enough for my purposes to point out that it is a conjecture. From my own digging in ancient history I incline to the view that we will never know the truth about Isocrates' end. Milton's version might be wrong, but there is no certainty about that, and such evidence as we have lends no support to Patterson's belief that the simile is "disingenuous."

I turn now to my third question: would a deliberate irony enhance or spoil *Sonnet X*? Patterson obviously admires Milton's cunning, and I too might welcome it at another time and in another place. But disingenuousness is exactly what is not wanted in *this* poem. *Sonnet X* is a compliment to Lady Margaret. At the pivotal moment Milton turns his praise of the earl into praise of the daughter:

> Though later born, than to have known the days
> Wherein your father flourished, yet by you,
> Madam, methinks I see him living yet;
> So well your words his noble virtues praise,
> That all both judge you to relate them true,
> And to possess them, honoured Margaret.   (9–14)

If Milton's real intent were to relate them false and hint that Isocrates and the earl were scoundrels, it would follow that Lady Margaret (who possesses the same qualities as her father) was also a scoundrel. What possible pleasure could she derive from this double insult? Patterson never asks this question, but she needs to ask it, since she believes that Milton's affection for Margaret was sincere. She even hints that it was a bit more than sincere. She uses the words "mildly scandalous."[34] I don't blame Patterson for fancying that Milton fancied his married neighbor. I confess I like the idea. But its very plausibility makes Patterson's case for a gratuitous insult seem fanciful.

Patterson wants *Sonnet X* to be deliberately ironic because she wants to distance Milton from Isocrates' political "allegiances."[35] She would be willing to take the sonnet at face value if Milton's simile had invoked Demosthenes, "that other eloquent old man who indeed lamented Chaeronea."[36] At first sight it does seem odd that Milton should invoke Isocrates. The puzzle can nevertheless be solved if we pay careful attention to the changing political views of Milton and Isocrates. Patterson misrepresents both. Ignoring "Letter III," she writes as if the real embarrassment to Milton's simile were Isocrates' *Philipus*, written in 346 B.C., eight years before Chaeronea. Patterson claims that the *Philipus* "initiated [Isocrates'] campaign to have Philip assume rule over a united Greece."[37] Isocrates would blanch at that "assume rule." Nowhere in his works, not even in "Letter III," does he propose that the Greek city-states merge their independence in a Macedonian empire. He dreamed of a confederacy of free states voluntarily united under one leader for a single military purpose—the conquest of Persia. His mythological model was Agamemnon and his historical model was the Delian league in its early days before Athens turned it into an empire. Isocrates' first hope, expressed in his *Panegyricus* (380 B.C.), was that Athens would lead the invasion. When it became clear that Athens was more interested in rebuilding her Aegean empire, Isocrates turned to a series of strong foreign monarchs.[38] Philip of Macedon was his final choice, but throughout the *Philipus* he makes it clear that he is willing to concede the hegemony only. The word "hegemony" can be misleading, for we have come to use it as a slack synonym for despotism. Isocrates uses ἡγεμονία to mean "leadership of a free confederacy." He repeatedly urges Philip not to repeat the errors of Athens, Sparta, and Thebes. These cities had betrayed the cause of Panhellenism by turning their hegemonies into empires. From the outset of the *Philipus*, Isocrates insists that force is for barbarians, persuasion for Greeks.[39] Philip must unite the Greeks by diplomacy.[40] Isocrates pointedly withholds the word "rule" (ἀρχή) when referring to Philip's leadership of the Greeks. In his penultimate paragraph he uses three distinct verbs for the three kinds of leadership Philip should exercise over Greeks, Macedonians, and Persians: "it is incumbent upon you to work for the good of [εὐεργετεῖν] the Hellenes, to reign as king over [βασιλεύειν] the Macedonians, and to rule over [ἄρχειν] the greatest possible number of barbarians."[41] Philip is to rule Macedonians and barbarians, but he is emphatically *not* "to assume rule" over Greece.

These distinctions are not mere niggles. They mattered to Isocrates, and they should matter to us because the man who made them might very well have lamented Chaeronea. The distinctions would also matter to Milton. Patterson sees an incongruous gap between Isocrates on the right and Milton on the left. The truth is much more complicated. Isocrates was never a monarchist so far as Greece was concerned. Milton, for his part, had not yet made the imaginative leap to regicide when he wrote *Sonnet X*. Most editors give 1642 as the poem's date of composition. Milton certainly supported Parliament at that time, but the point of the war, as he and Parliament then saw it, was to force Charles to be a constitutional king. This is more, not less, than Isocrates was willing to concede to Philip. But it is Isocrates' disillusionment that is the simile's real point. Having looked to Philip as a potential hegemon, respectful of Greek liberty, Isocrates is shocked to discover that his hero is, after all, willing to play the conqueror on Greek soil. Milton's simile makes no satirical point about Isocrates or the earl. It presents both as figures of disillusioned integrity. Isocrates and the earl have both tried to reconcile the claims of an ambitious king with the still greater claims of ancient liberty, and they have both been betrayed by the tyrant they trusted. Philip violates Greek liberty by military conquest; Charles violates English liberty by inaugurating the Eleven Years' Tyranny. Were it not for "Letter III," Milton's simile would be a perfect triumph. There is no contradiction between *Sonnet X* and any of

Isocrates' writings prior to "Letter III." The *Panegyricus*, the *Philipus*, and the *Panathenaicus* all deplore the conquest of Greek by Greek.[42] "Letter III" marks an unprecedented departure because it does accept force as a valid argument. "On account of the battle," the letter says, the Greeks must now abandon their squabbles and follow Philip.[43] It is "Letter III," then, not the *Philipus*, that puts *Sonnet X* in an ironic frame. All irony would be removed, and Milton's historical accuracy might be vindicated, if "Letter III" were spurious.

Let's assume the worst and concede that "Letter III" is genuine. Should it matter to a Miltonist? The easy answer would be: "No, it doesn't matter, because Milton is faithful to the scholarship of his own time." Many Miltonists will find this answer perfectly adequate, and I too am tempted to be content with it. But Christopher Ricks, in "Literature and the Matter of Fact," makes a strong case for holding poets accountable to high standards of historical accuracy. "The point," Ricks argues, "is not that writers are always right."

But we should prefer writers to be right, and we should particularly do so when their own standards would have been stringent precisely here. As so often, the alternative to respectfully holding people to high standards is the disrespect of condescension, and it would be condescending to murmur that, come now, such an error would not matter to us, as enlightened readers, even though it would have mattered to the author.[44]

It certainly would have mattered to Milton if someone had told him that Isocrates had betrayed the cause of liberty. Milton's own moral and political standards were most stringent "precisely here." The heart of his simile, and of his sonnet, are those potent words "fatal to liberty." Any compromise here would be fatal. Ricks illustrates his point by asking this hypothetical question about Marvell's "Horatian Ode":

To put it simply: would the poem be the same if historians were now to prove that the King had in fact been dragged kicking and screaming, blubbering and pleading, to the scaffold? Does not the poem make a claim to historical justice, and to the facts of power, which goes well beyond, though it never leaves behind, the power of words?[45]

Ricks's hypothetical case is not an exact parallel to the case we are now considering. Marvell knew the facts about Charles's death, and so can be expected to get them right. It is unfair to hold Milton accountable to such rigorous standards when classicists still dispute the facts about Isocrates' death. But Milton does make "a claim to historical justice" when he invokes Isocrates as a patriotic champion of liberty, and *Sonnet X* cannot be "the same" now that most classicists see Isocrates as a traitor. Perhaps some future classicist might vindicate Isocrates, but unless and until that happens, I think we have to admit that *Sonnet X* has been damaged by a change that Milton did not foresee. The damage is precisely commensurate with the relief that we Miltonists should rightly feel if Wilamowitz and Münscher were one day proved right, and Blass and Jebb proved wrong, about the provenance of "Letter III."

None of this is meant as a slur on Milton. As Ricks says, it is a compliment to hold people to high standards. Patterson is a generous critic (no one more so), but her reading of *Sonnet X* does not hold Milton to high standards. She is laudably vigilant against the dangers of high-minded idealism and the lordly pretence that poetry need not concern itself with history, but she has her own kind of evasiveness when she writes as if irony were always deliberate and always an asset. It is wiser to admit that even great poems can sometimes be overtaken by unforeseen ironies that entail unwanted complications. If "Letter III" is genuine, I think we have to admit that *Sonnet X* has been overtaken in just this way. Milton would not have been happy about it, but he would have preferred that fate to being praised for an even more damaging disingenuousness. He would prefer, in short, to be judged by Ricks's principles rather than Patterson's. Ricks's principles offer Milton the dignity of an honest defeat. Patterson argues in good faith, but in this instance her critical principles put Milton in a position where he can win only a dishonest victory, fatal to the virtues his poem sincerely praises. Dishonest victories always come at a price. In *Sonnet X* the price would be ruinous.

III. Likely Stories

I now turn from historical to literary errors. These present a new problem because they address matters of fiction, not fact. Different ancient poets often give different versions of the same myths, and later poets must choose between them. It is dangerous, in such cases, to use the word "inaccuracy," for what looks like an inaccurate allusion to Poet A may turn out to be an accurate allusion to Poet B. The danger is especially acute with Milton, for he is often drawn to arcane sources. Consider these lines from *Paradise Lost* describing pagan gods and Titans:

> The rest were long to tell, though far renowned,
> The Ionian gods, of Javan's issue held
> Gods, yet confessed later than Heav'n and Earth
> Their boasted parents; Titan Heav'n's first-born
> With his enormous brood, and birthright seized
> By younger Saturn, he from mightier Jove
> His own and Rhea's son like measure found;
> So Jove usurping reigned. (1.507–14)

Saturn's older brother Titan does not appear in Hesiod, Ovid, Apollodorus or Hyginus. As these authors tell the story, Saturn (Kronos) deposed his father Uranus. But Milton does have a source: Lactantius.[46] In speaking of "inaccurate" literary allusions, then, we need to distinguish cases like this from those places where Milton clearly distorts a recognizable source. In the following pages I will limit myself to instances where Milton targets a specific text—and gets it wrong.

Such allusions are frequent in Milton, and they recur throughout his poetic career. The earliest instance is probably this, from *Elegia Secunda*, written in the autumn of 1626. Describing how Richard Ridding, the Cambridge University Beadle, would deliver the vice chancellor's messages and instructions, Milton writes:

> Talis et Eurybates ante ora furentis Achillei
> Rettulit Atridae iussa severa ducis.   (15–16)

[You were like Eurybates when in the face of furious Achilles he delivered the stern command of his lord, Atrides.]

The allusion is to the moment in Homer's *Iliad* where Agamemnon sends his heralds Talthybios and Eurybates to Achilles with the "strong order" (1.326) to surrender Briseis. Milton's words "iussa severa" are a direct translation of Homer. But Milton changes one detail. He says that Eurybates delivered Agamemnon's command to Achilles' face. This, as Carey notes, "is inaccurate: the heralds were too frightened to say anything, and Achilles guessed why they had come from their silence." Homer's two heralds were "terrified and in awe" (1.331); Milton's one shows no sign of pusillanimity. It is hard to resist the inference that Milton has projected some of his own personality onto Eurybates. Milton throughout his life loved to brave authority in the name of a higher authority. In Homer the "strong order" is Agamemnon's alone. Milton allows Eurybates to participate in, and even enjoy, his commander's "iussa severa." Stern and austere ("severus" in the Latin sense), Eurybates speaks up like Abdiel "in a flame of zeal severe," or like Zephon, when "severe in youthful beauty," he confronts Satan face to face.[47] The posture is recognizably Milton's own. He had probably adopted it to his cost when he fell out with William Chappell, his college tutor, earlier in 1626.

This rewriting of Homer displays an idealizing tendency very like that we have seen in the allusion to Alexander in *Paradise Regained*. In each case Milton makes a real or fictional person appear more heroic or virtuous than we might have expected him to be. There is something attractive about this. We are often told that Milton had a low opinion of the human race, and there is some truth to that. But the equal and opposite truth is that Milton needed to have faith in his fellow men and women. The challenge for the critic is to decide whether the idealizing tendency in Milton's inaccurate allusions is ironic or sincere. In Milton's allusion to Isocrates we were able to discount the possibility that he was being disingenuous, but in some cases it seems hard to avoid attributing to Milton some kind of subversive irony, even if we want to. Indeed, part of the difficulty about Milton's allusions is that they lure us into *wanting* a subversive reading, even though such a reading would cause all kinds of trouble.

Consider the following simile from *Paradise Lost.* Departing from Adam's side on the morning of the Fall, Eve sets off to tend her flowers

> with such gard'ning tools as art yet rude,
> Guiltless of fire had formed, or angels brought.
> To Pales, or Pomona thus adorned,
> Likeliest she seemed, Pomona when she fled
> Vertumnus.   (9.391–95)

Pales was the Roman goddess of pastures; Pomona the nymph or goddess of fruit trees. Ovid equips Pomona with a pruning-hook and tells us that she used it to repress "the too luxuriant growth of her orchards."[48] The parallel with Eve is obvious. But the real heart of the simile is the claim that Pomona "fled" the wood-god Vertumnus. Ovid tells a different story. Pomona shut herself up in an orchard, but she did not take to her heels, and she even permitted men to visit her. Vertumnus "obtained frequent admission" (Met. 14.652) by disguising himself as a reaper, a herdsman, a vintner, a peasant, a soldier, and a fisherman. Disguised as an old woman, he urged Pomona to reject all suitors except Vertumnus. Pomona was indifferent to these overtures until Vertumnus "threw off his disguise" and appeared before her in his divine form. Her response then was unequivocal: "He was all ready to force her will, but no force was necessary; and the nymph, smitten by the beauty of the god, felt an answering passion" (14.770–71). Pomona was (frankly) easy. Milton's editors have been reluctant to admit this. Hughes refers to Pomona's "long resistance"; Orgel and Goldberg say that Vertumnus was "ultimately" successful. But Pomona offered *no* resistance and Vertumnus was *immediately* successful as soon as he revealed his identity and intentions. Pomona's indifference to the old woman cannot be characterized as resistance, for she did not know that there was anything to resist. In the moment Vertumnus "threw off his disguise," Pomona threw off her reserve and robes. Fowler is the only editor who even comes close to acknowledging the truth. In his 1968 edition Fowler has this telling note: "*fled*] Used ironically, for Pomona only fled Vertumnus until his guileful persuasions awakened 'answering passion.'"[49] But even this is too reticent, for Fowler still clings to the notion that there was a moment when Pomona "fled / Vertumnus." The fact of the matter, as Richard DuRocher succinctly notes, is that Milton "depicts a moment that is not in Ovid's myth."[50] What are we to make of this?

Fowler's word "ironically" points to one solution. "Fled / Vertumnus" might be calculated to provoke the response "a likely story." The irony would be at Eve's expense and would imply that she, like Pomona, will be easy. But DuRocher brings other possibilities to light when he sees Milton's "rewriting of myth" as "an instance of . . . moral imagination supplanting earlier poetry." DuRocher draws an analogy with Milton's "famous misprision in *Areopagitica* of the Palmer's role in Book Two of *The Faerie Queene.*"[51] Milton says that Guyon entered the cave of Mammon "with his palmer."[52] Critics usually see this as a genuine mistake emerging from Milton's own values. The same kind of argument might be made about "fled / Vertumnus." Milton's rewriting of Ovid might not be prompted by cynicism; he might have genuinely misremembered the myth because he wants Eve to flee. Although I prefer this reading, I don't think we can dismiss out of hand an intentional irony. This inaccuracy, like so many others, brings wishful idealism and wry irony into an igniting collision. The tension comes to a head in one memorable word:

> To Pales, or Pomona thus adorned,
> Likeliest she seemed, Pomona when she fled
> Vertumnus.   (9.393–95)

The 1667 version was "Likest she seemed." Most editors prefer "Likest," but Fowler in 1968 made a strong case for "Likeliest" when he invoked the editorial principle that "other things being equal" we should favor "the less usual word."[53] "Likeliest" makes perfect sense for (as Fowler points out) it means "[most] resembling the original" (*OED* "likely," A1). But "Likeliest" has other meanings in addition to this, and it is these that make it preferable. "Likeliest" implies (as "Likest" does not) that something is likely to happen. Robert Adams notes the pun: "Eve is like Pales or Pomona; she is also (like Pales or Pomona) a likely sort of female; the sort who is most likely to get in trouble with Jove, Vertumnus, or Satan."[54] It must be admitted that Adams's comment is not a triumph of tact. That "likely sort of female" might even provoke some to retort that it is the professor who is "most likely to get in trouble," these days. But Adams's basic point is sound. "Likeliest" does have ominous overtones—as is confirmed just twenty lines later when we see Satan searching for Eve "where likeliest he might find" her (9.414). Eve's likelihood is on a collision course with Satan's, and Pomona is leading her straight to him.

But the ironic reading does not have it all its own way. If "Likeliest" plays on Adam's ominous sense, it also plays on "strong or capable looking" (*OED* "likely," 4a), "giving promise of success or excellence" (*OED* 4b), "comely, good-looking" (*OED* 5), and "seemly, becoming, appropriate" (*OED* 6). That last sense is now obsolete, but the *OED* cites instances well into the eighteenth century. It also cites this, from Milton's draft for a tragedy about Sodom: "after likely discourses [Lot] præpares for thire entertainment."[55] "Likeliest" can have a lofty, dignified meaning, worthy of Lot's discourse with angels. Milton had put this lofty sense in Adam's mouth just thirty lines before "Likeliest she seemed":

> Seek not temptation then, which to avoid
> Were better, and most likely if from me
> Thou sever not. (9.364–6)

"Likely" there includes "likely to avoid" but it also implies that Eve's most "seemly, becoming, appropriate" act would be to stay with Adam. Now, as Eve leaves Adam's side, her "Likeliest" deportment answers his "most likely." Eve wants to show Adam that she can act in a "likely" (i.e., seemly) manner without his help. She fails, but the phrase "Likeliest she seemed" does not gloat over her failure. Milton even distorts Ovid so as to present Eve in the best light possible. Suspended between Adam's "most likely" and Satan's "likeliest," "Likeliest she seemed" could go either way. There is irony in the phrase, but it is not crude or heavy-handed, and it is distributed evenly between "Likeliest" and "seemed." Eve's tragedy is not that she was "a likely sort of female, the sort who is most likely to get in trouble"; her tragedy is that she was "strong or capable looking" and gave "promise of success," but failed to live up to her promise.

The clash between idealism and irony is especially difficult in my final example, for in this case it is unclear who is being idealistic, Milton or his dramatic speaker. The Elder Brother in *A Masque* assures his Younger Brother that no harm can befall their sister. To prove his point, he invokes Minerva's shield and challenges his brother to remember what it was:

> What was that snaky-headed Gorgon shield
> That wise Minerva wore, unconquered virgin,
> Wherewith she freezed her foes to congealed stone?
> But rigid looks of chaste austerity,
> And noble grace that dashed brute violence
> With sudden adoration, and blank awe. (447–52)

The face on Minerva's shield was that of Medusa. The Elder Brother gives no thought to *her.* He sees only Minerva. But his rhetorical question ("What was that snaky-headed Gorgon shield?") still brings Medusa into the picture. This is a problem because Medusa's story lends no support to the superstition that virgins enjoy supernatural protection. Ovid tells Medusa's story at the end of Book Four of the *Metamorphoses*. She had not always been a Gorgon. She had been Minerva's inviolable virgin priestess until Neptune violated her in Minerva's temple. Minerva did not intervene with "rigid looks." She "turned away and hid her chaste eyes behind her aegis" so that she would not have to look (4.799).[56] She then transformed Medusa into a Gorgon to punish her for being defiled. She later placed Medusa's head on her shield "to frighten her fear-numbed foes" (4.802). Minerva "freezed her foes," then, but the Elder Brother could not have chosen a more unfortunate or incongruous mythical analogue with which to allay his brother's fears. Has Milton merely forgotten Medusa's story? Or is he slyly invoking it?

I first asked this question in 1996 while engaging William Kerrigan in debate about virginity and sexual assault in *A Masque*.[57] I cited the Medusa analogue as evidence that Milton does not share the Elder Brother's beliefs. The point of the allusion, I argued, was to hint that the Lady's peril is greater than the Elder Brother realizes. I did not know, when I made that argument, that John Rumrich and Julia Walker were working on the same problem. We published our conclusions independently and almost simultaneously. We agreed about the Elder Brother. Walker calls him "blissfully unaware."[58] Rumrich dryly observes that "matters are more complex than the Elder Brother allows."[59] There was one matter, however, on which we did not agree. I had argued that Milton was soberly aware, not blissfully unaware. Walker at first seems to share this view. She calls the allusion "the most extreme manifestation of Milton's strategy of revision." A "strategy" is by definition consciously intended. But Walker changes tack just three sentences later: "In the Ludlow Mask, I would admit to the possibility of Milton's subconscious being a factor in the representation of those rape stories."[60] Walker wants to give Milton credit for his "strategy," but she finally admits that "Milton's subconscious" might be the real explanation for his distortion of Ovid. What Walker admits as a "possibility," Rumrich presents as a certainty. In his view, male "Renaissance authors," including Milton, "typically" misread Ovid because of their own fear of female sexuality. Ovid's "plain meaning," Rumrich writes, is that Medusa was "the victim and not the agent of violence," but Renaissance poets made Medusa's metamorphosis "the consequence of her unchastity, and not Neptune's."[61] This reading is the exact opposite of mine. I had supposed that Milton's allusion expressed sympathy for the Lady. For Rumrich, Medusa's story highlights "one of the more perplexing problems in *Comus:* whether it is possible to be an innocent victim."[62] So what place *does* Milton's simile allow for the author in his works?

Should we give Milton credit for his "strategy" or subject his "subconscious" to a psychoanalytic interpretation?

The best way to approach this problem, I now believe, is to stand back and ask the same three questions we asked about the Isocrates simile. These were: 1) Is the allusion *really* inaccurate? 2) If so, is it a deliberate irony? 3) If the irony is deliberate, does it enhance the poem? With Medusa as with Isocrates, it is the first question that yields the biggest surprise. Despite our differences, Rumrich, Walker, and I agreed about one thing in 1996. We all took Ovid to mean that Neptune raped Medusa. Rumrich calls Medusa "a rape victim"; Walker calls Milton's simile a "rape narrative."[63] But does Ovid *really* say that Medusa was raped? I made that inference via Lewis and Short's *Latin Dictionary*. Ovid uses the word "vitiasse" to describe Neptune's act. *Vitio* means "spoil, mar, corrupt," but Lewis and Short also give the specific sense "violate a woman" (*vitio* B). I therefore concluded that Neptune had raped Medusa and that Milton was aware of this. Rumrich agrees that Medusa was raped but thinks that "Renaissance authors" were unaware. It is this that makes me suspicious. I can believe that *some* Renaissance scholars and poets misread Ovid because of their own psychological shortcomings (an alleged "fascination with and envy of woman's procreative power"),[64] but I find it hard to believe that this explanation holds for several generations of male writers. If they really were unanimous in thinking that Ovid's Medusa consented, we should hear them out. They were good Latinists.

At risk of implicating my own male psyche I will now candidly admit that I am no longer so sure that Ovid's Medusa was a "rape victim." Lewis and Short tell us that *vitio* could mean "violate a woman," but J. N. Adams in *The Latin Sexual Vocabulary* advises caution with words like *vitio* and *violo*. The problem is that "a sexual act may be emotively spoken of as an act of violence or corruption, even if it is not regarded as such by its perpetrator (or even victim)." Adams concludes: "verbs meaning 'defile' and the like are not exclusively used of the aggressor's violation of an unwilling victim."[65] In the light of this, it is hard to know what to make of Ovid's line: "hanc pelagi rector templo vitiasse Minervae / dicitur" (4.798–99). Most modern translations render "vitiasse" as "raped" or "ravished," but a case might be made for "polluted." Some recent translations have "deflowered." One has "strumpeted."[66] If the latter versions are correct, Rumrich, Walker, and I have a problem. We have built our arguments on the assumption that Medusa was raped. Our arguments would collapse if it turned out that she consented. I do not say that all complications would be removed from Milton's simile. A lewd and lavish Medusa would raise even more problems. The Elder Brother equates Minerva's shield with Minerva's icy stare. But *Medusa's* stare (if she consented) would be anything but icy. Lascivious eyes darting contagious fire would be nearer the mark. Medusa's face threatens to contaminate the Elder Brother's supposedly pure icon. I can think of only one critic whose argument might survive (and be vindicated by) this turn of events. The redoubtable Kerrigan, undaunted by stern criticism (some of it mine), has bravely and steadfastly maintained that "the Lady's 'no' to Comus in some fashion means 'yes.'"[67] Can it be that the Elder Brother's allusion deconstructs itself and so gives the last laugh (the laugh of the Medusa) to Kerrigan?

This is possible (and more than I would have admitted in 1996), but I do not mean to concede defeat just yet. Rumrich is stretching a point when he tells us that Renaissance authors "typically" saw Medusa as wanton. The only author Rumrich cites in support of this claim is George Sandys, who allegorized Medusa as "lust and the inchantments of bodily beauty."[68] Sandys was not unique. Natale Conti in *Mythologiae* 7.11 writes of Medusa's "immoderatum desiderium."[69] Jean Beaudoin translates this as "trop excessive incontinence."[70] But some Renaissance commentators did take Ovid to mean that Neptune raped Medusa. Pierre Gautruche drew that inference in his *Histoire Poetique* (1659). I quote from Marius d'Assigny's 1671 translation:

Medusa, had been a rare beauty, so that when *Neptune* saw her in *Minerva's* Temple, he was mightily taken with her, and oblidged her to yield to his lust at the same time. This action did displease *Minerva* so much, that she changed *Medusa's* locks of hair into fearful Serpents, whose onely looks caused every one to be turned into Stones.[71]

Gautruche and d'Assigny attribute the "lust" to Neptune, not Medusa (though it is still Medusa who is punished for it). Other Renaissance authors lapse into ambiguity. Golding writes:

It is reported how she should abusde by *Neptune* bee
In *Pallas* Church: from which fowle facte *Joves* daughter turnde hir eye,
And with hir Target hid her face from such a villanie.
And least it should unpunisht be, she turnde her seemely heare
To lothly Snakes.[72]

Golding's "abusde," like Ovid's "vitiasse," might refer to rape or seduction.[73] We are left, then, with the frustrating but inevitable conclusion that Ovid's meaning is ambiguous and that we simply do not know what Milton made of it. Rumrich oversimplifies when he claims that Renaissance authors "typically" missed Ovid's "plain meaning." Ovid's meaning is not plain and responses to it have never been typical.

Since we do not know what Ovid's meaning is, we cannot know how Milton distorts it. I still think that Milton deserves better than to be lumped with Sandys, but I can no more assume his conformity with Gautruche or d'Assigny than Rumrich can assume his conformity with Sandys or Conti. No Renaissance commentator is going to solve this problem for us. We must look at Milton's own text if we are to have any hope of breaking out of our impasse. There is one piece of textual evidence that might support the view that Milton's simile is a deliberate and compassionate irony. The Elder Brother says that Minerva "freezed her foes to congealed stone." In the event, the Lady does not freeze Comus. He freezes her. It would be very odd if Milton just failed to notice that the Lady's immobilization is a complete reversal of what the Elder Brother had predicted. Yet this is exactly what psychoanalytic critics ask us to believe. Kerrigan believes that Milton himself was "root-bound" by an Oedipus complex when he wrote the masque. One cannot disprove a thesis of this kind, but one can challenge it on grounds of plausibility. The reversal of the Elder Brother's expectations is so complete, and so neat, as to make conscious authorial intent more plausible than any unconscious, debilitating "complex"—whether it be the plain old Oedipus complex or a more exotic "narcissistic, pre-Oedipal problematic."[74] The Elder Brother is simply wrong about the Lady's power to freeze male assailants, so it is at least plausible that he is also wrong (and that Milton meant us to see that he is wrong) about the "snaky-headed Gorgon shield." The point is not that the Elder Brother cuts a ridiculous figure. His idealism is a fault in the right direction, and it might be characteristic of Milton as he had been *when he was eleven.* The most sensible and sensitive response to the Elder Brother is that of the Attendant Spirit when he declares: "Alas good vent'rous youth, / I love thy courage yet, and bold emprise, / But . . ." (609–11). The Elder Brother's idealism is always vulnerable to that correcting "But." I see just such a "But" in the Ovidian subtext of the Minerva allusion. I cannot prove that the implied "But" is Milton's. My final (and perhaps strongest) argument is simply this: the poem is enhanced if we allow the poet to take some credit for his own works.

From the examples I have considered (especially this last one), some readers might conclude that it is pointless to try to locate the author in his works. Some might even be moved to protest that all this essay has really done is confirm that "the author" is dead. Much as I dislike premature death sentences, I have to admit that we can rarely, if ever, have absolute certainty about authorial intention. But it is a fallacy to suppose that we are therefore condemned to absolute uncertainty. We can answer some specific questions with reasonable confidence. The first step to finding the right answers is to ask the right questions. The three questions I have asked of the Isocrates simile in *Sonnet X* and the Minerva simile in *A Masque* are questions that should be asked of any seeming inaccuracy in Milton. I do not claim that these questions are particularly profound. On the contrary, they are basic. But a surprising number of critics (myself included) have failed to ask them when they should have done so. The first question ("Is Milton really inaccurate?") *can* sometimes be answered with certainty—as we saw with *Sonnet VIII* and the walls of Athens. Even when it cannot be so answered (as is the case in *Sonnet X*), that in itself is useful information that critics ignore to their cost. The second question ("Is the inaccuracy a deliberate irony?") is more difficult, and it may be that it can never be confidently answered in the affirmative. But by examining the sources available to Milton we can sometimes answer this question confidently in the negative (as we saw with *Sonnet X*), and we can also open at least the *possibility* of an affirmative answer (as I did with *A Masque* by citing Gautruche and d'Assigny). The third question ("Would a deliberate irony enhance the poem?") is the most subjective, but also the most fundamental, question for a literary critic. Patterson's reading of *Sonnet X,* for all its many insights, is finally unpersuasive because she fails to answer, or even ask, this question. To my mind, this question is the golden key. An affirmative answer here might, in doubtful cases, justify an affirmative answer to the other two questions, other things being equal. Conversely, if we decide that a deliberate irony would spoil a poem, we should be especially vigilant with the first two questions. We should, in any case, be vigilant.

I have tried to suggest some methods and principles for determining when, whether, and how an authorial inaccuracy is intentional. I have also argued that we have a responsibility as critics to distinguish between those inaccuracies that do deserve to be valued and those that do not. I suspect that it is this last point that will be the most contentious. If earlier generations of critics and editors were prone to sweep Milton's errors under the carpet, editors and critics of our own time too often fall into the opposite danger of carrying ingenious suspicion to bizarre extremes. This is a fault in the right direction, but it is still a fault. Milton does sometimes take liberties with history and myth, but he is also vulnerable to genuine errors and the irony of circumstance. We do no credit either to ourselves or him if we confuse his real achievements with mere accidents. The valuable inaccuracies are the ones where the author is in his works.

NOTES

1. Milton's errors have received occasional or intermittent critical comment but have rarely been the subject of inquiry in their own right. Those critics who do address the topic focus on Milton's literary errors to the exclusion of his historical ones. See Harold Bloom, *A Map of Misreading* (Oxford, 1975), Julia M. Walker, "The Poetics of Antitext and the Politics of Milton's Allusions," *SEL* 37 (winter 1997): 151–71, and John Leonard, "Milton's Counter-Allusions," in

Dialogues with Milton: Essays in Memory of Georgia Christopher, ed. Jane Hiles and Caroline McAlister (forthcoming). I also address the topic in my Penguin edition of Milton's *Complete Poems* (London, 1998), xiv–xx.

2. Bloom, *A Map of Misreading,* 128.

3. Christopher Ricks examines this danger in "Literature and the Matter of Fact," in *Essays in Appreciation* (Oxford, 1996), 280–310.

4. Annabel Patterson, "That Old Man Eloquent," in *Literary Milton: Text, Pretext, Context,* ed. Diana Treviño Benet and Michael Lieb (Pittsburgh, 1994), 22–44 (esp. 42).

5. The paragraph that follows is a condensed version of my article "Saving the Athenian Walls: The Historical Accuracy of Milton's 'Sonnet VIII,' " in *Milton Quarterly* 32 (March 1998): 1–6.

6. All citations of Milton's poetry are from my Penguin edition of the *Complete Poems.* See above, note 1.

7. Thomas Warton, ed., *Poems upon Several Occasions, English, Italian, and Latin, with Translations, by John Milton* (London, 1785).

8. Dennis H. Burden, ed., *The Shorter Poems of John Milton* (London, 1970).

9. Peter Goldstein, "The Walls of Athens and the Power of Poetry: A Note on 'Sonnet 8,' " in *Milton Quarterly* 24 (December 1990): 105–8.

10. See Plutarch *Lysander* 14.4, Xenophon *Hellenica* 2.220–23, Isocrates *Antidosis* 319, Lysias 14, Diodorus Siculus 13.57.4, Arrian *History of Alexander* 1.9. Robert Garland, in *The Piraeus from the Fifth to the First Century* B.C. (London, 1987), remarks of the Long Walls that "they and the Piraeus fortifications, but not the circuit wall of Athens," were "razed to the ground" (24). Warton was probably misled by Thomas North's paraphrase of Jacques Amyot's French translation of Plutarch. Where Plutarch speaks of the Long Walls, North has "the walles and fortifications of the city of ATHENS."

11. *John Milton: Paradise Lost,* ed. Alastair Fowler, 2nd ed. (London, 1998), note to *Paradise Lost* 1.586–87. Unless otherwise stated, all citations of Fowler are from this revised edition.

12. These events are related in Josephus, *Antiquities* 14.13–16 and *Jewish War* 1.13.3–4, 11. See also Tacitus, *Histories* 5.9 and Dio Cassius 37.15–16.

13. John Carey, ed., *Milton: Complete Shorter Poems* (London, 1997). See note to *Paradise Regained* 3.366–67. All further citations are from Carey's 1997 edition.

14. *Paradise Regained,* ed. Walter Mackellar, 172. Vol. 4 of *A Variorum Commentary on the Poems of John Milton,* 6 vols., ed. Merritt Y. Hughes (London, 1975).

15. Plutarch *Alexander* 21.5. All quotations from this text are from the Loeb edition of *Plutarch's Lives,* trans. Bernadotte Perrin (London, 1919), vol. 7.

16. Plutarch, *Alexander* 21.10–11.

17. Stephen Orgel and Jonathan Goldberg, eds., *The Oxford Authors: John Milton* (Oxford, 1991), 930.

18. Plutarch, *Alexander* 21.7–10. Cf. Quintus Curtius 3.13.14. Barsiné was in her late thirties or early forties when Alexander saw her. Peter Green gives Parmenio the credit for intuiting Alexander's fondness for older women. See *Alexander of Macedon, 356–323* B.C. (Berkeley, 1991), 245.

19. Quintus Curtius 6.5.23.

20. Plutarch, *Alexander* 67.8, 72.3.

21. Patterson, "That Old Man Eloquent," 41.

22. On the crucial question of Milton's intentions, Patterson gets bolder as she proceeds. Having cautiously conjectured that Milton's compliment "might have been disingenuous," she drops the "might have been" three pages later and refers to Milton's "disingenuities." She

concludes that Milton "had taken certain liberties" with Isocrates' "relationship to political liberty." See Patterson, "That Old Man Eloquent," 41 and 44.

23. See Friedrich Blass, *Rheinisches Museum* 20 (1865): 109–16 and *Die Attische Beredsamkeit* (Leipzig, 1868–80), vol. 2, 268–73, 299–304; Richard Jebb, *The Attic Orators: From Antiphon to Isaeus*, 2 vols., (London, 1893), vol. 2, 30–31; and Leslie Francis Smith, "The Genuineness of the Ninth and Third Letters of Isocrates" (Ph.D. diss., Columbia University, New York, 1940). On the other side, see Arnold Schaefer, *Demosthenes und seine Zeit*, 3 vols., (Leipzig, 1856–58), vol. 3, 5, Ulrich von Wilamowitz-Moellendorf, *Aristoteles und Athen* (Berlin, 1893), vol. 2, 391–99, and Karl Münscher, "Isokrates," in *Pauly-Wissowa Real-Encyclopädie*, 10 vols., (Stuttgart, 1916), vol. 9, 2146–2227.

24. Michael Grant, *The Classical Greeks* (New York, 1989), 223.

25. Dionysius of Halicarnassus *Isocrates* 1, Lucian *Longaevi* 23, Pausanias 1.18.8, Philostratus *Lives of the Sophists* 1.17.4, [Plutarch] *Moralia* 837e–f.

26. Hieronymus Wolf, ed., *Isocratis Scripta, Quae Nunc Extant, Omnia* (Basel, 1553), 1029. I am grateful to Stella Revard for letting me consult her copy of this text.

27. Carolus Stephanus [Charles Estienne], *Dictionarium Historicum, Geographicum, Poeticum* (Paris, 1596), 255.

28. See above, note 23.

29. Patterson, "That Old Man Eloquent," 40. Patterson is citing the 1937 edition of *The Oxford Companion to Classical Literature*, edited by Sir Paul Harvey. The second edition, edited by M. C. Howatson (Oxford, 1989), omits Harvey's conjecture.

30. Jebb, *The Attic Orators*, 2 vols., vol. 2, 31. Ernst Curtius proposed the theory in *Griechische Geschichte*, 3 vols. (Berlin, 1857–67), vol. 3, 715–49, see especially pp. 733–34.

31. The history of the days following the Athenian defeat at Chaeronea has to be put together from piecemeal references, many of them highly partisan. The primary sources are Demosthenes *Against Aristogeiton* 2.11 and *On the Crown* 248, Aeschines *Against Ctesiphon* 159, and Lycurgus *Against Leocrates* 37–45. See also Smith, "The Genuineness of the Ninth and Third Letters of Isocrates," 39–42 and J. B. Bury, *A History of Greece*, 3rd ed., rev. Russell Meiggs (London, 1963), 732–33.

32. Jebb, *The Attic Orators*, 257.

33. Jebb, *The Attic Orators*, 257.

34. Patterson, "That Old Man Eloquent," 42.

35. Patterson, "That Old Man Eloquent," 41.

36. Patterson, "That Old Man Eloquent," 40.

37. Patterson, "That Old Man Eloquent," 40.

38. These may have included Agesilaus II and Archidamus III of Sparta, Dionysius I of Syracuse, and Alexander of Pherae.

39. *Philipus* 16.

40. *Philipus* 30.

41. *Philipus* 154.

42. See e.g. *Panegyricus* 80–81, 166, *Philipus* 16, 30, 88, 154–55, *Panathenaicus*, 64–66.

43. "Letter III" 2.

44. Ricks, "Literature and the Matter of Fact," 282.

45. Ricks, "Literature and the Matter of Fact," 298.

46. Lactantius, *Divine Institutes* 1.14.

47. *Paradise Lost*, 5.807 and 4.845.

48. *Metamorphoses* 14.629.

49. *The Poems of John Milton*, ed. John Carey and Alastair Fowler (London, 1968), note to *Paradise Lost*, 9.393–96. In his 1998 edition Fowler omits the words "used ironically".

50. Richard DuRocher, *Milton and Ovid* (Ithaca, N.Y., 1985), 98. DuRocher has looked widely in Renaissance commentaries on Ovid, but he can find no text "that suggested this flight."

51. DuRocher, *Milton and Ovid.*

52. *Complete Prose Works of John Milton,* ed. Don M. Wolfe et al., 8 vols. (New Haven, 1953–82), vol. 2, 516.

53. Fowler opts for "Likest" in his 1998 edition, but even his 1998 note acknowledges that "Likeliest" might be the correct reading "as the less common word." Elision can easily accommodate the extra syllable in "Likeliest." Compare "Lovelier" in Book Nine, 505.

54. Robert Martin Adams, *Ikon: John Milton and the Modern Critics* (Ithaca, N.Y., 1955), 84.

55. *Complete Prose Works,* ed. Wolfe et al., vol. 8, 558.

56. Frank Justus Miller, ed. and trans., *Ovid: Metamorphoses* (London, 1916, rep. 1984). Unless otherwise stated, citations and translations of Ovid are from this Loeb Classical Library edition.

57. John Leonard, " 'Good Things': A Reply to William Kerrigan," *Milton Quarterly* 30 (October 1996): 117–27 (esp. 119–20).

58. Walker, "The Poetics of Antitext," 161. Mention should also be made of Walker's book *Medusa's Mirrors: Spenser, Shakespeare, Milton and the Metamorphosis of the Female Reader* (Newark, 1998), which appeared just as the present essay was going to press.

59. John P. Rumrich, *Milton Unbound* (Cambridge, 1996), 78.

60. Walker, "The Poetics of Antitext," 162.

61. Rumrich, *Milton Unbound,* 78.

62. Rumrich, *Milton Unbound,* 78.

63. Rumrich, *Milton Unbound,* 78, Walker, "The Poetics of Antitext," 160.

64. Rumrich, *Milton Unbound,* 79.

65. J. N. Adams, *The Latin Sexual Vocabulary* (Baltimore, 1982), 198–99.

66. For "ravished" and "raped" see, respectively, Frank Justus Miller's Loeb translation and Rolfe Humphries, *Ovid's Metamorphoses* (Bloomington, 1967). For "strumpeted" see A. E. Watts, *The Metamorphoses of Ovid: An English Version* (San Francisco, 1980).

67. William Kerrigan, "The Politically Correct *Comus:* A Reply to John Leonard," *Milton Quarterly* 27 (December 1993): 149–55 (esp. 152).

68. George Sandys, *Ovid's Metamorphosis Englished* (1632), ed. Karl K. Hulley and Stanley T. Vandersall (Lincoln, 1970), 221.

69. Natale Conti, *Mythologiae, sive explicationis fabularum* (Padua, 1616), 390.

70. Jean Beaudoin, *Mythologie* (Paris, 1627), 79.

71. Marius d'Assigny, *The Poetical Histories* (London, 1671), 125.

72. Arthur Golding, *The XV Bookes of P. Ovidius Naso entytuled Metamorphosis* (London, 1567), 960.

73. The *OED* lists instances of both consensual and non-consensual sex under the definition "violate, ravish, defile" (*OED* "abuse," 6).

74. Rumrich, *Milton Unbound,* 81.

MILTON AND THE PROGRESS
OF THE EPIC PROEMIUM

Stella P. Revard

T HE PROEMIUM IS A time-honored convention of heroic poetry,
dating back as far as the Hesiodic poem, *The Theogony*. It is where the
poet invokes his muses and introduces the theme of the poem he is about to
sing. It is also where he talks about himself, often revealing the only bio-
graphical information that we know about him. In the proemium to *The
Theogony*, Hesiod recounts how the muses came to him when he was shep-
herding his flock on Helicon and taught him glorious song. Though Homer is
usually given credit for inventing the epic proemium, the proemia to both
the *Iliad* and *Odyssey* include only brief invocations with summaries of the
poems that follow but no biographical data. It is really Hesiod who invents
the full-scale epic proemium and hands it down to future epic poets, princi-
pal among them being Virgil. In the *Georgics*, which was composed in imita-
tion of Hesiod's *Works and Days*, Virgil creates his own proemium, with a few
Roman innovations at the beginning of the third book. Summoning Hesiod's
muses from the Aonian mount Helicon, he presents himself as an epic poet
and begins to make plans for his own epic composition, the *Aeneid*. Both
Hesiod's and Virgil's proemia influenced John Milton. In this essay I shall
consider how the literary models Milton uses and the biographical details he
chooses enable him to create his own heroic persona—the epic *vates*. In
Milton's works biography as well as poetry is a literary act.

Sometime in the late 1630s an "epic" consciousness begins to get the
better of Milton. In the midst of two Latin poems, *Mansus* and *Epitaphium
Damonis*, he breaks off from the subject he is addressing to speak of a
proposed epic. The critical attention devoted to these passages usually fo-
cuses on the subject that Milton is announcing—an Arthurian epic—rather
than on the poetic structure of the passages or the epic persona that Milton
adopts for the first time. Like Virgil, he tells us that he plans to change his
voice from the pastoral to the heroic mode. As he does so, he intrudes a
personal tone by using the same Latin verb "dicam" ("I shall tell") both in
Mansus (82) and *Epitaphium Damonis* (103) to describe his plans for his
projected *Arthuriad*. It is almost as though he were speaking—or trying to
speak—the first line of a proemium.

In *Mansus* Milton addresses himself to his poet-friend Giovanni Battista Manso; in *Epitaphium Damonis* he speaks to the dead Damon, Charles Diodati, telling how he had wished on his own return to England to confide to Diodati plans for his projected epic. At this point in his life Milton seems more than a little affected with an epic urgency, perhaps because his Italian friends were pressing him to fulfill, as Tasso had, an epic promise, perhaps merely from his own inner urgings.[1] If the Arthurian epic that Milton outlines suggests a Spenserian influence, the way in which he describes it has a peculiarly Virgilian cast. Milton deliberately echoes passages from Virgil's *Eclogues* and *Georgics,* respectively, where Virgil deals with the question of his planned epic. In one way it is not particularly surprising that Milton— eager to produce a national epic for the glory of England—should echo Rome's national poet. Milton uses, in his lament for his friend Damon, a phrase that Virgil had used in the lament for his poet-friend Gallus, "concedite silvae" (give way, woods) (*Eclogues* 10.63). In adapting the phrase, however, Milton makes it something different. What is an impersonal moment in Virgil's eclogue becomes a personal moment for Milton. Virgil suppresses his own voice to express himself through the person of his dying friend. Milton, however, although speaking through the shepherd-singer Thyrsis, directly announces his future plans. At what is the turning point of the poem, he determines to sublimate his grief and to take up once more the task of being a poet. He recounts how, when playing upon the reeds of his rural pipe, it burst its fastenings because the strain he was playing was too sonorous. Rather than being discouraged, however, Thyrsis takes it for a sign of greater things to come: "dubito quoque ne sim / Turgidulus, tamen et referam" ("I doubt that I am overconfident; however, I shall proceed," 159–60). At that moment, the Virgilian echo occurs: "vos cedite, silvae" ("give way, you woods," 160).[2] Milton the pastoral poet is beginning to build an epic persona. But, is it truly (in spite of the Virgilian echo) a Roman persona?

When he includes his plans for an epic within his encomium to Manso and his lament for Damon, Milton clearly had in mind Virgil's inclusion within the *Georgics* of his own plans for the *Aeneid.* In the proemium to *Georgics* 3 Virgil announces his resolve to obey Caesar and compose a national epic, and in so doing he outlines the Roman themes that he will write of: Pales and Apollo; Caesar's conquests; the ancestors of the Roman race who were sprung from Jove. Prominent among the themes, of course, are Caesar's battles. It is significant also that Virgil here uses a first person plural verb, "canemus" ("we shall sing"), rather than the modest "incipiam canere" ("I shall begin to sing") with which he began the *Georgics.* It is almost as though the collective imperial theme demanded a collective effort, or as though Virgil were speaking in union with his patron Maecenas and with

Caesar when he set out his plans. In echoing this passage, Milton is taking just as great a risk as his predecessor, resolving to compose an English epic for an English audience, just as Virgil had proposed to write for Rome and Caesar.

Yet even though Milton is trying very hard to be a nationalistic poet like Virgil, there are significant differences between Milton and his would-be epic model that may have led him eventually to abandon Virgilian for biblical epic. True, Milton pronounces with gusto his intention to tell of Arthur's waging his wars under earth (*Mansus*, 81), but he does not do so in order to offer compliments to a contemporary British king, as Virgil undertook his theme to honor to Caesar's battles. His statement about Arthur's wars is curiously at odds, moreover, with his later declaration concerning warfare in *Paradise Lost*. There he confides that he was not "sedulous by Nature to indite / Wars" (9.27–28), forgetful apparently of his earlier ambition. Has his "nature" changed in the interim, or was this ambitious resolve even then alien to Milton, as he planned his future epic?

Another difference is Milton's use of a first person singular future verb, "dicam." Unlike Virgil's, his is not a collaborative effort, either with patron or with monarch. The old Marchese Manso to whom he relates his plans, though patron and friend to Tasso, is merely Milton's host in Naples, not the future sponsor of his poetry. Further, some twenty years later, when the hint comes that he might become the historian for the Commonwealth, not even Cromwell the general can command his pen.[3] In the 1650s as in the 1630s, wars and the patrons who sponsor wars were apparently alien to Milton's design.

On the other hand, Milton wants very much to be England's poet, as his declarations in both *Mansus* and *Epitaphium Damonis* indicate, and epic seems to be the proper form for undertaking a history of the British people. Making the pastoral hexameters of *Epitaphium Damonis* take on the weightiness of epic hexameters, he begins: "Dardanias Rutupina per aequora puppes / Dicam" ("I shall tell of the Dardanian ships embarking on the Rutupian sea," 162–63). In *Mansus* he sketches his story; in *Epitaphium Damonis* he begins to name those who make up the history: Inogen, and Arviragus, and old Belinus, and finally Igraine, the mother to Arthur, whose conception he alludes to. Gathering momentum, he seems almost ready to commence the epic itself. But of course, through necessity, he must break off, just as Virgil had in the proemium to *Georgics* 3, in order to return to the poem that he has interrupted with this epic interlude.

A few years later in *The Reason of Church-Government*, when Milton interrupts his discussion of God and true worship to outline subjects for poetry, nothing is said about Arthurian epic. He is still concerned with writing for the British people but proposes a Christian epic instead—with a hero such as Tasso's Godfrey, if someone comparable can be found in British history. Moreover, though he still speaks of Homer and Virgil as models for an epic poem, he is entertaining a host of other topics and forms for poetry, among them biblical and classical tragedy, odes and hymns both on classical and biblical models (CP, 668–69). Something has happened to the plans for a national epic and to the poet who was to write it. The persona that he is presenting to the world is still that of the future poet, but of a poet concerned with sacred themes, as he is occupied in *The Reason of Church-Government* with defending the liberty of the English Church.

When we come finally to the epic proemia of *Paradise Lost,* we find a significant difference between the voice adopted to speak of nationalistic epic in *Mansus* and *Epitaphium Damonis* and that adopted to introduce sacred epic. The transition from "dicam" to "I may assert . . . and justify" reflects the change from a Virgilian model for the epic persona to a model of a different sort. This process involves, curiously enough, not the abandonment of the woods or silvae of the early lyric and pastoral poems but a continued devotion to this world of intimate inspiration associated with the Hesiodic poems.

Hence Milton must refashion the epic persona of *Paradise Lost* on a Greek rather than Roman model. He must distinguish himself from the Virgil he had called up for his planned *Arthuriad,* just as Virgil had distinguished himself from the Greek poets Homer, Hesiod, and Pindar, who purportedly were to be his principal models for the muse-directed song. Let us look once again at the proemium to *Georgics* 3, for it has something more to tell us about both Virgil and Milton. In the proemium Virgil on the one hand proposes to bring the Greek muses from their Aonian peaks to Mantua (3.10–11); on the other he sets a task for them that is peculiarly Roman and imperial, not Greek. The Aonian muses that he refers to are those of Hesiod and Pindar, for they, not Homer, are the poets from Aonia. Although Homer's so-called muses and the Homeric poems are important to the epic he is writing, Hesiod and Pindar are the vatic poets of Greece who serve as models for the epic *vates.*

Homer speaks little about himself in either the *Iliad* or the *Odyssey,* whereas Hesiod and Pindar are always present in their poems. Homer may invoke the muses at the beginning of his epics, but Hesiod tells us specifically how the muses came to him on Helicon and made him a poet.[4] Throughout his epinician odes Pindar refers continually to the muses as the nourishers of his song and invokes them to be present when he creates his poetry. Even Virgil was conscious of the differences between Hesiod's rural poetry and the

Roman epic he is proposing. In the *Georgics,* he had been following Hesiod's *Works and Days* as a model, translating its rural Greek values to Italy. In the *Aeneid,* he was embarking on a different kind of poem.

The Romans already had native deities, the Camoenae, whose origin and functions were similar but not identical to those of the Greek muses. Yet Roman poets, when they imitated the Greeks, readily invoked the Greek muses in the place of their native deities.[5] There is a significant difference, however, between the Roman Camoenae and the Greek muses. The muses of Hesiod and Pindar are goddesses intimately associated with sacred places—springs and groves and mountains. They are the daughters of Zeus, who speak his sacred truths to human beings. They command the poet to a religious duty to be a spokesman for them, as they are the representatives for the highest god. In taking over the sacred goddesses of Hesiod and Pindar, Virgil and Horace and other Roman poets of his period tended to accept only the aspects of the muses that served their purposes. And the central purpose for them of the muses was as the patrons of poetry, who could with the poet serve his patron, Caesar.

Before he undertook the *Aeneid,* Virgil had a view of the muses closer to that of his Greek predecessors. In the first two books of the *Georgics* Virgil expresses his devotion to Hesiod's rustic muses and prays that they reveal to him knowledge of earth's and heaven's secrets:

> Me vero primum dulces ante omnia Musae,
> quarum sacra fero ingenti percussus amore,
> accipiant caelique vias et sidera monstrent,
> defectus solis varios lunaeque labores.   (*Georgics* 2.475–78)[6]

> But for me truly first, above all, may the sweet Muses,
> whose sacred emblems I carry, struck with great love for them,
> bring me to the highways of heaven and show me the stars,
> the many lapses of the sun and the labors of the moon.

This declaration of love occurs, moreover, after a passage that proclaims the supreme happiness of country life—a life that he hopes may be lived far from the court and the sound of contending arms. The Milton of *Paradise Lost* had no trouble identifying with this sentiment; indeed it is this very passage—rather than the proemium to *Georgics* 3—that he echoes in Book Three of *Paradise Lost*. Declaring his love of the places where the muses dwell, "Clear Spring, or shady Grove, or Sunny Hill," he also proclaims, like Virgil, that he has been "smit with the love of sacred Song" (27–29). He adds to Virgil's phrase one word only—"sacred"—that places him within biblical rather than classical authority.

It is remarkable that the sensitive passage of dedication that occurs in

Georgics 2 is followed by the polemics of *Georgics* 3. Has Virgil so quickly changed from a poet who prays to the muses for illumination to one who brashly declares that he will lead them in triumph from their Aonian peaks to be enshrined in a temple beside the Mantuan river Mincius, far from their sacred groves and springs? He is imperializing the rural muses he says he reveres. At the same time he appears to abandon Hesiodic inspiration; he expresses his ambition to become a Pindaric poet, referring implicitly to Pindar by choosing an epinician metaphor to describe his intentions as an epic poet. Like a victor in the Olympic games, he says that he will drive a hundred chariots before the marble temple of the muses that he has set up beside Mincius. Resplendent in Tyrian purple, he will do honor to Caesar. Now the festival sites where Pindar had sung his epinician songs will be transferred to Italy. No longer will Olympia be supreme. His hair bound with wild olive (the crown for Olympian champions), Virgil will lead the procession to Caesar's temple. On the doors of the temple will be memorialized Caesar's victories—those in the far east, in the far west, and in the Nile against Antony. The temple that Virgil speaks of is, of course, the heroic poem in Caesar's honor; its doors enshrine memorials of Caesar's victories. This passage both imitates and differs from the Pindaric passages it recalls. Pindar in *Olympian* 9 (81) describes himself borne along in the muses' cart; but he is not their charioteer. He conveys their song to earth; he does not command them to sing. They command him.

In adopting an athletic metaphor for his poetry-making and in portraying himself as driving the chariot of the muses, Virgil appears to be according honor to Pindar and to the Greek style of poetry. Yet in introducing Roman values and Roman attitudes into the Greek exordium, he has altered the Greek notion of poetry and the muses that inspire it. Ostensibly, of course, he is merely transferring to Caesar the honor that Pindar accorded the Sicilian tyrants, Hieron and Theron. But in both *Olympian* 1 and *Olympian* 2 Pindar names Olympian Zeus first and then Hieron or Theron. Virgil reverses the order that the Greek poet set down, naming Caesar first and bidding the muses sing—after he has already set forth his subject and theme. The muses do not command him; he commands them and they obey, bringing the poem into being. He puts them at the disposal of the god-man, Caesar, not Olympian Jove. Virgil's heroic poem will be man-centered.

"Of arms and the man I sing," wrote Virgil. Milton may include man in the first line of his epic, but he no longer follows the Virgilian prescription that he had adopted in his Latin poems. Abandoning in the opening lines of *Paradise Lost* the first person singular of *Mansus* and *Epitaphium Damonis,* Milton invokes the Muse to sing: but not of Arthur's wars: not of man's arms, but of his disobedience. Moreover, the subject is one ordained by his heavenly patroness, since she, not he, knows all that has been from the beginning. The universe of *Paradise Lost* is both god-centered and muse-centered. Although christianizing the Muse, Milton has restored her to the place of eminence the Greeks had assigned her, a place from which Virgil's epic displaced her. It is the Muse who will speak to him of things unseen to human beings and who will elevate his mind and spirit to the task before him.

In the proemia to Books One, Three, Seven, and Nine, Milton speaks most intimately to and of his Muse. What are the models for these proemia? Barbara Lewalski has provided us with a hint, in remarking how Milton has incorporated or imbedded lyric models within his epic.[7] If we look for the lyric models for the proemia we must leap over Virgil's proemium from the *Georgics* and go back to Hesiod's proemium to the *Theogony* and to the proemia and vatic asides that punctuate Pindar's odes. For Hesiod and Pindar were the first of the classical poets who claimed a personal relationship to the Muses and made their personae as poets continually present in their poetry. Other devices distinctive to Pindaric ode and classical hymn are also used in the proemia of *Paradise Lost:* invocation, personal digression, and *sententia* and concluding prayer. Of these, personal digression is the most important. Like Hesiod and Pindar, Milton in his proemia expresses both his hopes and fears as a poet. Thus we find that despite the farewell to pastoral poetry in *Epitaphium Damonis,* Milton had not abandoned the lyric mode when he turned to the epic. He had taken lyric along with him.

The proemium to Book One of *Paradise Lost* contains the three essential elements of classical ode—invocation, digression, and prayer. In it Milton lets fall his first and perhaps only allusion to Hesiod as a classical model. He begins by urging the Muse to sing of the subjects set forth—man's first disobedience, the fruit of the forbidden tree, the greater man to come. But Milton also includes in the proemium a statement of autobiographical intention that revises the goals and models his Latin poems had set forth. His is an "advent'rous Song" that "intends to soar / Above the *Aonian* Mount, while it pursues / Things unattempted yet in Prose or Rhyme" (1.14–16). Is this the Aonian mount of Virgil's proemium? Is Milton's bold statement simply a case of Virgil redivivus—another poet naming the Aonian mountain only to boast that he is going to outdo the Greek poets, Hesiod and Pindar? In a way it is, but in another, it is not. Like Virgil, Milton will outdo his Greek precursors; but he will not sing of Caesar or Arthur and military victory, but of the sacred themes that themselves inspire no middle flight. When he names the Aonian mount, moreover, Milton is aware that it is a place of vatic ordination. When Hesiod pastured his sheep on Helicon, he met the muses who commanded him to be a poet. Moses had a comparable experience on Horeb and became a prophet. As I have argued elsewhere, the reference to the Hebraic shepherd Moses also includes a glance at the Hellenic shepherd Hesiod, for Milton is describing an ordination both as poet and prophet.[8] In concluding his proemium with a prayer in which he abases himself before the heavenly spirit that inspires him, he places himself in the company both of Hebraic prophets and Hellenic poets who sought for instruction and illumination from the divine authority that the Muse represents. Pindar put it succinctly in one of the recorded fragments when he told his Muse to inspire that he might prophesy: μαντεύεο, Μοῖσα, προφατεύσω δ' εγώ.[9]

As Lewalski and others have noted, the so-called "Hymn to Light" at the beginning of Book Three replicates closely the tripartite structure of classical hymn or ode, beginning with an invocation, developing through a narrative digression, and concluding with a prayer.[10] But here personal digression—used in *Mansus* and *Epitaphium Damonis* to interrupt encomium and pastoral lament—becomes an integral part of the hymn structure, through which Milton can define his person and aims as an epic *vates*. Over forty lines in length, the digression commences as narrative. In Homeric Hymn the chief person in the so-called myth or digression is the god to whom the hymn is addressed. In Pindaric ode the central figure in the digression is usually a hero, often the son of a god, such as Perseus or Heracles. Light, sprung from God as first-born principle of Creation, is the so-called "goddess" or "deity" to whom the hymn is addressed. Even though she functions within the digression, she is not its main figure. Milton makes the epic *vates* the central figure of the hymn's digression.

The leap from god to hero to poet is not so astonishing as might first appear. Milton had made the poet-shepherd the central figure of *Lycidas* and of *Epitaphium Damonis*, a poet-visitor from a Hyperborean land the central figure in *Mansus*. Moreover, in the two Latin poems Milton had taken the license of speaking as a poet planning his future epic. In the comic digression of *Ad Ioannem Rousium* Milton had made his "little book" into the epic persona; and in the tragic digression in *Lycidas* he had made the archetypal poet Orpheus a heroic double for Lycidas. Now he creates a blind bard, whose epic adventures surpass those of the hero of Homer's *Odyssey*. He is a visitor to the realms of Chaos and Eternal Night, returned safely to the realms of light to sing Orphean hymns to the goddesses who control both realms. Milton has created this epic persona from the personae of poets who have preceded him in the business of writing epic. He only names the blind bards—Maeonides (Homer) and the legendary Thamyris. The Homer he calls upon, moreover, is primarily the poet of the so-called Homeric Hymns, still attributed to Homer in Milton's time. That the list of blind poets and prophets is a short one should not mislead us. Milton's epic persona is made up of many poets that came before him. The shade of Dante is present as a poet who returns from Hell and reascends to light. The Virgil of the *Georgics* is here too, as Milton proclaims his love of the muses of spring and grove and hill. Hesiod and Pindar cannot be far behind, as Milton depicts himself as a vatic poet taught by the Muse. Milton's persona is a deliberate composite.

What part, then, does the "real" John Milton, the blind defender of England's commonwealth, the blind poet who must dictate his epic to amanuenses, have in this composite? Many readers look to the central passage of Book Three's proemium simply as a personal outpouring by the real John Milton, rather than as the fictive complaint of the epic persona that Milton has carefully crafted. The passage, however, is replete with literary association. Not for the first time in his literary career does he compare himself to the nightingale; he had done so in *Elegia 5*. Yet now he makes comparison poignant, for like the "wakeful bird," he sings "darkling" of those things he cannot directly experience (38–39). His blindness cuts him off from direct experience with nature and human beings.

> Thus with the Year
> Seasons return, but not to me returns
> Day, or the sweet approach of Ev'n or Morn,
> Or sight of vernal bloom, or Summer's Rose,
> Or flocks, or herds, or human face divine;
> But cloud instead, and ever-during dark
> Surrounds me, from the cheerful ways of men
> Cut off, and for the Book of knowledge fair
> Presented with a Universal blanc
> Of Nature's works to me expung'd and ras'd,
> And wisdom at one entrance quite shut out.   (3.40–50)

The personal complaint has long been part and parcel of the poet's stock in trade. Classical poets—from Hesiod and Pindar to Ovid and Propertius— were masters of the art. They complained of the harshness of life, the insolence of fellow poets, the slim rewards of the poetic career, the neglect of their fellow men. Modern poets took up the tradition and were making it their own. In "The Complaint," for example, Abraham Cowley engages his Muse in conversation, reviewing his faithful dedication to her and complaining to her of Charles II's meager rewards for his service.[11] We might well rank in this tradition Milton's litany of the ills that beset him as a blind poet. Yet something in this passage sets it apart from either personal or literary complaint. Milton has carefully designed the passage as an integral part of a hymnic digression.

The hymn is addressed to Celestial Light, the very light that is instinctive with God's creation, of which the light of the world is both the physical manifestation and the symbol. Physical light brought the sighted poet the visual pleasures of "Clear Spring," "shady Grove," "Sunny Hill," and "flow'ry Brooks," whose attributes of clarity, shade, sun, and flower are now denied to the blind poet. Nature's light instilled in him the delight that brought him to the service of the muses. Echoing both Hesiod and Virgil, Milton declares that he yet dwells, though blind, in the landscape the muses taught him to love: "Yet not the more / Cease I to wander where the Muses haunt" (3.26–27). If we focus merely on the poignancy of the personal complaint, we miss the point of its literary application. Milton is using his own biography to develop the principal themes of the digression, relating the paradoxes of deprivation of light to the hymn's salutation to Celestial Light. In so doing, he carefully constructs the persona of the epic *vates*, first associating himself with poets of nature, then with the blind poets and prophets— Homer, Thamyris, Teiresias, Phineus—who continued, like him, to offer service to God, though blind. He also endows blindness with literary as well as divine prerogatives. Deprived of outer light, he comes to the inner light of the divinity, Celestial Light, through the medium of the heavenly Muse, who brings it directly to him. Dependent both on the Muse and on Celestial Light (who is now the light of prophetic illumination), he can speak with the authority of a divine poet and describe heavenly things. Through her he may inhabit a landscape that he cannot see and can be invited into the celestial vision that none of the seeing world can directly experience.

The closing prayer, addressed to Celestial Light, resembles those in the Homeric and Orphic Hymns in that it is a request for special favor from the "deity."

> So much the rather thou Celestial Light
> Shine inward, and the mind through all her powers
> Irradiate, there plant eyes, all mist from thence
> Purge and disperse, that I may see and tell
> Of things invisible to mortal sight.   (3.51–55)

Milton has made it something more, however; he is asking the deity to confer on him the genuine credentials of vatic authority that would also give authority to the poem he is composing. The Muse becomes perforce the intermediary between Celestial Light and the poet, placing as it were divine illumination at his disposal. Milton has in a sense rewritten the proemium to *The Theogony,* creating a "myth" comparable to Hesiod's but different.[12] Encountering the muses, he enters their service; now blind, he continues to dwell with them, obtaining from the heavenly Muse the kind of vatic authority that will make it possible for him to tell his own account of the "generation" of the gods. It is a triumphant, almost a sublime ascent from uncertainty to assurance. The hymn that began as an invocation to Light concludes by providing justification both for the epic poet and the poem in progress.

In the proemium to Book Seven, while employing once again the techniques of Homeric Hymn and Pindaric ode, Milton develops even further the potential of biographical digression. He begins with an invocation to the Muse Urania, now first named as his personal protectress, but here differentiated from the Greek Muse of the heavens. As in the proemium to Book Three, he progresses from invocation to biographical digression and concludes with prayer. The biographical digression assumes an even larger proportion of the hymn, picking up the theme of the poet's journey through space at the point the poet left it in Book Three. When he addressed Celestial Light in Book Three, he had referred to his escape from hell, assisted by Celestial Light and the Muse:

> Thee I revisit now with bolder wing,
> Escap't the *Stygian* Pool, though long detain'd
> . . . .
> Taught by the heav'nly Muse to venture down
> The dark descent, and up to reascend.   (3.13–14, 19–20)

In Book Seven, however, Urania alone is the recipient of the poet's request: to be returned to earth.

> Up led by thee
> Into the Heav'n of Heav'ns I have presum'd,
> An Earthly Guest, and drawn Empyreal Air,
> Thy temp'ring; with like safety guided down
> Return me to my Native Element.   (7.12–16)

In Book Seven Milton expands the metaphor of flight by mythic allusion, likening his flight to that of the mythic hero Bellerophon, who attempted to scale Olympus on Pegasus but was cast down.[13] Now it is he who faces fall and wandering and death:

> Lest from this flying Steed unrein'd, (as once
> *Bellerophon,* though from a lower Clime)
> Dismounted, on th' *Aleian* Field I fall
> Erroneous there to wander and forlorn.   (7.17–20)

Bellerophon's story was well known to Milton from various sources in antiquity and in the Renaissance.[14] Its appearance in two odes of Pindar—*Isthmian* 7 and *Olympian* 13—could not have failed to have interested Milton, for Pindar uses Bellerophon's fall as an admonitory example. As one of those heroes greatly favored by the gods, Bellerophon serves as a positive example for Pindar in one ode and a negative in the other. Having been guided by Athene to bridle Pegasus and conquer the Chimaera, Bellerophon was destroyed by the gods when in his pride and ambition he sought to ride Pegasus to Olympus. In *Olympian* 13 Pindar passes over Bellerophon's fall in silence and urges reverence toward the gods, praying that he may end his days in piety, acceptable to the gods and honored by men.

For Pindar the flight on the winged horse Pegasus was a symbol for those blessed by the gods, such as the poet, who risk danger in order to catch a glimpse of divine things.[15] Even in Pindar's time, Pegasus, sprung from Medusa and Poseidon, was associated with the muses. The winged horse, rising from the earth, caused Hippocrene, the spring of Helicon, to gush forth when he struck the ground with his foot. Ever since, by extension, Pegasus' flight became a symbol for the ambitious flight of the poet, who, hearing the muses and drinking from the horse-spring Hippocrene, ventures into the heaven of heavens. Such flight is approved—within limits. Pindar compares himself in *Olympian* 2 to the soaring eagle, Zeus' bird. In *Olympian* 13, however, he remarks that he himself must be cautious when casting his dart-like words and not miss the mark by trying to hurl too many.

Isthmian 7 offers a more personal account of Bellerophon, alluding to his fall and referring both to the poet's literary and indirectly to his political biography. The ode was composed after 456 B.C., when Thebes, Pindar's native city, had been defeated in battle by Athens and had been reduced to little more than an Athenian colony.[16] Pindar addresses the ode to a young Theban athlete, Strepsiades, who had been victorious in the Isthmian games. Its exordium recalls Thebes in happier days when Dionysus, her native son, rose to Heaven, or when Zeus visited earth to beget the Theban hero Heracles, or when Thebes (ironically now Athens' tributary) defeated the Athenian army led by the legendary general Adrastus and sent Adrastus home to Argos, bereft of his comrades. These memories of ancient glory wring from Pindar regret that men no longer remember their past. As a poet he proposes to rededicate himself to preserving in verse the best of human excellence, so that the highest flower not be shattered without poetic commemoration. At this point in the ode, he turns to lay the choral wreath both on the young victor Strepsiades, who has won the pancratium at the Isthmian games, and on his patriot uncle of the same name, who had also won an athletic crown at the Isthmia before he died fighting for Thebes' freedom. In honoring the dead Strepsiades, Pindar also honors the defeated warriors of legend, among them the Trojan Hector. By remembering these heroes in verse, Pindar implies that he removes a little of the stigma of their defeat, preferring to honor the loyalty to their country that spurred them to fight above the bitterness and ignominy of their death. When we view in context the account of the disgraced hero Bellerophon and of the poet who hopes to escape Bellerophon's fate, these cautious references to the recent political events that had brought defeat to his native city and anguish to him as a poet add a kind of tragic resonance to the ode. Concluding with his own personal prayer, he has made himself a foil to Bellerophon, reverent to the gods, hoping to avoid the erstwhile hero's tragic fate.

The poet prays first to Poseidon, the lord of the Isthmian games, to assure him calm after the storm: permission still to sing, as he moves towards old age, free from envy and suspicion, his hair circled with the poet's garlands. Pursuing whatever transient pleasure life may grant, may he walk softly, he prays, toward that allotted end of life all mortals must face. Death is certain, even though the destiny that brings men to death is different for each. At this point Pindar alludes to Bellerophon and his tragic end.

> . . . . . . τὰ μακρὰ δ' εἴ τις
> παπταίνει, Βραχὺς ἐξικέσθαι χαλκόπεδον θεῶν
> ἕδραν. ὅ τοι πτερόεις
> ἔρριψε Πάγασος
> δεσπόταν ἐθέλοντ' ἐς οὐρανοῦ σταθμοὺς
> ἐλθεῖν μεθ' ὁμάγυριν βελλεροφόνταν
> Ζηνός. τὸ δὲ πὰρ δίκαν
> γλυκὺ πικρότατα μένει τελευτά.   (*Isthmian* 7.43–48)

> But if anyone strains after things
> far off, it is too short to reach the bronze
> threshold of the gods; truly the winged Pegasus threw
> his master Bellerophon when he tried to come to the
> homes of heaven into the society of Zeus.
> A very bitter end awaits a sweet
> that is unjustly sought.

Reflecting on Bellerophon's destiny, Pindar offers another prayer, now to Apollo, the lord of the Pythian games and the patron of poets. May he, like the athletes for whom he writes, win the flowery crown, not by venturing, as Bellerophon did, but by service and prayer and the favor of the god.

Milton and Pindar are linked by political as well as poetical biography. Both poets use the myth of the ambitious Bellerophon to allude cautiously to their own political dilemmas. Regretting the unhappy sequel to the ancient hero's adventurous flight on Pegasus, the poets both seem to be glancing sideways at the risks of speaking too plainly in politically charged circumstances. Thus the passages in *Isthmian* 7 and *Paradise Lost* may refer to more than the vicissitudes of poetic vocation and involve the poet's political status in his native city or country. Also writing in old age and at a time of defeat,

Milton in Book Seven describes, as directly as he ever does in *Paradise Lost,* the evil days on which he has fallen as a poet and patriot, silenced after the restoration of Charles II both as a writer and as a citizen. His invocation, however, is not to a defeated England, remembered in happier days, but to the heavenly Muse, Urania, to descend to him and console him:

> though fall'n on evil days,
> On evil days though fall'n, and evil tongues;
> In darkness, and with dangers compast round,
> And solitude.   (7.25–28)

As in *Isthmian* 7, the reference to present evil is oblique. Milton does not elaborate on his own troubles or discuss his country's fate. Rather he determines that he must as a poet somehow vindicate himself and his song, finding (through the Muse) an audience "fit . . . though few" (31).

Now in the style of Pindaric ode, Milton adds a second mythic allusion to the first, coupling his first reference to Bellerophon, the rider of Pegasus, with a second to Orpheus, the poet torn apart by the Bacchantes. I say coupling, for both allusions are framed in terms of requests to the Muse. Throughout the proemium Urania is never distant from the poet's mind and is repeatedly invoked for assistance and protection. In Pindar's account in *Olympian* 13 Athene had guided Bellerophon when he reined Pegasus and subdued the Chimaera. She is absent, however, when Bellerophon attempts (as Pindar recounts in *Isthmian* 7) to venture into heaven on what Milton calls the "flying Steed unreined." Similarly, the muse Calliope was absent and unable to save her son Orpheus when he was assailed by the Bacchic rout, as Milton recounts in his retelling of the Orpheus myth in *Lycidas.*

Throughout the proemium Milton addresses Urania in the imperative mood, pleading for succor and protection, pleas that ironically remind us how goddess and muse failed to assist the mythic heroes to whom Milton alludes. "Return me to my Native Element," he prays to Urania, just before he alludes to Bellerophon's fall (passing over in silence, however, Athene's failure to secure Bellerophon's safe return to earth). "Still govern thou my Song," he prays to Urania, whose presence comforts him "in darkness" and "solitude" with "dangers compassed round." The third prayer is yet more insistent:

> But drive far off the barbarous dissonance
> Of *Bacchus* and his Revellers, the Race
> Of that wild Rout that tore the *Thracian* Bard
> In *Rhodope,* where Woods and Rocks had Ears
> To rapture, till the savage clamor drown'd
> Both Harp and Voice.   (7.32–37)

Here, however, he alludes specifically to the failed divine help—"nor could the Muse defend / Her Son"—before he urges the final imperative on Urania: "So fail not thou, who thee implores" (7.37–38)

Readers and critics alike have understood the allusions to the torn poet and the Bacchic rout as references to the potential violence Milton faced from the new political regime under Charles II.[17] And not without reason. In the wake of judicial acts that often included hanging and drawing and quartering, allusions to tearing and savage clamor are hardly poetic exaggerations of the violence Milton might have suffered from the returned royalists.[18] In *The Ready and Easy Way to Establish a Free Commonwealth*, moreover, Milton had anticipated the vengeance that the "tigers of Bacchus" might exact when the royalists and the restored monarch began to settle accounts (CP, 894).

Pindar had in a sense taught Milton how to interpolate biographical reference into a hymnic or odic passage.[19] Yet we must ask once again: what purpose does a biographical digression serve in a proemium that is essentially an invocation to the Muse? Do these personal allusions—joined with mythic examples—have, as they had in Book Three, an integral function within the proemium? First, we must note that the character of the poet has changed in a small but a significant way. The blind *vates* of Book Three has become the vulnerable political outcast of Book Seven, still dependent on the Muse, but now not only for illumination but also for protection. In Book Three the poet likens himself to mythic exemplars he wishes to emulate: the prophet-bards who, though sightless, won fame. But here, the poet regards resemblance to his mythic exemplars as threatening and wishes to differentiate himself from the destroyed hero and poet. Hence an element of danger enters the biographical digression. To counter it, he identifies himself as a Christian *vates*, no mere successor to the classical bards, moving beyond the classical authority he once relied on. Claiming the protection from a *heavenly* Muse, he endows both himself and his poem with divine privilege. Both he, the singer of the poem, and the poem itself (which remains half unsung) are imperiled, unless the Muse protects and guides. Through the biographical details and the mythic allusions, Milton has created a sense of endangerment not only for himself but also for the poem yet unfinished. Inextricably involved, the poet and the poem together either survive or perish.

Yet all is not danger and threat. In the midst of the heavily charged atmosphere he has created, Milton can also address Urania intimately and describe her nightly visitations with the most ineffable serenity:

> yet not alone, while thou
> Visit'st my slumbers Nightly, or when Morn
> Purples the East.   (7.28–30)

Here we are on the verge of another change in Milton's view of the poet and his Muse. But we must move on to the proemium to Book Nine, where Milton provides us a final look at the epic *vates* and at the same time revises for the last time those epic projections of the late Latin poems.

The proemium to Book Nine is the least formal of the proemia; it invokes neither Muse nor goddess, though it does refer (now in the third person) to the Muse. It abandons the tripartite structure of the proemia to Books Three and Seven, including neither mythic digression nor closing prayer. Its closest parallels are not the proemia that have preceded it but the passages in *Mansus* and *Epitaphium Damonis* that discuss his plans for a future epic. The subject of the proemium to Book Nine is (in retrospect) the choice of epic material. Milton does not inform us directly why he abandoned the *Arthuriad;* yet in defending his argument as more, not less, heroic than the wrath of Achilles, the rage of Turnus, or the ire of Juno or Neptune, he indirectly tells us. Weighing the anger of heaven and the just rebuke that will follow the sin of Adam and Eve against the wrath or rage or ire of any other epic argument tips the scales in favor of the sacred subject chosen in *Paradise Lost*.

The proemium to Book Nine does not develop further the epic persona we met in the proemia to Books One, Three, and Seven. Milton dwells on neither his blindness, his political alienation, nor his danger. Nor does he make any direct request of the Muse for inspiration, for illumination, or for protection. In the place of such elaboration is his confident assertion that his work is nearing completion:

> If answerable style I can obtain
> Of my Celestial Patroness, who deigns
> Her nightly visitation unimplor'd,
> And dictates to me slumb'ring, or inspires
> Easy my unpremeditated Verse.   (9.20–24)

To the claim of divine inspiration Milton only adds the claim of "visitation unimplor'd," thus enrolling himself once more with Hesiod, whom the muses commanded (in nightly visitation) to sing of the generation of the gods in *The Theogony,* and with Pindar, who was famed as the muses' trumpet.

The principal focus of the proemium to Book Nine is not the poet but the poem. Milton explains and defends the rationale for having chosen this specific heroic subject for his heroic poem. As he does so, we as readers and critics circle back once more to *Epitaphium Damonis* and *Mansus* and the choice of epic material. The longest and the most elaborate passage in the proemium to Book Nine dismisses those very epic subjects that he had once contemplated: "fabl'd Knights / In Battles feign'd. . . Races and Games, / Or tilting Furniture, emblazon'd Shields, / Impreses quaint, Caparisons and Steeds; / Bases and tinsel Trappings, gorgeous Knights / At Joust and Tournament; then marshall'd Feast / Serv'd up in Hall with Sewers, and Seneschals" (30–31, 33–38). This dismissal, of course, is deceptive; such descriptions exist in *Paradise Lost* and also in *Paradise Regained.* But that is not the point. What Milton is doing here is defining himself as the poet whose theme is "the better fortitude / Of Patience and Heroic Martyrdom" (31–32), whose ambition carries him not only over the Aonian mount but also over the fabled mounts of Christian poets of his own and previous generations. He has better things to do than to speak of Dardanian ships or the generation of British kings up to Arthur—or so he would present it. What is also remarkable is that the fear and doubt of the previous proemia have vanished, to be replaced by the kind of confidence that he exhibited in *Mansus* and *Epitaphium Damonis.* Perhaps age and climate might damp a little his "intended wing"; he is not the thirty-year-old who confidently announced, "dicam." But in its place the biographical construct of Muse and poet that he set in place in the proemium to Book One comes to his rescue: "much they may, if all be mine, / Not Hers who brings it nightly to my Ear" (9.46–47).

What I propose is that Milton has placed himself in his poetry, less to tell us something of his life and ambitions, but more to create a kind of support for the poetry itself. The persona of inspired bard vindicates the inspired poem on an atypical epic subject. If the biographical defenses of *The Reason of Church-Government,* of *Apology for Smectymnuus,* of the *Second Defense of the English People* had a function of justifying the arguments of these works, so the biographical content of the proemia support and sustain the progress of the epic itself. Milton the *vates* is at his most triumphant, just at the very time when he is changing his notes to tragic, anticipating the failure of Adam and Eve to choose rightly. There is no such danger for our epic *vates,* who has been "long choosing, and beginning late" (9.26). His choice has also been vindicated by his Celestial Patroness, who "inspires / Easy [his] unpremeditated Verse" (9.23–24). Perhaps there is a contradiction in terms between the claims of choice and unpremeditated song. If so, the paradox also embraces the Christian who chooses to be chosen or the Christian poet who aspires to raise his name above pagan poets and yet be nameless in the service of God. Although four books remain to the epic he set himself to write, Milton the *vates* speaks his final word here. He spares us the youthful enthusiasm of the poet of *Mansus,* who imagines himself on Olympus, his work completed, smiling with his face suffused with rosy light and applauding himself and his own accomplishments: "Ridens purpureo suffundar lumine vultus, / Et simul aethereo plaudam mihi laetus Olympo" (99–100).

The biographical construct of *Paradise Lost* is subtler. Milton leaves it to Urania to confer the laurels.

NOTES

1. Note particularly the epigram addressed to him by Selvaggi (printed in the 1645 *Poemata*) that compares him to Homer and Virgil as the ornament of his country (4).

2. Citations of Milton are from *Complete Poems and Major Prose*, ed. Merritt Y. Hughes (New York, 1957), hereafter cited parenthetically in the text as CP. In *Epitaphium Damonis* the confident "I" only emerges when Milton has Thyrsis speak of his poetry. "O ego quantus eram" ("O how great I was," 129) and "Ipse etiam" ("even I," 133) he exclaims when he tells how he competed with the shepherds of Tuscany in song. "Ipse ego" ("I myself," 162), he cries out, as he tells of the epic theme his pipes were playing. The passage where he announces his epic plans is simply a fulfillment of that growing confidence.

3. Milton responds to Henry Oldenburg on December 20, 1659: "I am far from compiling a history of our political troubles, which you seem to urge; for they are worthier of silence than of publication" (Letter 39, *Complete Prose Works of John Milton*, 8 vols., ed. Don M. Wolfe et al. [New Haven, 1980], vol. 7, 515).

4. Apart from the opening lines of both the *Iliad* and the *Odyssey*, where the goddess (thea) or the muse (mousa) are directly called upon to tell the story, or a passage in Book Two of the *Iliad*, where Homer calls on the muses to recite the catalogue of the ships, Homer's epics say almost nothing about the relationship of poet and muse, even though Homer enjoyed the reputation of a muse-inspired poet.

5. For a discussion of the Camoenae, particularly with reference to Milton's and other Renaissance poets' use of the term, see E.R. Gregory, *Milton and the Muses* (Tuscaloosa, Ala., 1989), 51–59.

6. Quoted from Virgil, *Bucolica et Georgica*, ed. T. E. Page (London, 1968).

7. See Barbara Kiefer Lewalski, *Paradise Lost and the Rhetoric of Literary Forms* (Princeton, N.J., 1985). As Lewalski demonstrates, Milton has embedded hymns, odes, and other lyric genres within *Paradise Lost*.

8. See "Milton's Muse and the Daughters of Memory," *ELR* 9 (1979), 432–41.

9. Fragment 137 in *Pindari Carmina*, ed. C. M. Bowra (Oxford, 1935). All quotations of Pindar, unless otherwise noted, are from this text.

10. Lewalski, *Paradise Lost and the Rhetoric of Literary Forms*, 31–33. See my discussion of the Hymn to Light, "Hymns and Anti-hymns to Light in *Paradise Lost*," in *"All in All": Unity, Diversity, and the Miltonic Perspective*, ed. Charles W. Durham and Kristin A. Pruitt (Selinsgrove, Pa., 1999), 174–88.

11. See "The Complaint," in *The Works of Mr. Abraham Cowley* (London, 1668).

12. Hesiod includes in the proemium to *The Theogony* a dramatic account of his interview with the muses. They address him, promising to reveal true things, and then they pluck an olive rod and give it to him, ordaining him as a poet. Breathing into him a divine voice to celebrate the present, past, and future that they will reveal, they command him to sing of the generation of the gods and always to sing of them first and last. (See Hesiod, *The Theogony* [London, 1914], ll. 22–34). The scene of ordination is imitated by Virgil and most of the Roman poets, as well as by Renaissance poets, such as Ronsard.

13. For Milton's use of the Bellerophon myth, see Stephen M. Fallon, "Intention and Its

Limits in *Paradise Lost:* The Case of Bellerophon," in *Literary Milton: Text, Pretext, Context,* ed. Diana Treviño Benet and Michael Lieb (Pittsburgh, 1994), 161–79.

14. In his odes Horace draws on such examples as Phaëthon and Bellerophon to advise moderation of desire: "terret ambustus Phaethon avaras / Spes, et exemplum grave praebet ales / Pegasus terrenum equitem gravatus / Bellerophontem" (Burning Phaëton scares away ambitious hopes, and another weighty example applies: winged Pegasus disdaining the weight of the earth-bound rider, Bellerophon.) (*Carmina* 4.11.25–28). The seventeenth-century English mythographer Alexander Ross has both cautionary and commendatory remarks on Bellero-phon's flight. He cautions, "By the example of Bellerophon beware of pride, which will spoil all good actions in us, and at last give us a fall." He notes also that "Christ is the true Bellerophon, the wisdom of God, who brought to us counsell and wisdom . . . and rides triumphantly on his Word, as on a winged horse, and by the power of his Divinity mounted up to Heaven." See "Bellerophon" in *Mystagogus Poeticus, or the Muses Interpreter* (London, 1647).

15. In his earliest poetry—the Latin elegies—Milton connects the "furor poeticus" with Pegasian flight and with a venturing beyond the human. In *Elegia* 5 (5–25), he anticipates the return of poetic inspiration with the coming of spring, describing, much as Callimachus had in his *Hymn to Apollo,* the onset of Apollonian "furor." Even without Pegasus, he is carried to the clouds, where he surveys the haunts of poets, the shrines of the gods, and even visits Olympus and the Tartarean world below. Milton's letter to Diodati in the 1630s also refers to his poetic ambitions as growing wings and mounting with Pegasus. (Letter 7, *Works of John Milton* [New York, 1936], vol. 12.27). His earliest allusion to Bellerophon is in *Prolusion* 6, where he alludes to the slaying of the Chimaera as a positive example of courage (CP, 618).

16. C. M. Bowra believes that these references to Bellerophon were Pindar's warning to Athens, which, by 454 B.C., was becoming too powerful and excessively bold. See Pindar, *The Odes,* trans. C. M. Bowra (London, 1969), 226. On Bellerophon also see Thomas K. Hubbard, "Pegasus' Bridle and the Poetics of Pindar's Thirteenth Olympian," *HSCP* 90 (1986), 27–48.

17. The doubling of Bellerophon with Orpheus is an especially interesting one, for in several accounts of the death of Orpheus, he too, like Bellerophon, angered the gods by impiety and became the victim of divine retribution. In one version of the story Dionysus is angry with Orpheus because the poet prefers Helios—the sun—to him as a deity; Dionysus consequently sends the Maenads to tear Orpheus apart. In another version it is Zeus who is offended because Orpheus has revealed divine secrets and so kills him with a thunderbolt. In these versions of the Orpheus story, Orpheus, like Bellerophon, ventured too far and incurred divine wrath. For accounts of the death of Orpheus, see Pausanias, *Descriptions of Greece,* trans. W. H. S. Jones (London, 1918). Also see Charles Segal, *Orpheus: The Myth of the Poet* (Baltimore, 1989).

18. See Michael Lieb's treatment of the theme of *sparagmos* in *Milton and the Culture of Violence* (Ithaca, 1994), 59–80.

19. Mary Lefkowitz has pointed out that much of the so-called biography of Pindar is a literary construct. She urges readers to be cautious in taking the first-person statements in the odes as personal statements of the poet. See "Pindar's Lives," in *Classica et Iberica, A Festschrift in Honor of the Reverend Joseph M.-F. Marique, S. J,* ed. P. T. Brannan (Worcester, Mass. 1975), 69–72. Also see Mary Lefkowitz. *First-Person Fictions, Pindar's Poetic 'I'* (Oxford, 1991).

PARADISE LOST AND MILTON'S POLITICS

Barbara Kiefer Lewalski

INTO *PARADISE LOST* Milton poured all that he had learned, expe-
rienced, desired, and imagined about life, love, artistic creativity, theology,
work, history—and politics. He had been thinking about writing some kind of
epic for decades, on the model of Homer and Virgil and Tasso, and with a
great national hero like King Arthur. When he came to doubt Arthur's histor-
icity he considered King Alfred. We cannot be sure just when Milton decided
that the great epic subject for his own times had to be the Fall and its
consequences: not the founding of a great empire or nation, but the loss of an
earthly paradise and with it any possibility of founding an enduring version of
the City of God on earth.[1] He probably settled on this subject for epic
sometime in the 1650s—"long choosing, and beginning late," as he put it in
the proem to Book Nine.[2] He may have begun writing around 1658 and
completed some part of the poem before the Restoration of 1660 brought
Charles II back to the throne. John Aubrey reports, citing Edward Phillips as
source, that Milton began the poem "about 2 yeares before the K. came-in,
and finished about 3 yeares after the K's Restauracion," working on it only
during the winter months and spending about four or five years on it (*EL*,
13).[3] The proem to Book Seven, with its dark references to the bard fallen on
"evil dayes" and encompassed round with dangers, suggests that much of the
final six books postdate the Restoration. He evidently had a complete draft in
hand by August, 1665, when his Quaker friend Thomas Ellwood reported
seeing it.[4] Most likely he continued working on it at Chalfont and in London,
during the eighteen months before its publication in 1667.

But those dangers and disappointments did not lead Milton, as some
critics believe, to write an epic that abandons politics and honors a quietistic
retreat to the spiritual realm, the "paradise within."[5] Several recent studies—
by, among others, Joan Bennett, Laura Lunger Knoppers, Sharon Achin-
stein, and most recently David Norbrook[6]—have challenged that view, un-
derscoring some political issues the poem engages. I mean to argue here that
Milton's poem is a more daring political gesture than we often realize, even as
it is also a poem for the ages by a prophet poet who placed himself with (or
above) Homer, Virgil, Ariosto, Tasso, and the rest. It undertakes a strenuous
project of educating readers in the virtues, values, and attitudes that make a

141

people worthy of liberty, and we need to recognize just how emphatic its political lessons were and are. In the moral realm the Miltonic bard exercises his readers in discernment, rigorous judgment, imaginative apprehension, and choice by setting his poem in relation to other great epics and works in other genres, thereby prompting a critique of the values associated with those other heroes and genres.[7] In the political realm, he involves them in thinking through the ideological and polemic controversies of the recent war, engaging them to think again, and think rightly, about monarchy, tyranny, rebellion, liberty, hierarchy, and republicanism. The long reception history of *Paradise Lost* demonstrates that it was quite possible to ignore, or to misread, the poem's politics. But that is not, I think, because Milton has obscured these issues out of confusion or misjudgment, or sought to give himself cover from the censors,[8] or multiplied difficulties in the reading process as a deliberate educational strategy. These considerations cannot be discounted, especially Sharon Achinstein's view that Milton's readers are made to struggle for right understanding as a means to form them as revolutionary readers. But it seems to me that Milton intends to make his political meanings clear, though of course when he challenges stereotypes he runs the inevitable risk of activating them. His fit readers may be few, but he wanted his poem to produce as many more of them as possible.

Throughout the revolutionary period, as Milton engaged his pen to the cause of reform, regicide, and a more nearly ideal church, state, and society, he continually sought to prod, goad, and educate his countrymen to understand the evils of monarchical government, the virtue of a republic, and above all the need to secure religious toleration for all Protestants and to separate church and state. Like others in the tradition of Plato, Aristotle, and Machiavelli, he believed that kinds of government—monarchy, aristocracy, democracy—must conform to the nature of the people, and that people get the government they deserve and are fit for. Monarchy is justified only when the king is vastly superior to the rest, but that condition seldom obtains, and when it does it should not: monarchy, and especially absolute monarchy, Milton came increasingly to believe, is a debased form of government only suited to a servile, debased people. Properly, government should be shared among the large body of worthy citizens who are virtuous and love liberty: as he put it in the *First Defense,* "It is neither fitting nor proper for a man to be king unless he be far superior to all the rest; where there are many equals, and in most states there are very many, I hold they should rule alike and in turn."[9] But the continuing disaffection of the majority of the English people after the regicide forced restrictive governments: first, by the unrepresentative Rump, and then by a Protectorate veering ever closer to monarchy. In supporting those governments, Milton recognized that England was not becoming the nation of prophets he had so hopefully envisioned in *Areopagitica,* nor yet the republic of worthy, virtuous, liberty-loving citizens he had projected in the *Tenure of Kings and Magistrates.*

Yet early to late he continued his efforts to educate his countrymen to the moral and political virtues he thought necessary to sustain a republican commonwealth. In *Of Education* (1645) he laid out a curriculum intended to fit students to be citizens, "to perform justly, skillfully and magnanimously all the offices both private and publike of peace and war" (YP 2:378–79). In his *History of Britain* (c. 1648–49) he sought to help Englishmen recognize and counter what he saw as a worrisome characteristic, displayed over and over again in their history: though valorous in war, they sadly lacked the civic virtues needed to sustain free governments and their own liberties, and should supply that lack by gaining "ripe understanding and many civil vertues . . . from forren writings & examples of best ages" (YP 5:451). In his *First Defense* he laments the disaffection of "a great part of the people [who] . . . longed for peace and slavery" [i.e., a restoration of the monarchy] but he hopes that a republican ethos will teach them better values:

I can still say that their sins were taught them under the monarchy, like the Israelites in Egypt, and have not been immediately unlearned in the desert, even under the guidance of God. But there is much hope for most of them, not to enter on the praises of our good and reverent men who follow earnestly after truth.   (YP 4:386–87)

In that tract and yet more earnestly in the *Second Defense* (1654), even as he justifies Cromwell's Protectorate on the ground that he alone has proved superlatively worthy to lead, he pleads passionately with his countrymen to display the political virtue that will fit them to participate in government:

By the customary judgment and, so to speak, just retaliation of God, it happens that a nation which cannot rule and govern itself, but has delivered itself into slavery to its own lusts, is enslaved also to other masters whom it does not choose. . . . Learn to obey right reason, to master yourselves. Lastly, refrain from factions, hatreds, superstitions injustices, lusts and rapine against one another. Unless you do this with all your strength you cannot seem either to God or to men, or even to your recent liberators, fit to be entrusted with the liberty and guidance of the state.   (YP 4:684)

In the *Readie and Easie Way to Establish a Free Commonwealth* (1660), published on the eve of the Restoration, he again proposes schools in each locale to train up children in "all liberal arts and exercises," as a means of spreading "knowledge and civilitie, yea religion through all parts of the land," and to make the people "flourishing, vertuous, noble and high spirited" (YP 7:460). And though he recognized that it was then all but hopeless to try to prevent the king's return, he still dared to hope his argument might have some effect: "I trust I shall have spoken perswasion to abundance of sensible and ingenuous men, to som perhaps whom God may raise of these stones to become children of reviving libertie" (YP 7:463).

After Charles II and the Anglican Church were restored in all courtly magnificence, Milton saw several of his regicide friends executed and Puritan dissenters harshly repressed. He himself was for some months in danger of execution for treason and spent some weeks in prison; in the proem to Book Seven of *Paradise Lost* he laments that he has fallen "On evil dayes . . . / In darkness, and with dangers compast round" (*PL* 7.26–27). He had reason to fear that his epic and any high poetry might be drowned out by the "barbarous dissonance" of the Restoration court's Bacchic revelers, and that he might meet the fate of the archetypal bard, Orpheus, who was killed and dismembered by other followers of Bacchus:

> But drive farr off the barbarous dissonance
> Of *Bacchus* and his revellers, the Race
> Of that wild Rout that tore the *Thracian* Bard
> In *Rhodope*, where Woods and Rocks had Eares
> To rapture, till the savage clamor dround
> Both Harp and Voice; nor could the Muse defend
> Her Son. So fail not thou, who thee implores:
> For thou art Heav'nlie, shee an empty dreame.   (7.32–39)

But he does not despair, because he can rely on the protective powers of his muse Urania, who is in part a figure for heavenly aid and inspiration. Nor does he hide or change his politics.

The poem's form makes its first overt political statement. For the first edition in 1667 Milton set aside Virgil's and Tasso's twelve-book epic format and chose instead the ten-book model of the Roman republican poet Lucan. That choice distances Milton's epic from Virgil's celebration of the glorious empire of Augustus predestined by the Gods, and from Tasso's celebration, through the story of the first crusade, of Counter-Reformation hegemony restored over all varieties of rebellion and dissent.[10] It also signals that *Paradise Lost* is not an epic of conquest and empire, though Satan conceives of his adventure in such terms. But another reason for Milton to gesture toward Lucan was surely that royalists had appropriated the Virgilian heroic mode both before and after the Restoration. John Denham's translation in heroic couplets of Book Two of the *Aeneid* under the title, *The Destruction of Troy* (1656), makes Aeneas' narrative of and lament for the death of King Priam and the destruction of Troy resonate with the regicide and the royalist defeat. Denham's poem ends well before Virgil's Book Two does, with a scene of Priam's beheading that evokes the beheading of Charles: "On the cold earth lies th'unregarded King, / A headless Carkass, and a nameless Thing."[11] After the Restoration, in what Laura Knoppers terms the "politics of joy," poets hailed the new era in Virgilian terms as a golden age restored, celebrating Charles II as a new Augustus; his coronation procession was designed as a magnificent Roman Triumph through elaborate Roman arches mythologizing him as Augustus, Aeneas, and Neptune.[12] Dryden's *Astraea Redux* (1660) rings changes on those motifs: "Oh Happy Age! Oh times like those alone / By Fate reserv'd for Great *Augustus* Throne."[13]

Also, Milton probably obtained and had someone read to him Dryden's *Annus Mirabilis*, which appeared in January, 1667.[14] Treating the naval losses and the great fire of 1666, that poem was carefully designed to recoup the king's reputation in the face of intense criticism. Patriarchal imagery covers over his barrenness and profligacy, representing him as a pious and tender father of his people: rebuilding the destroyed navy, directing rescue efforts in the fire, and giving shape to the vision of a reborn and far grander "Augustan" city.[15] With his own epic at some prepublication stage, Milton would have been especially interested in Dryden's essay defending this new model of a heroic poem based on contemporary events and serving royalist interests. Terming his poem "Historical, not Epick," Dryden nonetheless claims that kind as a branch of epic, insisting that his poem's "Actions and Actors are as much Heroick, as any Poem can contain." He also lays claim to the Virgilian legacy: his master, he proclaims, is Virgil and he has "followed him every where."[16] This new claimant to the modern heroic poem would surely goad Milton to offer the fit reader, promptly, his better version of epic. If Milton had not yet given his poem its Lucanian ten-book structure, Dryden's new royalist poem so explicitly claiming Virgil's mantle could have prompted republican Milton to find a formal means of withholding his poem from such Virgilian appropriations, even as he emphasizes in the opening lines of his epic that the true restoration will not be effected by an English Augustus, but must await a divine hero: "Till one greater Man / Restore us, and regain the blissful Seat."

Lucan's unfinished epic, *Pharsalia,* or *The Civil War,* was the font of a counter tradition. It celebrates the resistance of the Roman republic and its heroes, Pompey and Cato, who were finally defeated by the victorious tyrant Caesar in a bloody civil war. But, by ascribing that event to contingency and chance, not the Gods, and by having the spirit of the butchered Pompey enter into the future tyrannicide, Brutus (9.1–17), Lucan suggests an ongoing struggle against Caesarism.[17] Lucan's own career was readily assimilated to his story, since he was forced to commit suicide at age twenty-six for involvement in a botched conspiracy against Caesar's infamous successor, Nero. As David Norbrook has demonstrated, by Milton's time Lucan's epic was firmly associated with antimonarchical and republican politics through several editions and translations, especially the English version by the Long Parliament's historian-to-be, Thomas May (1627).[18]

Milton did organize his poem in twelve books for the second edition, 1674, by the simple expedient of splitting two books and adding a few lines. He did not intend to blunt the political import, but rather, I would suggest, to reclaim the central epic tradition for his better subject and nobler heroism, at a time when royalist Virgilianism was no longer such an issue. While Milton's poem includes the full range of topics and conventions common to the Homeric and Virgilian epic tradition,[19] it explicitly rejects the traditional epic subject (wars and empire) and the traditional representation of the epic hero as the epitome of courage and battle prowess. *Paradise Lost* celebrates, not an emperor or a debauched Charles II, but the only true king and kingdom in heaven; not the heroism of war but the "better fortitude / Of Patience and Heroic Martyrdom"; not a Virgilian earthly empire and new golden age but an earthly paradise now tragically lost. His protagonists are a domestic pair, Adam and Eve; the scene of their action is a pastoral garden, not a battle-field;[20] and their primary challenge is, "under long obedience tri'd" (7.159), to make themselves, their marital relationship, and their garden (as the nucleus of the human world) ever more perfect. The combats they fight and lose—but will ultimately win in conjunction with the "greater man" Christ— are moral and spiritual. Milton's epic in twelve books formally enlists that noblest genre in the service of his dearest values.

Another formal element of Milton's poem, blank verse, also carried political resonance, since rhyme, and especially the heroic couplet, had become the norm for heroic poetry and drama in the Restoration court. In *Annus Mirabilis* Dryden claimed that, while classical unrhymed verse gave poets more freedom, his four-line stanzas in alternating rhyme are "more noble, and of greater dignity, both for the sound and number, then any other verse in use amongst us."[21] Also, by coincidence Dryden's essay *Of Dramatick Poesie* was registered with the Stationers the same month as Milton's epic, August 1667, and it probably greeted the reading public at about the same time.[22] At the end of the essay Neander, Dryden's persona, makes a case for rhyme as the distinguishing excellence of modern poets and the best verse form for tragedy and heroic drama.[23] He affirms, categorically, that "Blank Verse is acknowledg'd to be too low for a Poem, nay more, for a paper of verses; but if too low for an ordinary Sonnet, how much more for Tragedy"— or for epic, he implies, since he considers drama and epic to be of the same genus.[24] Moreover, in the preface to the work Dryden notes that rhyme enjoys the favor of the court, "the last and surest judge of writing."[25] If

Milton's printer Samuel Simmons recognized that in this cultural milieu readers expected rhyme and needed an explanation for its absence, Milton was no doubt happy to take up the gauntlet thrown down by his erstwhile colleague in Cromwell's Secretariat, now the rising star on the poetic and critical horizon. He did so for the 1668 printing, challenging not only the new poetic norms but also the debased court culture and royalist politics that nurture them:

> The measure is *English* Heroic Verse without Rime, as that of *Homer* in *Greek,* and of *Virgil* in *Latin*; Rime being no necessary Adjunct or true Ornament of Poem or good Verse, in longer Works especially, but the Invention of a barbarous Age, to set off wretched matter and lame Meeter; grac't indeed since by the use of some famous modern Poets, carried away by Custom, but much to thir own vexation, hindrance, and constraint to express many things otherwise, and for the most part worse then else they would have exprest them. Not without cause therefore some both *Italian* and *Spanish* Poets of prime note have rejected Rime both in longer and shorter Works, as have also long since our best *English* Tragedies, as a thing of it self, to all judicious ears, trivial and of no true musical delight. . . . This neglect then of Rime so little is to be taken for a defect, though it may seem so perhaps to vulgar Readers, that it rather is to be esteem'd an example set, the first in *English,* of ancient liberty restored to Heroic Poem from the troublesome and modern bondage of Riming. (sigs. a 3v–a 4)

This language elevates Milton's blank verse above the practices of the barbarous gothic age and the vulgar taste of the present, and associates it not only with ancient poetic liberty but also, as Steven Zwicker notes, with the restoration of English liberty from the modern bondage of Stuart tyranny.[26] Milton makes his choice of blank verse the aesthetic complement to republican politics and culture.

Early responses to the poem indicate that it aroused political suspicion. As required by the Press Act of 1662 that revived the system of censorship for all books and periodicals, Milton submitted the *Paradise Lost* manuscript to the censors before its initial publication, and the censor, Thomas Tomkyns, who was a royalist, a high churchman, and domestic chaplain to the Archbishop of Canterbury, Gilbert Sheldon, reportedly denied it a license at first.[27] That censor would surely check carefully for subversion a poem by the notorious Milton, whose regicide and divorce treatises were still being cited and vigorously denounced in the press in the mid-1660s.[28] John Toland reports that Tomkyns objected especially to a passage in Book One:

> I must not forget that we had like to be eternally depriv'd of this Treasure by the Ignorance or Malice of the Licenser; who, among other frivolous Exceptions, would needs suppress the whole Poem for imaginary Treason in the following lines.

----------As when the Sun new risen
Looks thro the Horizontal misty Air
Shorn of his Beams, or from behind the Moon
In dim Eclipse disastrous Twilight sheds
On half the Nations, and with fear of change
Perplexes Monarchs.   (*EL*, 180; *PL* 1.594–99)

At first blush it seems odd that Tomkyns singled out these lines rather than, say, the overt republicanism of the Nimrod passage in Michael's prophecy (12.24–71). But the recent series of English calamities—the Great Plague of 1665, the Great Fire of 1666, and losses in the Dutch Wars—were being read as God's punishment for the nation's sins and linked with dire predictions attaching to comets and a recent solar eclipse (June 22, 1666), which church and government were eager to suppress. As one tract put it, eclipses are always attended by astounding effects such as "the death of Kings and Great persons, alterations of Governments, change of Laws."[29] However, Tomkyns probably thought that this complex poem posed little danger to the masses by comparison with the more overt subversion from dissenters' sermons and treatises, and so was prevailed upon to give it his (undated) imprimatur in late 1666 or early 1667.[30] The poem may have escaped harsher scrutiny because it was submitted, perhaps by Milton's design, at a time of weakened government and relaxed severities against nonconformists in the wake of the plague, the fire, and the fall of Charles's chief minister, Clarendon.[31] The first documented response to the poem, in letters from the royalist John Beale to John Evelyn, points to the Nimrod passage as evidence that "Milton holds to his old Principle"; he also found the "blasphemies" of the devils deeply disturbing.[32]

The early publication history of the poem also testifies to uneasiness about it and its author. *Paradise lost, a Poem in Tenne Bookes* was registered with the Stationers by Samuel Simmons on August 20, 1667; Milton is identified only by his initials, J. M.[33] The text of the first edition, a quarto, was well printed, in an attractive format and on good paper—gilt edged in some copies. But readers may well have been surprised at the stark presentation of the poem in the first three issues: it had no dedicatory or commendatory verses, no epistle from author or bookseller, no prefatory matter at all to engage the reader's interest or sympathy—not even the bookseller's name. That Milton's poem was sent forth into the world bare and unaccommodated suggests that the likely presenters and commenders had qualms about associating themselves with the rebel Milton's return to print. Yet Milton may have been willing enough to see his poem presented without the usual apparatus, wishing to separate himself decisively from the system of patronage and to present himself, as he had in his prose tracts, as a new kind of author in the market-oriented system aptly termed by Peter Lindenbaum a "Republican Mode of Literary Production."[34] Over the next three years the first edition was issued with six different title pages and distributed by six different booksellers—a strategy for making it more widely available, spreading the risk, and promoting sales.[35] The changing title pages with changing styles indicate continued anxiety on Simmons's part that a poem by the notorious Commonwealth polemicist might be shunned by prospective readers as treasonous or heretical. The title pages of the first three issues include, in large type, a message intended to reassure them: "Licenced, and Entred according to order." Two title pages dated 1667 bear Milton's name, but the second reduces that name to very small type, as if to avoid calling attention to it; a third (1668) identifies the author only as J. M.[36] With the fourth title page (1668) Simmons had gained confidence: Milton's name appears in full as does, for the first time, Simmons's name as printer, and the "Licenced, and Entred" line is omitted.

Milton's Arminianism, so vigorously defended in *De Doctrina Christiana*,[37] lies at the heart of the poem's politics, even as it also grounds the theodicy which is the stated intent of *Paradise Lost:* To "justifie the wayes of God to men." As a poet Milton works out that theodicy, not primarily by theological argument, but by the imaginative vision the entire poem presents of human life and the human condition as good, despite the tragedy of the Fall and "all our woe." That seems a quixotic, though also rather wonderful, affirmation from a poet who endured the agony of total blindness throughout his most creative years and experienced the utter defeat of the political cause to which he gave over twenty years of his life. But that continued belief in the goodness of the human condition is inextricably linked with the ideas of human freedom, moral responsibility, and especially the capacity for growth and change that make education, and politics, still possible for Milton.

Milton's politics are embedded in his representations of hell, heaven, and Eden, all of which challenge readers' stereotypes, then and now. All reflect aspects of human society and all are in process: their respective physical conditions are fitted to the beings that inhabit them, but the inhabitants then interact with and shape their environments, creating societies in their own images. By representing both Satan and God as monarchs and portraying Satan as a self-styled grand rebel against what he calls the "tyranny of heaven,"[38] Milton directly confronts the familiar royalist analogies—God and the king, Satan and the Puritan revolutionaries—and teaches his readers to find those analogies entirely false. The royalist analogy was spelled out very clearly in James I's celebrated speech to Parliament in 1609:

Kings are justly called Gods, for that they exercise in a manner or resemblance of Divine power upon earth. . . . They make and unmake their subjects: they have power of raising, and casting downe: of life, and of death: Judges over all their subjects, and in all causes, and yet accomptable to none but God onely. . . . Kings are not onely God's Lieutenants upon earth, and sit upon God's throne, but even by God himself they are called Gods.[39]

Continuing the analogy, James declared that as it would be blasphemy to "dispute what God may doe" so "is it sedition in Subjects, to dispute what a King may do in the height of his power." Milton's polemic antagonist Salmasius applied that analogy to Charles I: "If we lift up our eyes to the sovereign patron of all things, we will find that this fashion of commanding [absolute monarchy] is copied from that of God, who is the sole Sovereign of the world as he is therein the sole maker of it."[40] A few weeks before the Restoration, Matthew Griffith preached on Proverb 24:1: "My Son, feare God, and the King, and medle not with them that be seditious," deriving the familiar royalist analogy from its terms: "God is an heavenly King, and eternal . . . but the King is an earthly, and dying God . . . And yet in a qualified sence, they are both *Gods,* and both *Kings.*"[41] Royalists commonly described the king as God's anointed and his vicegerent on earth, thereby making revolution against the king rebellion against God. As Sharon Achinstein illustrates, after the regicide and in the months just before and after the Restoration several royalist treatises described "parliament in hell" scenes in which famous revolutionaries—Bradshaw, Vane, Cromwell, Nedham, and sometimes Milton— join forces with Satan to carry out the English revolution.[42]

Milton's treatises not only deny the analogy between the Heavenly King and earthly kings but also charge earthly monarchs with inspiring idolatry precisely because they seek to imitate God's rule. He also insists that God's preferred government for humans is a republic. A few examples must suffice. Answering Salmasius' claim that monarchy was patterned on the example of one God, Milton asks rhetorically in his *Defense:* "who, in fact, is worthy of holding on earth power like that of God but some person who far surpasses all others and even resembles God himself in goodness and wisdom? The only such person, as I believe, is the Son of God whose coming we look for" (YP 4:427–28). Milton's *Eikonoklastes* is a book-long critique of what he calls the peoples' "civil kinde of Idolatry in idolizing thir Kings," ascribing it to the "servility" taught them by prelates and Presbyterian ministers, and to King Charles's complicity in making himself an idol in *Eikon Basilike.*[43] In the *Ready and Easy Way* (1660) Milton finds evidence of God's disapproval of monarchy in the much-debated text in 1 Samuel 8, in which the Israelites ask God for a king and God chastises them for wanting to replace his kingship over them with that of gentilish kings who will be tyrants; he also finds that

Christ's reproof to the sons of Zebedee (Matthew 20:25–27) shows his strong preference for republics:

A free Commonwealth [is] not only held by wisest men in all ages the noblest, the manliest, the equalest, the justest government . . . most cherishing to vertue and true religion, but also (I may say it with greatest probabilitie) planely commended, or rather enjoind by our Saviour himself, to all Christians, not without remarkable disallowance and the brand of *gentilism* upon kingship. God in much displeasure gave a king to the *Israelites*, and imputed it a sin to them that they sought one: but *Christ* apparently forbids his disciples to admitt of any such heathenish government: *the kings of the gentiles*, saith he, *exercise lordship over them; . . . but ye shall not be so; but he that is greatest among you, let him be as the younger; and he that is chief, as he that serveth*. . . That he speaks of civil government, is manifest. (7:424)

Earthly kingship is idolatry in that the king usurps a role belonging only to God and his Son, and it is tyranny because the king exercises wrongful dominion over those who are "for the most part every way equal or superior to himself" (YP 7:429). Magistrates in a Commonwealth, Milton declares, "walk the streets as other men, may be spoken to freely, familiarly, friendly, without adoration. Wheras a king must be ador'd like a Demigod, with a dissolute and haughtie court about him" (YP 7:425). Kingship rightly belongs only to Christ, "our true and rightfull and only to be expected King, only worthie as he is our only Saviour, the Messiah, the Christ, the only heir of his eternal father, the only by him anointed and ordaind since the work of our redemption finishd, Universal Lord of all mankinde" (YP 7:445). On this understanding, kings themselves are the greatest rebels against God, and rebelling against kings may be piety to God.

This is the perception Milton asks the readers of *Paradise Lost* to adopt as, in Books One and Two, he portrays hell as a monarchy in the making, with royalist politics, perverted language, perverse rhetoric, political manipulation, and demagoguery. He presents hell first in traditional terms, with Satan and his crew chained on a lake of fire. But they soon rise up and begin to found a society: they mine gold and gems, build a government center (Pandemonium), hold a parliament, dispatch Satan on a mission of exploration and conquest, explore their spacious and varied though sterile landscape, engage in martial games and parades, perform music, compose epic poems, and argue hard philosophical questions. Hell's monarch, Satan, is not God's vicegerent but his presumptuous imitator: "To reign is worth ambition though in Hell: / Better to reign in Hell, then serve in Heav'n" (1.262–63). Satan has some claim to kingship according to the theory by which Milton and others justified rule by one who is out of all measure superior to the rest: he is "By merit rais'd / To that bad eminence" (2.5–6); and he readily assumes "as great a share / Of hazard as of honour" when (in parody of the Son's offer to die for fallen humankind) he offers to go as hell's emissary to subvert Adam and Eve. But his superiority is only relative: it bears no comparison to that of God over his creatures, or that of the Son of God who sacrifices himself for them. Satan's ambition has led him, the narrator reports, to "set himself in Glory above his Peers." To reinforce the evil of kingship, Milton's hell abounds in kings. Death, Satan's son by incestuous intercourse with his daughter Sin, wears "the likeness of a Kingly Crown" (2.673) and claims hell as his realm: "Where I reign King, and to enrage thee more, / Thy King and Lord" (2.678–79). Moloch, introduced first as the idol he will become in human history, is termed a "horrid king besmear'd with blood" (1.392). And Belial is introduced in terms of his continuing reign on earth in kingly courts:

> In Courts and Palaces he also Reigns
> And in luxurious Cities, where the noyse
> Of riot ascends above their loftiest Towrs,
> And injury and outrage.   (1.497–500)

During his long reign, the sons of Belial, "flown with insolence and wine" (1.502), riot not only in Sodom but also in Restoration England.

Pandemonium is "the high Capital / Of Satan and his Peers" (1.755–56); within it the "great Seraphic Lords and Cherubim" sit in conclave while the common angels, reduced to pygmy size, swarm without (1.777–97). The parliament in hell evokes, not a republican House of Commons, but a House of Lords controlled by a monarch.[44] Satan always addresses these superior angels as "Peers" and by their noble titles: "Powers and Dominions, Deities of Heav'n" (2.11); "Thrones, Dominations, Princedomes, Virtues, Powers" (5.772). He opens his council in hell in the style of an oriental sultan, a figure for the most extreme absolutism, luxury, and tyranny: "High on a Throne of Royal State, which far / Outshon the wealth of *Ormus* and of *Ind*, / Or where the gorgeous East with richest hand / Showrs on her Kings *Barbaric* Pearl and Gold / Satan exalted sat" (2.1–8). In the uneasy position of defeated military leader and de facto ruler, he begins by summarizing the grounds—all of them true enough—upon which his leadership of the angels was founded: first, "just right, and the fixt Laws of Heav'n" (legitimacy); next, their own "free choice" to follow him; and finally, his proven merit in counsel and in battle (2.18–20). In Book One he is addressed or referred to in terms relating to that leadership role, as "Chief of many Throned Powers" (128), "Leader of those Armies bright" (272), "their General" (337), "Their great Commander" (358), "Their dread commander" (589). But then, by a piece of rhetorical legerdemain, he simply assumes that these bases for *leadership* justify his assumption of *kingship*, and he proceeds to claim a "safe unenvied Throne / Yielded with full consent" (2.23–24). However, he cannot appeal to Heaven's laws to legitimate such a power grab, and he does not risk another free vote. Rather, he relies on the Hobbesian principle that a society's passive acceptance of a sovereign's power and protection establishes a binding social contract. Like a Machiavellian prince, he seeks to secure a new throne by manipulating his followers, and works to advance his goal—continued war against God—by Machiavellian force and fraud, "open Warr or covert guile" (2.41). He constructs his parliament as Charles I constructed his, as a consultative body only, not an independent legislature: "who can advise, may speak" (2.42). When the powerful peers venture to debate their own agendas, Satan sways the council to his will through the agency of his chief minister and spokesman, Beelzebub (Milton's readers might think of Strafford or Laud or Clarendon). The scene closes with Satan accorded divine honors: "Towards him they bend / With awful reverence prone; and as a God / Extoll him equal to the highest in Heav'n" (2.477–79). This is an exaggerated version of the idolatry Milton regularly associated with the Stuart ideology of divine kingship. As monarch of hell Satan alludes to Charles I but also to other Stuart Kings and to monarchs generally—including, perhaps, Cromwell, insofar as he was assuming quasi-monarchical powers and trappings in 1657, under the new constitution, *The Humble Petition and Advice;* he was also offered and was thought to be considering a crown.[45]

Some evidence that Milton's careful readers recognized his radical rewriting of the royalist "parliament of hell" trope is afforded by John Dryden's *State of Innocence*. Sometime in the 1670s Dryden sought and won Milton's permission to turn his epic into a drama in rhymed couplets—"Tagg'd his Lines" as Milton put it with wry humor (*EL,* 296). If Milton encountered the result he would not have been pleased. Not only were his soaring lines tamed and bounded by rhyme; Dryden also took care to restore the parliament in hell trope to the royalist meaning it conventionally carried, and to reinstate the royalist analogy between divine and human kingship. He does this by dividing Satan's speeches among several fallen angels (including new characters not in Milton's poem) so that the entire community, which he terms a "senate" or "States-General of Hell," plots the continuing rebellion against heaven and the seduction of Adam and Eve. In Milton's poem, rebellion is the act of a would-be usurping monarch against the only rightful kings, God and his vicegerent Son; for royalist Dryden it is the act of a parliament rising against a divine king, in analogy to the English revolution against a king claiming office by Divine Right.

In the temptation scene in heaven, when Satan tempts his followers to revolt after the Son is proclaimed king, Milton gives to Satan the rhetoric of republican virtue and the rights of a free citizenry that he himself used in the *Tenure of Kings and Magistrates*. In that work, Milton's argument for popular sovereignty and government based on contract begins with the declaration, "No man who knows ought, can be so stupid to deny that all men naturally were borne free, being the image and resemblance of God himself, and were by privilege above all the creatures, born to command and not to obey, and that they liv'd so" until the Fall (YP 3:198–99). It concludes with a declaration that kings and magistrates hold authority from the people, who retain sovereign power fundamentally in themselves, and so have always the right "as oft as they shall judge it for the best, [to] either choose him or reject him, retain him or depose him though no Tyrant, meerly by the liberty and right of free born Men to be govern'd as seems to them best" (YP 3:206). Satan offers a parallel argument:

> Will ye submit your necks, and choose to bend
> The supple knee? ye will not, if I trust
> To know ye right, or if ye know your selves
> Natives and Sons of Heav'n
>
> . . . .
>
> Who can in reason then or right assume
> Monarchie over such as live by right
> His equals, if in power and splendor less,
> In freedome equal? or can introduce
> Law and Edict on us, who without law
> Erre not, much less for this to be our Lord,
> And look for adoration to th'abuse
> Of those Imperial Titles which assert
> Our being ordain'd to govern, not to serve?   (5.787–802)[46]

This surprising republican rhetoric has led some readers to assume that Milton had a measure of sympathy with Satan the revolutionary, or that he had come to repudiate as Satanic the rebellion he had before promoted, or that he here convicts Cromwell of having used republican language to cover personal ambition, or that he intentionally or unintentionally sends a mixed message, confusing the reader.

But as the scene plays out, it demonstrates yet more decisively the fallacy of the royalist claim that rebellion against kings is rebellion against God, by showing that kings and aspirants to kingship are the true rebels. They usurp a role that belongs to God and take his place as false idols: "Affecting all equality with God," Satan addresses the angels from a splendid "Royal seat" high on a mount, like the one from which Messiah was pronounced king (5.756–66). Directly challenging Satan's republican argument, Abdiel underscores the absurdity of the royalist analogy between God and any other monarch: God is absolute monarch of heaven because he created all other beings, and the Son enjoys regal status by God's "just Decree" and as God's agent in Creation. Abdiel makes the crucial distinction that while Satan's republican argument against monarchy on grounds of equality is generally true, it is beside the point here because there can be no equality between Creator and creature:

> But to grant it thee unjust,
> That equal over equals Monarch Reigne:
> Thy self though great and glorious dost thou count,
> Or all Angelic Nature joind in one,
> Equal to him begotten Son, by whom
> As by his Word the mighty Father made
> All things, ev'n thee, and all the Spirits of Heav'n
> By him created in thir bright degrees.   (5.831–36)

Abdiel and Satan continue this political debate on the battlefield as Satan derides the loyal angels "traind up in Feast and Song" for having a servile and slothful spirit such as Milton often ascribed to royal courts and courtiers. The loyal angels will come off badly, Satan scoffs, when they match their "Servilitie" with the rebels' "freedom" (6.164–69). Abdiel counters with the natural law argument Milton spelled out in the *Second Defense* to support Cromwell's Protectorate: monarchy is justified "When he who rules is worthiest, and excells / Them whom he governs"—patently true of God if almost never of other rulers. Abdiel also makes the familiar Miltonic and Platonic distinction that relates liberty and tyranny in the first instance to states of soul, which are then replicated in the state:

> This is servitude,
> To serve th'unwise, or him who hath rebelld
> Against his worthier, as thine now serve thee,
> Thy self not free, but to thy self enthrall'd.   (6.177–81)

It is the followers of aspiring kings, not God's servants, who are servile since they mostly serve rulers enslaved to their own ambitions and passions.

Milton's presentation of the ensuing battle in heaven further identifies earthly kings as rebels against God. Observing that battle from his "gorgeous Throne," Satan is "exalted as a God / . . . Idol of Majesty Divine" (6.99–103). The rebel angels are referred to, significantly, as "Rebel Thrones" (6.199), and Moloch as a "furious King" (6.357). Finally, in sending the Son forth to end the battle, God proclaims that the title of divinely anointed king belongs to him alone: he only is "worthiest to be Heir / Of all things, to be Heir and to be King / By Sacred Unction, thy deserved right" (6.707–9). The reader also knows that the Son will display his superlative merit by his offer to die for fallen man: in Book Three God refers to that offer as proof that he indeed deserves his kingly office, "Found worthiest to be so by being Good, / Farr more then Great or High" (311–12).

Milton affirms republican principles quite explicitly in Book Twelve, as they pertain to the future history of the postlapsarian world. In the exchange between Michael and Adam about Nimrod, monarchy is equated with tyranny because it involves a man usurping over his equals the dominion that belongs only to God. Reporting that Nimrod subjected men to his empire by force, Michael explains the epithet ascribed to him, "mightie Hunter," in terms that associate him with Charles I's claims of Divine Right kingship and castigation of his opponents as "rebels": Nimrod, Michael states, claimed "from Heav'n . . . second Sovrantie; / And from Rebellion shall derive his name, / Though of Rebellion others he accuse" (12.33–37). Adam's immediate and fierce denunciation of Nimrod shows him to be, in Norbrook's terms, "instinctually republican."[47] He understands and appropriately applies the republican theory of Milton's *Tenure:*

> O execrable Son so to aspire
> Above his Brethren, to himself assuming
> Authoritie usurpt, from God not giv'n:
> He gave us onely over Beast, Fish, Fowl
> Dominion absolute; that right we hold
> By his donation; but Man over men
> He made not Lord; such title to himself
> Reserving, human left from human free.   (12.64–71)

Michael commends Adam for "justly" abhorring this descendant but reminds him—in terms reminiscent of many Milton tracts—that political liberty depends on inner liberty, which is the product of reason and virtue, and that the Fall allows "upstart Passions" to "catch the Government / From Reason, and to servitude reduce / Man till then free" (12.83–90). That analysis accounts for the Stuart Restoration and for absolute monarchy wherever it exists: inner servility leads to deprivation of outward freedom either as a natural consequence or as a punishment from God—but that does not justify tyranny or imply that it should not be resisted. Milton's poem means to help create a virtuous and liberty-loving people who might deserve, and so take steps to gain, a free commonwealth.

Heaven, of course, is not a republic but an absolute monarchy: it has no parliament, only assemblies in which the angels hear divine pronouncements or a dialogue between God and the Son. The imagery Milton uses to portray God, and the attributes Milton assigns him, often invite association with earthly monarchs, an association that many readers find disconcerting. That the Bible uses such imagery to portray God is a partial but not a sufficient explanation. A better one is that by this association Milton definitively removes absolute monarchy from earth to heaven, as the only place it rightly belongs.

Milton's heaven combines courtly magnificence and pastoral nature. Though hierarchical, it is designed to promote happiness, growth in virtue, and responsible citizenship in all its inhabitants. In this complex social order, God, though an absolute monarch, delegates power (presumably for merit) to many "Scepter'd Angels," described as "Princes, whom the supreme King / Exalted to such power, and gave to rule, / Each in his Hierarchie, the Orders bright" (1.734–37). Heaven's citizens of all ranks engage in a wide range of activities: elegant hymns suited to various occasions, martial parades, warfare, pageantry, masque dancing, feasting, lovemaking, political debate, the education of Adam and Eve, the protection of Eden. Their diverse pleasures and responsibilities give the lie to Satan's disparagement of their life as courtly servility. As messengers, Raphael and Michael have large liberty to decide how to carry out their educative and admonitory missions to Adam and Eve. Angels guard the Garden of Eden and its inhabitants against violent attack, though they cannot secure Adam and Eve against temptation. At God's command they fight heroically against the rebels threatening their society, though they cannot extirpate this evil by their own military might. That fact, along with the grotesque cannon-barrages and hill-hurlings, the near-destruction of Heaven's lovely landscape, and Michael's later denunciation (12.688–99) of the giants who sought glory in battle and conquest, suggests to some that Milton has become a pacifist, or that he means to repudiate the recent armed rebellion in England.[48] But these scenes rather invite a sober estimation of the costs and limitations of warfare, while allowing its necessity as a response to blatant evil. They undermine the epic ideal of *aristeia*, battle glory, by demonstrating that war is always, in its essence and its effects, tragic, not glorious. They also demonstrate war's limitations: however good the cause, however heroic the warriors, however divinely authorized and necessary—as the war in heaven clearly was, and as Milton always thought the English war had been—war cannot by itself eradicate evil.

The angels' mix of heroic, georgic, and pastoral activities and modes offers an ideal of wholeness, but an ideal involving process, not stasis, complexity not simplicity, and the continuous and active choice of good rather than the absence of evil. Most exegetes held that the loyal angels always were unable to swerve from grace, or that they at least became so after withstanding Satan's temptation. But Milton's angels, as Raphael explains to Adam, are exactly like prelapsarian humans in that they must continually and freely choose to act from obedience and love:

My self and all th'Angelic Host, that stand
In sight of God enthron'd, our happie state
Hold, as you yours, while our obedience holds;
On other surety none; freely we serve,
Because wee freely love, as in our will
To love or not; in this we stand or fall.   (5.535–40)

Also, though Milton's God does not hold parliaments, his decrees invite free
and thoughtful, not blind, obedience. At times he stages scenes that require
active participation by his creatures, to determine just what the decree means
for them, as is the case with the Dialogue in Heaven between God and the
Son, who in Milton's antitrinitarian theology is not omniscient or coequal to
God (3.80–343).[49] God first explains and defends his "high Decree" that
mandates contingency and freedom from all eternity and thereby secures to
both angels and humans a genuine freedom of choice, whose results he
foresees but does not determine. Responding to the dilemma God sets when
he foresees the Fall—the apparent conflict between Justice and Mercy that
seems to require damnation of Adam and Eve—"Dye hee or Justice Must"—
the Son works out for himself how Justice and Mercy might be reconciled
through his own sacrificial act and freely makes the appropriate offer. In
much the same way God stages a scene in which Adam must defend his
desire for and need of a mate in the face of God's apparent dismissal of his
request (8.354–451).

Another issue probed in Milton's epic is the politics of empire and
colonization. Language relating to those enterprises came readily to him,
given its contemporary currency.[50] Eden is described in terms often used of
the new world: lush, beautiful, prodigeously prolific, requiring to be culti-
vated and tamed. And both God and Satan seek to hold it as a satellite
colony.[51] However, God's relation to Eden is in virtually all respects the
obverse of Satan's. God created the lush garden and its inhabitants, he does
not discover it and conquer them. The epithet "sovran Planter" (5.641),
might seem to associate him with the plantation of settlements, but in context
it defines him as the gardener who produced the delights of Adam and Eve's
garden. The purpose of the angelic military guard in Eden is not to control
the inhabitants but to ward off external force. God forbids Adam and Eve one
tree but allows them free use of all else. He does not need or want any of
Eden's products but leaves them wholly to the inhabitants, whose labor he
requires, not for himself but because they themselves need to control the
garden's prolific growth and take responsibility for their environment. God
does not intend to settle any of the heavenly host on earth but wants the
inhabitants to increase, multiply, and spread through all the earth, cultivating

it for their own uses. At length he intends to bring Adam and Eve and their descendants to a still better place, heaven.

By contrast, Satan is represented as an explorer bent on conquest and colonization. He sets out courageously, like the sailors in Camoëns' *Lusiads*, to sail through an uncharted sea (Chaos), enduring as-yet-unknown dangers and difficulties. The fallen angels in Hell think of him as "their great adventurer" gone to seek "Forrein Worlds" (10.440–41). He discovers the Paradise of Fools and prepares for a future colony there. He discovers the paradise of Eden and intends, after conquering Adam and Eve, to settle the fallen angels in it. He practices fraud on Eve and causes her to lose her rightful domain. Upon first seeing Adam and Eve, he makes clear in soliloquy that he means to use Eden and its inhabitants for his own purposes, that his excursion aims at empire-building and the takeover of this idyllic place:

> League with you I seek,
> And mutual amitie so streight, so close,
> That I with you must dwell, or you with me
> Henceforth.   (4.375–79)

He justifies his enterprise by "public reason just, / Honour and Empire with revenge enlarg'd"—characterized by the narrator as "necessitie, / The Tyrants plea" (4.389–94).

This does not mean that Milton thought all exploration and colonization in the Americas necessarily Satanic, though, as with Satan's degradation of various versions of heroism, his language indicates how susceptible such enterprises are to evil purposes. Milton does formally link Satan's depredations with those of Spain: Michael's prophecy refers to "as yet unspoil'd / *Guiana*, whose great Citie *Geryons* Sons / Call *El Dorado*" (11.409–11), an allusion to Spanish conquests and exploitations of new world lands and peoples in their search for gold.[52] As for the English conquest and colonization of Ireland, nothing in *Paradise Lost* suggests that Milton has changed his mind about his earlier vigorous defense of that enterprise on the score of Irish barbarism and savagery in his *Observations upon the Articles of Peace, Made and Concluded with the Irish Rebels* (1649). Still, the imaginative force of Milton's representations may reach beyond his conscious intention. As the Genesis text prescribes, Milton's God gave Adam and Eve absolute dominion over the earth— a gift often cited in contemporary tracts to justify exploitation and subjugation of other races. But Milton does not allow such a gloss, for Michael's denunciation of Nimrod explicitly forbids such dominion to humans.

What then of the politics of Eden?[53] At the center of his epic, Milton set a richly imagined representation of prelapsarian love, marriage, and domestic society. It is a brilliant though sometimes conflicted representation, in which Milton's ideal of companionate marriage, contemporary views of gender hierarchy, his own life experiences, and his deeply felt psychic needs strain against each other. Some authoritative statements in the poem affirm gender hierarchy. Adam, after admitting to Raphael his unsettling passion for Eve, states that he knows she is inferior to himself in qualities both of mind and body; Raphael confirms Adam's judgment; and the Son, judging Adam after the Fall, reiterates that Adam's proper role is to act as Eve's head and governor:

> Was shee thy God, that her thou didst obey
> Before his voice, or was shee made thy guide,
> Superior, or but equal, that to her
> Thou did'st resigne thy Manhood, and the Place
> Wherein God set thee above her made of thee,
> And for thee, whose perfection far excell'd
> Hers in all real dignitie: Adornd
> She was indeed, and lovely to attract
> Thy Love, not thy Subjection, and her Gifts
> Were such as under Government well seem'd,
> Unseemly to beare rule, which was thy part
> And person, had'st thou known thy self aright.   (10.145–56)

Yet this conventional view of gender hierarchy is destabilized by elements of Milton's imaginative vision that invite a more egalitarian conception: if Milton could not fully work through these conflicts, he did provide liberalizing perspectives upon which later feminists could and often did build.[54] One such is the poem's unusually fluid concept of hierarchy, the concomitant of its monism: if, as Raphael explains to Adam and Eve, humans and angels differ only in degree, and humans can expect the gradual refinement of their natures to angelic status, the distance between male and female on the hierarchical scale must be minimal. Moreover, the fact that creatures hold their place on that scale "As neerer to him [God] plac't or neerer tending" (5.476) allows that their final places will depend on how they develop, whither they "tend." In Milton's unique representation of the state of innocence, Adam and Eve are both expected to grow, change, and develop in virtue by properly pruning and directing their own erroneous apprehensions and sometimes unruly impulses as well as their burgeoning garden.

Another complicating element is Milton's advanced notion of companionate marriage, argued in the divorce tracts and dramatized in more gracious terms in the poem. Adam asks God for an equal life partner: "Among unequals what societie / Can sort, what harmonie or true delight? / . . . Of fellowship I speak / Such as I seek, fit to participate / All rational delight" (8.383–91). In answer God states that he always intended exactly such a mate for Adam, "Thy likeness, thy fit help, thy other self, / Thy wish exactly to thy hearts desire" (8.450–51). Consonant with this vision of marriage, Adam and Eve's roles and talents are not sharply segregated by gender, as convention would dictate. Eve performs certain domestic tasks, ornamenting the couple's bedroom bower and preparing and serving the noonday meal when Raphael visits. Otherwise she shares with Adam in all the physical and intellectual activities of Edenic life and she enjoys certain areas of autonomy and initiative. The couple take equal responsibility for their world, laboring together to maintain its ecosystem and keep the garden from returning to wild. Unique to Milton is the role he assigns to Eve in naming the plants of Eden, and in thereby sharing in the authority over nature, the intuitive knowledge, and the power of symbolization that Adam's naming of the animals signifies, albeit in lesser degree. She also receives the same education as Adam, though not in the same manner. As decorum dictated, Adam asked Raphael questions (often framing them faultily) while Eve listened in silence, sitting at a distance but within earshot: for both, therefore, the Edenic curriculum included ontology, metaphysics, moral philosophy, history, epic poetry, and divine revelation.[55] Eve missed the astronomy lesson when she left to tend her flowers, but the Miltonic bard insists that she both delighted in and was fully capable of that knowledge and would obtain it later in discussion (mixed with kisses) with Adam—thereby gaining the educational benefit of dialogic interaction that Adam enjoyed with Raphael (8.48–50). She is portrayed as an accomplished reasoner and debater in the marital dispute in Book Nine, she often proposes issues for discussion and initiates action, and she constructs the first autobiographical narrative as she recounts her earliest recollections—with the implications autobiography carries of coming to self-awareness, probing one's own subjectivity, interpreting one's own experience, and so becoming an author (4.449–91). Also, she is as much a lyric poet as Adam—perhaps more so—with her elegant love lyric to Adam that begins "Sweet is the breath of morn" (4.641–56) and her lament-plea to Adam that opens the way to repentance, forgiveness, and reconciliation.

Milton further destabilizes the ideology of gender hierarchy by his treatment of Adam and Eve's different experiences and psychology. As a striking example, they offer very different accounts of their creation, first meeting, and marriage, producing versions of self that evidently reflect Milton's reading of female and male psychology. Eve tells of constructing herself first through pleasurable self-contemplation mistaken as response to another shape in the water, and then, after brief continued attraction to that "wat'ry image," freely accepting a marriage relationship urged by two who claim paternity over her, God and Adam. But she evidences no felt sense of need or lack, as Adam does, and her narrative resists interpretation of her story as a simple submission to patriarchy.[56] As she recounts the words spoken to her by God, they almost suggest that Adam was made for her, not vice versa, and they almost seem to institute matriarchy, not patriarchy:

> hee
> Whose image thou art, him thou shalt enjoy
> Inseparablie thine, to him shalt beare
> Multitudes like thy self [not, like himself], and thence be call'd
> Mother of human Race.   (4.471–76)

By contrast, Adam's narrative (8.355–99) testifies to a psychological and emotional neediness that in some ways undercuts gender hierarchy and recalls Milton's similar testimony in the divorce tracts.[57] Recounting his eloquent pleas with God for a mate, Adam emphasizes his keenly felt sense of incompleteness and loneliness; and he explains Eve's hesitation not as she herself did but by projecting onto her a serene consciousness of self-worth "That would be woo'd, and not unsought be won" and a demeanor of "obsequious Majestie" in accepting his suit (8.500–10). He also expresses a tension between what he "knows" of Eve's inferiority to him and what he experiences when he is with her:

> when I approach
> Her loveliness, so absolute she seems
> And in herself compleat, so well to know
> Her own, that what she wills to do or say,
> Seems wisest, vertuousest, discreetest, best;
>
> . . . .
>
> Authority and Reason on her waite,
> As one intended first, not after made
> Occasionally; and to consummate all,
> Greatness of mind and nobleness thir seat
> Build in her loveliest, and create an awe
> About her, as a guard Angelic plac't.   (8.546–59)

After Eve's fall, Adam's instant decision to fall with her arises from his desperate fear of a return to his lonely life before she came to him:

> How can I live without thee, how forgoe
> Thy sweet Converse and Love so dearly joyn'd,
> To live again in these wilde Woods forlorn?
> Should God create another *Eve,* and I
> Another Rib afford, yet loss of thee
> Would never from my heart.   (9.908–13)

If the politics of Milton's Eden remain uneasily hierarchical and patriarchal, he does dare to bring that ideology up against the testimony of experience and allow the conflicts to stand. He also explores through Adam and Eve the fundamental challenge of any love relationship: the uneasy, inevitable, and ultimately creative tension between autonomy and interdependence.

Milton designed the last segment of his poem, Michael's prophecy of the future history of humankind, around the issue of postlapsarian education for Adam, Eve, and the reader. Adam and Eve have to learn how to interpret the messianic promise of redemption signified by the metaphorical curse on the serpent: that the seed of the woman will bruise his head. But Milton also incorporates into Michael's prophecy the political issue closest to his heart: the misuse of civil power to force consciences. In a long passage that begins with popes and Roman emperors in the early Christian ages and then surveys subsequent history, Michael restates principles Milton urged in *Areopagitica, Of Civil Power, The Likeliest Means, De Doctrina Christiana,* and elsewhere: Christian liberty, the separation of spiritual and civil powers, the inviolability of conscience and individual faith, and the gift of the Spirit to all believers. That long passage also invites application to the harsh repression of Puritan dissent after the Restoration by prelates and magistrates who appropriate to themselves the "Spirit of God, promisd alike and giv'n / To all Beleevers," and who seek to force "Spiritual Lawes by carnal power / On every conscience" (12.519–22). Milton's voice echoes behind Michael's stern judgments:

> What will they then
> But force the Spirit of Grace it self, and binde
> His consort Libertie; what, but unbuild
> His living Temples, built by Faith to stand,
> Thir own Faith not anothers: for on Earth
> Who against Faith and Conscience can be heard
> Infallible? yet many will presume:
> Whence heavie persecution shall arise
> On all who in the worship persevere
> Of Spirit and Truth; the rest, farr greater part,
> Will deem in outward Rites and specious formes
> Religion satisfi'd; Truth shall retire
> Bestruck with slandrous darts, and works of Faith
> Rarely be found.   (12.524–35)

Adam and the reader are also to learn how to respond to the tragic course of history. They are shown, over and over again, one or a few righteous humans standing against the many wicked but at length overwhelmed. Michael sums up that pattern as he comments on the way of the world after Christ's ascension: "so shall the World goe on, / To good malignant, to bad men benigne, / Under her own weight groaning" until Christ's second coming (12.537–51). That tragic vision of an external paradise irretrevably lost, along with the promise of "A paradise within thee, happier farr" might indeed seem a recipe for quietism and retreat from the political arena, but it is not. The thrust of Michael's prophecy is against any kind of passivity, spiritual, moral, or political. He shows instead that in every age the few just have the responsibility to oppose, as God calls them to do so, the Nimrods, or the Pharaohs, or the royalist persecutors of the Church, even though (like the loyal angels in the battle in heaven) they can win no wholly decisive victories and can found no permanent City of God on earth until the Son appears. Michael's history-as-prophecy offers Adam and his progeny examples of two kinds of heroism: heroic martyrdom and heroic action. And Adam learns the lesson. He has come to understand that "suffering for Truths sake / Is fortitude to highest victorie," but also that God often accomplishes great things by unlikely means, "by things deemd weak / Subverting worldly strong" (12.565–70).

Harvard University

NOTES

1. Milton's nephew Edward Phillips saw the lines that now form the opening of Satan's address to the Sun (*PL* 4.32–41) some years before the poem was begun; the speech was then designed for the beginning of a tragedy on the subject of the Fall. See *The Early Lives of Milton*, ed. Helen Darbishire (London, 1932), 72–73 (hereafter, *EL*). John Aubrey had information from Phillips that he had seen the lines intended for a tragedy "about 15 or 16 yeares before ever his Poem was thought of" (*EL*, 13).

2. *PL* 9.26. Here and hereafter I cite book and line number of *Paradise Lost* (1674) from *John Milton's Complete Poetical Works, reproduced in Photographic Facsimile*, ed. Harris Francis Fletcher, 4 vols. (Urbana, 1943–48), vol 3.

3. Phillips's own account is less specific as to the years involved but suggests a somewhat longer period of composition and revision.

4. Thomas Ellwood, *The History of the Life of Thomas Ellwood*, ed. J[oseph] W[yeth] (London, 1714), 233.

5. Blair Worden offers a recent restatement of this common view in "Milton's Republicanism and the Tyranny of Heaven," *Machiavelli and Republicanism*, eds. Gisela Bock, Quentin Skinner, and Maurizio Viroli, (Cambridge, 1990), 244.

6. Joan Bennett, *Reviving Liberty: Radical Christian Humanism in Milton's Great Poems* (Cambridge, Mass., 1989); Laura Lunger Knoppers, *Historicizing Milton: Spectacle, Power, and Poetry in Restoration England* (Athens, Ga., 1994); Sharon Achinstein, *Milton and the Revolutionary Reader* (Princeton, 1994); David Norbrook, *Writing the English Revolution: Poetry, Rhetoric, and Politics, 1627–1660* (Cambridge, 1999).

7. See Barbara K. Lewalski, *Paradise Lost and the Rhetoric of Literary Forms* (Princeton, 1993).

8. Recently argued by Aschah Guibbory in *Ceremony and Community from Herbert to Milton: Literature, Religion, and Cultural Conflict in Seventeenth-Century England* (Cambridge, 1998).

9. *Complete Prose Works of John Milton,* ed. Donald M. Wolfe et al., 8 vols. (New Haven, Conn., 1953–1982), 4:366–67. Subsequent references to Milton's prose are from this edition, hereafter cited parenthetically in the text as YP, followed by volume and page number).

10. See David Quint, *Epic and Empire: Politics and Generic Form From Virgil to Milton* (Princeton, 1992), 21–31, 50–96, 213–47.

11. John Denham, *The Destruction of Troy* (London, 1656). Denham claims to have written it around 1636, but if so, he surely revised it after the regicide. He sets forth as his theory of translation a wish to make Virgil speak "not only as a man of this Nation, but as a man of this age."

12. Knoppers, *Historicizing Milton,* 67–122.

13. John Dryden, *Astraea Redux* (London, 1660), lines 320–21. The epigraph is from Virgil's fourth Eclogue, line 6: "Iam redit et Virgo, redeunt Saturnia regna" (Now the Virgin [Astraea] returns, and the reign of Saturn [the golden age] begins)."

14. Dryden, *Annus Mirabilis: The Year of Wonders* (London, 1667). It was dated in Dryden's prefatory letter to Sir Robert Howard, November 10, 1666.

15. For the skillful rhetoric of that attempt, see Steven N. Zwicker, *Lines of Authority: Politics and English Literary Culture 1649–1689* (Ithaca, N.Y., 1993), 90–107.

16. "An account of the ensuing Poem, in a Letter to the Honorable, Sir Robert Howard," *Annus Mirabilis: The Year of Wonders* (London, 1667), sig. A 5v.

17. See Quint, *Epic and Empire,* 131–57.

18. See Norbrook, *Writing the English Republic,* 23–62. Norbrook traces the association of Lucan with anticourt critique and an aristocratic republicanism in translations of the *Pharsalia* by Arthur Gorges (1614), Hugo Grotius (1614) and Thomas Farnaby (1619), as well as May.

19. Among many studies of such debts, see C. M. Bowra, *From Virgil to Milton* (London, 1944); Francis Blessington, *Paradise Lost and the Classical Epic* (Boston, 1979); and Lewalski, *Paradise Lost and the Rhetoric of Literary Forms.*

20. See Harold Toliver, "Milton's Household Epic," in *Milton Studies* 9, ed. James D. Simmons (Pittsburgh, 1976), 105–20; and T. J. B. Spencer, "*Paradise Lost:* The Anti-Epic," in *Approaches to Paradise Lost: The York Tercentenary Essays,* ed. C. A. Patrides (Toronto, 1968).

21. Letter to Sir Robert Howard, *Annus Mirabilis,* sigs. A5v–A6v.

22. John Dryden, *Of Dramatick Poesie, An Essay* (London, 1668). The bookseller Herringman registered the work in the *Stationers' Register* on August 7, 1667. The title page bears the date 1668, as was usual with late year publications.

23. He is answering the case against rhyme urged by Crites, the dramatist Sir Robert Howard, who was described by John Toland as a "particular Acquaintance" and "a great admirer of *Milton* to his dying day," as well as "a hearty Friend to the Liberty of his Country" and a vigorous critic of the "Heathen and Popish" Anglican clergy (*EL,* 185–86). Howard's strictures against rhyme in drama first appeared in the preface to his *Four New Plays* (London, 1665), sigs a 4v–b 1r, which includes *The Indian Queen* written with Dryden. It sets the topics for Dryden's defence of rhyme in his *Essay.* Howard excuses his own use of rhyme against his principles, "since it was the fashion," and he thought best "as in all indifferent things, not to appear singular."

24. Dryden, *Dramatick Poesie,* 66–67.

25. Ibid., sig. A 3.

26. See Steven N. Zwicker, "Lines of Authority: Politics and Literary Culture in the Restoration," in *Politics of Discourse: The Literature and History of Seventeenth-Century England,* eds. Kevin Sharpe and Steven N. Zwicker (Berkeley, 1987), 249.

27. Shortly after he dealt with Milton's poem Tomkyns published a tractate urging enforced uniformity in religion and strict control of dissenters, to obviate the dangers toleration would pose to political stability. [Thomas Tomkyns], *The Inconveniences of Toleration, or, An Answer to*

a Late Book, Intituled, A Proposition Made to the King and Parliament, for the Safety and Happiness of the King and Kingdom (London, 1667). See also [Thomas Tomkyns], The Rebel's Plea Examined: or Mr. Baxter's Judgment concerning the late War (London, 1660).

28. Eikonoklastes is cited as a "Villanous Book" in Thomas Sprat's Observations on Monsieur de Sorbier's Voyage into England (London, 1665), 58–59; [Pierre Nichole], The Pernicious Consequence of the New Heresie of the Jesuits against the King and the State (London, 1666), sig. A 4v, links Milton and the late republicans with the Jesuits as advocates of regicide. David Lloyd attacked Eikonoklastes in Memoires of the Lives, Actions, Sufferings, and Deaths of those Noble, Reverend, and Excellent Personages that Suffered . . . in our Late Intestine Wars (London, 1668), 221. Also, for seven consecutive years beginning in 1664 "Blind Milton" was mentioned as an object of ridicule in Poor Robin, a satiric almanac.

29. John Gadbury, Vox Solis: or, an Astrological Discourse of the Great Eclipse of the Sun (London, 1667), 2. See Nicholas von Maltzahn, "The First Reception of Paradise Lost (1667)," RES 47 (1996): 481–87.

30. "IMPRIMATUR: Tho. Tomkyns, RRmo. in Christo Patri ac Domino, Dno. Gilberto, Divina Providentia Archiepiscopo Cantuariensi, a sacris domesticis. Richard Royaston. Intr. per Geo: Tokefeilde Ck:" [Let it be Printed: Thomas Tomkyns, one of the religious servants of the most reverend father and lord in Christ, Lord Gilbert, by divine providence Archbishop of Canterbury. Entered by George Tokefield, clerk]," in The Life Records of John Milton, ed. J. Milton French, 5 vols. (New York, 1966), vol. 4, 433–34. The entry is now barely legible in the manuscript. The contract Milton signed with the printer Samuel Simmons on April 27, 1667 describes the poem as "lately licensed to be printed."

31. Maltzhan, "First Reception," 488–89.

32. Also, Beale cannot forget Milton's polemics: "he writes so good verse, that tis pitty he ever wrote in prose." And he mistakenly supposes that the elaborate demonology of the poem shows Milton's harsh Calvinism (British Library MSS, Evelyn Papers, 1EA 12, fal. 71). See Nicholas Von Maltzahn, "Laureate, Republican, Calvinist: An Early Response to Milton and Paradise Lost (1667)," in Milton Studies 29, ed. Albert C. Labriola (Pittsburgh, 1992), 187–94.

33. The entry reads: "Master Sam. Symons. Entred for his copie under the hands of Master Thomas Tomkyns and Master Warden Royston, a booke or copie intituled Paradise lost A Poem in Tenne bookes by J. M." Stationers' Registers, vol. 2, 381.

34. The legal contract Milton signed with Samuel Simmons was for sums that seem roughly consistent with contemporary levels of payment to writers, Lindenbaum, "John Milton and the Republican Mode of Literary Production," in The Yearbook of Literary Studies 21, ed. Andrew Gurr (London, 1991), 121–36. Also see Lindenbaum, "The Poet in the Marketplace: Milton and Samuel Simmons," in Paul G. Stanwood, ed., Of Poetry and Politics: New Essays on Milton and His World (Binghamton, N.Y., 1995), 258. The contract shows Milton exercising an author's right to his intellectual property at a time when copyright was granted only to stationers through entry in the Stationers' Register.

35. The first title page reads: "Paradise lost. A Poem. Written in Ten Books By John Milton. London: Printed, and are to be sold by Peter Parker under Creed Church near Aldgate; And by Robert Boulter at the Turks Head in Bishopsgate-street; And Matthias Walker, under St. Dunstons Church in Fleet-street, 1667." The first three issues list these three booksellers.

36. Von Maltzahn speculates that the poem may have been first presented for sale with the 1668 title page bearing just the initials, since that formula corresponds most closely to entry in the Stationers' Register, and that the 1667 title pages, though printed earlier, were used later. "First Reception," 488.

37. YP 6:151–202 . Also see Lewalski, "Milton and De Doctrina Christiana," in Milton Studies 36, ed. Albert C. Labriola (Pittsburgh, 1998), 203–28.

38. For some cogent analyses of God and Satan as monarchs, see Mary Ann Radzinowicz, "The Politics of *Paradise Lost*," in *Politics of Discourse*, ed. Sharpe and Zwicker, 204–29; Michael Wilding, *Dragons Teeth: Literature in the English Revolution* (Oxford, 1987), 204–58; Stevie Davies, *Images of Kingship in Paradise Lost: Milton's Politics and Christian Liberty* (Columbia, Mo., 1983); and Joan S. Bennett, *Reviving Liberty*, 33–58.

39. James I, *The Political Works of James I*, ed. C. H. McIlwain (Cambridge, Mass., 1918), 307–8.

40. Claude Saumaise [Salmasius], *Defensio Regia, Pro Carolo II* . . . ([The Hague]: Elzevir, 1649), 136 (my translation).

41. Matthew Griffith, *The Fear of God and the King*. London, 1660 (March 25), 53. Milton answered Griffith in *Brief Notes upon a Late Sermon* (London, 1660).

42. See Achinstein, *Milton and the Revolutionary Reader*, 187–99.

43. For historical perspective on this gesture, see Richard F. Hardin, *Civil Idolatry: Desacralization and Monarchy in Spenser, Shakespeare, and Milton* (Newark, 1992).

44. See Wilding, *Dragons Teeth*, 205–31.

45. See Bennett, *Reviving Liberty*, 33–58; and Blair Worden, "Milton's Republicanism and the Tyranny of Heaven," in *Machiavelli and Republicanism*, 242–44.

46. Satan's misapplication of this rhetoric is contextualized by Cataline's exhortation to his greedy and dissolute soldiers, as reported by Sallust: "Awake, then! Lo, here, here before your eyes is the freedom for which you have yearned, and with it riches, honor, and glory . . . unless haply I delude myself and you are content to be slaves rather than to rule" (Sallust, *The War with Cataline*, 20.1–17, trans. J. C. Rolfe [Loeb, Cambridge, Mass., 1965], 35–39).

47. Norbrook, *Writing the English Revolution*, 463.

48. For a critique of this position from another standpoint, see Robert T. Fallon, *Captain or Colonel: The Soldier in Milton's Life and Art* (Columbia, Mo., 1984), 202–34.

49. See *De Doctrina Christiana*, YP 6:203–80; also see Lewalski, "Milton and *De Doctrina Christiana*," in *Milton Studies* 36, ed. Albert C. Labriola (Pittsburgh, 1998), 203–28.

50. For such echoes see especially Quint, *Epic and Empire*, 253–67. J. Martin Evans, in *Milton's Imperial Epic: Paradise Lost and the Discourse of Colonialism* (Ithaca, 1996), argues that the pervasive influence of the conflicted discourses of exploration, Spanish, Portugese, and English produced a conflicted representation of that enterprise in Milton's poem.

51. Evans, *Milton's Imperial Epic*, 77–103, unwarrantably in my view, assimilates Adam and Eve to the condition of indentured servants working for God, or to new world Indians needing to be evangelized and controlled.

52. Spenser had presented Geryon as a type of political tyranny in *The Fairie Queen* 5.10.8–9, associating him specifically with Spain. Montezuma's empire had been spoiled by Cortez and Peru by Pizarro, but the fabulous El Dorado was not yet plundered by the Spanish explorers.

53. For a range of views on this point, see Diane K. McColley, *Milton's Eve* (Urbana, 1983; Christina Froula, "When Eve Reads Milton: Undoing the Canonical Economy," *Critical Inquiry* 10 (1983): 321–47; and Julia Walker, *Milton and the Idea of Woman* (Urbana, 1988).

54. For evidence of such liberalizing uses, see Joseph A. Wittreich, *Feminist Milton* (Ithaca, 1987).

55. See Barbara K. Lewalski, "Innocence and Experience in Milton's Eden," in *New Essays on Paradise Lost*, ed. Thomas Kranidas (Berkeley, 1969), 86–117.

56. For different readings of this episode, see Mary Nyquist, "The Genesis of Gendered Subjectivity," in *Re-membering Milton*, eds. Mary Nyquist and Margaret Ferguson (New York, 1987), 99–127, and Janet Halley, "Female Autonomy in Milton's Sexual Politics," in Walker, ed., *Milton and the Idea of Woman*, 230–53.

57. The leitmotif of man's loneliness without a wife fit for intelligent conversation echoes

through both versions of *The Doctrine and Discipline of Divorce,* even to the point of identifying the "burning" in the Pauline text (1 Cor. 7:9) as loneliness rather than lust: "What is it [that burning] then but that desire which God put into *Adam* in Paradise before he knew the sin of incontinence; that desire which God saw it was not good that man should be left alone to burn in; that desire and longing to put off an unkindly solitarines by uniting another body, but not without a fit soule to his in the cheerfull society of wedlock" (YP 2:251).

MILTON'S FETTERS, OR,
WHY EDEN IS BETTER THAN HEAVEN

Richard Strier

T HIS ESSAY JOINS the chorus of voices from Blake to Tillyard and
beyond who have seen *Paradise Lost* as a poem deeply divided against
itself.[1] This essay is not a "Satanist" reading, although it does share a number
of premises with the "Satanist" view. It adopts Blake's idea that Milton wrote
"in fetters" of God and the good angels, and it adopts Shelley's view that
heaven and hell in the poem are in a sense morally equivalent.[2] It addresses
Empson's feeling that even though the Shelleyan view is true, it "leaves the
mind unsatisfied" because, in holding it, one "becomes so baffled in trying to
imagine how Milton came to write as he did."[3] The most problematic and un-
satisfactory aspects of the poem, I will argue, flow directly from Milton's con-
scious and articulated intentions—indeed, from the "Great Argument" itself.
My understanding of the overall aim of the poem is almost the same as that of
Dennis Danielson: that it aims to show God to be good, or at least, not to be
wicked.[4] Where I differ from Danielson is that while he thinks that the aes-
thetic (and religious) success of the poem depends on the success of its the-
odicy, I think that the attempt at theodicy—whether one regards it as success-
ful or not—produces most of the aesthetic and religious failures of the poem,
Blake's "fetters." I see the great aesthetic and religious success of the poem,
where Milton wrote without fetters, as being in an area free of the Great
Argument: the presentation of Eden and of unfallen human life within it.

I. RATIONALISM (AND *CHRISTIAN DOCTRINE*)

It is important to be clear from the outset about the implications of
theodicy. It is essentially a rationalistic project.[5] Although many critics are
confused about this, it is not a project that an *echt* Calvinist would attempt.[6]
As John Rumrich has rightly noted, the context represented by the shared
beliefs of Luther and Calvin was "deeply inimical to the very notion of
theodicy."[7] The idea of showing God to be "good"—of showing divine actions
to correspond to some humanly intelligible conception of fairness—verged
upon blasphemy for Luther. He mocked those, like Erasmus, who refused to
acknowledge God to be good "when he speaks and acts above and beyond the

definitions of Justinian's code, or the fifth book of Aristotle's Ethics."[8] Calvin, citing Augustine, saw "wrong" ("iniuria") done to God whenever "a higher cause of things than his will is demanded."[9] The author of *Paradise Lost* stands squarely with Erasmus. While it is true that the desire to "assert Eternal Providence" is not necessarily rationalistic—something can be asserted, after all, in the face of evidence and common sense—but the intention to "justify the ways of God to men" is indeed a rationalistic project (*PL* 1.25–26).[10] There is, moreover, a slight but telling ambiguity in Milton's formulation. Either the poet is going to justify "the ways of God to men," meaning how God treats mankind, or the poet is going to justify "the ways of God" in general, and is promising to do so in terms that will be humanly intelligible. The difference, in other words, is (roughly) between stating a subject-matter ("the ways of God to men") and stating a philosophical-rhetorical project ("to justify . . . to men").[11] We cannot initially choose between the readings. The prominent "Man" in line 1 would probably favor the former, but as soon as the action gets underway, we recognize that Milton's topic is larger than "the ways of God to men." We come to realize that the second meaning, "justify . . . to men," must be the intended one. The goal is rational explanation; "justification" is used in its normal, rationalistic sense rather than in its specialized Reformation one.

This is where *Christian Doctrine* is helpful. Whatever its authorship, it can help us understand Renaissance theological rationalism.[12] Even if, as I believe and will assume, the internal evidence is overwhelming that the treatise is by Milton, W. B. Hunter has done a service not only in reopening an issue—always a good thing—but also in pointing to the intellectual lineage of the treatise.[13] It belongs, as Maurice Kelley had earlier argued, squarely in the line of the rationalist and biblicist critics of Reformation theology, the line of Servetus and Arminius.[14] This is the tradition in which both the poem and the treatise belong, and it is in demonstrating the shape and force of this tradition that the treatise can be most helpful. *Christian Doctrine* can also serve as an introduction to the counter-movement that we can see at work in *Paradise Lost*, since the treatise briefly and surprisingly manifests a flicker of this counter-movement, showing how potent its pull is.

Let us begin with Milton's anti-Trinitarianism. This will help us catch the flavor of this text. The major argument in *Christian Doctrine* against the traditional (Nicene/Athanasian) doctrine of the Trinity is *not* that the doctrine is unbiblical, though the treatise does dispute the biblical sources. The main argument is that the doctrine is unreasonable.[15] As in Milton's *Art of Logic*, so in *Christian Doctrine*, mystical mathematics does not compute: "The numerical significance of 'one' and 'two' must be unalterable" and "the same for God as for man" (*CD*, YP 6:212).[16] The oneness of God must be understood "in the numerical sense, *in which human reason always understands it*" (*CD*, YP 6:216; italics mine). Nothing can be said of the one God "that makes him both one and not one" (*CD*, YP 6:148). The Trinitarian argument with which *Christian Doctrine* has most difficulty is the recognition that while scripture "does not say in so many words that the Father and the Son are essentially one," this conclusion can be reasonably deduced from various passages (*CD*, YP 6:222). After momentarily granting (for the sake of argument) that this is true, the author (hereafter "Milton") renounces such a deduction in favor of extreme literalism. "We can," he says, "really base our belief only on God's word . . . at its clearest" and "not on mere reason." But Milton is not happy with this strategy, even "for the sake of argument." He does not, at this crucial point, renounce reason but instead strongly embraces it, since it turns out that by "reason" he does not mean the capacity to draw inferences but rather the stance of "common sense." To the question he poses, "I ask you, what can reason do here," Milton's answer is not "nothing" (as one might expect) but "everything" (*CD*, YP 6:222). In the face of formally correct inferences that produce mysterious conclusions, Milton insists that "the product of reason must be reason"—that is, "reasonable." Such conclusions cannot be "absurd notions which are utterly alien to all human ways of thinking" (*CD*, YP 6:222). Reasonableness is the key; it takes precedence over mere reasoning.

If anti-Trinitarianism, for Milton, protects Christianity against intellectual unintelligibility, anti-Calvinism protects it against moral unintelligibility. Nothing is more important to *Christian Doctrine* than the assertion of human free will. Only this doctrine, for Milton, can prevent God from being seen as wicked.[17] *Christian Doctrine* does, in fact, conceive of Luthero-Calvinism as a form of devil-worship. In *The Bondage of the Will*, Luther trumpeted his full awareness that "it gives the greatest possible offense to common sense or natural reason that God, who is proclaimed as being full of mercy and goodness and so on, should of His own mere will, abandon, harden, and damn men, as though He delighted in the sins and great eternal torments of such poor wretches."[18] For Luther, as I have suggested, it was the essence of Christianity to outrage "natural reason" in just this way.[19] For Milton, Christianity never offends natural reason. Among the opposers of the doctrine of human freedom, he notes, there are those who "do not hesitate to assert that God is, in himself, the cause and author of sin" (*CD*, YP 6:166). Our author could not be more shocked: "If I did not believe that they said such a thing from error rather than from wickedness, I should consider them of all blasphemers the most utterly damned." He cannot even conceive of their view of religion and of God: "If I were to attempt to refute them, it would be like inventing a long argument to prove that God is not the Devil" (*CD*, YP 6:166).

God's offer of salvation is conditional upon free human action. This conception of conditional divine decrees is not, as the author of *Christian Doctrine* rightly recognizes that Luther or Calvin would say, "unworthy of God" (*CD*, YP 6:160), but rather—as Luther would say mockingly, and as this author says complacently—"thoroughly reasonable" (*CD*, YP 6:164). The doctrine of double predestination must be false; it is "repulsive and unreasonable" (*CD*, YP 6:180). Pauline language must be contained. It must be "established at the outset" that even though all men "are dead in sin and children of wrath, *nevertheless some are worse than others*" (*CD*, YP 6:186; italics mine). Moral autonomy is an absolute premise: "everyone is provided with sufficient innate reason . . . to be able to resist evil desires by his own efforts" (*CD*, YP 6:186). Sufficient grace is necessary to enable sufficient reason, but God considers all persons "worthy of sufficient grace." And the reason for this is His justice (*CD*, YP 6:193). This view does not, as the Luthero-Calvinists say, swell man with pride, but rather it allows "the glory not only of divine grace, but also of divine wisdom and justice" to become apparent (*CD*, YP 6:190). God's wisdom and justice must be intelligible, and only if salvation and damnation depend on human freedom can they be so.

Christian Doctrine values freedom so highly that it tends to see all conceptions of necessity as negative. "From the concept of freedom," it says, "all idea of necessity must be removed" (*CD*, YP 6:161). This conception of freedom is entirely a conception of deliberation and choice. It is important to see that there are alternative conceptions of freedom. Luther vigorously espoused "the bondage of the will," yet the core of his entire system was the idea of "Christian freedom."[20] Freedom was his great watchword (when he was thinking of taking a Greek form of his name, he picked "Eleutherius" [free man]).[21] For Luther, what Christian freedom meant was precisely the opposite of deliberation. Freedom was freedom from calculation, from weighing of options, from attempting to live up to demands. It was freedom from self-conscious selfhood, a spontaneous outpouring of gratitude toward God that expresses itself in love for and happy service of one's neighbor—"works of the freest service, cheerfully and lovingly done, with which a [person] serves another without hope of reward," solely out of feeling "the fullness and wealth of his faith."[22] The "free" person, for Luther, acts out of an inner necessity, a necessity to express his joy and sense of liberation. This is a conception of "Christian freedom" entirely different from the deliberative one of *Christian Doctrine*.

Luther's conception has a mystical dimension—he edited and published the *Theologia Germanica*—and this dimension connects his thinking with the Neoplatonic tradition.[23] In many respects, Luther is an anti-Platonist, but the conception of goodness as involving non-ratiocinative spontaneity, abundance, and overflowing has its origin and home in the Platonic tradition.[24] This conception is part of what A. O. Lovejoy has called "the principle of plenitude." Lovejoy brilliantly traced how, in Plato (especially in *Timaeus*), "the concept of Self-Sufficing Perfection, by a bold logical inversion, was— without losing any of its original implications—converted into the concept of Self-Transcending Fecundity."[25] Plato's most important follower, Plotinus, contributed to both sides of this dialectic, but he was especially important in developing the fecundity idea. He asserted that "it is of the essence of things that each gives of its being to another"; "without this communication," he explained, "the Good would not be Good."[26] That "all that is fully achieved engenders" is a fundamental premise for Plotinus.[27] The cosmos "is due to a higher Kind of engendering in its own likeness," and this is (or is like) "a natural process." This means, as Plotinus quite explicitly holds, that the cosmos is "a product of Necessity, not of deliberate purpose."[28] He argues that the cosmos would be worse—less beautiful and less orderly—if it were the product of deliberation.[29] By the Middle Ages, the idea that "*omne bonum est diffusivum sui*" ("all good is diffusive of itself") had become, as Lovejoy puts it, "an axiom." This is a vision not of deliberation but of beneficent internal necessity. As Cassirer puts it in describing a major Renaissance Platonist, emanation stands "not in the sign of freedom, but in that of necessity."[30] This tradition came close to Milton. Jacobus Arminius insisted that "God is good by a natural internal necessity, not freely"; the English Platonist George Rust noted that "If you pitch upon the Platonick way," you must "assign the production of all things to that exuberant fulness of life in the Deity"—that is, to "the blessed necessity of his most communicative nature."[31]

Christian Doctrine is aware of this metaphysical-religious conception of "blessed necessity." At one point, in distinguishing between internal and external necessity, Milton acknowledges that while it can be said that in God there is "a certain immutable internal necessity to do good," he insists that this "can be consistent with absolute freedom of action" (*CD*, YP 6:159). Milton does not, however, stick to this "compatibilist" position.[32] He ends the discussion by withdrawing his initial tentative assent to its premise—"Nor, incidentally, do I concede the point that there is in God any necessity to act" (*CD*, YP 6:159). He prefers to believe that God is "not impelled by any necessity" (*CD*, YP 6:154). Milton has trouble seeing any type of necessity as positive, so fixed is he on his conception of freedom as the deliberate exercise of the will. In an anti-Trinitarian interpretation of the birth of the Son, he asserts that "this particular Father begot his Son not from any natural necessity but of his own free will"—a method, Milton assures us, "more excellent and more in keeping with paternal dignity" (*CD*, YP 6:209). Similarly, he argues that the Holy Spirit was "produced, from the substance of God, not by natural necessity but by the free-will of the agent" (*CD*, YP 6:298). Finally, in a remarkable passage on creation, Milton attempts to reconcile a vision of diffusion with a vision of will: "It is, I say, a demonstration of God's supreme power and goodness that he should not shut up this heterogeneous and substantial virtue within himself, but should disperse, propagate, and extend it as far as, and in whatever way, he wills" (*CD*, YP 6:308). This passage attempts to bring the vision of plenitude ("such heterogeneous, multiform, and inexhaustible virtue"), of propagation, and of "substance" under the aegis of will. As to the coherence of this attempt, opinions differ; as to the motive of the attempt, there is no doubt: to make deliberative choice cosmically central.

II. Reason or Force? Politics Everywhere

We know from the initial statement of the Great Argument (1.24–26) that in *Paradise Lost* Milton is going to attempt a rational explanation of God's ways. In immediately asking the Muse to "say first . . . what cause" (1.27–28), he is proceeding in what we know he considers the most rational manner, since in the *Art of Logic*, he characterizes providing a cause as "the source of all knowledge."[33] We do not yet know, however, what sort of rational-causal explanation we are going to be given. It turns out that we are going to be given an explanation through an account of a malicious agent—"Who first seduc'd them to that foul revolt?" (1.33). The focus has already shifted from the Fall of Man, the announced subject of the poem, to the agent who was the "cause" of the Fall. Understanding the agent is presented as the necessary context for understanding the Fall. In Milton's initial description of the agent, we receive our first indication of the terms in which he will carry out the rational explanation that he has promised. Out of the poet's loathing for the event and the malicious agent of it ("foul revolt . . . infernal serpent"), a larger story, with more specific terms of description, begins to emerge:

> hee it was, whose guile
> Stirr'd up with Envy and Revenge, deceiv'd
> The Mother of Mankind; what time his Pride
> Had cast him out from Heav'n, with all his Host
> Of Rebel Angels, by whose aid aspiring
> To set himself in Glory above his Peers,
> He trusted to have equall'd the most High,
> If he oppos'd; and with ambitious aim

> Against the Throne and Monarchy of God
> Rais'd impious War in Heav'n and Battle proud.   (1.34–43)

This explanation of the Fall notably shifts from moral terms—"Envy and Revenge . . . Pride"—to political terms—"aspiring . . . above his Peers"; "ambitious aim / Against the . . . Monarchy." The narrator wants us to think in political terms about the situation and the behavior of all the key agents in his story. The framework for rational theodicy that Milton will offer will be political. As Empson says, "it is all weirdly political."[34] Milton is fully committing himself to the tendency toward politicization of the "war in heaven" narrative that Stella Revard has shown to be characteristic of Renaissance treatments.[35] When, in a wonderful moment, the narrative shifts from description to dramatization, and Satan is allowed to speak, he presents his story in military and political terms as well. He acknowledges God's superior weaponry ("the stronger prov'd / He with his Thunder"), and asserts that neither for thunder,

> Nor what the Potent Victor in his rage
> Can else inflict, do I repent or change,
> Though chang'd in outward lustre; that fixt mind
> And high disdain, from sense of injur'd merit,
> That with the mightiest rais'd me to contend,
> And to the fierce contention brought along
> Innumerable force of Spirits arm'd
> That durst dislike his reign, and me preferring,
> His utmost power with adverse power oppos'd.   (1.95–103)

Satan seems to have a clear and recognizable sense of himself. The discontented courtier, servant, or military figure suffering from "sense of injur'd merit" was a familiar figure in Elizabethan and Jacobean drama—think of Bosola, Iago, or Coriolanus. We know how complex these figures can be. We do (or should) immediately recognize that we are witnessing here one of these complex portrayals.[36] The difficult question is not how to think about Satan but how to think about Satan's portrayal of God.

For Satan, God is only "the Potent Victor"; Satan sees God's only attribute (aside from wrath) as power, for which He desires to be worshiped ("To bow . . . and deify his power" [1.111–12]). Instead of seeing a monarchy in heaven, he sees a tyranny, the rule of a whimsical absolutist. This characterization continues throughout Book One. In his third speech, Satan presents a completely Nominalist view of God. Through power, God "can dispose and bid / What shall be right" (1.246–47). Power is the only issue: "Whom reason hath equall'd, force hath made supreme" (248). Satan's insistence that his mind has remained unchanged is part of the framework of physical coercion.[37] As he puts it epigrammatically in his final speech in Book One, "who overcomes / By force, hath overcome but half his foe" (648–49). The view of God that the fallen angels consistently present is of a sadistic, vindictive, and implacable conqueror who takes pleasure in their suffering: "Will he . . . give his Enemies their wish, and end / Them . . . whom his anger saves / To punish endless?" (2.157–58). The fallen angels see God's consciousness as exactly parallel to their own: "terms of peace yet none / Voutsaf't or sought" (2.331–32). The key point here is not "none . . . sought" by the fallen angels, but "none / Voutsaf't" by God. The challenge that Milton has set for himself in using political terms is to distinguish heaven from hell *in these terms*. He must show the monarchy of God not to be a tyranny and not to be based merely on superior power. Conversely, he must show hell to involve an especially debased form of political life.

One of Milton's problems is the difficulty of keeping political life in hell demonic rather than merely—and non-pejoratively—political. A spectacular example of this problem occurs in the narrator's comment on Belial's speech: "Thus Belial . . . Counsell'd ignoble ease and peaceful sloth, / Not peace" (2.226–28). This is perhaps an apt comment on the speech in general political terms, but it makes no sense whatever in the narrative context. Apart from the paradoxes of felix culpa, wouldn't it be better for the cosmos if the fallen angels had adopted a policy of "ease" and "sloth," and been "ignoble"?

A case that might initially seem easier but that actually turns out to be quite complex is presented by the unanimity of the fallen angels. Satan claims this as a positive distinguishing feature of hell—"a safe unenvied Throne / Yielded with full consent" (2.23–24). This is echoed in the "full assent" (2.397) of the fallen angels to the plan proposed by Beelzebub and Satan. Such agreement might seem merely to confirm how "diabolical" they all are. Yet Milton is quite struck by this unanimity and by the faith and trust that Satan's followers have in him. The narrator returns to these phenomena—"Thus they thir doubtful consultations dark / Ended rejoicing" (2.486–87)—and he describes the collective state of mind of the legions in a stunningly beautiful and innocent (not to say "heavenly") simile comparing this newly hopeful group to a "dark'n'd lantskip" which responds spontaneously to a last glimpse of "the radiant sun": "the fields revive, / The birds their notes renew, and bleating herds / Attest their joy, that hill and valley rings" (2.492–95). Milton finds himself in the anomalous position of admiring the fallen angels. He attempts to untangle the situation by turning his odd admiration for the political life of fallen angels into an attack on the political life of fallen humans:

> O shame to men! Devil with Devil damn'd
> Firm concord holds, men only disagree

Of Creatures rational, though under hope
Of heavenly Grace; and God proclaiming peace,
Yet live in hatred, enmity, and strife. (2.496–500)

Yet this is clearly a desperate move. The "devilishness" of the devils is bracketed. And surely it is odd for "disagree" to have to function as a term for a worse-than-demonic moral failure.

The ironies of Satan's status as "by merit rais'd / To that bad eminence" (2.5–6) seem under control. Yet the presentation of his "eminence" gets more complex as Book Two proceeds. The speech that produces the cheerful unanimity of the devils is introduced thus: "at last / *Satan,* whom now transcendent glory rais'd / Above his fellows, with Monarchal pride / Conscious of highest worth, unmov'd . . . spake" (2.427–30). This might seem straightforwardly pejorative, but "Monarchal" cannot be a negative term in itself given the epic narrator's apparently neutral reference to "the Throne and Monarchy of God" (1.42); and while "pride" seems negative, Milton certainly believed that consciousness of "worth," if appropriate, was a virtue.[38]

Critics often speak as if there were something rigged and stagy about Satan's role in the council in hell, but his consciousness of highest worth seems justified.[39] Any of the fallen angels could have volunteered for what was, in fact, a dangerous and uncertain mission. And "unmov'd" is one of Milton's great words of Stoic heroism.[40] "Monarchal pride" of the sort that Satan is manifesting here is not, in short, necessarily intended to be a negative judgment rather than a neutrally accurate assessment. Satan does feel that he has to earn his position—"I should ill become the Throne, O Peers . . . if aught propos'd / And judg'd of public moment, in the shape / Of difficulty or danger could deter / Mee from attempting" (2.445–50). I cannot see any undercutting irony here. I am not even sure that Satan's behavior in preventing others from volunteering for the mission after the fact, and thus taking credit for having volunteered, is to be seen as somehow wicked rather than, with all of its inherent complexity, "Prudent"—as Milton says (2.467–73). It is the presentation of the fallen legions celebrating Satan, "that for the general safety he despis'd / His own" (2.480–82), that leads Milton to the first of the moments when he is forced *to praise* the devils: "Neither do the Spirits damn'd / Lose all their virtue" (482–83). To try to restore the moral balance, Milton makes the connection to human behavior—"lest bad men should boast / Their specious deeds on earth, which glory excites" (483–84), but the condemnation of "glory," especially civic glory, is always complex for him.[41]

So Milton has a hard time keeping politics in hell diabolical. We must now ask whether he is any more successful in keeping heavenly politics heavenly. The challenge is to counter the view of God as He whom "force hath made supreme." This means that mockery of Satan for being weaker than God or for fighting against an overwhelmingly more powerful force is irrelevant to Milton's purpose (not to say morally contemptible). Moreover, such mockery does not respond to the challenge of ethical and political justification that Milton has set himself—the challenge, to repeat, of showing God to be supreme not only in force. The key texts for examining Satan's claims about God are Books Five and Six, since the war in heaven is the immediate context of all the actions and speeches in Books One and Two, and, as virtually all attentive readers of *Paradise Lost* have noted, the "history" that the poem includes begins with the exaltation of the Son to the angels dramatized toward the end of Book Five.

This exaltation is a pure fiat:

> Hear my Decree, which unrevok't shall stand.
> This day I have begot whom I declare
> My only Son, and on this holy Hill
> Him have anointed, whom ye now behold
> At my right hand; your Head I him appoint;
> And by my Self have sworn to him shall bow
> All knees in Heav'n, and shall confess him Lord.   (5.603–9)

All the major verbs here denote divine action—"begot . . . declare . . . anointed . . . appoint." The responses of the angels are themselves commanded—"shall bow / All knees . . . and shall confess." The next lines attempt to present this event as beneficent toward the angels—"Under his great Vicegerent Reign abide / United as one individual Soul / For ever happy" (609–11a)—but this vision is still governed (not just grammatically) by an imperative ("abide") and is, in any case, fairly obscure. Rather than explicating this benevolent command, God immediately turns to a warning in which only Milton's Latinate treatment of English keeps the focus on the Son rather than on the wicked ("Him who disobeys / Mee disobeys"). This warning then leads to a detailed, terrifying threat: "Cast out . . . Into utter darkness . . . without end" (613–15). I do not mean to suggest that Satan's response to this speech, "envy against the Son of God, that day / Honor'd" (662–63), is a rational one, but I do mean to suggest that Satan's specific claim, "new Laws thou seest imposed" (679), is true, and that the lie he tells—"I am to haste . . . Homeward . . . there to prepare / Fit entertainment to receive our King" (686–90)—is plausible. Moreover, it is important to recognize that in the exaltation speech, God gives no reason for His decision. We are close here to a Nominalist God "for whose will no cause or ground [*ratio*] may be laid down," but this is acceptable to Luther, not Milton.[42] In Milton's text, the Messiah is supposed to be He "who by right of Merit reigns" (6.43), but this is not even asserted in the key passage. It is asserted and demonstrated in Book Three, but that occasion—the heavenly parallel to Satan's demonstration of his merit—takes place later in the history.

The only answer to Satan's account in Book Five is that given by Abdiel. He accuses Satan of ingratitude—given Satan's high and favored position in heaven—and then asks the great biblical-Nominalist-Reformation question, "Shalt thou give Law to God?" (5.822). But this cannot be where Milton leaves the matter. Abdiel then argues that the angels have abundant evidence of God's beneficence and notes that God in fact proclaimed beneficence to them in "Under his . . . Vice-gerent . . . abide / United." After another argument from power—the Son was the instrument of God's creation of "All things, ev'n thee [Satan]"—Abdiel finally attempts to explicate the claim that the exaltation of the Son benefits the angels:

> nor by his Reign obscur'd,
> But more illustrious made, since he the Head
> One of our number thus reduc't becomes,
> His Laws our Laws, all honor to him done
> Returns our own.   (5.841b–45)

This argument is clearly hard going, since the key line—"One of our number thus reduc't becomes"—is, even by Miltonic standards, contorted. The idea seems to be that the Son, by becoming the "Head" of angels, is "reduced" to being one of them, which in turn raises the status of the angels. This is tricky, and the next lines sound like a sophistical argument for how special treatment of one member of a group is not actually special treatment ("all honor to him done / Returns our own").

More importantly, Abdiel claims that the exaltation is rational—meaning, for Milton, based on merit. Satan and his followers must be seen as refusing not an arbitrary decree but reason. God implies this in asserting that the Son "by right of Merit reigns" (6.44), and Abdiel, in perhaps the most important speech in Book Six, explains that there is a difference between service and servitude, and that it cannot be servitude to serve one who is objectively worthier; in such a case, "God and nature [meaning natural reason] bid the same" (6.174–78). So the question remains, in what does the Son's objective worth (merit) consist? In Book Five, God had spoken of Satan intending "to try in battle what our Power is, or our Right" (5.728), a line which leaves the two abstractions uneasily related. In Book Six, after the (I do not believe intentionally grotesque) *Sturm und Drang* of the war between the angels, God decides "To honor his Anointed Son" (676) by having him end the war:[43]

that the Glorie may be thine
Of ending this great Warr, since none but Thou
Can end it. Into thee such Virtue and Grace
Immense I have transfus'd, that all may know
In Heav'n and Hell thy Power above compare,
And this perverse Commotion govern'd thus,
To manifest thee worthiest to be Heir.   (6.701–7)

It is hard to see how "Virtue" can here mean anything but potency, and it is hard to see what "Grace" means at all. The speech is a paean to power. "Worthiest" here can only mean most powerful. In the next lines, the assertion of the Son's "deserved right" is followed immediately by the description of him as "Mightiest in thy Father's might" (6.709–10). The Son suggests, very briefly and abstractly, a rational basis for his actions (6.741), but the whole emphasis of this section of the poem is, as Michael Lieb has recently reminded us, on the Chariot of Paternal Deity as an immense war machine.[44]

Milton recognizes the problem at this point. Before presenting the scene of military terror, he does have the Son restore heaven's beauty (6.781–84), and he does present Satan's legions unmoved by this and "harden'd more by what might most reclaim" (6.791). This latter line, however, is very opaque. A demonstration of power cannot be supposed to "reclaim" the rebels in any moral sense. Milton's major strategy for getting out of the problem is to acknowledge it. He has the Son inform the good angels that the Father has "assign'd" the suppression of the revolt to the Son in order that the rebel angels

may have thir wish, to try with mee
In Battle which the stronger proves, they all,
Or I alone against them, since by strength
They measure all, of other excellence
Not emulous, nor care who them excells.   (6.818–822)

This is another brilliant but desperate maneuver.[45] The "might equals right" perspective that has dominated this entire section of the poem is presented, retroactively, as a kind of accommodation to the diabolical perspective— which it does not, in any case, accurately capture, since the fallen angels seem, in fact, to appreciate many kinds of "excellence" (see the account of their music-making, athletic contests, and philosophical discussions in Book Two [528–69]).[46] In the final narrative lines of Raphael's discourse, moreover, the "Saints," meaning the good angels, are presented as seeing the Son's military triumph as what proves him to be "Worthiest to Reign" (886–88).[47] Milton cannot keep this framework demonic.

III. HEAVENLY MINDS? CHOICE EVERYWHERE

We have now seen how the political framework in which Milton presented his theodicy creates the continuity between heaven and hell that Shelley thought was the deepest meaning of the poem. But what of Milton's presentation of life in heaven apart from the great rebellion? C. S. Lewis has acknowledged (along with many other critics from the eighteenth century on) that there are problems with this presentation, but Lewis has classified these problems as merely matters of "poetical prudence" into which, he warns, "it is easy to look too deep."[48] But surely the presentation of heavenly life in the poem is something into which we should "look deep." When we do, we find that the problems with Milton's heaven flow directly from his most fundamental and consciously held values—his commitment, as we have already seen, to rational moral explanation. The problems flow directly from this bed-rock commitment. Here a contemporary (with us) moral philosopher can help. Bernard Williams has argued that it is a mistake to assume "that the moral point of view must be ubiquitous"—that all actions are to be evaluated from a moral point of view.[49] Williams has also argued that it is a mistake (of a similar sort) to maintain "a rationalistic conception of rationality," a view that holds, for instance, that only acts done out of rational deliberation are reasonable.[50] Milton holds both these views. They determine the limits of his heaven—of his ability, that is, to present a distinctively heavenly consciousness.

Let me begin, as seems proper, with God. At the beginning of Book Three, we actually meet this figure and, probably to our surprise, directly hear His reactions to the events that were narrated and dramatized in Book Two. Milton's decision to have God speak, and to have Him speak as He does here, has troubled a multitude of critics. The most successful defense of the speech has assured us that this speech is meant to trouble us, that we are meant to see this trouble as a sign of our depravity, and that, properly seen, the speech is a totally toneless and affectless "unfolding" of a state of affairs.[51] Apart from whether these claims are true, or even plausible, there is something wrong with this approach. It is purely formal. A satisfactory account of this speech must focus not on its (supposed) logical form but on its content.[52] In the (first) *Defense of the English People,* Milton noted that "it is the custom of poets to place their own opinions in the mouths of their great characters."[53] Milton gives this speech to God, and puts it where he does, *because of what it says.* For reasons that we have been exploring all along, Milton's God had to be able to give a rational account of Himself.[54]

The speech falls into three major parts and a coda. Its first section moves twice from mock-bemusement in the dramatic present—"seest thou what rage / Transports our adversary, whom no bounds . . . can hold" (80–84a); "And now / Through all restraint broke loose" (86b–87a)—into a fierce certainty with regard to the future—"that shall redound / Upon his own rebellious head" (85b–86a); "Hee and his faithless Progeny" (96a). Neither of these moments is "toneless." And if we look ahead to the third part of the speech, where it becomes directly theological, it seems absurd to say that God does not anticipate objections, since it is precisely in response to an anticipated (or foreseen) accusation that Milton's God, like Homer's Zeus, and with the same distinctive tone of mock-bemusement, makes His point about human responsibility. "My word," says Zeus, "how mortals take the gods to task! / All their afflictions come from us, we hear./ And what of their own failings?"⁵⁵ This passage is alluded to in a discussion of divine will in *The Doctrine and Discipline of Divorce* and directly quoted to conclude the chapter on predestination in *Christian Doctrine*.⁵⁶ Milton flouts the Calvinists in having God speak of His "Decree / Unchangeable" as the decree which "ordain'd" human freedom (126–27) . The language of "decree" is entirely assimilated to the language of freedom and moral responsibility— "they themselves *decreed* / Thir own revolt . . . they themselves *ordain'd* thir fall" (116–17, 128–29).

What is characteristically Miltonic in God's speech is the extraordinary value it places on free will. The central section of the speech (96b–111a) is entirely devoted to justification of this valuation. *Pace* Fish, the progress to this section is not straightforwardly logical. One could easily imagine a narrative continuation to "So will fall / Hee and his faithless Progeny" (95b–96a). The topic of moral responsibility ("whose fault?") enters this line not inevitably but with a jolt, after a strong caesura, as a new topic (line 96b). Milton inserts the topic because it is his central concern. While it is true that "ingrate" in the following line—"Whose but his own? ingrate, he had of mee" (97)—is not an insult, the tone here is unquestionably defensive, since what God is doing is precisely defending.⁵⁷ He is working, as the prose Argument to Book Three says, to clear "his own Justice and Wisdom from all imputation." The point that God develops is the parallel between the moral condition that will be granted to man—"Sufficient to have stood, though free to fall"—and that of the angels: "Such I created all th' Ethereal Powers . . . Freely they stood who stood and fell who fell" (100–2). The argument for the special importance of this follows. Its form is that of a series of rhetorical questions that progressively lose their status as questions:

> Not free, what proof could they have giv'n sincere
> Of true allegiance, constant Faith or Love,
> Where only what they needs must do, appear'd,

> Not what they would? what praise could they receive?
> What pleasure I from such obedience paid,
> When Will and Reason (Reason also is choice)
> Useless and vain, of freedom both despoil'd,
> Made passive both, had serv'd necessity,
> Not mee.   (103–11a)

This is perfectly intelligible. It is what Aristotle said a legislator concerned with assigning honors and punishments needs to consider.[58] In explaining the same point in *Areopagitica,* Milton appealed to what "we our selves esteem."[59] But this is also very odd. Shelley's point clicks in. This passage makes God *exactly* like us. Yet why should He be concerned with "proof" of sincerity, and with the proper assignment of praise? Why must His "pleasure" derive only from sincerity arising from deliberation? And, the most theologically and philosophically interesting question (as we saw with regard to *Christian Doctrine*), why must "necessity" and acting out of necessity be negatively conceived?

This is where Milton's insistence on the ubiquity of the moral starts to seem odd and can be seen as having eliminated possibilities—especially heavenly ones.[60] As a number of critics have noted, the presentation of God's speech is immediately followed by an aggressively sensuous and lyrical narrative moment:

> Thus while God spake, ambrosial fragrance fill'd
> All Heav'n, and in the blessed Spirits elect
> Sense of new joy ineffable diffus'd.   (3.136–38)

As the impersonal syntax suggests, this does not seem to be a moment of choice or will on anyone's part. It seems merely to happen—"while God spake . . . fragrance fill'd"—and the agent of the "Sense of new joy" in the "Spirits elect" is the fragrance itself.[61] The angels simply respond to what is "diffus'd" into them. Milton knows the importance of such spontaneous moments, but his ideological framework—"Reason . . . is choice"—does not allow him to give them much value. As in *Christian Doctrine,* this is true even in high metaphysical and ontological contexts. In speaking of creating the cosmos, God explains (as Raphael reports):

> Boundless the Deep, because I am who fill
> Infinitude, nor vacuous the space.
> Though I uncircumscrib'd my self retire,
> And put not forth my goodness, which is free
> To act or not. Necessity and Chance
> Approach not mee, and what I will is Fate.   (7.168–73)

This passage is remarkable for its mixture of ontological and voluntaristic terms; "fill" hovers between the realms, though Pleroma, "fullness," is a term from the realm of emanation.[62] God's substance is not equivalent to his "goodness," which is (somehow) "free / To act or not." This "goodness" is conceived not only as independent of God's being but as if "goodness" could intelligibly withhold itself. Such withholding is exactly what the "diffusion principle"—which sees generativity as intrinsic to, analytic to, goodness— means to deny: *omne bonum est diffusivum sui*. At the beginning of the tradition, Plato denied that goodness could be "grudging" or "envious"; Plotinus developed this; Arminius insisted that it was blasphemous (as well as false and absurd) to think of God's goodness as "free"—as if it could be otherwise.[63] After Milton's odd account of "free" goodness, he ends with a Nominalist or Calvinist–sounding assertion, put in pagan terms, of the divine generation of necessity ("what I will is Fate"). The odd, perhaps unintelligible, mix of conceptions continues.[64] Raphael explains that in the creation of man, God "ordain'd . . . instead / Of Spirits malign a better Race to bring / Into their vacant room, and thence diffuse / His good to Worlds and Ages infinite" (7.188–91). But this vision of "diffusion" of divine goodness is illusory; it has to work through the creature whose moral constitution is exactly that of "All th' Ethereal Powers . . . both them who stood and them who fail'd." So diffusion is replaced by contingency.

Interestingly, the character in *Paradise Lost* who enunciates the principle of diffusion, and who has the clearest experience of being compelled into goodness, is Satan. In whispering into the sleeping Eve's ear, Satan employs the vocabulary of abundance versus "reserve" (5.61), and it is he who states that "good, the more communicated / The more abundant grows" (5.71–72). The principle takes on a sinister cast, since it is not stated elsewhere. The experience of "sweet / Compulsion" is not valued. The phrase occurs when Satan is psychologically, almost physically, struck by Eve's beauty (9.473–74). Milton describes him as having been momentarily rendered "stupidly good" (9.465). At a similar moment in Book Four (also with regard to Satan), Milton had commented on the "awful" power of beauty and goodness (4.845–48), but this kind of instinctive awe is not the characteristic experience of Milton's heaven. It is an experience of necessity, not of deliberative choice. Milton knows that there are morally positive states that are non-deliberative—"a grateful mind / By owing owes not, but still pays, at once / Indebted and discharged" (4.55–57)—but his presentation of heavenly life is not based on these.[65] It is based on tests of sincerity and obedience.

Only a positive conception of necessity (or a conception of positive necessity) can keep heaven from being a realm of ordinary psychology and politics. Dante saw this clearly. Early in the *Paradiso*, Dante the pilgrim initially fails to recognize a Florentine woman he knew named Piccarda. Finally recognizing her, and being impressed by her "wondrous looks" ("mirabili aspetti"), Dante asks her a question about her lowly status in heaven—"tell me, do you who are happy here desire a higher place, that you may see more and become more dear?" She answers as follows:

Brother, the power of charity quiets our will and makes us will only what we have and thirst for nothing else. Did we desire to be more exalted, our desire would be in discord with His will who appoints us here, which thou wilt see cannot hold in these circles if to be in charity is here *necese* and if thou consider well its nature. Nay, it is the very quality of this blessed state that we keep ourselves within the divine will, so that our wills are themselves made one; therefore our rank from height to height is pleasing to the whole kingdom, as to the King, who wills us to His will.[66]

There is no question here of deliberation and testing. "To be in charity is here *necese.*" That is what blessedness means for Dante. It is not in the beatified Piccarda's will "to love or not" or to "forget to love" (*PL* 5.540, 550). It is not clear, moreover, that it is in *anyone's* will to do these things, or that "to love" is the kind of thing that can be chosen (or forgotten)—this is another point on which Platonism and Reformation theology agreed. Milton, with his insistence that all praiseworthy action had to spring from choice, could not agree to this.

Raphael describes the angels who later fell as "perfect while they stood" (5.568), but while this claim may be ontologically true, it is not morally or spiritually so.[67] Toward the end of Book One, Mammon is characterized by the epic voice as the "least erected Spirit that fell / From Heav'n" because

> ev'n in Heav'n his looks and thoughts
> Were always downward bent, admiring more
> The riches of Heav'ns pavement, trod'n Gold,
> Then aught divine or holy else enjoy'd
> In vision beatific.   (1.680–84; italics mine)

This is an admirable evocation of a degraded spirit but an odd account of a heavenly one. Similarly, the description of Belial in Book Two as a skillful and dangerous sophist who "could make the worse appear / The better reason" and whose "thoughts were low" (2.113–16) is an account of a long-standing character, not of one newly destroyed. The moral capacities of the fallen angels seem exactly the same as those of the unfallen ones. The parallel between the "muteness" of the fallen angels in response to Satan's challenge in Book Two (420) and that of the unfallen angels in response to the Son's in Book Three (217) is a lovely structural feature of the poem, but it has the effect of establishing a moral equivalence.

Milton is extremely interested in the Vergilian question of what sorts of negative emotion can dwell in heavenly minds: *"tantaene animis caelestibus irae"* ("Can there be so much anger in celestial spirits?" [*Aeneid* 1.11]). This line is paraphrased or directly alluded to four times in *Paradise Lost*.[68] In Book Four, the narrator tells us that "heavenly minds" are free of the kinds of passion that "disfigured" Satan on Mount Niphates (4.18–19), though later in the passage the difference seems to be merely one of degree—"more than could befall / Spirit of happy sort" (127–28). In the second (most distant) allusion, Satan states that he had thought that "Liberty and Heaven / To Heav'nly Souls had all been one"—exactly Piccarda's position—but that he had learned this to be false (6.164–65). Later in Book Six, the line is almost directly translated—"In heav'nly Spirits could such perverseness dwell?" (788)—and the answer, as in Vergil, is "yes." The final allusion to the line again almost directly translates it. In tempting Eve, Satan asks with mock-ingenuousness, "Can envy dwell / In heav'nly breasts?" (9.729–30). The rhetorical situation requires that the implied answer be negative, and Satan can rely on Eve's innocence to provide this answer. Yet in the context of the poem as a whole the answer is less clear. Satan claims that one of the features that distinguishes hell from heaven is precisely that in hell envy is incoherent, whereas in heaven "the happier state . . . which follows dignity, might draw / Envy from each inferior" (2.24–26). This is phrased in an oddly hypothetical way—"might draw"—but we know that in at least one case (his own), this occurred. Satan's pre-fallen eminence "in favor" as well as "in Power" (5.661) is never made morally intelligible.[69] The allegory of the "birth" of Sin is perhaps an attempt at dealing with the problem of the genesis of sin within a "perfect" creature (2.749–60), but the naturalistic mode of the poem as a whole leaves the possibility of envy in heavenly minds unfortunately intelligible.

The fallen angels present a view of devotion in heaven as merely a matter of "Knee-tribute" (5.782). Mammon gives a full picture of what forced devotion would be like; it would

> celebrate his Throne
> With warbl'd Hymns, and to his Godhead sing
> Forc't Halleluiahs; while he Lordly sits
> Our envied Sovran, and his Altar breathes
> Ambrosial Odours and Ambrosial Flowers,
> Our servile offerings.   (2.241–46)

Surely this should be impossible, and the imagination of it the product (and symptom) of a fallen nature. Yet one of the strangest episodes in the poem is that in which "Uriel . . . Regent of the Sun, and held / The sharpest-sighted

Spirit of all in Heav'n" is shown to be unable to detect hypocrisy, "the only evil that walks / Invisible, except to God alone, / By his permissive will, *through Heav'n and Earth*" (3.682–85; emphasis mine). So hypocrisy in heaven is treated not just as a possibility but as a fact. And it is dramatized in the poem. After the exaltation of the Son and the explicit demand for "knee-tribute" to Him, Milton provides a wonderful picture of the angels dancing "about the sacred Hill" in "Mystical dance" and eating and drinking "in communion sweet" (5.619–20, 637). This is the sort of picture on which the defenders of Milton's heaven rely. But this is all merely external. The fact of the matter is that "All seem'd well pleas'd, all seem'd, but were not all" (5.617). At *least* one of the highest angels—Satan—was, at that moment, participating in the "Mysticall" dances and festivities in exactly the way that Mammon describes. At the end of Book Three, Satan was presented as "bowing low" to Uriel "As to superior Spirits is wont in Heav'n, / Where honour due and reverence none neglects" (3.736–38). Satan's punctiliousness there about the outer signs of reverence exactly mirror his long-standing behavior in heaven. A (presumably) authoritative speaker (Gabriel) describes Satan as having "Once fawn'd, and cring'd, and servilely ador'd / Heav'ns awful Monarch" (4.959–60). Satan was the chief of the hypocritical adorers. No wonder this monarch is concerned with proof "Of true allegiance" and sends his servants on pointless errands to test and "enure" their "prompt obedience" (8.237–40).[70]

IV. DIFFUSION AND SPONTANEITY

Thus far, I have concentrated on the problems and limitations that are created in *Paradise Lost* by Milton's commitment to rational explanation and his understanding of the nature of this commitment. A whole set of religious and ethical possibilities are precluded by this commitment and this understanding. This commitment and this understanding of it create the "fetters" that Blake sensed and the surprising continuities that Shelley perceived. Yet there are some moments in *Paradise Lost* in which Milton escapes from his preoccupation with deliberation and choice. To find Milton writing without "fetters," in my view, is not to turn to his treatment of Satan but to turn primarily to his treatment of two other topics, nature and innocence.[71] In relation to these, Milton escapes—or at least provides the material for escaping—the framework of choice, deliberation, and anxious duty.

The sun is one of the great images, in Christian as in Neoplatonic contexts, of overflowing, non-deliberative, and diffusive bounty.[72] In the magnificent passage describing the sun in Book Three, Milton is (almost) freed from his obsession with freedom. The "great Luminary" is at first a great lord, "aloof," dispensing "Light from afar," but, as the description continues, a sense of happy natural process supervenes; we hear of

> his Magnetic beam, that gently warms
> The Universe, and to each inward part
> With gentle penetration, though unseen,
> Shoots invisible virtue even to the deep.   (3.583–86)

In this context, the fact that the sun's "virtue" is of the power rather than the moral sort makes it more rather than less benign. The same effect occurs when Milton justifies his fantasia on the sun as a place where "fields and regions . . . Breathe forth Elixir pure" by appealing to how, "with one virtuous touch / Th' Arch-chemic Sun" produces "with Terrestrial Humor mixt / Here in the dark so many precious things" (3.606–11). Even gold is allowed a non-moralized existence here as a wonderful natural substance.

We have seen how the deliberative dimension complicates the imagery of diffusion in the account of divine omnipresence ("I am who fill / Infinitude") and in the claim that the creation of man is supposed to "diffuse" God's "good to Worlds and Ages infinite." The account in Book Seven of the creation of the non-human cosmos happily celebrates "vital virtue" and benign natural processes like fermentation and generation (7.236, 281, 387).[73] Genesis and Lucretius happily mix. This presentation allows Milton to evoke a sense of divine goodness independent of the (for him) tense realm of freedom. The sense in which the creation is seen as "good," here and in Genesis, has little to do with passing a test. But even more than the account of the creation, the presentation of nature in Eden is Milton's great success in evoking a benign process independent of moral categories. Edenic nature is notably not rulebound:

> Flow'rs worthy of Paradise which not nice Art
> In Beds and curious Knots, but Nature boon
> Pour'd forth profuse on Hill and Dale and Plain.   (4.241–43)

In Book Five, Milton repeats the theme, even more emphatically rejecting any kind of regulation or inhibition. Eden is

> A Wilderness of sweets; for Nature here
> Wanton'd as in her prime, and play'd at will
> Her Virgin Fancies, pouring forth more sweet,
> Wild above rule or art, enormous bliss.   (5.294–98)

"Wanton'd" is here a positive term—without, I think, any "testing" of the reader—and it is notable that this vision allows for a positive sense of play.

"Will" here is a term for happy spontaneity, not for deliberation. Diffusion ("pouring forth") is unchecked.

Perhaps the most successful metaphysical passage in *Paradise Lost* is the vision Raphael presents of what seems to be a natural movement of matter up the scale of being to spirit. Various sorts of matter are "to thir several active Spheres assign'd, / Till body up to spirit work" (5.477–78). This cosmic process of sublimation (483) is illustrated by two purely natural processes: the way in which a flower produces fragrance, and the way in which, in Galenic physiology, the human blood system produces "animal" ("intellectual") out of "vital" spirits (479–87).[74] The culmination of this process would be that human bodies would "at last turn all to spirit" and allow the resulting "ethereal" creatures to exercise choice in a purely preferential, non-moral manner—they "may at choice / Here [in Eden] or in Heav'nly Paradises dwell" (497–500). But this whole cosmic process turns out to have an ethical basis—"If ye be found obedient" (501). This is perhaps Milton's most successful mingling of the ontological and the ethical—here ethical behavior allows a cosmic *entelechia* to be realized—but the question remains as to whether it makes sense, in terms of the vision of Edenic life that Milton gives us, for the "obedience" necessary to this cosmic process to be conceived in such a narrow, specific, and negative way ("not to taste that only Tree," 4.423). Why couldn't Adam and Eve be "obedient" by following the "dictates" of their unfallen natures?

It is a measure of the profound difference between Milton's heaven and his Eden that when in heaven Satan protests against the superfluity of "Law and Edict" to those who "without law / Err not" (5.798–800), his claim seems merely rhetorical; in Eden, it seems pertinent. Joseph E. Duncan points out how extraordinary it was for Milton not to have presented Adam and Eve in Eden as following a "Covenant of Works."[75] They are not following prescriptions in order to obtain a reward. They do not have to be constantly instructed in virtue. Their impulses are trustworthy. With "instinctive motion," Adam stood upright (8.259).[76] Eve, "with unexperienc't thought," falls victim to an illusion but responds immediately and spontaneously to a correcting "voice"— "what could I do / But follow straight . . . ?"—and quite quickly responds to Adam's words and gestures by recognizing in her experience a complex moral lesson (4.456–92).[77] Adam and Eve do not have to be told to be grateful to "the Power / That made us . . . and plac't us here / In all this happiness" (4.412–18); they do not have to be told how to worship and do not have to deliberate about how to do so—"Lowly they bow'd adoring, and began / Thir Orisons . . . in fit strain pronounct or sung / Unmeditated" (5.144–49). They do not have to be told to be willing. They learn moral lessons directly from their environment, from Eden where "Nature multiplies / Her fertile growth, and by disburd'ning grows / More fruitful, which instructs us not to spare" (5.318–20). It is not even clear that they need to have work "appointed" to them (4.619), since they seem to have a natural aversion to the messiness of Eden ("those dropping Gums, / That lie bestrown unsightly" [4.630–31]) as well as an intuitive sense of how to intervene usefully in it (5.212–16).[78]

The moment when Milton first has evil enter (in some sense) the minds of these creatures who truly are "perfect" in their unfallen state bears close attention. As epic narrator, Milton comments on this moment in a way that is completely appropriate, even admirable, within his rational-moral scheme. Yet it is strikingly inappropriate to the lives of the morally perfect beings that he has created. In a wonderful evocation of the difficulty of Satan's task, Satan is described, when squatting at the ear of the sleeping Eve, as seeking "to taint / Th' animal spirits that from pure blood arise / Like gentle breaths from Rivers pure" (4.805–6). This is an image of benign natural process that has, as we have seen, potentially cosmic reach. Satan does succeed in giving Eve a vision of "high exaltation" (5.90), but Eve, instead of being disappointed to wake up and find her vision of flying false, immediately characterizes the dream as a nightmare—"O how glad I wak'd / To find this but a dream" (5.91–92).[79] Adam then—presumably with the voice of authority—first gives her a lecture on the psychological mechanism by which dreams are produced (5.100–13), and then reassures her with a moral point:

> Evil into the mind of God or Man
> May come and go, so unapprov'd, and leave
> No spot or blame behind.   (5.117–19)

This is, as I suggested, an admirable assertion of the juridical independence of mere thoughts from actions—a major issue in Milton's period, both before and after the Civil War and Interregnum—but it is strikingly inappropriate to Eve's situation.[80] Evil did not spontaneously "come into" her mind; it was put there by an outside agent. Adam should have stopped at "evil whence?" ("Yet evil whence? In thee can harbor none, / Created pure" [5.99–100]). His moral comment is no more relevant to Eve's situation than is his lecture on dreams (she has had, as she says, dreams before, and this experience was nothing like those [5.30–34]). My point is that while what Adam says is fully appropriate to the consciousness of angels (called "Gods" elsewhere in the poem), and to that of fallen men, it is not appropriate to Milton's presentation of unfallen persons. Evil would not spontaneously have "come into" their minds.[81] They do not need injunctions, promises, or threats in order to be good; they are good because they are creatures of a certain kind. They do not need constantly to choose the good. Tillyard's declaration that "no human being can conceive or represent evil entering into a mind quite alien to it" eliminates one of Milton's greatest achievements by denying that it could have occurred.[82]

I hope that I have given a sense of how extraordinary it is that the apostle of moral deliberation, of reason as choice, should have created one of the most compelling pictures of an alternative vision of the ethical life. Let me conclude by arguing that what Milton has presented in his Eden really is a vision of the ethical life, and not something inferior and less truly, rigorously desirable. Aristotle's *Ethics* helps here; its project is to encourage the development of creatures of a certain kind rather than of perfect rational calculators. The goal of the ethical life, for Aristotle, is not to make perfect choices but to become, through training, education, and moral experience, the sort of creature who does not have to be constantly making moral choices.

C. S. Lewis nicely describes the difference between Aristotle's view and one that stresses moral effort. Lewis notes that "where we incline to think that 'good thews inforced with pains' are more praiseworthy than mere goodness of disposition," for Aristotle, the ease with which good acts are done, precisely the absence of moral effort, is what defines virtue.[83] Bernard Williams's attack on "the moral" in the name of the ethical is getting at this same idea. In discussing the importance for social life of being able to rely on certain things not routinely happening (not being killed, etc.), Williams notes that one way of assuring this is to instil into persons dispositions to give the considerations against such actions a very high "deliberative priority." But Williams goes on to argue that, alternatively, "an effective way for actions to be ruled out is that they never come into thought at all," and he claims that "this is often the best way." Lest this seem mere dogmatizing, he gives an example: "One does not feel easy with the man who in the course of a discussion of how to deal with political or business rivals says, 'Of course, we could have them killed, but we should lay that aside right from the beginning.'" Williams comments, "It should never have come into his hands to be laid aside" (recall Adam's inability to understand ingratitude).[84] Williams's large conclusion is that "it is characteristic of morality that it tends to overlook the possibility that some concerns are best embodied in this way, in deliberative silence."[85]

So how was it possible for Milton to present the picture of life in Eden that he did? The answer might be that unfallen life was not part of the project of theodicy. In Eden, there was no problem of evil; there was no pressure on God's goodness. By contrast, we never see heaven solely as a place of bliss. Heaven is always the place where the great rebellion has happened. But about life before the Fall, Milton does not have to argue anything—except, of course, the propriety of the single prohibition, which need not be focused on until the very moment of disaster. Finally, I should say that I am not sure that the counter-currents to deliberative moralism were unconscious to Milton. His most unfettered imaginings of happiness always involved relying on "the faultless proprieties of nature."[86]

The University of Chicago

NOTES

1. "The Marriage of Heaven and Hell," in *The Poetry and Prose of William Blake*, ed. David V. Erdman (New York, 1965), 35; E. M. W. Tillyard, *Milton*, rev. ed. (New York, 1967; orig. pub. 1930), Pt. 3, ch. 4 ("The Unconscious Meaning"). I owe my awareness of the kinship of Tillyard's view with my own to Michael Lieb.

2. "Milton has so far violated the popular creed (if this shall be judged to be a violation) as to have alleged no superiority of moral virtue to his God over his Devil." *A Defence of Poetry*, in *The Selected Poetry and Prose of Percy Bysshe Shelley*, ed. Carlos Baker (New York, 1951), 512.

3. William Empson, *Milton's God* (London, 1961), 35. For Empson's commitment to authorial intention, see Richard Strier, *Resistant Structures: Particularity, Radicalism, and Renaissance Texts* (Berkeley, 1995), 15–16.

4. Dennis Richard Danielson, *Milton's Good God: A Study in Literary Theodicy* (Cambridge, 1982).

5. Danielson knows this, but he finds the idea so attractive that he does not present any sense of its distinctness. At one point he finds himself having to assure us that a "reasoned" justification of God's ways is not a rationalistic one, though he never clarifies wherein the distinction lies (*Milton's Good God*, 117).

6. Many critics, most notably Stanley Fish in *Surprised by Sin: the Reader in Paradise Lost* (New York, 1967), take *Paradise Lost* to be Calvinist in its theology. The most surprising (and contradictory) in this regard is Dennis H. Burden, *The Logical Epic: A Study of the Argument of Paradise Lost* (London, 1967), 124–25, which seems to see the poem as *both* Calvinist and rationalist.

7. John Peter Rumrich, *Matter of Glory: A New Preface to Paradise Lost* (Pittsburgh, 1987), 10.

8. Martin Luther, *The Bondage of the Will*, trans. J. I. Packer and A. R. Johnston (New Jersey, 1957), 282. The fifth book of the *Ethics* concerns justice.

9. John Calvin, *Institutes of the Christian Religion*, ed. John T. McNeill, trans. Ford Lewis Battles (Philadelphia, 1960), 1.14.1. A more literal rendering would translate "will" as "pleasure" in "Et recte Augustinus iniuriam Deo fieri conqueritur ubi *superior eius voluptate* flagitur rerum causa." Joannis Calvini, *Opera Selecta*, ed. P. Barth and W. Niesel, vol. 3 (Munich, 1928).

10. Quotations from Milton's poetry are from *John Milton: Complete Poems and Major Prose*, ed. Merritt Y. Hughes (New York, 1957).

11. Danielson, *Milton's Good God*, 10 n.14, obliquely notes the ambiguity but does not make anything of it.

12. See Willam B. Hunter, *Visitation Unimplor'd: Milton and the Authorship of De Doctrina Christiana* (Pittsburgh, 1998).

13. Virtually all scholars now agree with Hunter that the physical evidence, the name and initials in the manuscript, does not settle the authorship question; see Gordon Campbell, Thomas N. Corns, John K. Hale, David I. Holmes, Fiona J. Tweedie, "The Provenance of the *De Doctrina Christiana*," *Milton Quarterly* 31 (October 1997): 92–93. My discussion therefore

focuses on what the text says. Neither the supposed references to practices that were non-English nor the claims for ideological divergence (from Milton's known writings) hold up.

14. See Hunter, *Visitation Unimplor'd*, ch. 5, and Kelley's "Introduction" to *Christian Doctrine*, ed. Maurice Kelley, trans. John Carey, *The Complete Prose Works of John Milton*, ed. Don M. Wolfe, et al., 8 vols. (New Haven, 1963), vol. 6, 54–58 (on Servetus), and 74–86 (on Arminianism). This eight volume edition of the prose will hereafter be cited as YP (Yale Prose). *Christian Doctrine* will hereafter be referred to parenthetically in the text as *CD*.

15. Compare Andrew Milner, *John Milton and the English Revolution: A Study in the Sociology of Literature* (Totowa, N.J., 1981), 115.

16. In the discussion of "number" in *The Art of Logic*, Milton interposes the following words into the passage he is quoting: *Evigilent hic Theologi* ("Here let the Theologians take notice"), YP 8:233. See T. K. Scott-Craig, "The Craftsmanship and Theological Significance of Milton's *Art of Logic*," *HLQ* 17 (1953), 2–3.

17. For the importance of the free will argument, see D. P. Walker, *The Decline of Hell: Seventeenth-Century Discussions of Eternal Torment* (Chicago, 1964), 42–48; and Danielson, *Milton's Good God*, ch. 4.

18. Luther, *The Bondage of the Will*, 319.

19. See Brian Gerrish, *Grace and Reason: A Study in the Theology of Luther* (Oxford, 1962); Richard Strier, *Love Known: Theology and Experience in George Herbert's Poetry* (Chicago, 1983), ch. 2 ("The Attack on Reason").

20. Luther saw his little book on *The Freedom of a Christian* as containing "the whole of Christian life." See John Dillenberger, ed., *Martin Luther: Selections from His Writings* (New York, 1961), 52.

21. Roland H. Bainton, *Here I Stand: A Life of Martin Luther* (New York 1950), 97.

22. Luther, *Freedom of a Christian*, Dillenberger, ed., 74.

23. See *The Theologica Germanica of Martin Luther*, trans. Bengt Hoffman (New York, 1980). For Luther's relation to mysticism, see, inter alia, Heiko A. Oberman, "*Simul Gemitus et Raptus:* Luther and Mysticism," in *The Reformation in Medieval Perspective*, ed. Steven E. Ozment (Chicago, 1971), 220–51.

24. For Luther's anti-Platonism, see "Preface to Romans," in Dillenberger, ed., *Luther Selections*, 19–34.

25. Arthur O. Lovejoy, *The Great Chain of Being: A Study of the History of an Idea* (Cambridge, Mass., 1936), 49.

26. Plotinus, *The Enneads*, trans. Stephen MacKenna, abridged and with an introduction by John Dillon (London, 1991), 2.9.3.

27. *Enneads* 5.1.6. For Lloyd P. Gerson, the importance of this passage "cannot be overestimated" (*Plotinus* [London and New York, 1994], 23).

28. *Enneads* 3.2.3. I am grateful to Janel Mueller for a question that led me to see the importance of this point to Plotinus.

29. *Enneads* 4.4.10–12.

30. Ernst Cassirer, "Giovanni Pico della Mirandola," in *Renaissance Essays*, ed. Paul O. Kristeller and Philip P. Wiener (New York, 1968), 22.

31. "Certain Articles to be Diligently Examined" in *The Works of James Arminius*, trans. James Nichols (Auburn and Buffalo, 1853), vol. 2, 480; George Rust, *Letter of Resolution Concerning Origen* (1661), 25. I owe my awareness of the importance of this theme to Arminius and Rust (and others) to Stephen M. Fallon, " 'To Act or Not': Milton's Conception of Divine Freedom," *JHI* 49 (1988): 425–49.

32. For the view that *Christian Doctrine* consistently (and coherently) does maintain this position, see Fallon, " 'To Act or Not.' "

33. YP 8:222.

34. Danielson, *Milton's Good God*, 138 (see also 123–24).

35. Stella Purce Revard, *The War in Heaven: Paradise Lost and the Tradition of Satan's Revolt* (Ithaca, 1980), 204.

36. For this perspective on Satan, see Helen Gardner, "Milton's 'Satan' and the Theme of Damnation in Elizabethan Tragedy,"in *Milton: Modern Essays in Criticism*, ed. Arthur E. Barker (London, 1965), 205–17.

37. For a reading of *The Tempest* as an exploration of the limits of coercing, see Richard Strier, "'I am Power': Normal and Magical Politics in *The Tempest*," in Derek Hirst and Richard Strier, eds., *Writing and Political Engagement in Seventeenth-Century England* (Cambridge, 1999), 10–30.

38. See Richard Strier, "Milton against Humility," in *Religion and Culture in the English Renaissance*, ed. Claire McEachern and Debora Shuger (Cambridge, 1997), 258–86.

39. Irene Samuel, inter alia, unfavorably contrasts the genuineness of the dialogue in heaven in Book Three with the falseness of the dialogue in hell in Book Two ("The Dialogue in Heaven: A Reconsideration of *Paradise Lost*, III, 1–417," in *Milton: Modern Essays in Criticism*, ed. Barker, 233–45). In fact, the opposite seems to me to be true. The response of the Son to God's opening speech sounds, as Samuel says, "remarkably unlike mere assent" (235), but that is what it is. God's speech ends by asserting and explaining why Man (but not the fallen angels) "therefore shall find grace" (3.129–34). The Son's account (150–67) of the undesirability of the destruction of man describes a possibility that has already been forestalled.

40. On Jesus as "not mov'd" in *Paradise Regained*, see 2.407 (also 4.420, "unshak'n"), culminating in "and stood" (unmoving) at 4.561.

41. Even here, Milton feels impelled to add something worse than the desire for "glory" in condemning men; the next line substitutes "close ambition varnisht o'er with zeal." Compare the qualifications in *Paradise Regained* 3.100–4. For the complexity of "glory" in *Paradise Lost*, see Rumrich, *Matter of Glory*, esp. ch. 9.

42. Luther, *Bondage of the Will*, 209.

43. For the claims that the "farce" in the war is intentional, and that the military trappings in the poem are meant to undercut themselves and conduce to a paficist message, see Arnold Stein, *Answerable Style: Essays on Paradise Lost* (Minneapolis, 1953), 22–26. On the unlikeliness of the latter, see Robert Thomas Fallon, *Captain or Colonel: The Soldier in Milton's Life and Art* (Columbia, Mo., 1984), 204–5. On the unlikeliness of the former, see Revard, *The War in Heaven*, 154–55 and passim.

44. Michael Lieb, *Children of Ezekiel: Aliens, UFOs, the Crisis of Race, and the Advent of End Time* (Durham, N.C., 1998).

45. Compare the discussion of demonic concord above.

46. The fact that the narrator denigrates these pleasures—"Thir song was partial" (2.552), their discussions inconclusive (2.557–65)—does not affect the point about the capacities of Satan's followers to appreciate "excellence" other than military.

47. In *The War in Heaven*, Revard notes that the Son's return "at first suggests a martial victor" (262), but she then goes on to explain how we have to discount this impression. Similarly, in *Images of Kingship in Paradise Lost: Milton's Politics and Christian Liberty* (Columbia, Mo., 1983), Stevie Davis has a difficult time rationalizing the imperial Roman association of Christ's triumph here (121–24).

48. C. S. Lewis, *A Preface to Paradise Lost* (Oxford, 1942), 130.

49. Bernard Williams, *Morality: An Introduction to Ethics* (New York, 1972), 75.

50. Bernard Williams, *Ethics and the Limits of Philosophy* (Cambridge, Mass., 1985), 18. I am indebted to Mark Miller for reminding me of this phrase.

51. Fish, *Surprised by Sin,* ch. 2.

52. On Fish's general tendency to focus on form rather than on content, see Strier, *Resistant Structures,* ch. 2. For some important reflections on why Fish's approach to *Paradise Lost* has been so successful, see John Rumrich, *Milton Unbound: Controversy and Reinterpretation* (Cambridge, 1996), chs. 1–2.

53. YP 4:446.

54. Compare Milner, *John Milton and the English Revolution* 157.

55. Homer, *Odyssey* 1.32–34.

56. YP 2:294; *CD,* 202.

57. If this entire line (97), or at least its third foot ("ingrate"), is perceived as perfectly regular iambic, the tonal problem disappears, since the stress falls on the second syllable of "ingrate," and the word becomes an adjective rather than a noun.

58. See *Nicomachean Ethics* 1109b, 30–35, trans. Terence Irwin (Indianapolis, 1985), 53 (hereafter *NE*). Hughes's reference to *NE* 3 as the source for "Reason also is choice" (*Complete Poems and Selected Prose,* 260) is puzzling, since Aristotle distinguishes, in book 3, between deliberation and other uses of reason—holding opinions, for instance (see 1111b2–1112b15).

59. YP 2:527.

60. It is important to recall that, in Williams' account, the "moral" is a specialized subsection of the ethical, a subsection that is characterized by its insistence on "bright lines" between itself and everything else. The ethical realm, for Williams, is a much larger and looser realm of heterogeneous considerations. See especially "Morality, the Peculiar Institution," *Ethics and the Limits of Philosophy,* ch. 10.

61. "Spirits elect" here, and throughout Book Three, does not imply Calvinist predestination. As in "Decree / Unchangeable," Milton uses the terminology of Calvinism in an anti-Calvinist sense.

62. For the "Pleroma," see Hans Jonas, *The Gnostic Religion: The Message of the Alien God and the Beginnings of Christianity,* 2nd ed. (Boston, 1963), esp. ch. 8.

63. See Plato, *Timaeus,* 29e, in *Collected Dialogues of Plato,* ed. Edith Hamilton and Huntington Cairns (Princeton, 1961), 1162; Plotinus, *Enneads* 5.4; Arminius, "The Apology or Defence of James Arminius," *Works* 1:345–46.

64. For the view that Milton's position is coherent here, as in *CD,* and is based on a coherent position in Aquinas, see Fallon, "'To Act or Not.'" I would deny that Milton accepts Aquinas' position (even mediated through Wollebius and Ames), and I would also deny (with Lovejoy) that Aquinas' position is itself coherent (*Great Chain,* 73–79).

65. These lines attempt to conceptualize freedom from obligation, but they feel strained and do not seem to escape from the language of obligation. For a vision that does seem to escape from these problems, see "Gratefulnesse" in *The Works of George Herbert,* ed. F. E. Hutchinson (Oxford, 1945), 124.

66. Dante's *Paradiso, Italian Text with English Translation* by John D. Sinclair (New York, 1961), 50–53 (3.64–84).

67. Michael Murrin has urged me to take into account that this line is spoken by Raphael and not by God or the epic narrator. While it is surely true that one has to consider to whom an utterance in a narrative is assigned, I do not think that this is relevant to the truth of the assertion here. The line is meant, I think, to introduce the extent of the tragedy of the rebellion, not the limits of Raphael's perceptions.

68. I believe that it is therefore the line of classical poetry most frequently alluded to in the poem, though I would be eager to hear of other contenders.

69. Revard's statement that Satan "uses the beauty of his unfallen nature to draw allegiance"

from the angels who follow him paraphrases the poem accurately (5.708–9) but remains, I think, entirely morally opaque (*War in Heaven*, 98).

70. See Empson, *Milton's God*, 111, on the qualities of character demonstrated in the "prompt obedience" speech, and the appropriateness of these qualities of character to the conditions of angelic (heavenly) existence.

71. In seeing Milton's treatment of nature as escaping from some of his more explicit views, I have been anticipated by John Rogers, *The Matter of Revolution: Science, Poetry, and Politics in the Age of Milton* (Ithaca, 1996). However, where for Rogers rationalism and "vitalism" (what I call "the diffusion principle") stand together against authoritarianism, I see a major tension between rationalism and "vitalism." Milton's presentation of and relation to what Michael Murrin calls "the mysterious figure alluded to in the Invocations" might be seen as another "unfettered" area in *Paradise Lost*, another area free from the framework of deliberation, though I do not agree with Murrin that this figure is as present in the poem as "the rationalist deity." See *The Allegorical Epic: Essays in Its Rise and Decline* (Chicago, 1980), 163–64.

72. See, for instance, Dionysius, *The Divine Names*, ch. 4, in *The Divine Names* and *The Mystical Theology*, trans. C. E. Rolt (London, 1940), 86–87.

73. This kind of passage is part of what Empson had in mind in suggesting that it was not totally unintelligible or despicable for Satan to imagine being self-begotten through "our own quick'ning power" (5.860–61; *Milton's God*, 88–89). Rogers' book provides a great deal of convincing support for Empson's view. See especially Rogers' treatment of "the non-authoritarian logic of the principle of the ferment," *The Matter of Revolution*, 121–51.

74. See, inter alia, Robert Burton, *The Anatomy of Melancholy*, 3 vols., ed. Holbrook Jackson (New York, 1932), vol. 1:147–48. It is interesting and, I think, significant, that "aspire" can be used positively here ("Man's nourishment, by gradual scale sublim'd / To vital spirits aspire").

75. Joseph E. Duncan, *Milton's Earthly Paradise: A Historical Study of Eden* (Minneapolis, 1972), 134–147.

76. When the Father speaks of the privilege Adam had "freely" to dislike the possible mates presented to him before the creation of Eve (8.443), the term works in an interestingly ambiguous and non-straightforward way. It seems to mean primarily "with impunity" (see "freedom . . . permissive" at 434–35), but while the word attempts to put Adam's responses into the moral framework, and while the whole passage stresses "rational delight" (391), the sense of "freely" here remains close to "instinctively"—as the passage suggests by ending, wonderfully, on "thy heart's desire" (451). There is no contrast between "rational" and "instinctive" delight in this presentation.

77. As this account suggests, I am in sharp disagreement with critics who see Milton as, in Tillyard's words, "faking" with regard to prelapsarian life. See E. M. W. Tillyard, "The Crisis of Paradise Lost," in *Studies in Milton* (London, 1951), 11. I am opposed to all versions of the "fall before the Fall" view. The view that this scene dramatizes Eve's "successful" internalization of a patriarchalist system is less easily answered, and perhaps unanswerable. See, inter alia, Christine Froula, "When Eve Reads Milton: Undoing the Canonical Economy," *Critical Inquiry* 10 (December, 1983), 321–47, esp. 326–30. A Lacanian reading of Eve's narrative might present it as not an account of the origin of gendered subjectivity, but simply an account of the origin of subjectivity *tout court*, describing stages through which every (normal) human infant goes in becoming a subject. This reading would need to deal with the fact that gender seems a marked feature of this narrative, but such an objection could certainly be dealt with by such a reading. In any case, the two accounts need not be seen in opposition to one another but as layered (or intertwined) in the passage. Linda Gregerson seems to see them this way in *The Reformation of the Subject: Spenser, Milton, and the English Protestant Epic* (Cambridge, 1995), 151–61.

78. In *Bodies of Rule: Physiology and Interiority in Early Modern English Literature* (Cambridge University Press, 1999), ch. 5, Michael Schoenfeldt asks, "Are we to imagine a paradise strewn with over-ripe fruit?" Milton's answer, I believe, is "yes." It is part of the special dynamism and future-orientation of Eden that Barbara K. Lewalski first emphasized in "Innocence and Experience in Milton's Eden," in Thomas Kranidas, ed., *New Essays on* Paradise Lost (Berkeley, 1971), 86–117.

79. Compare Diane Kelsey McColley, *Milton's Eve* (Urbana, 1983), 99.

80. I have dealt with the opposition to legal and other proceedings seen as "reaching even to men's thoughts" in "From Diagnosis to Operation: The 'Root and Branch' Petition and The Grand Remonstrance," in *The Theatrical City: Culture, Theatre and Politics in London, 1576–1649*, ed. David L. Smith, Richard Strier, and David Bevington (Cambridge, 1995), 230–33.

81. I do not think that anything in the dialogue about division of labor in Book Nine contravenes this. I think that Milton there does a remarkable job of presenting a disagreement that does honor to both speakers. As Addison says, "It is such a Dispute as we may suppose might have happened in Paradise"; it "proceeds from a Difference of Judgment, not of Passion, and is managed with Reason, not Heat" ("The Spectator," no. 351, in *The Spectator*, ed. Gregory Smith [London, 1907], vol 3., 98).

82. Tillyard, "Crisis," 11. See also A. J. A. Waldock, *Paradise Lost and Its Critics* (Cambridge, 1947), 61.

83. C. S. Lewis, *The Allegory of Love: A Study in Medieval Tradition* (Oxford, 1936), 59. Lewis has in mind Aristotle's distinction between temperance (*sophrosyne*) and continence (*enkratia*); Aristotle does not consider the latter, the condition of the person who feels temptations, but resists them, virtuous (*NE* 1104^{b}5 and 1152^{a}1).

84. See Adam's puzzled response to the conditionality of Raphael's "If ye be found obedient" at Book Five, 513–18. ("What meant that caution . . .?").

85. Williams, *Ethics and the Limits of Philosophy,* 185.

86. YP 2:237.

"A THOUSAND FORE-SKINS": CIRCUMCISION, VIOLENCE, AND SELFHOOD IN MILTON

Michael Lieb

I

A MONG THE MOST MEMORABLE scenes in the biblical account of Samson's exploits is his slaughter of the Philistines with the jawbone of an ass. Commemorating that exploit, the place at which the massacre occurs comes to be known as *Ramath-lehi* or "height of a jawbone" (Judg. 15:15–17). It is to this event that the Chorus of *Samson Agonistes* alludes when it recalls how the once-mighty Samson with "the Jaw of a dead Ass" smote the Philistines so ruthlessly that "a thousand fore-skins fell" in "*Ramath-lechi* famous to this day" (*SA*, 143–45).[1] Although the reference to the thousand foreskins is obviously a synecdoche for the Philistine troops as a whole, one might observe (a bit facetiously perhaps) that in felling such a multitude of "fore-skins," Milton's Samson no doubt proved himself the greatest *mohel* of all time. At the very least, Milton's trope points up the all-important distinction between Samson as the circumcised champion of the Israelites and the Philistines as the uncircumcised enemy. Focusing upon the implications of this distinction, I wish to invite an interpretation of how Milton's works in general and his dramatic poem in particular provide a renewed understanding of the significance of violence to his outlook and his sense of self. This is a sense that I have already explored at length in a discussion of *sparagmos* or bodily mutilation and dismemberment as a crucial feature of the Miltonic psyche.[2] In keeping with that earlier discussion, I wish now to focus on what might be called the violence of the cut. Through an examination of circumcision as the consummate expression of that violence, I seek to gain a clearer idea of the forces that shaped Milton both as individual and as author.

In order to address the issue of circumcision in Milton's thought and writings, one must come to terms with the practice both as a biblical phenomenon and as an event of major import to the world that Milton inhabited. As a biblical phenomenon, the covenant of circumcision (*brit milah*) first makes its presence known in the patriarchal narratives.[3] There, it is the rite that sanctifies God's promise to the "exalted father," Abram, that he will be the "father of multitudes," Abraham, through whose fruitful seed many nations will be produced (Gen. 17:4–7).[4] As a signifier of that promise, the "fruitful cut" is ordained.[5] So God says to Abraham: "This is my covenant [*zot briti*], which ye shall keep, between me and you and thy seed after thee; Every man child among you shall be circumcised [*hamol*]. And ye shall circumcise the flesh of your foreskin [*bsar arlatchem*]; and it shall be a token of the covenant betwixt me and you" (Gen. 17:10–11).[6] To cut the fore-skin (*arlah*) is to remove that portion of flesh (commonly known as the prepuce) that paradoxically renders one not only "naked" or "exposed" but in later usage "unclean."[7] Those not circumcised (that is, those who are "fore-skinned"), moreover, shall be deemed to have broken the covenant and shall therefore be "cut off" from God and his people (Gen. 17:14). The idea of being "cut off" is ironically appropriate, for in biblical terms the very act of making a covenant is already conceived as a cutting, so that when God makes a covenant with Abraham, the expression is literally that of "cutting a cove-nant [*karat brit*]" (Gen. 15:18).[8] Whereas *karat* denotes the act of "cutting" or "cutting off," it bears the derivative idea of "exterminating."[9] Encoded in *karat* is already the possibility of violence in the extreme. The idea is implicit in the act of cutting and dismembering the calf, goat, and ram that commem-orates Abraham's covenant with God (Gen. 15:9–11; cf. Jer. 34:10–19).

Within this violent context, the rite of circumcision that follows hard upon this *karat brit* is thereby seen as a "special case of general cutting or dismembering rites by which covenants or treaties were established."[10] As a fulfillment of the *brit*, circumcision served as a kind of "knife rite" that inscribed on the flesh the cutting that was essential to the covenant from the very beginning.[11] At the heart of the *brit milah* or covenant of circumcision, then, is the concept of violence. Consistent with the violence implicit in *karat*, the verb *mul* (circumcise) not only denotes the idea of "cutting off" (as in the cutting of the foreskin) but implies as well a "cutting to pieces" or "annihilating" the enemy "by force of arms."[12] The violence implict in the *brit milah* as a manifestation of the act of cutting the covenant can either turn inward in a generative sense to seal a relationship between the individual and his deity, or it can turn outward in a destructive sense to wreak vengeance upon those who violate all that the relationship between the individual and his deity implies. Either way, circumcision in its most archaic form is indeed a "knife rite" infused with the notion of violence.

This violence is variously portrayed throughout the Hebrew Bible.[13] As a generative notion of the so-called "knife rite," it is delineated in the Book of Joshua as a large-scale event. Having passed over the river Jordan, the chil-dren of Israel must be purified in order to fulfill their desire to enter the Promised Land. This involves an act of mass circumcision. So "the Lord said unto Joshua, Make thee sharp knives, and circumcise again the children of Israel the second time. And Joshua made him sharp knives, and circumcised the children of Israel at the hill of foreskins [*gibeat-haaralot*]" (Josh. 5:3). Although those who first came out of Egypt had already been circumcised, those born in the wilderness during the journey had not yet undergone the ritual. Because those originally circumcised had perished in the wilderness sojourn as the result of their disobedience, it is their uncircumcised children who must be circumcised now in order to enter the Promised Land. Significantly, the act of circumcising the foreskin is commemorated by its own hill, known as the hill of foreskins, a name that suggests the piling up of the *aralot* (foreskins) of an entire male population as a monument to reestablishing the covenant between God and his people. Such a hill or mound encodes within the landscape the visible sign of the *karat brit*. Having undergone circumcision, the Israelites "abode in their places in the camp, till they were whole," that is, until they healed from the wound. In their new state of purity, they celebrate Passover (Josh. 5:2–12; cf. Exod. 12:48). To emphasize even further the significance of the event and in particular the importance of circumcision as that which renders pure, the narrator of the Joshua account observes that the place of the encampment is named *Gilgal* (related to *galal*, "to roll"), because, as God proclaims, "This day have I rolled away [*galoti*] the reproach of Egypt [*cherpat mitzraim*] from off you" (Josh. 5:9). Liberated from the bondage of the slavery they were made to endure in Egypt, they are cleansed of their "reproach" or "shame" (*cherpah*). Emblematized in the "rolling off" of the foreskin from the head or crown of the penis, circumcision is the means by which they regain their purity, strength, and virility. As such, they stand cleansed before God. Inscribed as a seal of the covenant upon the flesh of the Israelites by the violence of the cut that binds, this is circumcision in the generative sense.[14]

The destructive implications (circumcision as a "cutting to pieces" or "annihilating" the enemy "by force of arms") are equally important to the rite. Once again, violence is an integral part of the "knife rite." A case in point is the vengeance that the sons of Jacob take upon the Shechemites for the rape and defilement of Dinah by Shechem, the son of Hamor (Gen. 34:2). For the sons of Jacob, such an act is rendered that much more abominable because it is committed by a member of an alien people, one whose state of uncleanness is signified by the fact of their uncircumcision (*arlah*) (Gen. 34:7, 14). In the minds of the Israelites, such a people are by their very nature "unclean."[15] It is by means of the distinction between clean and unclean that the sons of Jacob seek to avenge Dinah, for when Shechem seeks permission to marry Dinah as a duplicitous way of gaining power over Jacob and his possessions (Gen. 34:8, 23), the sons of Jacob, in turn, deceive the enemy into thinking that there can be a reconciliation only if every male of the Shechemites is circumcised: "And they [the sons of Jacob] said unto them [the

Shechemites], We cannot do this thing, to give our sister to one that is uncircumcised; for that *were* a reproach unto us: But in this will we consent unto you: If ye will be as we *be*, that every male of you be circumcised; Then will we give our daughters unto you" and accept your daughters in return (Gen. 34:14–16). Agreeing to the arrangement, the Shechemites undertake a mass circumcision that renders them vulnerable to the slaughter they bring upon themselves, as the sons of Jacob descend upon the newly circumcised enemy. "And it came to pass on the third day, when they [the Shechemites] were sore, that two of the sons of Jacob, Simeon and Levi, Dinah's brethren, took each man his sword, and came upon the city boldly, and slew all the males. And they slew Hamor and Shechem his son with the edge of the sword, and took Dinah out of Shechem's house, and went out." Thereafter, "the sons of Jacob came upon the slain, and spoiled the city, because they had defiled their sister" (Gen. 34:25–27). The violence that is turned upon the self as a fruitful sign of binding in the act of cutting the covenant is here turned upon the enemy as a means of retribution. One might suggest that in savagely slaying the newly circumcised (and therefore vulnerable) Sheche-mites, the sons of Jacob are in effect performing a "true" circumcision upon them, rendering them sons of the covenant in a manner that they had little anticipated. Now, the Shechemites truly know what it means to be circum-cised! In this triumphant act of savagery on the part of the sons of Jacob, circumcision by "the edge of the sword" becomes the vehicle through which rape and defilement are met with a brutality undreamt among those who have been forcibly "circumcised" in the true Israelite fashion.[16]

When Saint Paul undertook to redefine the significance of circumcision in his epistles, he was at pains to overcome this sense of savagery. In the process, he spiritualized and internalized the *brit milah* in a manner consis-tent with an impulse already discernible in the Hebrew Bible.[17] There, Paul found that the Deuteronomist speaks of circumcision of the heart (30:6; cf. Lev. 26:41), a metaphor adopted later by Jeremiah (4:4; 9:25) and Ezekiel (44:7, 9). He likewise discovered that other texts speak of circumcision of the lips (Exod. 11:12, 30), as well as of the ears (Jer. 9:25; cf. Acts 7:51). Such a reorientation, already present in the Hebrew Bible, prompted Paul to re-move the emphasis that literal circumcision placed on the flesh and to refor-mulate the idea of circumcision so that its proper emphasis was on the spirit. This spiritual orientation is crucial to the Pauline teachings. For Paul, true circumcision is accordingly not of the flesh but of the heart. It belongs to those who worship God in the spirit, who glory in Christ, and who put no confidence in the flesh (Rom. 2:25–27; Phil. 3:2–5; Col. 2:11–13). According to Paul, not circumcision but faith in Christ is required for one to be accepted by God (Rom. 4:9–12; 15:8–9). Reliance upon literal circumcision alone is reliance upon the law, which leads to death (Rom. 3:9–19), whereas justification and acceptance come in Christ and are the reward of faith (Rom. 3:21–5:5). Far from insuring acceptance before God, circumcision, as an actual cutting of the flesh, condemns anyone who trusts it.[18] In the Christocentric perspective that Paul embraces, the truly faithful are "circumcised with the circumcision made without hands" and buried in Christ in baptism and risen with Christ through faith (Col. 2:11–12). No longer requiring literal circumcision as a signature of the covenant, the faithful "glory in the cross of our Lord Jesus Christ," in whom "neither circumcision availeth any thing, nor uncircumcision, but a new creature" born of the suffering of Jesus Christ, by whom "the world is crucified" unto them, and they "unto the world" (Gal. 6:12–15). It is in this manner that Paul banishes "carnal Israel."[19]

As much as Paul distances himself from the violence wrought upon the flesh, his determination to spiritualize the ritual of circumcision has its limits, for in the very act of devaluing circumcision as a literal cut, he engages in a rhetoric that revels in a corresponding cut of the most brutal sort. This is a rhetoric that ironically gives rise to its own form of violence, indeed, a savagery all its own. It is precisely this violence that Paul would unleash upon those who adhere to the cut. Preaching the efficacy of spiritual circumcision as opposed to the folly of circumcision in the flesh, Paul accordingly admonishes those who persecute his brethren by declaring, "I would they [the persecutors] were even cut off [apokopsontai in the Greek; abscindantur in the Latin] which trouble you" (Gal. 5:11–12). "Cut off" is not only derisive in its force but violent in its implications. Especially in the Greek but also in the Latin, the text suggests precisely what Paul would have happen to the circumcised persecutors of his brethren: "would that they [the persecutors] might make eunuchs of themselves." (The Latin adds insult to injury, for abscindo means "to break or tear off as with the hand.")[20] In a brutal act of vilification, Paul does not hesitate to counter circumcision with castration. As early as Paul's epistle to the Galatians, the association of the two is canonized in the New Testament. By virtue of such an association, the violence encoded in the brit milah is subsumed with renewed virulence into the Pauline point of view, so much so, in fact, that it is transformed through a rhetoric of vilification into the unkindest cut of all. All the anxieties engendered by circumcision as a "knife rite" coalesce here, as Paul brings to the fore fears of the cut that emerge unexpectedly in moments of confrontation with those who rely on the literal cut to confirm their beliefs. Needless to say, the violence made evident in the Pauline text engaged biblical exegetes from the time of the Church Fathers throughout the early modern period and beyond.[21] In whatever form it might be perceived, then, the ritual of circumcision is imbued from the outset with a sense of brutality, if not savagery, that renders its proper milieu one of aggression and fear.

This milieu typifies the repulsion that has greeted both circumcision and its purveyors throughout history. In the ancient world, two rulers outlawed circumcision on pain of death: Antiochus IV Epiphanes, the Greek Seleucid ruler, hurled mothers and their circumcised babies from the walls of Jerusalem; and Hadrian, the Roman emperor, looked upon circumcision as the moral equivalent of castration and outlawed both.[22] For the Roman poets, the *"curti Iudaei"* were the constant objects of derision, as Horace's slighting references to "the bob-tailed Jews" and Martial's impugning of Jews as impotent figures of lust attest.[23] The anxieties surrounding the "unforeskinned race" were correspondingly present in early modern England, a period during which Jews were putatively absent from English soil as a result of their expulsion in 1290 until the time of their readmission in 1656.[24] Whatever the extent of their actual presence during this long span, Jews were conceived in such a way that their association with circumcision amounted to something like a national obsession. This fact is especially fascinating if one considers that in early modern England, "there is no evidence that circumcisions took place," at least among the Christian population.[25] Given this circumstance, the early modern English obsession with the Jew as circumciser (not to mention abducter and crucifier) of male victims is "nothing less than extraordinary."[26] In keeping with this obsession, Raphael Holinshed and John Foxe, for example, describe in detail how Jews were punished in the early Middle Ages because they circumcised and mutilated Christian boys. Anthony Wood lists among the "enormities" performed by medieval Jews at Oxford "enticing the young scholars and the children of the inhabitants to be of their religion, and forcing them to be circumcised."[27] As an argument against the prospect of readmitting the Jews to England, William Prynne provides detailed accounts of the medieval Jew as abducter, circumciser, and barbarian. Jews, Prynne declares, were known to steal children from their parents and to imprison them for "a years space from the sight of Christians," with the barbaric idea of circumcising them "on the feast of *Easter*," of all times. Once abducted, these children were not only circumcised but "tortured, spat upon, whipped, blasphemed, disembowelled, and cast into a pit."[28]

What might aptly be called the "Jewish crime" appears "to have touched deeply on fears that no doubt stretch across cultures but seem to have had a special urgency in early modern England."[29] In his study of the impact that this culture of fear had upon Shakespeare's own works, James Shapiro makes a compelling case for the symbolism of circumcision/castration implicit in the cut that Shylock would wreak upon poor Antonio, who comes to fear that he will amount to nothing more than a "tainted wether," or castrated ram.[30] Many years later, corresponding anxieties are manifested in Alexander Pope's malicious depiction of the forced circumcision that the bookseller Edmund Curll endures by a company of merciless Jews equipped with "a large Pair of Sheers" and "a red hot Searing Iron." At the critical moment of the procedure, Curll in his fright jerks upward and loses "five times as much as ever Jew did before."[31] In the minds of those for whom circumcision is the very embodiment of violence against the body, such an account might well serve to intensify deep-seated fears about how the ritual is conducted and the havoc it wreaks.

The early modern period was hardly lacking in accounts that served to bring this ritual to life. These accounts confirmed the all-pervasive conviction that those who engaged in the practice of circumcision were guilty of something amounting to barbarity. Such an outlook is present in the works of Samuel Purchas, who goes far to describe in gruesome detail circumcision as then practiced in different parts of the world. Where it is practiced, violence and barbarity are the keynote of the day. Accordingly, Purchas does not hesitate to focus unflinchingly on the organ to be cut, as he describes how the "Mohel" or circumciser "layeth hold on [the child's] member, and holding the *fore skinne*, putteth back the top thereof" in order to "cut off the fore-part of the skin." This, the *mohel* in a decisive gesture "presently hurleth" into the sand dish. To make certain that the head of the penis is entirely bare of the foreskin, the *mohel* next "rendeth" what remains with his "sharp-pointed thin nayles." (A *mohel*, Purchas avers, "may be known by his thumbes, on which he weareth the nayles long and sharpe, and narrow-pointed" for just this purpose.) Next, the *mohel* "taketh the member of the child in his mouth, and sucketh out the blood," which he then spits into a cup of wine.[32] Washing his bloody mouth and hands, the *mohel* takes the cup of wine with the spittle and offers it to all the young men to drink. In such a manner, Purchas declares, the child "is made a Jew."[33] A correspondingly gruesome first-hand account is ventured by John Evelyn as a result of his visit to the Jewish ghetto in Rome on January 15, 1645. Witnessing there an actual circumcision, he provides his own insight into the way in which the English mind responds to what it considers so alien a ritual. On the occasion of the circumcision, the company (no doubt, the *minyan*) "fell a singing of an hebrew hymn, and in as barbarous a tone wav[ed] themselves to & fro," during which the *mohel* (here, a "Rabbie"), taking hold of the penis, "Chaf'd it with his fingers till it became a little stiff," and then with a "Razor, did rather Saw, then cutt it [the Praeputium] off; at which the miserable babe cry'd extreamly," while all in attendance "continu'd their odd tone, rather like howling then singing." Consistent with Purchas's portrayal, the *mohel* in Evelyn's account, "taking the yard [or penis] all blody into his mouth, suck't it a pretty while," spit the blood into a glass filled with wine, and then drank the remains. Evelyn abruptly concludes his description with a dismissive gesture of disgust: "So ended the slovenly ceremony."[34] This attitude of repulsion is characteristic of the English view of circumcision as it was practiced among the Jews during the early modern period.

These accounts are invoked to suggest that the violence associated with circumcision from the biblical time onward remains an essential constituent of its delineation. As much as circumcision might have been viewed as the "fruitful cut" by its practitioners, it became a source of horror, if not repulsion, among those for whom it was an alien and savage act, one amounting to castration. Even as the ritual was celebrated as a crucial event in the church calendar in the early modern period, the anxieties surrounding circumcision were hardly alleviated. For evidence of these anxieties, one need only examine John Donne's treatment of the subject in his sermon preached at Saint Dunstan's upon New-Years-day, 1624, commemorating the circumcision of Christ.[35] Despite all Donne's appeals to "the *spirituall Circumcision* of our hearts," lips, and ears (vol. 6, 186, 193, 196–97, 201) and to the function of circumcision as a prefiguration of baptism (vol. 6, 193, 201) as a means of elevating the ritual from the realm of flesh to the realm of spirit, the horror and repugnance associated with the cut as a carnal act are ever present in the sermon.[36] Putting himself in the place of Abraham commanded to circumcise the foreskin of his flesh (Gen. 17:24), Donne has the patriarch cry out to his God, "*Quare sigillum?* What needs a seale betweene thee and me," especially so painful and indeed "base" and "troublesome" a seal of this sort in the flesh, in the "most rebellious part of the body"? For this is a seal that is "too obscene a thing to be brought into the fancy of so many Women, so many young Men, so many Strangers to other Nations, as might bring the Promise and Covenant it selfe into scorne, and into suspicion." Intuiting the repugnance that Abraham must have felt, Donne continues in the person of the patriarch to ask, "why does God command me so base and uncleanne a thing, so scornful and mis-interpetable a thing as Circumcision and Circumcision in that part?" Moreover, Donne as patriarch asks why he must perform this abomination not only on himself but on his entire family, "which could not be (in likelyhood) of lesse than 400"? The excruciating pain that the procedure must have caused the patriarch and his family is ever on Donne's mind, as he conceives Abraham's house as "a *Spittle* of so many impotent Persons, unable to helpe one another for so many daies," once the members of the family had endured such an indignity. The newly circumcised males, Donne remarks, would then be like the *"Sichemites,"* who were "unable to resist or defend themselves, and so were slaine" by the sons of Jacob (vol. 6, 190–91). No

matter how much Donne interprets that which defies interpretation, the
doubts and anxieties that crowd this sermon continue to trouble. The repug-
nance remains, the sense of the absurdity of it all persists, the dilemma of the
unwarranted violence to so vulnerable and finally rebellious a part of the
body is an ever-present part of the discourse. Donne is candid about so much
of what is occluded in the attempt to render as spiritual that which is embed-
ded in the flesh and leaves its indelible mark upon the body from one genera-
tion to the next. John Donne is part of a milieu that suggests the disturbing
presence of circumcision as both a biblical concept and a site of deep-seated
anxieties in the early modern period.

II

The place of circumcision in Milton's own thought is no less conflicted. To
gain a sense of his views on the subject, we might well begin with the theolog-
ical perspective delineated in his *De Doctrina Christiana,* a work that brings
to the fore some of the basic assumptions upon which his other writings are
founded.[37] Much of what Milton says on the subject of circumcision is dis-
cussed in his chapter on "The External Sealing of the Covenant of Grace"
(1.28). There, he treats circumcision as a sealing of the covenant under the
law that prefigures baptism as a sealing of the covenant under the gospel.
With its putative ties to the sacrament of baptism, circumcision is often
looked upon in sacramental terms. If circumcision is sanctified under the law,
Milton says, it occasionally "signifies sanctification even under the gospel."
But this sacramental outlook ultimately gives way to a view that not only
desacramentalizes circumcision but questions what might be called the fig-
ural relationship between circumcision and baptism. "There is," Milton con-
cludes, "no necessary analogy between circumcision and baptism; and it is
our duty not to build our belief on vague parallels." At most, circumcision is
"a seal in the flesh [*in carne sigillum*], indistinctly and obscurely given [*et
quidem perobscurum*], of that grace which was at some distant period to be
revealed," as opposed to baptism, which is a "seal of grace already revealed,
of the remission of sins, of sanctification" and "a sign of our death and
resurrection with Christ." This act of isolating circumcision as a seal of an
earlier covenant superseded by an entirely new dispensation moves Milton to
localize and problematize what in his theology becomes a decidedly con-
flicted phenomenon. Viewed in this way, circumcision, according to Milton,
"was given under the law and the sacrifices, and bound the individual to the
observance of the whole law (Gal. v. 3), which was a service of bondage, and a
schoolmaster [*paedagogicus*] to bring its followers to Christ." Milton's refer-
ence to the text from Galatians ("For I testify again to every man that is

circumcised, that he is a debtor to the whole law" [5:3]) immediately places him in conflicted territory, one whose landscape, we recall, is that of persecution ("Why do I yet suffer persecution" [5:11]) and recrimination ("I would they were even cut off which trouble you" [5:12]). This realm is also that of biting and devouring ("But if ye bite and devour one another, take heed that ye be not consumed one of the other" [5:15]). As it appears in Milton's discourse, "schoolmaster [*paedagogicus*]" is also an integral part of Galatians territory: "Wherefore the law was our schoolmaster to *bring us* unto Christ" (3:24). From the perspective of Milton's own outlook, the term "schoolmaster" is charged with potentially conflicted meanings. One need only recall John Aubrey's life of Milton and its anecdotal allusions to Milton's being whipped by the schoolmaster and to Milton himself having whipped, in turn, unruly students after he had become a schoolmaster.[38] The term "schoolmaster" resonates with pain, harshness, "discipline," and with that which is singularly unpleasant. Such are the associations to which circumcision as a sealing of the covenant of the law gives rise in Milton's theology. Opposed to the harshness of circumcision is baptism. Through it "we are initiated into the gospel, which is a reasonable, manly, and in the highest sense free service." For Milton, there is nothing reasonable, manly, or free about the ritual of circumcision. In fact, this ritual is little more than an operation performed by an individual such as a "surgeon [*chirurgus*]," Milton's version of a *mohel,* whose purpose is essentially to cut in the service of the law. This is a law that keeps its denizens slaves and infants in its adherence to that which is "outward." As a sign of that which has been superseded by the New Dispensation, circumcision is a ritual enacted only by those who subscribe to a set of practices that have "either already come to an end, or will eventually be terminated" (CM 16:165–67, 179–81, 369).

Such views are discernible elsewhere in Milton's prose works. So in his discussion of dispensations in *The Doctrine and Discipline of Divorce,* Milton decries the customs of the Jews bound by the rigors of the law, especially as it is manifested in those rites from which Christians have been liberated. Once again, circumcision is invoked as the prime example of such rites. In keeping with the theological outlook reflected in *De Doctrina Christiana,* circumcision is noted in Milton's divorce tract as the one rite most distinguished by its barbarity because of the violence it perpetrates upon the flesh. In a gesture of horror at all that circumcision represents, Milton recoils at "that severe and rigorous knife" that refuses to spare "the tender fore-skin of any male infant" but "carve[s] upon his flesh" the mark of the "covnant." Among those bound by the rigors of the law, Milton declares, "how vain then and how preposterous must it needs be to exact a circumcision of the Flesh" as an outward sign of purity (YP 2:302). One can almost behold Milton's grimacing at the very

thought of such a mutilation for the purpose of adhering to ways that are so
repugnant. The idea enunciated here is rendered with renewed vigor in *A
Treatise of Civil Power.* There, Milton addresses the notorious reading of
circumcision made evident in the epistle to the Galatians (5:11–12). This is a
text that clearly causes Milton discomfort, for he is very much aware of the
view voiced by the Church Fathers as well as more recent exegetes who
"interpret that *cutting off* which S. *Paul* wished to them who had brought
back the Galatians to circumcision" as an "amercement of thir whole virili-
tie." Such an amercement or infliction is what Milton calls a "concising
punishment of circumcisers." Alluding to Philippians 3:2 ("beware of the
concision" [*katatome* in the Greek; *concisionem* in the Latin]), Milton's refer-
ence to "concising punishment" is nothing less than a "cutting down" or
"cutting off" that amounts to a mutilation of one's "virilitie" (YP 7:252–53).[39]
Ever on Milton's mind is the horrifying specter of genital mutilation associ-
ated with circumcision, a mutilation that he seeks to mitigate in his own
reading of the Pauline epistles but that haunts him in his understanding of (if
not obsession with) circumcision as a cutting off or concision, nonetheless.[40]

What then is to be made of his early poem *Upon the Circumcision*
(1633–37?), which, along with *On the Morning of Christs Nativity* (1629)
and *The Passion* (1630), might well be part of a calendrical cycle commem-
orating the feast days of the Christian year?[41] If one considers other poems
written during Milton's time that commemorate the circumcision as a crucial
event in the church calendar, one is struck by the celebratory nature of the
tone that these poems reflect. So Robert Herrick's *The New-yeeres Gift, or
Circumcision Song* celebrates the infant Christ's circumcision as an occasion
to rejoice. Even though the babe must be circumcised, he is surrounded by
flowers. In this sweet, aromatic, indeed, cloying environment, violence to the
body has no place. In the midst of springing tulips, Herrick calls for those
who perform the cut to "touch gently, gently touch" the member to be
circumcised; and even from the "sacred Bloud" of the babe "here shed," the
poet would have "roses grow, to crown His own deare Head" (13–23). Once
the ritual is performed, the babe is lovingly carried with song "unto His
Mother *Marie*," as Herrick's own "Rites are ended" (24–29).[42] Anything that
might possibly compromise this festive atmosphere is banished from the
ritual that Herrick celebrates.

I offer the context of Herrick's poem to suggest how different it is from
what one finds in Milton's poem. *Upon the Circumcision* is a poem not of cel-
ebration but of mourning, not of festivity but of lamentation: "Now mourn,"
Milton declares to the angelic hosts, and "borrow / Seas wept from our deep
sorrow," for this is a child that "bleeds to give us ease" (6–11).[43] As John T.
Shawcross wisely observes, this is a poem in which the "blood sacrifice" is of

central concern.[44] Confronting the brutality of the blood sacrifice, Milton writes a poem about *pain*, specifically, the pain of the cut that follows inevitably upon the birth of the messiah as an anticipation of the ultimate pain that he shall suffer in the crucifixion.[45] The two are bound in grim succession as painful markers between the beginning and the end of the savior's life. Addressing the first signifier of pain, Milton laments: "Alas, how soon our sin / Sore doth begin / His infancy to sease" (12–14). This "wounding smart" anticipates an even greater suffering the savior must endure. Addressing that ultimate signifier, Milton looks upon the crucifixion as an event when "Huge pangs and strong / Will peirce more neer his heart" (24–27).

In Milton's poem, there is no attempt to mitigate the fact of pain, no admonition to "touch gently, gently touch" the part to be cut, no calling upon tulips to spring or roses to blossom. Far from it: at the core of Milton's poem is an almost obsessive (if not a disquieting) focus upon the physicality of suffering that arises from the brutal act, first of circumcision, then of crucifixion. (One blanches at the "soreness" of the staccato four-beat pronouncement "Sore doth begin" that verbally reenacts the violence of the cut. This gesture finds its counterpart in the correspondingly abrupt four-beat declaration "Huge pangs and strong" that reenacts the violence of the final thrust.) Nor is there any attempt to spiritualize or internalize the circumcision as a covenantal act. Milton's poem resists any notion of a movement from body to spirit in its treatment of what it calls "that great Cov'nant" (20).[46] There is no suggestion of being "circumcised with the circumcision made without hands," no glorying in the cross as a symbol of being crucified to the world in preparation for the birth of a new creature as there is in Pauline theology.

In Milton's poem, the "sealing" of obedience with "wounding smart" is all about "seasing" the body (and, as the result of *kenosis*,[47] the "naked" body at that) with the pain that comes with the cutting of the flesh in infancy, followed by the "Huge pangs and strong" that overwhelm the body in adulthood. Milton may extol Christ, who "bleeds to give us ease" (11), but the anxieties that attend upon the cut do little to reassure. Projecting those anxieties onto the body of the circumcised and ultimately crucified savior, Milton as poet undergoes the very soreness and pain that he relives in the body of the one whose agony the poem mourns. Here, as elsewhere, the violence of circumcision is never far from Milton's thought.[48]

That violence assumes its most virulent form in *Samson Agonistes*. For here once again is the culmination of what I have elsewhere called the inclination to violence that underscores Milton's sense of himself both as an individual and as a writer. Consumed by a fear of *sparagmos*, Milton appropriated all the energies that coalesce in the violence of the cut and unleashed them in his conception of the blind and fallen Nazarite. From the perspective of the events at *Ramath-lehi*, the remembrance of how the foreskinned race was slaughtered by God's sanctified warrior brings into focus the place of circumcision in Milton's outlook. To suggest that, in effecting the fall of "a thousand fore-skins" at *Ramath-lehi*, the once-mighty champion of God has ironically proven himself to be the greatest *mohel* of all time is perhaps not as questionable as it might first appear. As we have seen in the terrible slaughter of the Shechemites, the inclination to transform the ritual of circumcision into an act of war is not without warrant in the biblical text. A crucial distinction in the Judges account between Samson and the Philistines is that Samson as an Israelite is among the circumcised who does battle against the "uncircumcised" Philistines (15:18; cf. 14:3). Felling the choicest youth of the foreskinned race with a trivial weapon in *Samson Agonistes* is tantamount to the violent removal of those very foreskins that most distinguish the Philistines both in their own eyes and in the eyes of the Israelites. Samson does not require either a flint knife or the edge of the sword to effect his "surgery": the trusty jawbone of a dead ass serves his purpose admirably. Although the circumcision of Samson himself is not specifically described in the narrative of Judges, it is certainly assumed. In fact, it is the *sine qua non* of Samson's status as an Israelite to defend God's cause against all those who have not been circumcised and who therefore do not share in the covenant. In the Miltonic text, the distinction between Samson as circumcised and the Philistines as uncircumcised is brought home repeatedly. So Milton's Samson himself recounts how he was yielded by his own countrymen to "the uncircumcis'd a welcome prey" and bound with cords (Judg. 15:12), but, despite the cords (which to him were as "threds / Toucht with the flame"), "on their whole Host" he flew "unarm'd," and "with a trivial weapon fell'd / Their choicest youth" (258–64).

That this confrontation is between the circumcised and the uncircumcised is emphasized throughout Milton's dramatic poem: not only does Samson refer to the enemy as "th' uncircumcis'd" (640) but in a kind of *quid pro quo* the enemy refers to the Israelites as "the Circumcis'd" (975) or "the unforeskinn'd race," of whom Samson "bear'st" the "highest name" (1100–1101). Referring to Samson's initial unwillingness to appear before the Philistines at the temple of Dagon, the Chorus notes that, in his state of abjection, Samson is already serving the Philistines, who are at once "idolatrous, uncircumcis'd, . . . [and] unclean" (1363–64). Not to have undergone circumcision is implicitly to be guilty of idolatry and uncleanness. By ultimately appearing before the enemy at the very temple of their god, Samson is willing to risk even greater impurity as a means of cleansing himself in a final act of retribution as God's "faithful Champion" (1751). In that role, Samson is imagined by the Chorus as "dealing dole among his foes," as he walks his way "over heaps of slaughter'd" (1529–30).

Having destroyed himself along with the Philistines as a result of his final act, Samson, of course, is hardly capable on this occasion of glorying in the slaughter of the enemy. But the fantasy of the champion of the Israelites walking triumphantly over "heaps" of slaughtered Philistines in Milton's dramatic poem recalls the very scene at *Ramath-lehi* in the biblical account. After the slaughter of the Philistines in that battle, Samson declares, "With the jaw of an ass, heaps upon heaps, with the jaw of an ass have I slain a thousand men" (15:16). The Chorus's reference to Samson's "heaps" in what amounts to the final confrontation at the temple of Dagon conflates the two scenes (that of *Ramath-lehi* and that of Dagon's temple) in such a manner that the one must be read in light of the other. In this respect, the heaps of the slain at the temple of Dagon are correspondingly bereft of their foreskins, that is, symbolically circumcised, as their *aralot* are piled up in heaps.

Drawing upon the idea of those heaps as piled up *aralot,* one might suggest that the "heaps of slaughter'd" (amid which Samson is purported to walk in the Chorus's fantasy) constitute a veritable "hill of foreskins" (*gibeat-haaralot*), ironically reminiscent of the hill of foreskins piled up in the mass circumcision of the Israelites at Gilgal. Although one might be loath to push this analogy too far, the ironic juxtaposition of the scenes at Ramath-lehi and Gilgal, on the one hand, and at the temple of Dagon, on the other, suggests something of the dynamics that would underlie a reading of *Samson Agonistes* as a dramatic poem drawing upon the violent implications of circumcision as a motif of fundamental importance to Milton's outlook. In my reading of circumcision, I do not necessarily claim the presence of overt correspondences, but I do maintain that the history of the ritual as an event grounded in a culture of violence leaves its mark on a poet whose own views of the ritual were essentially conflicted. It is the psychology of these conflicts as they are manifested in Milton's works that engages us here.

This is a psychology made evident in the commonplace association of circumcision and castration. As we have seen, the association is already canonized in the biblical text, a fact that prompts Milton to address the issue in his own writings. In the world of psychoanalytic discourse the issue looms large, of course, in the works of Sigmund Freud and his followers.[49] Throughout his writings, Freud makes a point of suggesting that embedded in the ritual of circumcision one finds anxieties that surround the castration complex. This is a complex that Freud argues is fundamental to the establishment of Jewish identity. Thus, in *Moses and Monotheism* (1939), Freud observes that "among the customs by which the Jews made themselves separate, that

MICHAEL LIEB

of circumcision has made a disagreeable, uncanny impression, which is to be explained, no doubt, by its recalling the dreaded castration and along with it a portion of the primaeval past which is gladly forgotten" (vol. 33, 91).[50] Such a statement no doubt reflects Freud's own anxieties as much as the anxieties he would discern in others.

Compounding the association of circumcision with castration as an archaic event, Freud in *Totem and Taboo* (1913–14) views the act of cutting the hair "among primitive peoples" as the symbolical equivalent of circumcision and castration (vol. 13, 153n.1). This association assumes renewed impetus in his treatise on *The "Uncanny"* (1925). There, Freud engages in a detailed discussion of castration anxieties through the figure of the "Sand-Man." As one who tears out children's eyes, this is a figure who haunts our dreams in childhood and underlies our fear of going blind. What Freud calls "the substitutive relationship between the eye and the male organ" accounts for our corresponding "dread of being castrated" (vol. 17, 227–31). Finally, the association between circumcision and castration for Freud centers in the figure of the cruel father (a sand-man in his own right). According to Freud's study *From the History of an Infantile Neurosis* (1918), it is the cruel father as a God figure who becomes in effect the primal castrator (vol. 17, 86–87). This point is explored in depth by Bruno Bettelheim, who, in his discussion of "symbolic wounds," maintains that circumcision "may lead to castration anxieties in particular or to the general fear of the true father or religious father figure which so much characterizes Jewish religion."[51]

Particularly within the framework of the anxieties surrounding castration, such notions have been brought to bear upon the poet of *Samson Agonistes* in several studies. Consistent with my own interpretation of Milton's dread of *sparagmos,* Frank Kermode looks upon Milton as a figure plagued by "a special horror of physical mutilation," a horror of being not only psychologically but physically "mangled" in what Samson calls his "apprehensive tenderest parts" (624). For Kermode, this condition manifests itself in a particular fear of emasculation. Kermode singles out Freud's Daniel Paul Schreber as one most befitting the kind of pathology that distinguishes a Nazaritical obsession with things "clean" and "unclean" and a belief in one's "chosenness." Schreber was convinced that in order to fulfill his role as *electus*, he must suffer emasculation and become a woman.[52] In accord with this outlook, such scholars as Herman Rapaport and Jackie DiSalvo have made a great deal of the "emasculatory" dimensions of *Samson Agonistes*.[53] Drawing upon the Freudian idea of the castration complex and the relationship between castration and blindness, Rapaport views Samson as one immobilized by the feminine "other." For Samson, his is Dalila, a Medusa-like serpentine figure (indeed, a "manifest Serpent" [997]) who at once attracts and repels. With her head containing (in Rapaport's words) "a proliferation of phallus symbols" that preserve "the element of terror that accompanies the castration fear," Dalila-as-Medusa is the "castrating woman" who is also herself a "castrate" (what Germaine Greer calls the "female eunuch"). Through Dalila as castrator and as castrate, Samson, in turn, becomes "feminine," a "female castrate" cut off from the "truth" of God's ways.[54]

In a somewhat similar vein, DiSalvo argues that Samson, having been betrayed by Dalila, must confront the "woman" within, a confrontation that amounts to what DiSalvo calls an "agon of masculine identity." As a result of his seduction by Dalila, the fallen Samson becomes a child, indeed, an infant, one whose "blindness," "hairlessness, and even his soiled weeds, all evoke early infancy." For this reason, we behold him at the outset of the dramatic poem as one who "lies, infantlike, in complete passivity" and entirely "in power of others," never in his own power. In that position, he must emerge from the infancy into which he has fallen by overcoming the temptations of those who would undermine his attempts to achieve full masculinity. Most grievous in this respect is, once again, Dalila who, having earlier received his "head" in her "lascivious lap," proceeded to "shear" him like "a tame Weather" (a trope, we recall, adopted earlier by Shakespeare in the reference to Antonio as a "tainted wether"). Having so castrated her lover by cutting his hair, Dalila then turned him out "ridiculous, despoil'd, / Shav'n, and dis-arm'd" among his "enemies" (535–39). Now in the power of others, Samson is made to grind at the mill (435), an act that for Milton had distinctly sexual connotations.[55] Like Kermode and Rapaport, DiSalvo views Samson as one who is beset by anxieties that threaten to undermine his sexuality, indeed, as one who, in his state of castration, must in some way regain his masculinity by overcoming what Samson himself calls the "foul effeminacy" that holds him "yok't" (410) as a slave to the woman within.[56]

As one might surmise from my reading throughout, my views are consistent with those of Kermode, Rapaport, and DiSalvo. To their emphasis upon the relationship between the act of cutting the hair, suffering blindness, and undergoing the trauma of castration, I add what I consider to be the all-important element of circumcision, an element through which these other acts coalesce. Emphasizing this element and all that it implies, I have attempted to bring into focus a dimension of Milton's outlook that has received scant attention, perhaps in part because its presence in his works is so conflicted. This fact is nowhere more nearly in evidence than in *Samson Agonistes*. There, in particular, the ritual of the *brit milah* must be taken into account as a crucial aspect of the psychology that constitutes Milton's depiction of his fallen hero. The covenant of circumcision underscores Samson's sense of self throughout Milton's dramatic poem. This covenant not only justifies Samson's acts of doing battle against the uncircumcised enemy before his fall but distinguishes the suffering that Samson must undergo in his state of abjection once the violation has occurred. This is the suffering of one whose original cut becomes the source of the trauma that marks him as a fallen warrior. The cut that seals is a constant reminder of the cut that severs. Samson's effeminization, his subjection to the woman within, results in a battle to restore his sense of virility in the face of an emasculation brought about by his violation of the cut. In countering the effects of that violation, Samson must attempt to regain his status as the true circumcised of God. He must regain his status, that is, as one for whom the cut is a mark not of shame but of glory.

From the Nazaritical perspective to which Kermode alludes, the terms of Samson's dilemma assume a special significance. If the Nazarite in his glory is one who is separate *to* God (*nazir*) by being "cut off" from all that might undermine his purity, Samson now as fallen Nazarite is one who has brought that impurity upon himself and is separate *from* God.[57] The hair that crowns (*nezer*) his head is cut off, and he stands bare and exposed, that is, paradoxically uncircumcised (*arel*), as one whose very circumcision becomes a mockery of his fallen state (Judg. 16:17–21). To regain his purity, he must vindicate himself by unleashing upon his enemies the violence of the *brit milah*. This he does in his final act of destroying the Philistines. The extent to which he is successful in fulfilling his mission, of course, remains to be seen. Samson's final act is consistent with a point of view that subsumes the all-important notion of the *brit milah* and all that it implies for Milton as the true poet of the cut.

NOTES

1. References to Milton's poetry are to *The Complete Poetry of John Milton,* ed. John T. Shawcross, 2nd rev. ed. (Garden City, 1971). References to Milton's prose by volume and page number in my text are to *The Complete Prose Works of John Milton,* 8 vols. in 10, ed. Don M. Wolfe et al. (New Haven, 1953–82), hereafter designated YP. Corresponding references to the original Latin (and on occasion to the English translations) are to *The Works of John Milton,* 18 vols. in 21, ed. Frank Allen Patterson et al. (New York, 1931–38), hereafter designated CM.

2. See my book *Milton and the Culture of Violence* (Ithaca, 1994), esp. 226–63.

3. Biblical references in English are to the Authorized Version of 1611. References to the Hebrew Bible are to the *Biblia Hebraica Stuttgartensia* (Stuttgart, 1967); and references to the Greek and Latin New Testament are to the *Novum Testamentum Graece et Latine* (London, 1926).

4. The transformation from *Abram* as "exalted father" to *Abraham* as "father of multitudes" involves phonetic word-play that is not etymologically present in the Hebrew roots. This kind of

word-play is present elsewhere in the Hebrew Bible. See the entry on Abram/Abraham in *The New Brown-Driver-Briggs-Gesenius Hebrew and English Lexicon*, trans. Edward Robinson (Peabody, Mass., 1979), 4 (hereafter cited as *BDB*).

5. The phrase "fruitful cut" is borrowed from Howard Eilburg-Schwartz's excellent study *The Savage in Judaism: An Anthropology of Israelite Religion and Ancient Judaism* (Bloomington, 1990), 141–76. It is well known that circumcision was not peculiar to Israel. This fact is made evident not only by Egyptian bas reliefs from the third millennium but by historians such as Herodotus. In the Hebrew Bible, Jeremiah refers to circumcision in connection with "Egypt, and Judah, and Edom, and the children of Ammon, and Moab" (9:25–26). For an illuminating account of the origins of circumcision among both Semitic and non-Semitic cultures, see the *Encyclopaedia of Religion and Ethics*, ed. James Hastings, 12 vols. (New York, 1922), vol. 3, 659–80; and the entry on circumcision in *The Encyclopedia of Religion*, ed. Mircea Eliade, 16 vols. (New York, 1987), vol. 3, 511.

6. In viewing the establishment of the covenant in Genesis 17:4–7 as an anticipation of the circumcision narrative, I am aware that I am juxtaposing two separate covenant narratives. Whether or not the text is composite here, the overall narrative moves toward the circumcision as the culminating event.

7. So *aral* ("be counted uncircumcised") as *heyarel* in the *niphal* means "to be uncovered" or "exposed." See *heyarel* in Hab. 2:16, which biblical versions render variously as "expose your own nakedness" or "be exposed." In later biblical usage, *aral* as *arel* ("uncircumcised") becomes a term of contempt. In Isaiah 52:1, it is associated with moral and spiritual uncleanness, and Ezekiel uses it in the sense of that which is polluted and defiled (32:28–30). See the *Theological Wordbook of the Old Testament*, ed. R. Laird Harris et al., 2 vols. (Chicago, 1980), vol. 2, 696–97, for an account of these meanings. According to the *BDB*, *aral* as *heyarel* also implies the condition of being the object of mockery (790).

8. For an examination of this aspect, see the entry on *brit* in the *Theological Dictionary of the Old Testament*, ed. G. Johannes Botterweck and Helmer Ringgren, 8 vols. (Grand Rapids, 1975), vol. 2, 253–63. The locution "cutting a covenant" is one of several that denote the establishment of a covenant with God. The etymological origins of *brit* are obscure. The term denotes "covenant," but in conjunction with *karat* it assumes other meanings as well (Erich Isaac, "Circumcision as a Covenant Rite," *Anthropos* 59 [1964]: 446). Of particular interest to the violence implicit in cutting a covenant is Regina M. Schwartz's *The Curse of Cain: The Violent Legacy of Monotheism* (Chicago, 1997), 21–38.

9. Isaac, "Circumcision as a Covenant Rite," 446.

10. Isaac, "Circumcision as a Covenant Rite," 444.

11. *The Anchor Bible Dictionary*, ed. David Noel Freedman, 6 vols. (New York, 1992), vol. 1, 1026.

12. See the entry on *mul* in the *BDB*, 557–58. See also the entry on *mul* in the lexicon that accompanies James Strong's *Exhaustive Concordance* (Grand Rapids, Mich., n.d.), 63. The notion of "cutting to pieces" or "annihilating" the enemy "by force of arms" is, according to the *BDB*, attested in the *hiphil*: "in the name of. . . , I will make them to be circumcised (enemies, by force of arms; but . . . cut to pieces, . . . mow, . . . annihilate [?],´. . .)."

13. It emerges, for example, in Exodus in an extremely perplexing passage that lies beyond the purview of this study: "The Lord met him [Moses], and sought to kill him. Then Zipporah took a sharp knife, and cut off the foreskin of her son, and cast *it* at his feet, and said, Surely a bloody husband *art* thou to me. So he [God] let him [Moses] go: then she [Zipporah] said, A bloody husband *thou art,* because of the circumcision" (4:24–26). The passage, which is inserted into the narrative that follows upon Moses' receipt of his call on Horeb, is no doubt part of an older tradition. Although the precise import of the passage is uncertain, it appears that in

neglecting to circumcise his son as required, Moses incurred the wrath of God. To appease God, Zipporah performed the function that Moses was to have fulfilled. She does so in a violent manner by taking a sharp knife, cutting off the foreskin of her son, and then thrusting it at the feet of her "bloody husband." For commentary, see Lawrence A. Hoffman, *Covenant of Blood: Circumcision and Gender in Rabbinic Judaism* (Chicago, 1996), 30–33, among other studies.

14. It is this sense that is discussed in great detail by Eilberg-Schwartz, *The Savage in Judaism,* esp. 141–76.

15. The idea of uncircumcision is applied most often to the Philistines and other non-Israelites (Judg. 14:3; 1 Sam. 14:6, 31:4).

16. The idea is one the author of 1 Samuel might well have understood: "And Saul said, thus shall ye say to David, The king desireth not any dowry, but an hundred foreskins of the Philistines [*bmaeyah arlot plishtim*], to be avenged of the king's enemies" (18:25). Although literal circumcision is not at issue, the act of slaughtering figured as a mass circumcision of the enemy to satisfy the desire for revenge certainly is implied. Saul's desire for a hundred foreskins is outdone by the "thousand fore-skins" of Milton's Samson.

17. See especially Daniel Boyarin, *A Radical Jew: Paul and the Politics of Identity* (Berkeley, 1994) for a full account of Paul's treatment of circumcision.

18. *The Anchor Bible Dictionary,* vol. 1, 1029.

19. See Daniel Boyarin, *Carnal Israel: Reading Sex in Talmudic Literature* (Berkeley, 1993), 233. See also Daniel Boyarin, " 'This We Know to Be the Carnal Israel': Circumcision and the Erotic Life of God and Israel," *Critical Inquiry* 18 (1992): 474–505.

20. For *apokopsontai,* see the entry under *apokopto* in *A Greek-English Lexicon of the New Testament and Other Early Christian Literature,* trans. and ed. W. F. Arndt (Chicago, 1957), 92. The translation (*"would that they might make eunuchs of themselves"*) is that of the *Greek-English Lexicon.* It is a rendering that is attested in the later translations, such as the New Revised Standard Version (1991), among others. For *abscindantur,* see the entry under *abscindo* in *A Latin Dictionary,* ed. Charlton T. Lewis and Charles Short (Oxford, 1879), 10. There, a distinction is made between *abscido* and *abscindo.* Whereas *abscido* means "to cut off with a sharp instrument," *abscindo,* as indicated, means "to break or tear off as with the hand" (cf. *praecidere* vs. *avellere*). The form that appears in the Latin text, then, has the force of tearing or rending, if not mutilating, an act that even intensifies the violence of the Greek.

21. See the *Greek-English Lexicon* commentary on *apokopsontai* in Gal. 5:12 as "make a eunuch of, castrate." The *Lexicon* cites figures such as Chrysostom and Ambrosiaster (92). As I discuss later in this paper, the association of circumcision and castration is fundamental to psychoanalytic discourse in this century.

22. *The Anchor Bible Dictionary,* vol. 1, 1028.

23. *Encyclopaedia of Religion and Ethics* (vol. 3, 663). See Horace's Satires (1.9) in *Satires I,* trans. P. Michael Brown [Warminster, Wiltshire, 1993]) and Martial's Epigrams (7.30, 35, 82; 9.46) in *Epigrams,* trans. Walter C. A. Ker, 2 vols. (Cambridge, Mass., 1928–29).

24. For an enlightening account of the myths surrounding the expulsion and readmission of the Jews in England, see James Shapiro, *Shakespeare and the Jews* (New York, 1996), 43–88. "While medieval chroniclers recounting the events of 1290 made it clear that the Jews had indeed left England in that year, no parliamentary or even royal decree to this effect could be found to substantiate these accounts." Contrary to popular belief, moreover, "there was no formal or legal Readmission in 1656." To complicate matters further, those engaged in the debate for readmission were very much aware "that there were Jews already living in England who practiced their faith in private, and that there had been a Jewish presence in England since at least the turn of the century, and perhaps earlier as well." In fact, "small numbers of Jews

began drifting back into England almost immediately after the Expulsion, and began to arrive in larger numbers during the Tudor period" (58–62).

25. Shapiro, *Shakespeare and the Jews,* 115. Shapiro notes the exception of "a handful of infants circumcised by the radical Puritan group led by John Traske around 1620, and a few self-circumcisors [sic] like Thomas Tany and Thomas Ramsey thirty years later." My own research confirms Shapiro's observation.

26. Shapiro, *Shakespeare and the Jews,* 111. This stereotype persisted well beyond the early modern period. According to Frank Felsenstein, Jews in the later periods were viewed also as "compulsive circumcisers" (*Anti-Semitic Stereotypes: A Paradigm of Otherness in English Popular Culture, 1660–1830* [Baltimore, 1995], 123). So all-pervasive is the stereotype, in fact, that in modern times the Jew as *shochet* or ritual butcher becomes associated with Jack the Ripper. See Sander Gilman, *The Jew's Body* (New York, 1991), 119.

27. Cited by Shapiro, *Shakespeare and the Jews,* 111. See Samuel Purchas, *Purchas his Pilgrimage* (London, 1626), 152; Raphael Holinshed, *The Chronicles of England, Scotlande, and Ireland* (London, 1587), 219; John Foxe, *Actes and Monuments* (London, 1570), 296; and Anthony Wood, *Athenae Oxonienses,* 4 vols. (London, 1691–92), vol. 1, 329.

28. William Prynne, *A Short Demurrer to the Jews* (London, 1656), 17, 27.

29. Shapiro, *Shakespeare and the Jews,* 111.

30. Shapiro, *Shakespeare and the Jews,* 120. See *The Merchant of Venice,* 4.1.114.

31. Alexander Pope, *A Strange but True Relation How Edmund Curll of Fleetstreet, Stationer . . . was converted from the Christian Religion by certain Eminent Jews . . . And . . . circumcis'd* (1720), in *The Prose Works of Alexander Pope,* ed. Norman Ault, 2 vols. (Oxford, 1936), vol. 1, 317–22. I am indebted to Felsenstein, *Anti-Semitic Stereotypes,* 143–46, for this reference.

32. This step is known as *metzitzah.* For a statement of the practice, as well as all the steps involved in ritual circumcision, see Moses Maimonides, *Hilchot Milah,* in the *Mishneh Torah,* trans. R. Eliyahu Touger (New York, 1991), 220–21.

33. Purchas, *Purchas his Pilgrimage,* 179–81. For corresponding accounts, see Thomas Godwyn, *Moses and Aaron, Civil and Ecclesiastical Rites by the Ancient Hebrewes* (London, 1641), 213–17; Leo Modena, *The History of the Rites, Customes, and Manner of Life, of the Present JEWS, throughout the WORLD* (London, 1650), 201–8; and Alexander Ross, *PANSEBEIA: Or, A View of all Religions in the World* (London, 1655), 54–55.

34. John Evelyn, *The Diary of John Evelyn* (Oxford, 1955), vol. 2, 292–94.

35. John Donne, *The Sermons of John Donne,* ed. Evelyn M. Simpson and George Potter (Berkeley, 1953), vol. 6, 186–204. Further references to this edition will be noted parenthetically in the text.

36. For other attempts to "spiritualize" circumcision, see the commentaries of Jeremy Taylor, *The Life of Our Blessed Saviour Jesus Christ* (Philadelphia, 1819), 42–43; and John Diodati, *Pious and Learned Annotations upon the Holy Bible* (London, 1648), 14, 152.

37. Although I am very much aware that the authorship of *De Doctrina Christiana* is in dispute, I shall (for the sake of argument) assume Miltonic authorship here. For the issue of authorship, see William B. Hunter, *"Visitation Unimplor'd": Milton and the Authorship of "De Doctrina Christiana"* (Pittsburgh, 1998).

38. See John Aubrey's "Life of Milton," anthologized in *John Milton: Complete Poems and Major Prose,* ed. Merritt Y. Hughes (New York, 1957): At the university, "his 1st tutor . . . was Mr. Chapell, from whom receiving some unkindness [whipped him], he was afterwards . . . transferred"; and, as a schoolmaster himself, he punished his nephews so severely that poor Mary Powell "oftentimes heard his nephews beaten and cry" (1023–24).

39. For a discussion of the topical allusions to this passage, see William B. Hunter's notes to *A Treatise of Civil Power* (YP 7:252–53), as well as Barbara K. Lewalski's notes to the same work in *The Prose of John Milton*, gen. ed. J. Max Patrick (Garden City, New York, 1967), 472. In addition to the Church Fathers, Milton cites Desiderius Erasmus and Hugo Grotius, who view the Galatians and Philippians texts as evidence of the ideas of castration and mutilation.

40. Countering what he views as an Erastian arrogation of power in matters of religion, Milton warns against the "dangerous example of beginning in the spirit to end . . . in the flesh." He would like to read the Pauline act of "cutting off" as a "cutting off from the church," but the other form of "cutting off" (as concision) is something he cannot dispel (YP 7:252–53).

41. I follow the dating of the poems indicated in the Shawcross edition of *The Complete Poetry of John Milton*. The calendrical dimension is noted by E. Richard Gregory, among others, in his entry on *Upon the Circumcision, A Milton Encyclopedia*, gen. ed. William B. Hunter, 9 vols. (Lewisburg, 1980), vol. 8, 105–6. Commemorated by Milton's poem, the Feast of the Circumcision in the Christian calendar is January 1, eight days after the birth of the male child. For the liturgical basis of the holy day in the Church of England, see *The Book of Common Prayer* (Oxford, 1928), 122–23.

42. In *The Poetical Works of Robert Herrick*, ed. L. C. Martin (Oxford, 1956). Both Herrick's *The New-yeeres Gift, or Circumcision Song* and *Another New-yeeres Gift, or Song for the Circumcision* approach the event from a Pauline perspective that emphasizes the circumcision of hearts, hands, lips, ears, and even eyes. Circumcision is idealized, and rather than emphasizing the crucifixion as antitype, Herrick highlights baptism as much more palatable. In its emphasis upon the body and the function of the foreskin, Francis Quarles's *Of our Saviours Circumcision, or New-yeares day* more nearly approaches the Miltonic outlook. See Quarles's *Hosanna, or Divine Poems on the Passion of Christ*, ed. John Horden (Liverpool, 1960).

43. For various studies of the poem's conventions and affiliations, see, among others, F. T. Prince, *The Italian Element in Milton's Verse* (Oxford, 1954), 61–63; Alex B. Chambers, "Milton's 'Upon the Circumcision': Backgrounds and Meanings," in *Texas Studies in Literature and Language* 17 (1975): 687–97; and M. Thomas Hester, "Typology and Parody in 'Upon the Circumcision,'" in *Renaissance Papers*, ed. Dale B. Randall and Joseph A. Porter (Durham, 1985), 61–71.

44. John T. Shawcross, *John Milton: The Self and the World* (Lexington, 1993), 154.

45. Significantly, there is no mention of the baptism, a staple of Christocentric exegesis that is called into question in *De Doctrina Christiana*.

46. As much as one might view that covenant as crucial to the dispensational outlook of the poem, the notion that the circumcision of Jesus marks a renewal of the relationship originally established between God and Abraham is called into question by the way in which Milton delineates the significance of the cut. Specifically, the lines "Alas, how soon our sin / Sore doth begin / His infancy to sease" suggests that the circumcision of the savior is viewed not as a sign of sealing a relationship but as a willingness to undergo punishment for man's transgression. Moreover, this is a transgression that plagues mankind throughout history until the "full wrath" of "vengefull Justice" is "Intirely satisfi'd" (21–23) by the ultimate sacrifice of the savior in the crucifixion. For an enlightening exploration of the place of the covenant in Milton's works, see John T. Shawcross, "Milton and the Covenant: The Christian View of Old Testament Theology," in *Milton and Scriptural Tradition: The Bible into Poetry*, ed. James Sims and Leland Ryken (Columbia, Mo., 1984), 160–91.

47. For a discussion of *kenosis* in Milton, see my *The Sinews of Ulysses: Form and Convention in Milton's Works* (Pittsburgh, 1989), 38–52.

48. Although limitations of space do not permit an examination of Milton's *On the Forcers of Conscience*, this is a poem that implicitly reenacts the violence of the cut as the final "assault" of

the sonnet's "tail": "That so the Parlament / May with their wholsom and preventive sheares / Clip your [the presbyters's] Phylacteries though bauk your eares" (15–17). As Mathew Biberman has demonstrated, the idea of shearing the phylacteries here is implicitly sexual. At issue is the multiplicty of meanings that accrue to the notion of the cut ("Milton's Tephilin," *Milton Quarterly* 31 [1997]: 136–45).

49. References by volume and page number are to *The Standard Edition of the Complete Psychological Works of Sigmund Freud*, ed. and trans. Alix Strachey and Alan Tyson (London, 1964).

50. Freud had earlier arrived at similar conclusions in his study of the castration complex in his other works. See, for example, his study *From the History of an Infantile Neurosis* (1918). There, the relationship between circumcision and castration is centered on the cruel father (that is, God) as castrator (vol. 17, 86–87). Among those in the psychoanalytic school who arrive at similar conclusions (circumcision/castration/cruel father/God), see Bruno Bettelheim, *Symbolic Wounds: Puberty Rites and the Envious Male* (Glencoe, Ill., 1954), 130–43.

51. Bettelheim, *Symbolic Wounds*, 131 and passim. Circumcision has become a recurring topic in Jacques Derrida's philosophy as well. See his *Glas*, trans. John Leavey and Richard Rand (Lincoln, Neb., 1986).

52. Frank Kermode, "Milton in Old Age," *Southern Review* 11 (1975): 513–29. Daniel Paul Schreber's *Memoirs of My Nervous Illness* (1903) served as the basis of Freud's *The Case of Schreber*, in *The Standard Edition*, vol. 12, 12–82.

53. Herman Rapaport, *Milton and the Postmodern* (Lincoln, Neb., 1983), esp. 131–64; Jackie DiSalvo, "Intestine Thorn: Samson's Struggle with the Woman Within," in *Milton and the Idea of Woman*, ed. Julia M. Walker (Urbana, 1988), 211–29.

54. Rapaport, *Milton and the Postmodern*, 150–53. See Germaine Greer, *The Female Eunuch* (New York, 1971). In the context of the circumcised male, it is interesting to note Daniel Boyarin's treatment of circumcision as an act of "feminizing the male" as a positive sign. According to Boyarin, such feminizing as a concept in midrashic thought renders one "open to receive the divine speech and vision of God" ("'This We Know to Be the Carnal Israel,'" 495–96).

55. In the *The Doctrine and Discipline of Divorce*, Milton speaks of grinding at the mill "of an undelighted and servile copulation" (YP 4:258). In the Hebrew, the word is *tachan* (Judg. 16:21) and carries with it the idea of wifely submission (Job 31:10). See *Theological Wordbook of the Old Testament*, vol. 1, 347–48. The sexual dimensions of *tachan* were commonplace in rabbinical commentary. See the *Midrash Rabbah*: "'And he did grind in the prison-house': This teaches us that 'all and sundry brought him [Samson] their wives to prison so that they might conceive from him'" (*Midrash Rabbah*. ed. H. Freedman and Maurice Simon, 10 vols. [London, 1951]), vol. 5, 286.

56. DiSalvo, "Intestine Thorn," 211–12, 217–18, 222, 225. For the concept of Samson as a slave bound to his effeminacy, see Mary Beth Rose, "'Vigorous Most / When Most Unactive Deemed': Gender and the Heroics of Endurance in Milton's *Samson Agonistes*, Aphra Behn's *Oroonoko*, and Mary Astell's *Some Reflections Upon Marriage*," in *Milton Studies* 33, *The Miltonic Samson*, ed. Albert C. Labriola and Michael Lieb (Pittsburgh, 1997), 83–109.

57. For an account of the rituals surrounding the figure of the Nazarite, see the detailed account in Numbers 6. Only after the days of the Nazarite's separation have been concluded is he obliged to shave his head: "And the Nazarite shall shave the head of his separation *at* the door of the tabernacle of the congregation, and shall take the hair of the head of his separation, and put *it* in the fire which *is* under the sacrifice of the peace offerings" (Num. 6:18).

THE SPUR OF SELF-CONCERNMENT: MILTON IN HIS DIVORCE TRACTS

Stephen M. Fallon

I F ANY AUTHOR IS in his or her texts, Milton is in his.[1] And Milton is nowhere more present than in his divorce tracts. If they lack the extended autobiographical digressions of *The Reason of Church-Government, An Apology for Smectymnuus,* or the *Second Defense,* Milton liberally salts them with laudatory self-representations, as diligent prosecutor of the common good, as prophetic rescuer of God's word and law from monkish misconstruction, as heroic champion of an unpopular position. Carrying Milton's anxieties and wishes on or near the surface, the divorce tracts are not disinterested texts. Making a virtue of necessity, Milton acknowledges the role of what he calls in the second edition of the *Doctrine and Discipline of Divorce* "the spurre of self-concernment."[2] He speaks more truly than perhaps he knew. The imperatives of self-conception and self-representation help to form and ultimately to distort the argument for divorce. The manner in which self-representation drives and then deforms Milton's argument betrays itself in differences between the *Doctrine and Discipline* and *Tetrachordon,* two works that have much in common but whose crucial differences are often glossed over by critics.

Milton had established a pattern of prose self-representation in the antiprelatical tracts that were published just before the divorce tracts. There Milton presented himself as speaking for God, elect by virtue of his unstained character and unstinting diligence in learning. In the *Reason of Church-Government,* for example, he counted himself among those who are "in Gods prime intention and their own, selected heralds of peace, and dispensers of treasure inestimable" (YP 1:802); his words were inspired not by profligacy, as do those that flow "at wast from the pen of some vulgar Amorist, or the trencher fury of a riming parasite," but from "that eternall Spirit who can enrich with all utterance and knowledge, and sends out his Seraphim with the hallow'd fire of his Altar to touch and purify the lips of whom he pleases" (YP 1:820–21). In *An Apology* he again emphasizes his unspotted chastity as a qualification for his election as divine spokesperson (YP 1:889–93).

The events of the mid-1640s, Milton's failed marriage and the withering response to the divorce tracts, were corrosive to Milton's sense of himself as above the fray. The story is familiar. In the late spring of 1642, the thirty-three-year-old Milton marries Mary Powell, whom he meets while collecting a debt in Oxfordshire. A month or two later, she leaves him. The experience contributes to his decision to compose several works advocating divorce for incompatibility, a topic that interested him before his marriage. In both the *Doctrine and Discipline* and *Tetrachordon,* Milton argues that divorce was not prohibited by the Gospels, and that the Mosaic law allowing divorce continues to be necessary given the blameless incompatibilities and the infirmities resulting from the Fall.

There is some mystery surrounding Milton's courtship and marriage: why did Milton marry a woman he had known for so short a time, particularly one from a Royalist family? Why exactly did Mary Powell leave Milton? Was the marriage consummated before her departure? But there is no doubt that the experience challenged the self-representation he had nurtured in the antiprelatical tracts. For one used to thinking of himself as untouched by frailty and as heroically and uniquely virtuous, the experience of arguing for (and in all probability desiring) a remedy that seemed to be expressly prohibited by Christ could only be disorienting. How could a person of virtue and discernment make a catastrophically mistaken marriage choice? How could he now require a remedy suited not to strength but to weakness? Arthur Barker is persuasive when he argues that Milton's "self-esteem had suffered a blow of the utmost severity, and he had been forced to recognize his own humanity."[3] This surprised recognition of shared humanity, according to Barker, leads to a revision in the perfectionist thinking that marked the antiprelatical tracts:

He has come to recognize that the reformation cannot be sudden; more than that, he has had proof of his own infirmity and imperfection. So far is he from discounting the significance of the Fall that, here at least, the idealist gives place to the realist. The divorce problem and its attendant difficulties not only lead him to remark on the impossibility of Atlantic and Utopian polities, but to justify liberty in terms of fallen nature.[4]

But if Milton excuses his mistake and acquits himself of sin by reinterpreting Christ's apparent prohibition of divorce, the problem for the revival of his self-esteem is evident. Justification comes at the expense of implicating himself in the general weakness of fallen humankind, a weakness from which he had seemed exempt in his earlier self-representations. Self-justification and the argument for divorce drive Milton toward inclusion in what he calls the "common lump" of men, company with whom he is never comfortable.

Milton's dilemma, I will argue in this essay, leads to a succession of self-representations in the divorce tracts, as Milton claims heroic status, obscurely contemplates the possibility of alienation from God, justifies himself by the argument of shared imperfection, and then recoils from participation in general infirmity with implicit and ultimately incoherent gestures toward unfallen status. In suggesting that Milton comes to terms with infirmity and imperfection, and makes an accommodation with fallen nature, Barker tells only half the story, eliding, as we shall see, a significant difference between the *Doctrine and Discipline* and *Tetrachordon*. Ernest Sirluck picks up this partial story when he argues that the painful experience of a failed marriage explains why Milton wrote so little poetry in the 1640s. If Milton derived his inspired status from heroic virtue and special election by God, evidence of imperfection shared with others could undermine that status: "Milton's concept of his role as poet developed in such a way as to make the failure of his marriage a direct blow to his poetic inspiration (or, what amounts to the same thing, to his faith in it)."[5] Although Barker and Sirluck recognize ways in which *Tetrachordon* goes beyond or departs from the *Doctrine and Discipline* in argument, they treat them interchangeably as evidence of Milton's self-conception.[6] Much of the drama of these extraordinary works lies in the progression and variations of Milton's self-representations. The central argument of the divorce tracts exerts real pressure on Milton's familiar self-representation, and in turn the imperatives of self-conception and self-representation, Milton's need to see and present himself as outstanding, exert a very real counterpressure on the argument. Ultimately the counterpressure distorts the argument.

THE DOCTRINE AND DISCIPLINE OF DIVORCE:
DESPAIR/DIS-PAIR/REPAIR

In the first divorce tract, *The Doctrine and Discipline of Divorce*, one can begin to trace the splintering of self-representation that would characterize Milton's work from this point on. Milton represents himself as a prophetic restorer of divine mercy, but in a second and conflicting self-representation Milton obscurely contemplates the possibility that he is alienated from God.

In one of the more remarkable self-representations in the first edition, Milton implies that recorded history does not contain a contribution to human good comparable to his own: "he that can but lend us the clue that windes out this labyrinth of servitude to such a reasonable and expedient liberty as this, deserves to be reck'n'd among the publick benefactors of civill and humane life; above the inventors of wine and oyle" (YP 2:240). The reading public apparently did not agree; Milton was attacked as a promoter of heresy and license.[7] The anonymous author of *An Answer to a Book, Intituled, The Doctrine and Discipline of Divorce* charges that Milton's argument "smels very strongly of little lesse than blasphemie against Christ himself."[8]

Milton reacted vigorously in the greatly expanded second edition to the hostility and ridicule elicited by the first. He attacks those of "a waterish and queasy conscience" who "rail and fancy to themselves, that injury and licence is the best of this Book," calling them "the brood of Belial, the draffe of men, to whom no liberty is pleasing" (YP 2:225–26).

Milton's self-representation as godly hero is more pronounced in the second edition. Milton associates himself with heroes from the epic/romance and the biblical traditions.[9] At the outset he confronts Custom's female face atop Error's serpentine body, a figure adapted from the dragon Errour, whose den the reader and the Redcrosse Knight encounter at the outset of *The Faerie Queene* (1.1.13–24). Identifying, and so proleptically defeating, his enemy, Milton claims the role of romance hero. Milton closes the heroic frame with an addition near the end of his work, proudly claiming the "purity and wisdom" of God's law permitting divorce as "buckler" and mournfully boasting that it is "a labour of no mean difficulty and envy to defend" the law (YP 2:351). The implicit comparison with Hercules here looks forward to an explicit comparison in *Colasterion* for his labor of answering the voluminous but sordid arguments of the Answerer: "Yet *Hercules* had the labour once impos'd upon him to carry dung out of the *Augean* stable" (YP 2:756). In his last substantial addition to the first edition he ranges himself alongside God and Moses; criticism of his argument "lights not upon this book, but upon that which I engage against them, the book of God, and of *Moses*" (YP 2:354).

Standing forth in roles borrowed from the Bible, classical myth, and the "sage and serious Spenser," Milton seems above and immune to weakness. But countercurrents of anxiety and doubt, perhaps stronger for their being unconscious, emerge particularly at moments of most heroic self-representation. Even the opening Spenserian allegory of Error and Custom—in which Milton assumes the role of St. George—is subject to eruptions and counterpressures. Milton introduces the allegory with a surprising analogy between Custom's book of knowledge and the prophetic scroll in Ezekiel: "her [Custom's] method is so glib and easie, in some manner like to that vision of *Ezekiel*, rowling up her sudden book of implicit knowledge, for him that will, to take and swallow down at pleasure; which proving but of bad nourishment in the concoction, as it was heedlesse in the devouring, puffs up unhealthily, a certaine big face of pretended learning" (YP 2:222–23). Milton's opponents swallow Custom's empty confections, but their swallowing is compared with Ezekiel's swallowing of the scroll. Expected roles are reversed, feeding a sense of uncertainty and dis-ease echoed in the murky syntax.[10] Another surprise awaits us at the end of the allegory. In *The Faerie Queene* Errour is a grotesquely fecund mother; in the *Doctrine and Discipline* Truth is the mother: "Error and Custome . . . with the numerous and vulgar train of their followers, make it their chiefe designe to envie and cry-down the industry of free reasoning, under the terms of humor, and innova-tion; as if the womb of teeming Truth were to be clos'd up, if shee presume to bring forth ought, that sorts not with their unchew'd notions and supposi-tions" (YP 2:224). Milton as mother/father of teeming truth (the gender confusion surrounding the metaphor of birth is so common as to be a signa-ture of Milton's) is uncomfortably close to the image of Error the mother of her swarming and devouring litter.[11] Having placed himself metaphorically as mother and father, Milton in the next breath positions himself as the paradox-ically unique culmination of a teeming brood: "now the duty and the right of an instructed Christian cals me through the chance of good or evill report, to be the sole advocate of a discount'nanc't truth: a high enterprise Lords and Commons, a high enterprise and a hard, and such as every seventh Son of a seventh Son does not venture on" (YP 2:224). Out of miraculous and pro-digious fertility comes not the promiscuous spawn of Error but the unprece-dented and unparalleled chosen son.[12]

The anxiety finds more direct expression. Already forming in the first edition and fully developed in the second is a pattern that will mark the works of the remainder of Milton's career. Veering between antithetical extremes, he will claim heroic stature, grounded in an exercise of virtue uncommon—and even improbable—in fallen creatures, even as he contemplates behind veils the possibility of mortal error. Annabel Patterson has unlocked the working of encoded autobiographical micro-narratives in the *Doctrine and Discipline,* narratives providing Milton a space in which to confront that which he cannot or will not confront publicly, the possibility of guilt and failure.[13] We recognize Milton in the third-person description of those "so-berest and best govern'd men" who, because they "have spent their youth chastly" and "are lest practiz'd in these affairs," are liable to innocent error in choice of a marriage partner (YP 2:249). When this happens, the natural burning for companionship is frustrated, giving rise to an innocent hate, "not that Hate that sins" (YP 2:253). The paradox suggests that the blamelessness of Milton's veiled self-representation is sustained tenuously at best. He pro-ceeds nonetheless, suggesting that this natural hate, like the natural loneli-ness that gives rise to it, "hath not the least grain of a sin in it, *if he be worthy to understand himself"* (YP 2:253; emphasis mine). However much Milton attempts to assert this other self's blameless purity, by the next page he teeters at the edge of a chasm:

though he be almost the strongest Christian, he will be ready to *dispair* in vertue, and mutin against divine providence: and this doubtles is the reason of those lapses and that melancholy despair which we see in many wedded persons, *though they under-*

stand it not, . . . and is of extreme danger; therefore when human frailty surcharg'd, is at such a losse, charity ought to venture much, and use bold physick, lest an over-tost faith endanger to shipwrack. (YP 2:254; emphasis mine)

Both passages raise the question of self-understanding; significantly, the positive statement is conditional ("if he be worthy to understand himself"). Self-understanding and the self-representation built on that understanding are crucially important to Milton; the displaced uncertainty glimpsed here is a threat to his authority as a writer and to his status as a Christian. The struggle for equilibrium marking the tract is played out here in small compass. I am the strongest Christian, Milton seems to be saying, and I am ready to divorce virtuously, or to "dis-pair in vertue"; though the strongest Christian, owing to an intolerable law I am in danger of despair, loss of faith, and mutiny against God.[14] What is missing is a third possibility: I am a reasonably virtuous and conscientious Christian, struggling to understand and follow God's will while seeking companionship in marriage.

As was evident in the allegory of Custom and Error, anxiety emerges even—or especially—in those moments when Milton is self-assertive, as in this passage recalling the *Apology*'s declarations of heroic virtue and spotless probity:

Hee who shall indeavour the amendment of any old neglected grievance in Church or State, or in the daily course of life, if he be gifted with abilities of mind that may raise him to so high an undertaking, I grant he hath already much whereof not to repent him; yet let me arreed him, not to be the foreman of any mis-judged opinion, unlesse his resolutions be firmly seated in a square and constant mind, not conscious to it self of any deserved blame, and regardles of ungrounded suspicions. (YP 2:224)

Milton again distances himself from any spot or blame and derives his authority as a disputant from his purity. Examinations of conscience yield assurance rather than conviction. But, as things now are, of how many actions can it be said, as Milton said of the natural hatred of ill-yoked spouses (his own experience, as is palpable in the tract), that it "hath not the least grain of a sin in it" (YP 2:253). The psychological and theological pressures attending a claim of freedom from "any deserved blame" are substantial. Milton himself in his *Apology* had rebuked the author of *A Modest Confutation* for writing as if unfallen, ridiculing his claim to freedom from prejudice in his adherence to truth: "Which unlesse he only were exempted out of the corrupt masse of *Adam*, borne without sinne originall, and living without actuall, is impossible" (YP 1:909). Despite seeing the danger and absurdity in claiming exemption from fallen frailty, Milton repeatedly lays himself open to similar rebuke.

The resulting pressures betray themselves inevitably. The other self who would amend old grievances is one who will be the "foreman of any misjudged opinion." While Milton clearly means that the true opinion may be misjudged by others as false, the syntax invites a reading of misjudgment on the part of the "foreman." What if the tract's rereading of Christ's apparent proscription of divorce in Matthew 19 and its opposition to a settled majority opinion is the result of improper judgment? What if the same faulty judgment errs in failing to recognize "deserved blame"? When Milton offers one of his typical, and typically nervous, knotted negatives, "he hath already much whereof not to repent him," the cumbersome construction evokes precisely what Milton means to exorcize, the taint of guilt.

Given that Milton's unhappy marital situation made him an interested participant in the controversy, the traces of anxiety are not surprising. In one of the most revealing moments of the tract, Milton wrestles with the demon of "self-concernment," running the phrase through hoops to make it work for rather than against him, deflecting it from self-servingness toward disinterested service to God and country. His critics blaspheme in their arguments against divorce, reproaching God

whom they doe not deny to have belawgiv'n his owne sacred people with this very allowance, which they now call injury and licence, and dare cry shame on, and will doe yet a while, till they get a little cordiall sobriety to settle their qualming zeale. *But this question concerns not us perhaps:* Indeed mans disposition though prone to search after vain curiosities, yet when points of difficulty are to be discusst, appertaining to the removall of unreasonable wrong and burden from the perplext life of our brother, it is incredible how cold, how dull, and farre from all fellow feeling we are, without *the spurre of self-concernment.* Yet if the wisdome, the justice, the purity of God be to be cleer'd from foulest imputations which are not yet avoided, if charity be not to be degraded and trodd'n down under a civil Ordinance, if Matrimony be not to be advanc't like that exalted perdition, writt'n of to the *Thessalonians, above all that is called God* [emphasis Milton's], or goodnesse, nay, against them both, then I dare affirm there will be found in the Contents of this Booke, that which *may concern us all. You it concerns chiefly,* Worthies in Parlament, on whom, as on our deliverers, all our grievances and cares, by the merit of your eminence and fortitude are devolv'd: *Me it concerns next,* having with much labour and faithfull diligence first found out, or at least with a fearlesse and communicative candor first publisht to the manifest good of Christendome, that which calling to witnesse every thing mortall and immortall, I beleeve unfainedly to be true. Let not other men thinke their conscience bound to search continually after truth, to pray for enlightning from above, to publish what they think they have so obtaind, & debarr me from conceiving my self ty'd by the same duties. (YP 2:226; emphasis mine, except where noted)

In the middle of the passage we hear the unmistakable cry of outraged suffering: those not spurred by self-concernment are blind and deaf to the suffering, the burden and perplexity, caused by the human prohibition of divorce. But in short order self-concernment is transmuted into disinterested service. His attackers are actually God's attackers, and they need "a little cordiall sobriety to settle their qualming zeale." How they will reach this sobriety is not specified; instead Milton adds, "this question concerns not us perhaps." But after the intervening admission of self-concernment, it turns out that punishing the scoffers will in fact concern Milton, now not as one suffering burden and perplexity but as one selflessly fighting God's (and Parliament's) battles. This is not the first or the last time that Milton takes on the role of God's defender; what is interesting here is the quick move from the hint that God's action will repay the scoffers to the conclusion that Milton will repay them. Along the way, the notion of self-concernment is trans-formed; if it is the concern of everyone that God's justice be vindicated, it is the special concern of Parliament, the guardians of the nation, and of Milton, the searcher after truth. Milton is self-concerned now not as a suffering husband but as a godly interpreter facing ignorant opposition and calumny.

In arguing for a relaxation of divorce laws, then, Milton not only claims his birthright as a son of God, he engages in theodicy. He does so from above and from below. Milton speaks as if alongside God and above the frailties of human beings, as if untouched by human misery (except as a compassionate observer) and as if free from sin. Unconscious of any blame, shoulder to shoulder with God and Moses, Milton is a superhuman benefactor, rarer in virtue and favor than anyone in history. At the same time, Milton speaks from below, out of painful, fallen experience. He wants to demonstrate that divine law concerning marriage and divorce is properly adapted to the weakness of fallen human beings, to those who are not "heroically vertuous" but belong to "the common lump of men" (YP 2:253). If it were not so adapted, a person of good will saddled because of natural disaffection with the blameless hatred that is not sin would be led to despair, or the sin against the Holy Spirit: "the whole worship of a Christian mans life should languish and fade away be-neath the waight of an immeasurable grief and discouragement" until he (as opposed to she) is driven "at last through murmuring and despair to thoughts of Atheism" (YP 2:259–60). Even if a bad marriage does not damn him, it can kill him: "they ofttimes resent one anothers mistake so deeply, that long it is not ere grief end one of them" (YP 2:273). The third-person portrait that culminates in this language of despair is at the outset indistinguishable from Milton himself. This language of despair, heavy with the weight of anguished personal experience, contributes to a self-construction more disguised but no less authentic than the more familiar heroic one.

The tension between the explicit self-representation as heroically vir-tuous, divinely chosen, and untouched by fallen frailty and the implicit self-representation as potentially alienated from God is highlighted by the fact that the central argument of the *Doctrine and Discipline* is built around the distinction between what is appropriate before and after the Fall.[15] The Fall ushered in not only sin but also sinless imperfection, the human equivalent of natural as opposed to moral evil. Nature and natures change with the Fall; from that date planets meet in "synod unbenign" and sinless animals make mutual war (*PL* 10.661, 710).[16] Analogously, sinless people will not be able to live in harmony together if kept apart by a clash of natural tempers. This theory of natural, sinless antipathy serves Milton's psychological purposes well; as one perhaps in need of a divorce, he would not be anxious to ascribe his suffering to his own sin. Repeatedly in this text Milton argues that natural incompatibility is free of sin.[17] Considering his own case as he explores the biblical warrant for divorce as accommodation to the fallen, Milton redefines the Fall to allow for weakened but sinless individuals.

But the admission of imperfection, even morally blameless imperfection, entailed in the argument runs counter to Milton's former practice and his deep inclination. He argues that blameless thralldom in an unfit marriage can lead to neglect of duty toward God, "if there be not a miracle of vertue on either side" (YP 2:260). But Milton has consistently represented himself as miraculously virtuous, as uniquely worthy of blessing. In a particularly revealing moment, Milton argues that divorce is necessary for the man (such as himself) who finds himself in an unhappy marriage, "unlesse he be a thing heroically vertuous, and that are not the common lump of men for whom chiefly Laws ought to be made, though not to their sins, yet to their unsinning weaknesses" (YP 2:253–54). Within ten lines of implicitly associating himself with the "common lump of men," Milton externalizes and neutralizes this admission by describing the wife as "an image of earth and fleam [i.e., phlegm]" (YP 2:254). Not surprisingly, his self-representations as imperfect are unstable, in part because Milton cannot for long think of himself as common and in part because he has difficulty keeping culpable and non-culpable imperfection separate. The difficulty of keeping morally neutral and morally suspect weaknesses separate is evident in the opening lines of the *Doctrine and Discipline*. The second edition begins with the Fall: "whether it be the secret of divine will, or the originall blindnesse we are born in, so it happ'ns for the most part, that Custome still is silently receiv'd for the best instructer." The result is "counterfeit knowledge" that "depress[es] the high and Heaven-born spirit of Man, farre beneath the condition wherein either God created him, or sin hath sunke him" (YP 2:222–23). Is the following of custom natural, as inevitable as bad weather, or is it morally culpable? It seems to be a general failing, but it turns out that some are exempt.[18] In refusing the easy teaching of custom, Milton implies that he is in that respect at least not subject as are others to "the originall blindnesse we are born in," to say nothing of the "condition wherein . . . sin hath sunke" man. Milton's rhetoric holds out the possibility not only of resisting the teaching of custom but in doing so of not sinking below the created condition. Milton in other words seems to exempt himself not merely from moral weakness but also from the blameless imperfection attendant on the Fall. If there are inconveniences in the postlapsarian state (north winds, dropsies, blindness and susceptibility to custom, inability to predict the unfitness of mates?), some few seem to be untouched even by blameless weaknesses.

The acknowledgment of imperfection that Barker identified in the *Doctrine and Discipline* triggers a volatile, double reaction. Unable or unwilling to maintain the distinction of culpable and blameless weakness upon which his own argument depends, Milton contemplates despair and alienation, a typical Puritan experience most familiar to us perhaps in Bunyan. And immediately, in a counterreaction, Milton reasserts his freedom from all varieties of imperfection, and thus implicitly dissociates himself from the Fall.[19] This perspective must remain implicit, to Milton as well as to the reader, for it is incompatible with his Augustinian belief in the universality of the Fall. This implicit and unacknowledgeable claim nevertheless betrays itself as Milton introduces a line of argument placing the injured husband in a position that uncannily foreshadows the unfallen Adam's in *Paradise Lost*.[20] In the epic, after the fallen Eve has decided that, if she must die, she will take Adam with her, Adam throws in his lot with his spouse:

> some cursèd fraud
> Of Enemy hath beguiled thee, yet unknown,
> And mee with thee hath ruined, for with thee
> Certain my resolution is to die;
> How can I live without thee, how forgo
> Thy sweet convérse and Love so dearly joined,
> To live again in these wild woods forlorn? (*PL* 9.904–10)

While Adam does not consider divorce, the *Doctrine and Discipline* offers one of the only ways (if not the only way) for him to avoid falling, in its proposing divorce when one's spouse conspires against one's life, whether physical or spiritual. This reason for separation is recognized even in Canon Law, otherwise so cold to the plight of the unhappily married:

The Canon Law and Divines consent, that if either party be found contriving against the others life, they may be sever'd by divorce; for a sin against the life of mariage is greater then a sin against the bed: the one destroys, the other but defiles it. The same may be said touching those persons who beeing of a pensive nature and cours of life, have summ'd up all their solace in that free and lightsom conversation which God & man intends in mariage: wherof when they see themselves depriv'd by meeting an unsociable consort, they ofttimes resent one anothers mistake so deeply, that long it is not ere grief end one of them. When therfore this danger is foreseen that the life is in perill by living together, what matter is it whether helples greef, or wilfull practice be the cause? This is certain that the preservation of life is more worth then the compulsory keeping of mariage. (YP 2:273–74)

In *Paradise Lost* we find both "helples greef" and "wilfull practice," the former proleptically in Adam's fear of being deprived of "sweet converse" ("lightsom conversation") and the latter in Eve's fallen design ("Confirm'd then I resolve, / *Adam* shall share with me in bliss or woe" [9.830–31]). Curiously, the disappointed (as opposed to the warring) spouses in the *Doctrine and Discipline* "resent one anothers mistake" rather than their own; even in this moment of apparent mutuality, fingers are pointed. In the interval between Eve's fall and Adam's, Adam could legitimately absolve himself and resent Eve for her mistake; he chose wisely, but his spouse is no longer what she was. The discursive gap between mutual blamelessness and the guilt of the woman, which will widen in *Tetrachordon,* is mediated by the example of Adam and Eve, never far from the surface in texts built on the tension between prelapsarian and postlapsarian marriage. In his increasing emphasis on the innocence of the man facing a guilty, idolatrous, and dangerous woman, Milton returns to a moment when a recuperation of the original Fall of man can be enacted.

Tetrachordon—"Temptation even in the Faultless Person"

The *Doctrine and Discipline* reveals that Milton's experience of marriage caused him to recognize and implicitly acknowledge his imperfection. The reaction to this recognition, in the form of implicit gestures toward asserting his own unfallenness, is already present in the *Doctrine and Discipline,* particularly in the second edition, but in *Tetrachordon* it dominates Milton's self-representations. In the *Doctrine and Discipline* Milton emphasizes natural incompatibility and a kind of "no fault divorce" for unfortunate couples who through no fault of their own cannot love one another. But as he moves to *Tetrachordon,* despite a new reading of Matthew 19 that should promote the language of mutual blamelessness, he exchanges that language for language bewailing the plight of the innocent party shackled to a faithless, heathen, or sinning partner. Missing along with the language of mutual blamelessness are the veiled representations of himself as a man in despair, replaced by equally veiled representations of himself as one who has escaped or undone the Fall.

Tetrachordon, like the 1644 *Doctrine and Discipline,* begins with a heroic self-representation. Thanking Parliament for refusing to censure or censor him, Milton hints at the value of his gratitude: "such thanks perhaps they may live to be, as shall more then whisper to the next ages" (YP 2:579).[21] If he is no less confident than he was in first setting out his arguments in 1643, he is now embittered by what he views as ignorant attacks on the *Doctrine and Discipline*. He invokes two heroic predecessors, one explicitly and one implicitly.[22] He compares himself to Socrates, who for his wisdom was accused of making the worse appear the better reason (YP 2:583). And he assigns himself a role later claimed by his own Samson: "if men want manlinesse to expostulate the right of their due ransom, and to second their own occasions, they may sit hereafter and bemoan themselves to have neglected through faintnesse the onely remedy of their sufferings, which a seasonable and well grounded speaking might have purchas'd them" (YP 2:585).[23] Having experienced the treachery of those he has sought to help, Milton characteristically invokes classical and biblical predecessors.

A new element in *Tetrachordon*'s attempt to remedy the sufferings of the English has great implications for Milton's self-representations. Milton revisits Christ's answer to the Pharisees, "Moses because of the hardness of your hearts suffered you to put away your wives: but from the beginning it was not so" (Matt. 19:8). Earlier Milton, taking hard-heartedness as characterizing a subset of the Jews, argued that God allowed divorce for the relief of the conscientious despite knowing that the hard-hearted—such as the questioning Pharisees—would abuse the law by divorcing for trivial reasons. Now finding in hard-heartedness two senses, the conscious sinfulness of the few evoked earlier ("a stubborne resolution to doe evil" [YP 2:662]) and the imperfection or weakness among even the good after the Fall ("infirmity, and imperfection, which was in all the Apostles" [YP 2:661]), Milton assigns the latter innocuous meaning to hardness of heart in Matthew 19:8. In so doing, he salvages for virtuous Christians (such as himself) the Mosaic permission of divorce as glossed by Christ, without having to evoke a complex and ironical interpretive setting. This reinterpretation, that is, has the virtue of allowing Milton to read Matthew 19:8 as spoken directly to all and not obliquely as a coded teaching for the Pharisees.[24] The new definition of hard-heartedness and rereading of the verse dovetails with the argument in the *Doctrine and Discipline* that, had we remained in paradise, we would not need permission to divorce, for in the perfect state we would be perfect mates and helpmeets to each other. All are weakened at the Fall, and all are subject to blameless error in marriage choices. But if the overarching argument remains the same, Milton now has Christ speaking directly in its support.

The newly interpreted sense of Christ's teaching on "hardness of heart" would seem to promise a firmer foundation for the argument for no-fault divorce advanced in the *Doctrine and Discipline*. It is curious, then, that this argument all but disappears from *Tetrachordon*. The generous recognition that both parties might be equally blameless for the failure of a marriage, that their incompatibility can be traceable to immutable and involuntary differences in temperament, is frequent in the *Doctrine and Discipline*. Milton writes, for example, that "ofttimes the causes of seeking divorce reside . . . deeply in the radical and innocent affections of nature" or in "the guiltles instinct of nature" (YP 2:345, 346). Some marriages fail through no one's fault but because of "natures unalterable working" (YP 2:249).[25] These gestures toward mutual blamelessness, despite Milton's adoption of the new and innocent interpretation of "hardness of heart," disappear from *Tetrachordon*. In the very first description of a failed marriage in *Tetrachordon* there is no question of a blameless, natural, and mutual antipathy:

seeing woman was purposely made for man, and he her head, it cannot stand before the breath of this divine utterance, that man the portraiture of God, joyning to himself for his intended good and solace an inferiour sexe, should so becom her thrall, whose wilfulnes or inability to be a wife frustrates the occasionall end of her creation, but that he may acquitt himself to freedom by his naturall birthright, and that indeleble character of priority which God crown'd him with. If it be urg'd that sin hath lost him this, the answer is not far to seek, that from her the sin first proceeded, which keeps her justly in the same proportion still beneath. She is not to gain by being first in the transgression, that man should furder loose to her, because already he hath lost by her means. (YP 2:589–90)[26]

There is a trace of blamelessness in the "inability to be a wife," but the remainder of the passage tips the scales toward the other alternative, the wife's "wilfulness." Carried away as he imagines objections to his argument, Milton evokes Eve's transgression and imagines that women's aim is to enthrall husbands and "to gain by being first in the transgression."

This passage sets the tone for the rest of the work. Where in the *Doctrine and Discipline* Milton suggests that contrariety of natural tempers lies behind the failure of at least some marriages, in *Tetrachordon* the cause again and again comes down to the wife's wilfullness and hostility.[27] Men look for helpmeets when they take wives, he argues, "But if they [the men] find them neither fit helps, nor tolerable society, what thing more natural, more original and first in nature then to depart from that which is irksom, greevous, *actively hateful,* and *injurious eevn to hostility,* especially in a conjugal respect, wherin antipathies are invincible, and wher the forc't abiding of the one, can bee no true good, no real comfort to the other" (YP 2:621–22; emphasis mine). This passage, like the one examined a moment ago, looks in two directions. Hatefulness and hostile injuriousness point toward wilfulness; such wives are active in their opposition to their husbands. Invincible antipathies, on the other hand, recall the blameless natural tempers evoked repeadedly in the *Doctrine and Discipline*. But now Milton treats the two reasons for divorce as interchangeable. In the following sentences, Milton returns apparently to natural and blameless dislike, only to conclude with a distinction between guiltless and guilty: "For if hee find no contentment from the other, how can he return it from himself, or no acceptance, how can hee mutually accept? what more equal, more pious then to untie a civil knot for a natural enmity held by violence from parting, to dissolv an accidental conjunction of this or that man & woman, for the most natural and most necessary disagreement of meet from unmeet, guilty from guiltless, contrary from contrary?" Milton discusses invincible antipathy in both works; the difference is that in the *Doctrine and Discipline* these discussions are accompanied by reminders that they can arise from what he calls "the faultles proprieties of nature" (YP 2:237), while in the later work they are accompanied by reminders of the woman's guilt and, inevitably and crucially, the man's innocence. The emphasis on guilt informs the remarkable anatomy of ill-yoked marriages near the conclusion of *Tetrachordon*'s section on Deuteronomy:

And what confusion els can ther bee in separation, to separat, upon extrem urgency, the Religious from the irreligious, the fit from the unfit, the willing from the wilfull, the abus'd from the abuser, such a separation is quite contrary to confusion. But to binde and mixe together holy with Atheist, hevnly with hellish, fitnes with unfitnes, light with darknes, antipathy with antipathy, the injur'd with the injurer, and force them into the most inward neernes of a detested union, this doubtles is the most horrid, the most unnatural mixture, the greatest confusion that can be confus'd! (YP 2:635)

The urgent, wrenching tone of the passage points to its roots in painful experience. The lone phrase suggesting mutuality and perhaps blamelessness, "antipathy with antipathy," is overwhelmed by a tide of anger, injury, and accusation.

The distance between the two works can be gauged by juxtaposing two related passages:

There is indeed a twofold Seminary or stock in nature, from whence are deriv'd the issues of love and hatred distinctly flowing through the whole masse of created things, and that Gods doing ever is to bring the due likenesses and harmonies of his workes together, except when out of two contraries met to their own destruction, he moulds a third existence, and that it is error, or some evil Angel which either blindly or maliciously hath drawn together in two persons ill imbarkt in wedlock the sleeping discords and enmities of nature lull'd on purpose with some false bait, that they may wake to agony and strife. (*Doctrine and Discipline of Divorce;* YP 2:272)

Besides the singular and substantial differences of every Soul, there is an intimat quality of good or evil, through the whol progeny of *Adam,* which like a radical heat, or mortal chilnes joyns them, or disjoyns them irresistably. (*Tetrachordon;* YP 2:606)[28]

The earlier passage is complex to the point of obscurity. Is it that some things come from the seminary of love and others from the seminary of hate? The opening seems to admit that reading, but the rest of the passage makes more likely the reading that hatred arises from the mixture of things from two seminaries. In any event, the agent of the ill-yoked marriage here is neither spouse but "error, or some evil Angel."[29] The spouses are presented as hapless and blameless victims of an accident or cosmic joke. The later passage parallels the first, and Milton seems to have the same phenomenon in mind, but now in place of a two-fold seminary one finds "an intimat quality of good or evil." The new terms epitomize the perspective of *Tetrachordon* as it diverges from the *Doctrine and Discipline.* Despite a new definition of hardness of heart as a kind of blameless imperfection incident to our universal status as fallen, Milton cannot seem to pass by any discussion of incompatibility without asserting blame or evil on one side and innocence or good on the other. Blameless error is repeatedly transmuted into the woman's blamable and "most unnatural fraud" (YP 2:626); mutual blamelessness is replaced by "anothers fault against him" (YP 2:625). At one point even "inability" becomes culpable:

I argue, that man or wife who hates in wedloc, is perpetually unsociable, unpeacefull, or unduteous, either not being able, or not willing to performe what the maine ends of mariage demand in helpe and solace, cannot bee said to care for who should bee dearest in the house; therefore is worse then an infidel . . . ; either in undertaking a duty which he cannot performe, to the undeserved and unspeakable injury of the other party so defrauded and betrai'd, or not performing what he hath undertaken, . . . to the perjury of himselfe more irreligious then heathenisme. (YP 2:691)

The inability to love, formerly a tragic but blameless result of fallen nature, is now evidence of deception and breach of promise. Although Milton includes man as well as woman as potentially guilty here, the larger context firmly blames the woman.

    Tetrachordon comes closest to echoing the *Doctrine and Discipline*'s argument for mutual blamelessness when Milton writes of the innocence of the man "who puts away by mutuall consent" with love and gentleness, or of one who divorces because of "causes rooted in immutable nature, utter unfitnesse, utter disconformity, not concileable, because not to be amended without out a miracle" (YP 2:669–70). A moment after this interlude of tender concern for the woman and acknowledgment of mutual blamelessness, however, Milton refers to the poorly matched wife as "a helpelesse, unaffectionate and sullen masse" (YP 2:670), in a reprise of the *Doctrine and Discipline*'s "image of earth and fleam."

How does one account for the all but complete disappearance of the argument of mutual blamelessness from *Tetrachordon*? The answer cannot lie simply in *Tetrachordon*'s insistent patriarchalism, for it shares that characteristic with the *Doctrine and Discipline*.[30] While the *Doctrine and Discipline* makes a case for mutual blamelessness, it does not argue for the equality of the sexes (though it does gesture now and then in that direction); Milton presents instead the possibility of two unequal partners being equally blameless along with the possibility of the unfit woman's stubborn refusal to be a wife. In *Tetrachordon*, the first possibility is elided, despite the fact that the new reading of "hardness of heart" would seem to invite it.

If not patriarchalism, what? I suggest that the change springs from Milton's need to represent himself to us and to himself as heroic, as chosen because of eminent virtue. He can argue for a universal yet not necessarily sinful hardness of heart after the Fall, but when push comes to shove he does not want to count himself among the herd, even concerning qualities wherein the herd is sinless. Ernest Sirluck is right to see that "hardness of heart" in *Tetrachordon* becomes "a description of the fallen condition of man" (YP 2:154). But Milton disowns this sense of "hardness of heart" as a self-description as soon as he offers it. Yes, Moses allows divorce because of the imperfection after the Fall of even the virtuous, and, yes, Christ seconds this permission, but Milton cannot own to that imperfection. James Grantham Turner rightly identifies Milton's distinction between intention and practice, between "pursui[ing] the full Edenic ideal" and "fight[ing] for such regulations 'as reason and present nature can bear.' "[31] But the disappearance from *Tetrachordon* of veiled representations of himself as despairing or even imperfect reveals Milton's deep reluctance to apply to his own case what is otherwise universally applicable. The reading of "hardness of heart" as universal, blameless natural imperfection evokes the same ambivalence and tension as the claim in the *Doctrine and Discipline* that a law the author contemplates availing himself of is made not for the "heroically vertuous" but for the "common lump of men" (YP 2:253). Milton scrambles on a precipice between two slippery slopes: either acknowledgment of shared weakness will undermine his self-representation as heroically virtuous, or disavowal of weakness will involve him in untenable claims of unfallenness (and eviscerate his argument for divorce). The tendency to slip into the claim of unfallenness is on display in a passage introduced earlier:

If it be urg'd that sin hath lost him [his birthright and priority], the answer is not far to seek, that from her sin first proceeded, which keeps her justly in the same proportion still beneath. She is not to gain by being first in the transgression, that man should furder loose to her, because already he hath lost by her means. Oft it happens that in this matter he is without fault; so that his punishment herein is causeles. (YP 2:590)

The primary meaning of "this matter [in which] he is without fault" is the unhappy marriage. But the immediate allusive context is that of the Fall, in which Eve is "first in the transgression." If the man (or Milton) loses "by her means," he nevertheless remains "without fault," in the first instance in the marriage but by allusion in the Fall.

Milton argues that divine permission to divorce accommodates not our sinfulness (God does not accommodate and thus abet sin) but what he had called in the earlier tract our "unsinning weaknesses." But as he projects himself onto the schema that he has articulated, he redefines and even distorts the schema to fit his self-construction. Milton begins to undo the new signification of "hardness of heart" even before he has finished articulating it. He pivots on the term "weakness," which signifies both an effect of original sin and an innocent source of error. This ambiguous signification allows Milton to shift from weakness as the effect of sin first to innocent weakness and then to entire innocence. The passage, noted above, in which he differentiates significations of "hardness of heart" illustrates the complexity of the relationships among sin, weakness, and innocence in Milton's conception of the effects of the Fall. It repays closer inspection:

hardnesse of heart hath a twofould acception in the Gospel. One, when it is in a good man taken for infirmity, and imperfection, which was in all the Apostles, whose weaknesse only, not utter want of beleef is call'd hardnes of heart, *Marke* 16. partly for this hardnesse of heart, the imperfection and decay of man from original righteousnesse, it was that God suffer'd not divorce onely, but all that which by Civilians is term'd the *secondary law of nature and of nations* [Milton's emphasis]. . . . [H]ee suffer'd divorce as well as mariage, our imperfet and degenerat condition of necessity requiring this law among the rest, as a remedy against intolerable wrong and servitude above the patience of man to beare. Nor was it giv'n only because our infirmity, or *if it must be so called,* hardnesse of heart could not endure all things, but because the *hardnes of anothers heart might not inflict all things upon an innocent person,* whom far other ends brought into a league of love and not of bondage and indignity. . . .

In a second signification hardnes of heart is tak'n for a stubborne resolution to doe evil. (YP 2:661–62; emphasis mine)

Milton's first examples of hardness of heart are the Apostles, who betray moments of weak faith but do not fall into faithlessness. Hardness of heart in this sense is not sinfulness revealed in breaking the law but the weakness or frailty that makes law necessary. But even in the middle of the passage introducing this sinless hardness, Milton begins to speak of injury inflicted by the hardness of one on the *innocence* of another; one might not think from the clause "if it must be so called" that it was Milton himself who made the identification of "hardness of heart" with general infirmity the moment before; as he contemplates membership in this universal set, he can only grudgingly and with difficulty accept the label of hardness of heart himself. He immediately goes about distinguishing the innocent from the guilty or hardhearted; now it is "anothers heart" that is hardened, and this hardness inflicts injury on "an innocent person." This distinction might seem to fit more logically under the discussion of the second meaning of hardness of heart, a "stubborn resolution to doe evil," which governed the interpretation of the *Doctrine and Discipline*. No sooner does Milton name a category in which he fits with all others than does he begin to divide and distinguish, to open a gap between himself and the imputation of imperfection, even from an imperfection derived from the universally shared guilt of original sin.[32] Imperfection may come and go in Milton's self-representation; upon departing it leaves no spot or blame behind.

Having isolated the man's guilt, Milton not surprisingly claims a special perfection for the divorcer:

Him I hold *more in the way to perfection* who forgoes an unfit ungodly & discordant wedloc, to live according to peace & love, & Gods institution in a fitter chois, then he who debarrs himself the happy experience of all godly, which is peaceful conversation in his family, to live a contentious, and unchristian life not to be avoided, in temptations not to be liv'd in, only for the fals keeping of a most unreal nullity, . . . the remedy whereof God in his law voutsafes us. Which not to dare use, he warranting, is not our perfection, is our infirmity, our little faith, our timorous and low conceit of charity: and in them who force us, it is their masking pride and vanity, to seem holier & more circumspect then God. *So far is it that we need impute to him infirmity*, who thus divorces: since the rule of perfection is not so much that which was don in the beginning, as that which now is nearest to the rule of charity. This is the greatest, the perfetest, the highest commandment. (YP 2:666–67; emphasis mine).

Milton writes that one should not impute "infirmity" to the one who divorces, but of course this is precisely the characteristic that provides the gloss for hardness of heart and that makes the divine permission to divorce not only merciful but just. Within several pages Milton has insulated the innocent party to divorce, and by extension himself, from just these properties. While the language of "greater perfection" need not be more than relative, in a context where the Fall and its effects are central it calls to mind Edenic perfection. While Milton at one point gestures toward celibacy as proper to and possible only for the "supernaturally gifted," he seems more in character when he claims, on several occasions, greater perfection for one like himself:

"Men of most renowned vertu have sometimes by transgressing, most truly kept the law" (YP 2:588).[33] The greater perfection refers literally to the action of the man who dissolves an unfit marriage relative to that of the man who suffers in one, but again Milton's language seems to point beyond the local meaning to a greater perfection absolutely conceived. The language of "greater perfection" in *Tetrachordon* marks a step beyond the language of "lesse evil and lesse in scandal" with which he makes the same point in the *Doctrine and Discipline* (YP 2:328).

To explain how someone neither imperfect nor infirm could make a poor marriage choice, as Milton believed he had done, Milton relies on the Uriel defense: the unavoidability and moral neutrality of intellectual or perceptual error. Milton argues that one's life should not be ruined "meerly for a most incident error which no warines can certainly shun" or for "the most irreprehensible mistake in choosing" (YP 2:601). The analogy to Uriel is apt not only for innocence of the error but also for its arising from fraud. For the unfortunate husband as for the angel, "goodness thinks no ill / Where no ill seems," and the husband, like the angel later, is thus unable to see through a "fraudulent impostor" (*PL* 3.688–89, 692). Those who would forbid divorce say that the unfortunate husband should have discerned potential adultery in the woman he chooses, in "every glaunce of her eye, every step of her gate" (YP 2:629). But the unfortunate husband is in the position of one defrauded by a trickster, who can disguise her bad faith and unsuitability. Milton asks, "Why should his own error bind him, rather then *the others fraud* acquit him? . . . [I]t is not equal that error and fraud should be linkt in the same degree of forfeture, but rather that error should be acquitted, and fraud bereav'd of his morsel" (YP 2:630; emphasis mine).[34]

Tetrachordon at this point foreshadows the path *Paradise Lost* would take from Uriel on the sun to Adam in Eden; once again the paradoxical position Milton carves out for himself in *Tetrachordon* resembles Adam's just before his fall. If one finds oneself in an unfit marriage, "Then follows dissimulation, suspicion, fals colours, fals pretences, and wors then these, disturbance, annoyance, vexation, sorrow, *temtation eevn in the faultles person*, weary of himself, and of all action public or domestic; then comes disorder, neglect, hatred, and perpetual strife, all these the enemies of holines and christianity" (YP 2:631; emphasis mine). This catalogue looks forward to the effects of the Fall in *Paradise Lost*,[35] but the italicized phrase looks back to before the Fall. The driving apart of the guilty and the innocent, along with the figuring of the prelude to an ill marriage as a successful seduction of one who expects no ill, suggests once again the position of Adam before his fall and after Eve's, only now perhaps a greater Adam who would not fall if not deceived. Milton's argument depends for its plausibility on general weakness, but inasmuch as he identifies with the wronged husband he tends to assign the woman the role of seductress in the garden and the man the role of still innocent Adam. Divorce, then, holds out the promise of a return to Eden, an undoing of the fatal error in Eden. Here is a way to recapture the pristine state and to make metaphoric sense of oneself as unfallen, and this I conclude is perhaps what Milton, despite his theological beliefs, most wants to do.

NOTES

The earliest version of this essay was discussed by the Newberry Milton Seminar, Chicago, in February, 1996. Later versions were delivered in a session at the Modern Language Association Convention, Washington, D.C., in December, 1996, and as a lecture at the University of Texas, Austin, in March, 1999. For valuable questions and comments, I am grateful to the editors of this volume and to Joi Chevalier, David Loewenstein, Janel Mueller, Jason Rosenblatt, Regina Schwartz, John Shawcross, Richard Strier, and Henry Weinfield. Stephanie Thomas provided reliable and discerning research assistance. I owe special debt to John Rumrich, who responded to several versions of the essay.

1. I understand that my conditional clause is open to dispute. From the perspectives of, for example, Barthes's argument for the death of the author or Derrida's attack on the metaphysics of presence, authors, in the sense of historical figures who stand behind, precede, and compose texts, are not in their texts. I address the reciprocal implications of Milton's works and of attacks on biographical and intentionalist criticism in a work-in-progress on self-representation across Milton's career. My understanding of the relation between the historical author and his self-representation is agnostic: the self-representation is neither identical to an extra- or pre-textual self, nor is it merely fictional and unrelated to that self.

2. *The Complete Prose Works of John Milton*, 8 vols., ed. Don M. Wolfe et al. (New Haven, 1953–82), vol 2, 226, hereafter cited parenthetically in the text as YP, with volume and page number.

3. Arthur Barker, *Milton and the Puritan Dilemma, 1641–1660* (Toronto, 1942), 116.

4. Barker, *Milton and the Puritan Dilemma*, 115.

5. Ernest Sirluck, "Milton's Idle Right Hand," *JEGP* 60 (1961): 754.

6. Reuben Sánchez Jr., though he writes mainly about *Tetrachordon*, similarly elides the difference between the two works (see *Persona and Decorum in Milton's Prose* [Madison, N.J., 1997], 94–96). Much published criticism of the divorce tracts, including my own ("The Metaphysics of Milton's Divorce Tracts," in *Politics, Poetics, and Hermeneutics in Milton's Prose*, ed. David Loewenstein and James Grantham Turner [Cambridge, 1990], 69–83), has treated the two works as interchangeable. Lana Cable, for example, subtitles her excellent chapter on the *Doctrine and Discipline* "The Coupling Rhetoric of the Divorce Tracts," despite devoting only a passing reference each to *Tetrachordon* and *Colasterion* (see *Carnal Rhetoric: Milton's Iconoclasm and the Poetics of Desire* [Durham, N.C., 1995], 90–116).

7. See William Riley Parker, *Milton's Contemporary Reputation* (1940; rpt. New York, 1971). Parker provides excerpts from contemporary attacks on Milton's divorce tracts.

8. Anon., *An Answer to a Book, Intituled, The Doctrine and Discipline of Divorce* (London, 1640), 28. Parker reproduces this entire work in facsimile in *Milton's Contemporary Reputation*, 170–216. One wonders which rankled more, the answerer's attack on Milton as theologian ("this is a wilde, mad, and frantick divinitie, just like to the opinions of the Maids at Aldgate," 36) or

his dismissal of Milton as stylist ("This frothie discourse . . . sugred over with a little neat language," 41).

9. For a view of the narrator in the *Doctrine and Discipline* as medieval romance hero, see Charles Hatten, "The Politics of Marital Reform and the Rationalization of Romance in *The Doctrine and Discipline of Divorce*," in *Milton Studies* 27, ed. James D. Simmonds (Pittsburgh, 1991), 95–113. Hatten's discussion of the historical and socio-political context of the tract's insistence on the subordination of women is perceptive; his discussion of the text as representative of elite Puritan cooptation and containment of the radical sects is less persuasive.

10. I note the paradoxical relation of this passage to the passage in *The Reason of Church-Government* in which Milton compares himself to the evangelist John eating the book (Rev. 10:9–10) in "Intention and Its Limits in *Paradise Lost*," in *Literary Milton*, ed. Diana Treviño Benet and Michael Lieb (Pittsburgh, 1994), 168–69.

11. On the metaphor of birth and Milton's appropriation of both gender roles, see chapter five, "The Art of Generation," in John Rumrich's *Milton Unbound* (Cambridge, 1996).

12. In the Bible the parenting of seven sons appears to be a token of rare good fortune (see Ruth 4:15, where Ruth is more precious than seven sons, and Job 1:2, where having seven sons is the first and highest sign of Job's wealth and good fortune). Admittedly, being one of the seven does not guarantee special favor or sanctity, as witness Acts 19:14, where an evil spirit rebukes the seven sons of a priest for their attempt at exorcism. I am not aware of any passage in the Bible in which the rarity of seven sons is squared to the seventh son of a seventh son.

13. Patterson, "No Meer Amatorious Novel," in *Politics, Poetics, and Hermeneutics in Milton's Prose*, ed. Loewenstein and Turner, 88–95.

14. The punning spelling "dispair" in this passage is not unique, but it is unusual, with variants employed once in *The Reason of Church-Government* and one other time in the *Doctrine and Discipline* (YP 1:847 and 2:339). Variants beginning "des," on the other hand, appear thirteen times in Milton's prose published before his blindness. For additional gestures toward despair, see YP 2:259–60, 273, 275.

15. For the centrality of the relation of prelapsarian to postlapsarian states in the divorce tracts, see James Grantham Turner's *One Flesh: Paradisal Marriage and Sexual Relations in the Age of Milton* (Oxford, 1987), ch. 6.

16. *Paradise Lost* 10.661 and 710, in *John Milton: The Complete Poems*, ed. John Leonard (Harmondsworth, 1998). All further references to Milton's poetry are to this edition, and the book and line numbers will be cited parenthetically in the text.

17. See YP 2:235–37, 249, 253, 260, 272, 328, 342, 345, 346, 355.

18. The psychological and rhetorical situation requires that Milton not be alone in exemption from what otherwise appears the universal lot of fallen humanity. If the many are deluded by Custom and the empty shows of human authority, he will depend on the wise and knowing few, an increasingly familiar audience: "the wise and right understanding handfull of men" and "the choisest and the learnedest, who have this high gift of wisdom to answer solidly, or to be convinc't" (YP 2:232, 233). Milton's heroic task is to bring truth to a world from which it has fled, and the likelihood of a hostile reception is a measure of his singularity and his courage.

19. In a private communication, Jason Rosenblatt suggests that the *Doctrine and Discipline's* Hebraic teaching that "the law incarnates deity" might help to account for Milton's implicit pretensions to unfallenness, inasmuch as a "corollary of the Hebraic emphasis on law would be an absence of reference to original sin." For Rosenblatt's excellent discussion of the Law and Gospel in the divorce tracts, see his *Torah and Law in "Paradise Lost"* (Princeton, N.J., 1994).

20. On the applicability of the teaching of the divorce tracts to Adam's situation in Eden after Eve's fall, see Rosenblatt, *Torah and Law*, pp. 196–203; as Rosenblatt observes, "Adam

speaks to Eve fatalistically, 'Submitting to what seem'd remediless' (*PL* 9.919), and all four tracts offer divorce as the remedy of a sick marriage" (196). On the *Doctrine and Discipline* as prophetic of *Paradise Lost*, see Barker, *Milton and the Puritan Dilemma*, 98.

21. He echoes the pledge in *The Reason of Church-Government* to "leave something so written to aftertimes, as they should not willingly let it die" (YP 1:810), and he anticipates the pose adopted a decade later in the *Second Defense*, when he represents himself as a worthy singer of heroic deeds and by extension a hero himself (YP 4:553–55).

22. In between the *Doctrine and Discipline* and *Tetrachordon*, Milton had invoked a more recent heroic predecessor, a Reformation hero who had anticipated his argument for divorce. In his signed address "To the Parlament" prefaced to the *Judgement of Martin Bucer*, Milton is caught on the horns of a dilemma, claiming on the one hand originality and on the other the authorizing precedent of Bucer. He recounts the story of finding Bucer's similar arguments only after he had published the *Doctrine and Discipline* and concludes, "I may justly gratulat mine own mind, with due acknowledgement of assistance from above, which led me, not as a lerner, but as a collateral teacher, to a sympathy of judgment with no lesse a man then *Martin Bucer*" (YP 2:435–36).

23. See *Samson Agonistes:*

> I was no private but a person raised
> With strength sufficient and command from Heav'n
> To free my country; if their servile minds
> Me their deliverer sent would not receive,
> But to their masters gave me up for naught,
> Th'unworthier they; whence to this day they serve.   (1211–16)

24. This paragraph follows Ernest Sirluck's introduction to the divorce tracts, YP 2:153–58. Sirluck notes a second major change in the later tract: a far-reaching discussion of the primary and secondary laws of nature, with the secondary law fitted to our fallen condition and providing a basis for the law of nations.

25. For additional passages in which Milton argues for no-fault divorce based on immutable differences in temperament, see note 17.

26. In an example of the psychological complexity of the divorce tracts, a moment earlier Milton had acknowledged that the woman should rule the husband "if she exceed her husband in prudence and dexterity."

27. Previous commentators have not seen the difference between the tracts that I discuss here. Barker, for example, curiously elides the distinction between culpable hostility and blameless incompatibility of temper. In his discussion of the divorce tracts, he offers a passage from the *Second Defense* as an example of temperamental incompatibility: "a consideration of divorce was particularly necessary 'when man and wife were often the fiercest enemies, he being at home with his children, while she, the mother of the family, was in the camp of the enemy, threatening slaughter and destruction to her husband.' The consistent argument of the divorce tracts is *therefore* that 'indisposition, unfitness, or contrariety of mind, arising from a cause in nature unchangeable,' provide a sounder reason for divorce than frigidity or adultery" (*Milton and the Puritan Dilemma*, 66–67 [emphasis mine]; Barker quotes the *Second Defense* from *The Works of John Milton*, 20 vols., ed. F. A. Patterson et al. (New York, 1931–40), vol. 8, 133; the passage from the *Doctrine and Discipline* can be found in YP 2:242). Milton presumably thought that one's choice of sides in the Civil War was a matter of principle rather than temperament.

28. In an earlier discussion ("The Metaphysics of Milton's Divorce Tracts," 79–80), I identified the difference between these two passages, but I did not see at the time that the difference epitomized a more thoroughgoing difference between the tracts.

29. In describing the agent as acting "either blindly or maliciously," Milton translates to the abstract or supernatural realm the qualities elsewhere viewed as underlying the wife's failure to be a fit help: inability or willfulness.

30. See, for example, the earlier work's claim that "the freedom and eminence of mans creation gives him to be a Law in this matter to himself, beeing the head of the other sex which was made for him" (YP 2:347).

31. Turner, *One Flesh,* 193, quoting *Tetrachordon* (YP 2:666).

32. Sánchez argues that in *Tetrachordon* Milton finds a middle way: "Milton will have it both ways by placing himself somewhere in the middle, between the two extremes of *altogether* good and *altogether* evil" (*Persona and Decorum in Milton's Prose,* 89). While such a placement would make sense given the argument of the *Doctrine and Discipline* and the premises of *Tetrachordon,* I argue that Milton reacts in *Tetrachordon* precisely against such a placement.

33. The mention of celibacy occurs in a passage in which Milton attacks as Romanizing any tampering with divine law (YP 2:595).

34. For fraud in the tract, see also YP 2:626. In the passage concerning hard-heartedness discussed above, we saw that Milton only grudgingly admits a sense he has just himself evoked ("our infirmity, or if it must be so call'd, hardnesse of heart" [YP 2:661–62]); the same gesture of reluctance appears in his discussion of error in judgment: "With great reason therfore and mercy doth it heer not torment an error, *if it be so,* with the endurance of a whole life lost to all household comfort and society" (YP 2:629; emphasis mine).

35. This is true both in general of Books Ten through Twelve and in particular of passages such as that at 9.1121–31.